27

Handbook of Pottery and Porcelain Marks

also by J. P. Cushion

POCKET BOOK OF BRITISH CERAMIC MARKS

Handbook of
Pottery and Porcelain
Marks

compiled by
J. P. CUSHION
Lately Senior Research Assistant
of the Department of Ceramics
Victoria and Albert Museum London

in collaboration with
W. B. HONEY
Former Keeper of the Department of Ceramics
Victoria and Albert Museum London

faber and faber

First published in 1956
by Faber and Faber Limited
Second edition (revised) 1968
Reprinted 1962
Third edition (revised) 1965
Reprinted 1966, 1968, 1970
Fourth edition (revised and expanded) 1980
Reprinted 1981 and 1983
Printed in Great Britain by
Redwood Burn Limited, Trowbridge, Wiltshire
All rights reserved

British Library Cataloguing in Publication Data

Cushion, John Patrick
  Handbook of pottery and porcelain marks.
  – New ed.
  1. Pottery – Marks
  2. Porcelain – Marks
  I. Title
  738′.02′78   NK4215

ISBN 0–571–04922–2

Contents

MARKS

Preface to Fourth Edition

Following the first publication of the major *Handbook of Pottery and Porcelain Marks*, which I compiled with the collaboration of the late W. B. Honey, I produced three small pocket books dealing exclusively with English, German, and French and Italian ceramic marks, and catering primarily for the specialist collector. These books have proved popular with the collector and dealer alike for many years.

In this new edition of the *Handbook of Pottery and Porcelain Marks*, all the material embodied in those four previous volumes has been included to make what must be the most comprehensive volume of recorded pottery and porcelain ever produced. Nearly 1,000 new marks and nearly 2,000 new entries have been incorporated, another most useful addition being the substantial index to designs patented in Britain between 1842 and 1883, which provides the reader with material only available otherwise through personal application to the patenting authorities.

J. P. CUSHION

Introduction

THE SCOPE AND ARRANGEMENT OF THE BOOK

It is usual for the compiler of a mark-book to claim for his work a larger number of examples than his predecessors had assembled. Yet such comprehensiveness is not necessarily a merit, especially if (as is usually the case) the number of marks is swelled by the inclusion of many unexplained workmen's and painters' inscriptions which were never intended as factory marks in the strict sense. Such comprehensiveness defeats the true purpose of a mark-book, which is to help the collector by means of avowed or recognized factory marks to identify the place of manufacture of a piece and if possible to determine its date. He can only be confused by the presence of great numbers of single letters which might have been used anywhere and were in many cases added only for the information of the management. They are seldom factory marks, and are in fact usually a hindrance rather than a help in identification. Therefore the marks recorded here are restricted to true factory marks and those others which by their frequent occurrence or in other ways are of actual use in identifying the place of manufacture of a piece.

But the scope of this book has on the other hand been extended beyond the usual by the inclusion of many nineteenth- and twentieth-century marks not hitherto recorded. The general use of factory marks in the last century increased their number to a point making it impracticable to include them all. Nor would it be desirable to record all the names of all the partners of all the firms, many of whom never made wares worth remembering or collecting. The modern English marks given, however, include those of all the more important factories.

Of modern Continental marks, only a selection is given of those most frequently encountered; a complete list would be unnecessary and confusing, adding mere bulk to a handbook in which compendiousness must be counted as a virtue.

Factory marks in the Western sense are practically unknown on Oriental (Chinese, Japanese, Indo-Chinese, and Near Eastern) wares, while those purporting to record the period of manufacture are so liable to be 'commemorative', or even deliberately fraudulent, as to be a frequent cause of dispute among students and worse than useless to the inexperienced. Thus marks of the Ming (Chinese) Emperors, Hsüan-tê, Ch'eng-hua and Chia-ching are commonly found on wares of the reign of the Ch'ing Emperor K'ang-hsi, while the reign-name of K'ang-hsi himself, rare on the abundant porcelain of his period, is chiefly found on nineteenth- and twentieth-century wares. Only Ming and Ch'ing reign-names are accordingly included, for reference. It must be insisted that the wares bearing these are so often imitations as to make them useless for purposes of identification unless interpreted critically with knowledge of the period and factory styles. This applies also to the cyclical dates sometimes found, while the 'marks' of commendation and 'good augury' and the 'hallmarks', though common on eighteenth-century wares, are so often of disputed date and origin as hardly to justify their inclusion here. With Japanese wares the task is still more difficult. A piece of pottery may be referred to by its place of manufacture or the province in which the place is situated, or by the family name of the potter or by his art-name or 'studio name' (which may have been changed several times) or by the name of a tea-master who ordered it, or by the princely patron under whose protection it was made. Any of these names may be inscribed on the piece honestly or fraudulently. Japanese marks are thus utterly untrustworthy, and only a few potteries and place-names often found are covered.

Without knowledge of the actual wares, marks European and Oriental alike are at all times liable to prove deceptive and must be interpreted with caution. It is especially important to have regard to the type of ware bearing a mark as well as its proper date. Thus an anchor on soft-paste porcelain may be a mark of Chelsea; on the greyish hybrid Italian porcelain it is a Venice mark; on French soft-paste it is a mark of Sceaux; on English nineteenth-century bone-china it was used by the firm of Davenport of Longport; in purple, it was used on faïence made about 1800 at Cologne or Poppelsdorf; while on modern German hard-paste in the style of eighteenth-century Meissen and Chelsea, it was avowedly used by Ernst Bohne at Rudolstadt from 1854 onwards.

To help the enquirer in this matter, for every mark an approximate date is given and a word of description on the kind of ware on which each is likely to be found. But unlike most other mark-books, old and new, the present work does not as a rule stray from its proper field to give general information about pottery. A note on the history of its pottery is given for each country covered; but for the accounts of the evolution of technique and design in pottery and the work of particular factories, the reader is referred to the various monographs and dictionaries. We are concerned here only with the recording and interpretation of marks. These will always hold a fascination for the collector in spite of all demonstrations of their untrustworthiness; the tempting short cut to certainty which they offer appeals to a gambling instinct in most of us and to a universal love of cryptograms. Finally (and this is their principal value), they often supply a clinching argument in support of an attribution already conjecturally based on the more trustworthy ground of style.

The marks are arranged by countries alphabetically, subdivided into towns also in alphabetical order. This has been the customary arrangement and is on the whole the most convenient; the marks of each factory may be kept together in this way, and the difficulty offered in a single alphabetical series, by marks not easily decipherable, and by monograms which can be read in more than one way, can be avoided. That alternative has, however, some advantages which are here secured by a provision of an index of letters, monograms and heraldic or other devices. (It should be mentioned that a very full table of marks down to about 1815, classified alphabetically or by devices and the like, is included in *European Ceramic Art*: Vol. II *Dictionary*, by W. B. Honey.) The index also includes place-names and personal-names. The marks are given here for the most part in facsimile, the chief exception

being those numerous modern marks consisting of the names or initials of the maker, or of the place of manufacture, which are reproduced by using printers' type, as has so often been done in the marks themselves on the actual wares.

To each mark is appended the place-name of the factory and the name of the principal proprietor where that explains the mark, the date or approximate period, and a word or so of description of the type of ware on which the mark is generally found.

This enlarged and revised new edition includes that part of the Class IV Design Index for Great Britain which relates to pottery and porcelain (Appendix B, page 173). It is included by the kind permission of the Public Record Office and will enable readers not only to date their wares by using the tables on page 172, but also to determine the name of the manufacturer or person or firm who initially registered the design to protect it from 'piracy' for a period of three years.

The Use of Marks on Pottery and Porcelain

1. *Factory marks*. The practice of inscribing a seal of origin on pottery is a very old one. The impressed names or 'seals' of makers on the Roman red ware ('Samian Ware'), called on that account *terra sigillata*, and the signatures of painters on Greek pottery are outstanding instances dating from Classical times. In the Middle Ages in Europe 'fine' pottery was virtually unknown and the practice lapsed. On the Near Eastern wares of the same period, however, dedicatory inscriptions are sometimes found on pottery, but are by no means common; they are normally round the rim or elsewhere on the 'show-side' of the vessel.

The modern practice of inscribing a name or symbol of origin on the base was undoubtedly suggested by the marks on Chinese porcelain. As mentioned already these are for the most part not potters' marks but the reign-names of emperors, words or phrases of commendation, and symbols of good omen. This was not understood in the fifteenth and sixteenth centuries when the Chinese wares began to become familiar in the West and Nearer East. The marks were evidently taken to be potters' marks, for we find Islamic blue-and-white pottery in Chinese style, probably of fifteenth-century date, from Fostat in Egypt, bearing such signatures as '*El Shami*' ('the Syrian'), while the 'Medici Porcelain' of the late sixteenth century (commonly decorated '*alla porcellana*') as a rule bears a fully developed factory mark, the earliest of its kind, in the form of a sketch of the cathedral dome of Florence. This was perhaps suggested by the marks on the Near Eastern earthenware just referred to, which the 'Medici porcelain' so often resembles.

No regular marks however appear on the Hispano-Moresque ware or on Italian fifteenth- and sixteenth-century maiolica, and the cryptic signs and initials found on them are a perpetual source of confusion and bewilderment to the collector. The occasional inscriptions (such as '*fata i Siena da mº Benedetto*', '*Mº Giorgio*' or '*1508 a di 12 de Setēb. facta fu Castel Durat Zouan Maria Vro*') are in many cases potters' marks, since '*maestro*' ('*Mº*' for 'master') and '*vasaro*' ('*vro*' for 'potter') are included in them, but often this is not at all certain, and there is always the possibility of confusion with ownership marks, such as appear also in the field of decoration (the '*Bº*' on a class of Faenza drug-pots is an example of these, probably the mark of a monastic pharmacy). Further, '*in botega di ...*' does not necessarily imply a work by the hand of the person named. Undoubted painters' signatures, also on the bases or backs of the pieces, are however occasionally found, but these often leave the factory uncertain. The painter Melozzo de Forli was born at that place and retained the name when working elsewhere, while '*Iacomo da Pesaro in Venetia*' and '*Giovanni Batista da In Verona*' are recorded on maiolica, so that '*da ...*' may not indicate the place of making a specimen so marked, though '*Nicola da Urbino*' and '*Giorgio da Ugubio*', both of them believed to have been born elsewhere, are instances to the contrary. A further doubt arises from the probability that '*in Siena*', etc., like '*in Verona*', indicate that the master was working exceptionally away from his normal place of abode. Signatures on pottery, in fact, generally indicate work that is exceptional in some way, and are thus likely to be misleading.

On seventeenth-century maiolica, the shield of Savona, the lighthouse of Genoa, and the rest are virtually factory marks in the modern sense, though never apparently the declared marks of particular makers; the Delft practice was perhaps in view here. In fact the random signs that appear on faïence of the seventeenth century were in no sense authorized or the exclusive property of the users, though sometimes having (as on Delft ware), the character of factory marks. But that these were freely imitated is clear from the attempts made at Delft to register the marks on the 'red teapots' in 1680, and the regulations as to marking imposed on the faïence-makers later, in 1764.

It was not until the declared adoption on Meissen porcelain of the 'K.P.M.' in 1723 and eventually in 1724 of the crossed swords (from the arms of Saxony) that marks began to be used at all regularly in Europe. The placing of the mark under its foot and the use of blue are clear indications that the Chinese model was being followed. The Meissen practice was then adopted at other German and indeed most porcelain factories of repute. Heraldic charges were usually adapted for the purpose. The faïence-factories followed (Bayreuth was one of the earliest), though by no means universally. A rare instance of marks systematically added on faïence is that of Marieberg and Rörstrand (Stockholm), where day, month and year, a painter's mark and sometimes a sign indicating price were included in addition to the factory mark and the manager's initial. These take a characteristic three- or four-storeyed form and were copied by others in the Baltic region. Eventually the practice of marking received the sanction of the law. From 1766 in France the porcelain-makers were required to place upon their wares a mark previously registered with the police authorities, while two years earlier (when their industry was already in rapid decline) the Delft faïence-makers had agreed to place registered marks upon their wares.

The normal system of marking was extended at Sèvres, Vienna and Frankenthal, where blue-painted or impressed date-letters and numerals were added, and eventually in the nineteenth century at the first-named two factories and at Berlin it became the practice to use one mark (generally in underglaze colour) at the time of making and another in red or other enamel colour when the piece was decorated; dates were often included in both these marks. A further development of the regular marking-system to be noted is the cancellation of the mark as a disclaimer, when outmoded pieces were sold undecorated or spoilt pieces (*Ausschuss*) were disposed of cheaply; instances will be found under Sèvres, Meissen, Vienna and Berlin. This was usually done by a cut on the engraver's wheel, and forgers have been known to remove this disclaimer mark by grinding it completely away, leaving a small cavity bare of glaze.

But the practice throughout the eighteenth century was never regularized, and except for a brief late period in the countries just mentioned there was no compulsory marking of wares. The factories of repute, proud of their productions, added a recognized mark (and even used it as part of the decoration, as at Nymphenburg); their imitators left their wares unmarked or employed a mark likely to be mistaken for a more famous one. Weesp and Tournay both adopted a version of the Meissen crossed swords; the torches of La Courtille, the hooks of Rauenstein, the hay-forks of Rudolstadt, the 'L's' of Limbach, and the 'W' of Wallendorf, were all drawn in such a way as to resemble the Meissen mark. Many other imitations could be cited, apart from modern forgeries; in eighteenth-century England the crossed swords were openly copied on Bow, Lowestoft, Derby and Worcester, and it is believed that the marks on the earlier Delft ware (which are often of uncertain significance) were used by different factories imitating one another.

It should be obvious from what has been said that marks by themselves are untrustworthy evidence of origin on pottery of the whole period here in question, being seldom compulsory (unlike those placed upon precious metals) and at no time efficiently protected against imitation. The initials and numerals which are commonly found alone are ambiguous and often mis-leading, not strictly factory marks at all, and of little use for purposes of identification. Moreover, on porcelain and muffle-decorated faïence they may be fraudulently added to a piece long after its making.

It should be further added here that dates cannot always be taken at their face value, being sometimes commemorative (as of birthdays, etc.) and instances are known of their being copied from much earlier engravings, used for the designs.

2. *Painters' and workmen's marks.* Apart from factory marks and the full signatures of potters and painters (which are naturally much more likely to occur on *Hausmalerei* or on spare-time or special work done outside the factory), it was in the seventeenth and eighteenth centuries a common custom for workmen to add, solely for the information of the management of the pottery, a numeral or initial letter or some other identifying sign on their work; throwers and 'repairers' or assemblers used a scratched mark, painters and gilders one in colour or gold. Where surviving factory-records are so complete as to include the registers of these marks, it is possible with their aid to identify the workmen, but this is altogether exceptional. A statement of the numerals in use at a particular date (as at Derby) is likely to be misleading, since they would be variously assigned at different times; and the pattern numbers commonly found are distinguishable from these only by the high numbers to which they naturally run. It is obvious that a gilt letter or number is more likely to be a gilder's mark than a painter's and the inferences sometimes drawn as to Meissen painters from the gilt letters and numerals frequently found are on this account open to question. The signs used by the Sèvres painters are of a different order and are comparatively well authenticated; and in some other instances (such as Rörstrand and Marieberg) where initials were used and lists of painters and their dates are available it is possible to identify some of the artists with fair certainty.

Marks scratched or impressed in the paste may also refer to its composition and have been added for the guidance of manager and workmen, especially the kiln-master. The scratched cross on a class of Bristol (or Worcester) porcelain, and some of the numerals found in association with the mark of Joseph Adam Hannong of Strasbourg are instances; others used at Berlin and Nymphenburg are believed to indicate the part of the kiln in which the object was to be placed. The 'T B O' on Wedgwood ware (formerly thought to refer to a modeller named Tebo) is now known to mean 'Top of Biscuit Oven'. But the cryptic signs presumed to be of this order are naturally hard to distinguish from those of the throwers and 'repairers'. Identification of these last is an exceedingly hazardous affair, and actually of little importance. But it should be noted that on occasions the modeller added his initials or signed his name; instances will be found under Sèvres (le Riche) and Nymphenburg (Bustelli), probably indicating that the specimen was approved. The full signature of the modeller himself is rarely found, but that of Melchior on a Höchst figure should be noted here. It is unlikely that a modeller's initial or name would ever be added in enamel-colour as has sometimes been claimed.

Incised or impressed numerals may be mould numbers as on late Meissen and Derby porcelain.

3. *Ownership marks* on maiolica have already been mentioned; dedicatory inscriptions including the names of persons and places are also common on faïence and porcelain and liable to be mistaken for evidence of origin.

Destination marks are sometimes easily recognizable (as in the case of the 'Château marks' on late Sèvres porcelain of the *Restauration* period), but others (such as the 'Villers Cotteret' of Chantilly, the *'Pridvornia Kontora'*, an inventory mark of the St.

Petersburg palaces, like the 'K.H.C.' for *Königliche Hof-Conditorei*' or Court Pantry, found on Meissen porcelain, and the 'Anet' of Sceaux) are liable to be mistaken for factory marks. Such marks, again, especially in the nineteenth century, were similar to the pattern names which in some English instances were actually borrowed from them.

A quite exceptional series of ownership 'marks' is found on the wares, chiefly Oriental and Meissen porcelain, from the Johanneum at Dresden, some of which were sold in 1919 and 1920. These consist of an initial (for the class of ware, 'W' for Meissen, a cross for 'Japanese', and so on) and an inventory number, and were engraved on the wheel on the base of the piece and coloured black. They are of course easy to imitate for the purpose of fraud and appear on Chinese porcelain from Near Eastern collections, in some cases dating from the sixteenth century.

Ownership marks similar to the *Hausmarken* (usually monograms) of the German merchants of the sixteenth and seventeenth centuries are occasionally found on faïence (e.g. that of Hamburg), and Jan Emens' mark on Raeren stoneware is of the same character. Others are found on Kreussen stoneware.

In the late eighteenth and nineteenth centuries, dealers' marks ('Jan Derks Delft', 'Mist, London', 'Mortlock's Cadogan', etc.) appear on wares made or decorated to their order.

The belief that certain marks, such as the 'A.R.' on Meissen and the wheel with electoral hat on Höchst written in underglaze blue, indicate pieces originally intended for the use or gift of the Court may be well founded, but they cannot be marks of quality, since this could not be proved until after the final firing, that is to say, at a stage much later than that at which these marks were added.

4. Marks may be *written on pottery* in any of the following ways:

A. BY INCISING (SCRATCHING) IN THE SOFT UNFIRED CLAY. This is one of the oldest methods, and when covered with glaze such marks may be accepted as genuine. When in the bare paste, they should be scrutinized carefully, since it is possible to cut or etch them after the making of a piece. When scratched in the soft clay the lines usually show a 'burr' or raised edge.

B. BY IMPRESSING IN THE UNFIRED PASTE A STAMP OR STAMPS. It is sometimes claimed that the modern use of these marks begins with the commercializing Wedgwood, but at Nymphenburg from 1754, and at Strasbourg or Frankenthal about 1753 to 1755, impressed signs were introduced as factory marks long before Wedgwood's practice is known to have started. The ancient Roman seals (which provide an early instance) were apparently made by impressing separate letters, but the usual modern impressed marks are rows of letters resembling printers' type stamped at a single operation. Impressed devices, such as the curious Striegau mark and those on the Delft red-wares, and the castles and crosses, etc., on a class of Paterna ware,

are all marks of this order, which cannot well be added fraudulently after the making of the ware.

C. BY PAINTING OR TRANSFER-PRINTING UNDER THE GLAZE, in blue only before about 1850, when underglaze chrome-green also began to be used for the purpose (as at Sèvres and Minton's). It is said that a method has recently been discovered by which marks in blue may be fraudulently added to porcelain in such a way as to appear to be under the glaze; but marks so written must be exceedingly rare. On the fusible glaze of Capodimonte and Buen Retiro, and on Vincennes and Sèvres, the overglaze enamel colours used commonly sink so deeply as to appear to be under the glaze.

D. BY PAINTING, TRANSFER-PRINTING OR STENCILLING OVER THE GLAZE. Such marks may always be added to a specimen, for purposes of fraud or otherwise, at any time after its making. A colour used in the decoration was commonly used for these marks, except when (as at Sèvres and Derby) workmen were specially employed to write the marks on the wares. Transfer-printed marks are commonly in black on printed wares, and were frequently in England in the early nineteenth century made by 'thumb-printing'—the impression from the engraved plate being taken and applied with the thumb or some part of the hand of a workman. Bloor-period Derby, Swansea porcelain and Liverpool pottery are examples. Stencilled marks are common on late eighteenth- and early nineteenth-century French porcelain, such as that of Lille and several of the Paris factories.

An exceptional type of overglaze mark is painted in pale reddish or brownish lustre-colour. These in the form of letters or numerals were added to outmoded early Meissen decorated at Augsburg with gilt pseudo-Chinese figure-subjects and borders, and also to pieces repaired by Bristol and other china-menders who added their names ('Coombes', 'Daniel', etc.) to the pieces passed through their hands for repair with glassy frit. The marks in both cases were apparently produced by lightly firing marking-ink or gall-solution; their purpose on the Meissen porcelain has not been satisfactorily explained, though it is thought that they were added for purposes of sorting and grading, or even for pricing.

From 1891, when the American McKinley Tariff Act was introduced, it became necessary to mark export wares with the country of origin, hence the name 'ENGLAND', 'GERMANY', 'JAPAN', etc., suggests a date post-1891. The full term of 'Made in England', as with other countries, was certainly a twentieth-century practice, whilst 'Ltd' is rarely seen or used prior to about 1880.

The so-called 'diamond-mark' (page 172) was in use from 1842–83 and signified that the form or decoration had been registered at the Patent Office and was 'protected' for three years. From 1884 a series of consecutive numbers was used, with the prefix 'Rd' or 'Rd. No'. Up until 1900 approximately 350,000 designs had been so registered.

Acknowledgements

The author wishes to express his gratitude to the many officers and colleagues at the Victoria and Albert Museum, numerous collectors, English Ceramic Circle members and ceramic dealers, all of whom have assisted him in the recording of elusive marks for the guidance of future seekers.

The author is indebted to Mr. Geoffrey Godden for information concerning the dates of nineteenth-century factories and potters.

Thanks for information concerning recently established factories, closures, take-overs etc. are due to the proprietors of *Tableware International* (formerly *Pottery Gazette and Glass Trade Review*, established 1877), and to Mr. Terence Woolliscroft of Milton, Stoke-on-Trent, who so generously carried out the research concerning the recent, and often very complicated, changes of proprietorship of many Staffordshire factories. Mr. Woolliscroft noted that by January 1972 only one hundred and forty-four factories (individual producing units) remained in the Stoke area, employing thirty-four thousand workers.

Austria

Among the many towns in Austria, Salzburg seems to have been the centre of *Hafner*-ware or pottery stove-making during the sixteenth and seventeenth centuries, their wares all related to those of Germany, sometimes being coloured with tin-enamels. Wels, Enns, and Steyr were from the sixteenth century also engaged in this type of potting.

The faïence of the former Austrian Empire consists for the greater part of peasant pottery of admirably vigorous design. Its ascriptions to localities is often difficult. Peasant maiolica in bright colours was being made at Salzburg and Wels during the late seventeenth century.

The only porcelain factory in Austria of any importance in the eighteenth century was that of Vienna which was established in 1719. During its first period (1719–44) the productions of Vienna include some of the most beautiful examples of the Baroque style in porcelain, while the figures and groups of its second period (1744–84) and the highly wrought tablewares made under Sorgenthal (1784–1805) are also of great importance.

From 1716 onwards the Viennese court official, Claudius Innocentius Du Paquier, had experimented in porcelain-making, but it was not until 1719 that he succeeded, aided by two workmen from Meissen—Hunger and Stolzel—who apparently communicated to him the processes, for despite their departing in 1720, Du Paquier continued to make porcelain with great distinction on his own account until 1744, when through financial difficulties he was forced to sell to the Austrian state. Under the state, after various successive directors and a marked decline, there was another financial crisis, largely due to extravagance in experiments towards the imitations of Sèvres, and the concern was once again offered for sale. It remained unsold but Konrad von Sorgenthal came forward and undertook its direction, finally bringing it into prosperity and making a famous type of porcelain, decorated with great refinement in the Neo-Classical taste.

Following the death of Sorgenthal in 1805 the factory began a decline which continued until its final closing in 1864.

(See map on page 57)

FRAUENTHAL
Neumann, Ludwig
1920–
hard-paste porcelain

MILDENEICHEN
Robrecht, G.
1850–
hard-paste porcelain

SCHWAZ
Hussl, Jos. Ant.
1801– earthenware
1883– faïence & 'majolika'

Schwaz

VIENNA
Claudius Innocentius Du Paquier's factory
1719–1864
hard-paste porcelain

Du Paquier period (1719–1744)
mark on Chinese style pieces
c. 1720–30

9

in blue

State period before Sorgenthal
(1744–1784)

1744–1749

in red or other overglaze
colours

1744–1749

impressed

usual form of shield

impressed

incised

1750–1780
(probably on wares
for Court use)

in blue

1749–1780
examples of shield-mark

in blue

Sorgenthal period and later
(1784–1864)

1820–1827

in blue

c. 1827–1850

impressed

c. 1850–1864

in blue

cancellation marks on
wares sold in the white
('Ausschuss')

in blue cancelled by
cuts on the wheel

in blue, the 'A' in red
or green

in addition to the factory marks
given above there occur two or three
numerals of the date from 1783
onwards, e.g. '88' for 1788, '806' for 1806,
etc.

Decorators:

Anreiter von Zirnfeld, J. K. W.
b. about 1702, *d.* 1747

J: Earl JBendelin Anreiter ♉

Anreiter, Anton, *d.* 1801   Ant^{us} Anreiter
Ʋ♉: 1755

Helchis (or Helkis or Helchs), J.
c. 1730–1747   *J. H.*

'Jacobus Helchs fecit'

Jünger, Christoph
c. 1768   *'Ch: v. Jünger'*

Böck, Josef
1829–
decorator of hard-
paste porcelain

Dörfl, Franz
1880–
decorator of
porcelain & enamels

Vater, Josef
second half of 19th century
decorator of
hard-paste porcelain

WILHELMSBURG
Wilhelmsburger Steingutfabrik
Lichtenstern, Gebr.
1835–
earthenware

WILHELMSBURG
impressed

Belgium

By the second decade of the sixteenth century, and probably earlier, Italian potters and their pupils were at work in Antwerp making the tin-glazed pottery, painted in colours, to which the name 'maiolica' should be applied in preference to 'delftware'.

Antwerp remained the chief pottery centre until 1568, when the Spanish persecutions under Alva and the subsequent long war commenced.

Faïence was made at several factories in Brussels from the seventeenth century, the most important being that of Mombaers started in 1705. Apart from its colour and the tureens in natural forms, the Brussels faïence was in general similar to the commoner Delft and Northern French wares. Faïence was also produced at Andenne, Liége and Tournay.

White and cream-coloured wares were made at several factories from the late eighteenth century; among those worthy of note are Andenne, Brussels and Namur.

One of the most important eighteenth-century manufactures of soft-paste porcelain was founded in 1751 at Tournay. The porcelain was at first greyish, but from about 1755 onwards generally of fine quality, with a faintly yellowish tone. Much of the earlier decoration was quite frankly in imitation of Meissen and Sèvres, but the forms were in many instances original. The figures were seldom marked and there is sometimes doubt about their identification. In style they often show a strong resemblance to those of Chelsea, Derby and Mennecy. Much Tournay porcelain was sold 'in the white' for decoration at The Hague, and any soft-paste bearing the stork-mark of the latter factory in overglaze blue enamel is likely to be of Tournay manufacture. In recent years forgeries of old Tournay porcelain itself, very thin in body and marked with a large tower, have been made actually in Tournay.

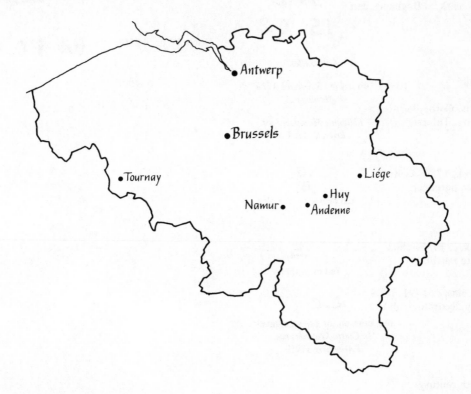

ANDENNE
Wouters, Joseph
1783–
faïence

J̇W̧A̧Ḑ   A̧ḐW̧

Lammens, B.
c. 1794–1820
white and
cream-coloured wares

BD LS & CE
impressed
'Grande Manufacture Andenne'
impressed in cartouche

late mark on transfer-printed wares

ANTWERP
16th and 17th century
maiolica
probably mark of Boghaert, Jan
1552–1571

15 G2

BRUSSELS
1705–1825
faïence
Mombaers, Corneille
Witsenburg, Thierry

'A Bruxelles'

'Brussel le 15 Novemb 1746
P Mombaers'

'Philippus Mompaers tot
Bruxelle 1769'

Schaerbeek, 1786–1790
hard-paste porcelain

B
red or underglaze blue

Etterbeek, *c.* 1787–1803
hard-paste porcelain

ÆE
red or purple

Cretté, Louis, *c.* 1791–1803
(probably decorator only)

L.C.
red, crimson, or brown enamel
'L. Cretté Bruxelles rue
d'Aremberg 1791'

HUY
1740–19th century
faïence
L'Homme, Charles
early 19th
century

C L et P L
A HUY   impressed

J : P B   impressed

LIÈGE
1752–1811
faïence
Boussemaert, Joseph, *c.* 1770–

L   G

TOURNAY
1751–
soft-paste porcelain
Peterinck, F. J.
1751–1796
early marks

in blue, gold, crimson or
other colour

1756–1781

in blue, gold, crimson or
other colour

Boch *frères*, 1850

6✳ ✵ G ✳🕭

China

There can be little doubt that the cradle and nurturing-ground of the Chinese race were the valley and plains of the Yellow River (Huang-Ho), in what are now the provinces of Shensi, Shansi, Honan and Shantung. But that the people dwelling there in pre-historic times were already subject to invasions from the north and west, from Mongolia and Central Asia, as early as the end of the Stone Age, is suggested by some pottery of that period lately discovered in China showing a remarkable resemblance to some Western and Neolithic wares.

Neither the legendary Hsia period nor the Shang and Yin periods (1760–1120 B.C.) produced ceramics of any account; recent finds at Anyang, a late Shang-yin capital in Honan, being either of slight artistic importance or too fragmentary.

During the succeeding Chou period (1120–249 B.C.) the early wares were relatively crude, but there is evidence of finer work being done towards its close, whilst during the Ch'in period (221–206 B.C.), there is some probability that glazed stoneware was being made.

In the Han period which began in 206 B.C. we have clear evidence of outside contacts with the eastern part of the Roman Empire in the introduction of lead-glaze; whilst purely Chinese is the feldspathic-glazed stoneware.

In the following period known as the Six Dynasties (A.D. 220–589), something of the sculptor's inspiration was shared by the maker of pottery figures, which in accordance with a widespread custom were largely used in the furnishing of tombs. The development of stoneware seems to have continued during the Six Dynasties and it is highly probable that a vitrified ware of almost porcellanous character was being made as early as the third century A.D.

We now enter the T'ang Dynasty (A.D. 618–906), which is generally agreed to be the most creative period in Chinese history, the abundant surviving pottery producing vigorous painting, varied techniques and a wide range of colour. By the ninth century A.D. at the latest we have the Yüeh ware, our first example of 'celadon' wares, which together with a white translucent stoneware conforming to the European definition of porcelain were being made and even exported.

During the succeeding Sung period (A.D. 960–1279) the Imperial taste in porcelain inclined to prefer reproductions of the shapes of ancient jades and bronzes, whilst the skill of the potter was directed more towards the development of a material that should have all the qualities of jade, and fine quality 'celadon' ware was made not only in China but in Indo-China, Siam, and Korea. These wares continued during the short-lived Yüan Dynasty (A.D. 1279–1367) and a wider export market was encouraged with the resulting influences from abroad including the use of cobalt for painting in blue on porcelain.

Under the rule of the Ming emperors (A.D. 1368–1644) the Sung ideals in pottery were largely rejected in favour of the brighter colour and variety of T'ang, and with the vogue of fine-grained white porcelain is heralded the beginning of a new period in Chinese ceramic history with its centre in the town of Ching-tê-chên in Kiangsi province where a new Imperial factory was started in 1369 with a prolific output of early Ming blue-and-white and fine enamel-painted porcelain both for the court and later for general use and export. Alongside these fine porcelains were also made earthenware and stoneware decorated with richly coloured glazes or with carved or incised or applied ornament all in the traditional T'ang form.

By the beginning of the seventeenth century an export trade with Europe was flourishing with the Portuguese, the Dutch East India Company and both English and French companies.

Following the fall of the Ming Dynasty in 1644 the decline in culture was reversed by the Ch'ing Emperor K'ang-hsi (A.D. 1662–1722) who was a great patron of the arts and the European influence of the French and Netherlandish Jesuits at his court is seen in the Baroque character of early Ch'ing porcelain, and in the introduction of the use of pink enamels, Western flower-painting and pastoral scenes.

There was a backward-looking tendency during the reign of both Yung-chêng (A.D. 1723–35) and Ch'ien-lung (A.D. 1736–95) when exact copies of the classical Sung wares and of the early Ming painted porcelain were made.

The Imperial porcelain of the nineteenth century was as a rule carefully and weakly correct in following earlier styles and models, until the factory was burned in 1853 by the T'ai-ping rebels only scarcely to recover before the Revolution of 1912 ended the dynasty.

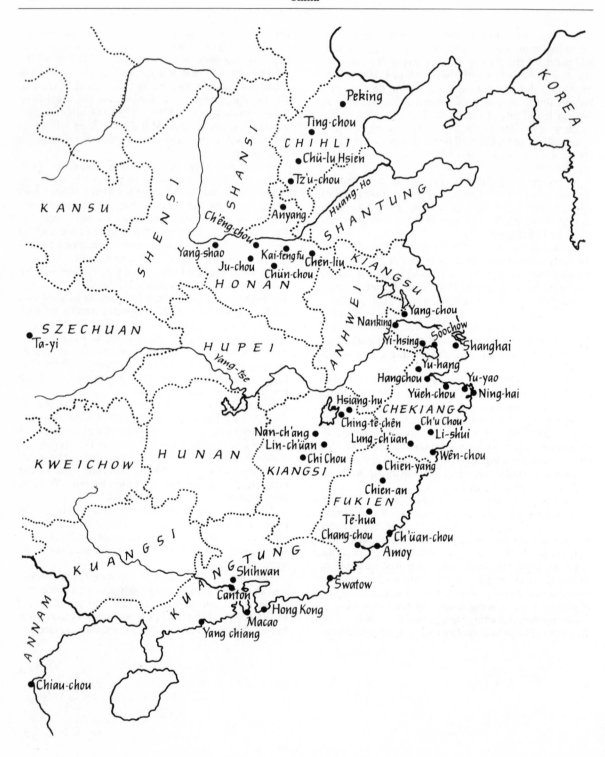

CHINESE DATE MARKS

The Chinese have two methods of indicating a date. First, by a *nien hao*, or name given to the reign, or part of the reign, of an emperor; second, by reference to a 'cycle' of sixty years.

A reign-name is chosen after the emperor has ascended the throne, and dates from the beginning of the first new year after his accession. Like the name of the dynasty, it is an epithet of good augury drawn from some classical text. Thus 'K'ang-hsi' means 'Joys of Peace', and 'Yung-chêng', 'Inviolable Righteousness'. 'Ming' means 'Bright', and the character for it consists of a conventionalized representation of the sun and moon side by side; the name of the Manchu dynasty, the 'Ch'ing', means 'Pure'. Under the older dynasties the reign-name was frequently changed on the occurrence of some catastrophic or otherwise notable event, but after the accession of the Ming in 1368 there was but one instance of such a change, when the Emperor Chêng-t'ung returned after seven years of exile and resumed his reign in 1457 under the name of T'ien-shun. A reign-name should be distinguished from an emperor's family name and also from his posthumous title; reign-names and dynastic names are the names of periods, and a pot is therefore spoken of as belonging to a period rather than to a reign.

Chinese, it is well known, is read from right to left, usually in columns running downwards. The 'six-character mark' is usually written in two columns, composed as follows: two characters signifying the name of the dynasty prefaced by the word great (*ta*), two the reign-name and two more meaning 'period' (*nien*) and 'make' (*chih*); occasionally the last character is *tsao* or *tso* (also meaning 'make' or 'made'), and in the case of a small class of eighteenth-century palace porcelain the word *yü*, meaning 'to Imperial order', replaces *nien*. The six-character mark is occasionally written in one horizontal line. In the 'four-character mark' the name of the dynasty (or, in rare instances, the reign-name) is omitted. The seal-marks are similar combinations of words written in an archaic script known as seal character. This script is naturally commoner in archaizing periods such as those of Yung-chêng and Ch'ien-lung.

CHINESE REIGN-MARKS

MING DYNASTY

Hung-wu (1368–98)

Chien-wên (1399–1402)

Yung-lo (1403–24) (In archaic script)

Yung-lo (1403–24)

Hung-hsi (1425)

Hsüan-tê (1426–35)

(In seal characters)

Chêng-t'ung (1436–49)

Ching-t'ai (1450–57)

T'ien-shun (1457–64)

Ch'êng-hua (1465–87)

(In seal characters)

Hung-chih (1488–1505)

Chêng-tê (1506–21)

Chia-ching (1522–66)

Lung-ch'ing (1567–72)

Wan-li (1573–1619)

T'ai-ch'ang (1620)

啟年製 大明天
T'ien-ch'i (1621–27)

年製 崇楨
Ch'ung-chêng (1628–43)

光年製 大清道
Tao-kuang (1821–50)

(In seal characters)

CH'ING DYNASTY

治年製 大清順
Shun-chih (1644–61)

(In seal characters)

(In seal characters)

緒年製 大清光
Kuang-hsü (1874–1908)

(In seal characters)

隆年製 大清乾
Ch'ien-lung (1736–95)

豐年製 大清咸
Hsien-fêng (1851–61)

(In seal characters)

熙年製 大清康
K'ang-hsi (1662–1722)

(In seal characters)

(In seal characters)

統年製 大清宣
Hsüan-t'ung (1909–12)

(In seal characters)

年製 嘉慶
Chia-ch'ing (1796–1821)

治年製 大清同
T'ung-chih (1862–73)

年製 洪憲
Hung-hsien (1916)
(Yüan Shih-kai)

正年製 大清雍
Yung-chêng (1723–35)

(In seal characters)

16

CHINESE CYCLICAL DATES

Dates named on the cyclical system, by which time is reckoned in periods, beginning with the year 2637 B.C., are much rarer and less easy to read. Each of the sixty years composing a cycle has a name made up of two characters—one of the 'ten stems' combined with one of the 'twelve branches', taken in turn and repeated. As the least common multiple of ten and twelve is sixty, the same pair of characters does not recur until the sixty-first year, which begins a new cycle. As no indication is as a rule given of the particular cycle intended, these marks are of no use by themselves in determining the date of a piece of porcelain on which they occur. Where a reign-name is given, as in the first and fourth of the marks reproduced below, the year may be ascertained without difficulty. With the assistance given by the style of a piece a precise date may often be obtained. An example of this kind is given in the second of the marks reproduced below. The mark *yu hsin ch'ou nien chih* (made in the thirty-eighth year recurring) occurs on a piece of early *famille rose* porcelain; the date 1721 is to be read for this, as the Emperor K'ang-hsi reigned for over sixty years and the *hsin ch'ou* thus recurred at the end of his reign. The third example appears on a pair of vases in late Ch'ien-lung style. The cycle intended is evidently that beginning in 1804 and the date is thus 1808.

ta Ming Ch'êng Hua yüan nien i-yu

First year of the reign of Ch'êng-hua of the Great Ming Dynasty, in the twenty-second year (of the cycle beginning in 1444) (1465).

yu hsin ch'ou nien chih

Made in the thirty-eighth year recurring (see above).

mou ch'ên nien liang t'ou chih

Fifth year: good picture record (see above).

T'ung-chih shih êrh nien kuei-yu

Twelfth year of the reign of T'ung-chih in the tenth year (of the cycle beginning in 1864) (1873).

TABLE OF CYCLICAL DATES FROM A.D. 4

Cyclical Signs	CYCLE BEGINNING 4 304 604 904 1204 1504 1804	64 364 664 964 1264 1564 1864	124 424 724 1024 1324 1624	184 484 784 1084 1384 1684	244 544 844 1144 1444 1744
甲 午	34	94	54	14	74
乙 未	35	95	55	15	75
丙 申	36	96	56	16	76
丁 酉	37	97	57	17	77
戊 戌	38	98	58	18	78
己 亥	39	99	59	19	79
庚 子	40	100	60	20	80
辛 丑	41	101	61	21	81
壬 寅	42	102	62	22	82
癸 卯	43	103	63	23	83
甲 辰	44	104	64	24	84
乙 巳	45	105	65	25	85
丙 午	46	106	66	26	86
丁 未	47	107	67	27	87
戊 申	48	108	68	28	88
己 酉	49	109	69	29	89
庚 戌	50	110	70	30	90
辛 亥	51	111	71	31	91
壬 子	52	112	72	32	92
癸 丑	53	113	73	33	93
甲 寅	54	114	74	34	94
乙 卯	55	115	75	35	95
丙 辰	56	116	76	36	96
丁 巳	57	117	77	37	97
戊 午	58	118	78	38	98
己 未	59	119	79	39	99
庚 申	60	120	80	40	100
辛 酉	61	121	81	41	101
壬 戌	62	122	82	42	102
癸 亥	63	123	83	43	103

Cyclical Signs	CYCLE BEGINNING 4 304 604 904 1204 1504 1804	64 364 664 964 1264 1564 1864	124 424 724 1024 1324 1624	184 484 784 1084 1384 1684	244 544 844 1144 1444 1744
甲 子	04	64	24	84	44
乙 丑	05	65	25	85	45
丙 寅	06	66	26	86	46
丁 卯	07	67	27	87	47
戊 辰	08	68	28	88	48
己 巳	09	69	29	89	49
庚 午	10	70	30	90	50
辛 未	11	71	31	91	51
壬 申	12	72	32	92	52
癸 酉	13	73	33	93	53
甲 戌	14	74	34	94	54
乙 亥	15	75	35	95	55
丙 子	16	76	36	96	56
丁 丑	17	77	37	97	57
戊 寅	18	78	38	98	58
己 卯	19	79	39	99	59
庚 辰	20	80	40	100	60
辛 巳	21	81	41	101	61
壬 午	22	82	42	102	62
癸 未	23	83	43	103	63
甲 申	24	84	44	104	64
乙 酉	25	85	45	105	65
丙 戌	26	86	46	106	66
丁 亥	27	87	47	107	67
戊 子	28	88	48	108	68
己 丑	29	89	49	109	69
庚 寅	30	90	50	110	70
辛 卯	31	91	51	111	71
壬 辰	32	92	52	112	72
癸 巳	33	93	53	113	73

THE TEN STEMS

十干　*Shih kan*

1	甲	*chia*
2	乙	*i*
3	丙	*ping*
4	丁	*ting*
5	戊	*wu* or *mou*
6	己	*chi*
7	庚	*kêng*
8	辛	*hsin*
9	壬	*jên*
10	癸	*kuei*

THE TWELVE BRANCHES

十二支　*shih erh chih*

1	子	*tzǔ*	rat
2	丑	*ch'ou*	ox
3	寅	*yin*	tiger
4	卯	*mao*	hare
5	辰	*ch'ên*	dragon
6	巳	*ssǔ*	serpent
7	午	*wu*	horse
8	未	*wei*	sheep
9	申	*shên*	monkey
10	酉	*yu*	cock
11	戌	*hsü*	dog
12	亥	*hai*	boar

NUMERALS

一	1	*i*
二	2	*êrh*
三	3	*san*
四	4	*ssǔ*
五	5	*wu*
六	6	*liu*
七	7	*ch'i*
八	8	*pa*
九	9	*chiu*
十	10	*shih*

Denmark

Late-medieval lead-glazed wares and later slipware show a kinship with the contemporary English pottery. The principal manufacture in Denmark of faïence was at Copenhagen where in 1722 the Store Kongensgade factory was founded; its best period was from 1727–49, when its wares were evidently derived from the blue-and-white of Nuremberg, with a strong Baroque element. The factory of Kastrup was started around the middle of the eighteenth century and produced its best wares from 1755 to 1762 when its decoration was in the Strasbourg Rococo style painted in muffle-colours. The factory at Kastrup together with those of Gudumlund and Bornholm Island produced cream-coloured wares in English style from the eighteenth and early nineteenth centuries.

The chief manufactories of porcelain were the short-lived undertaking of Louis Fournier making soft-paste (1759–65); and F. H. Müller's, afterwards the Royal, factory, making true porcelain from 1771–2 onwards and still existing. That of Bing and Gröndahl dates from about 1853.

The Fournier soft-paste porcelain is usually a faintly yellowish colour and has a somewhat dull glaze; its productions were chiefly tablewares of modest dimensions painted in soft enamel colours.

The Royal factory adopted for its mark in 1775 the well-known device of three wavy lines (for the Sound and the Great and Little Belts). Prior to its Royal period (1779 onwards) its wares under Müller were in general painted in underglaze blue, purple or iron-red; from the beginning of the Royal period the forms adopted were of a severe Classical character.

Some colossal vases, mirror frames and large columns with figures of women and cupids were also made towards 1800. It should be noted that the well-known biscuit figures after Thorvaldsen were not made before 1867. The word 'Eneret' stamped on many of them means 'copyright'.

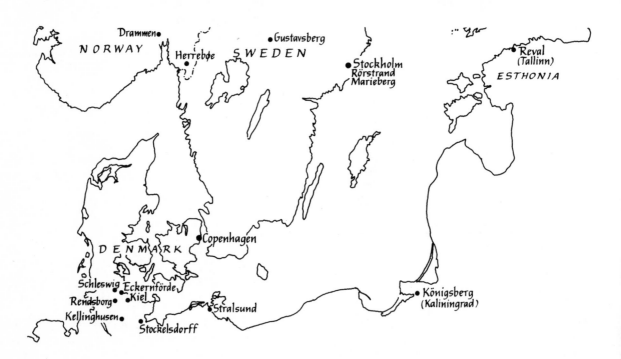

BORNHOLM ISLAND
1792–1858
cream-coloured earthenware

Spietz, Johann   *Spietz* impressed

COPENHAGEN
The Store Kongensgade factory
1722–*c*. 1770
faïence

Pfau, Johann Ernst
1727–1748

Kastrup 1754–*c*. 1814
faïence

Fortling, Jacob, 1754–1762

Mantzius, Jacob C. L.   C W   impressed in an oval
1781–1794   M

Østerbro 1763–1769
faïence
'Øster Bro Fabrik' and
painter 'J. Hasrisz

Fournier, Louis, 1760–1766
soft-paste porcelain
'Frederik V' of Denmark

in blue enamel

The Royal Factory 1779–
hard-paste porcelain
Müller, F. H., 1771–
mark on early trial piece

impressed

'wave-mark' adopted 1775

in underglaze blue

mark found on figures

1889–

1890–   1894–

1897–   1905–

1923–

1929–

Faïence Manufactory Aluminia
1863–

1903–

1929 'iron porcelain'

Bing & Gröndahl, 1854

1925–
hard-paste porcelain
Dahl-Jensens

GUDUMLUND
1804–1820 cream-coloured earthenware and faïence
mark in use 1804–1814

1808–1814 three brown spots

MORS 1774–*c*. 1784
faïence and stoneware
mark of Thomas Lund (owner)
and S. Aschanius and
H. Meulengracht

SØHOLM 1826–
earthenware

'*Söholm*'

Estonia

A faïence factory at the Baltic town of Reval was started about 1775 by Karl Christian Fick of Stralsund, and came to an end at his death in 1792.

The wares show the influence of Stralsund. The forms are for the most part in Rococo style, including figures and vases pierced in openwork as well as tureens with applied leaves and flowers, and other tablewares. Some rare figures of dogs, bulls and elephants were made.

(See map on page 20)

REVAL

1775–1792 Fick, Karl Christian faïence

factory mark with that of painter H. G. Pauel

Reval
Fick
Paul

marks with those of painter Otto

probably mark of painter Otto

France

The earliest French earthenwares are probably of fourteenth-century date and consist of unglazed buff material decorated with grouped vertical stripes in red, whilst a little later the unglazed grey wares are of excellent form. Probably of fourteenth- or fifteenth-century date are a class of yellow-glazed jugs, lobed cups, and a distinct group of pieces marked by the use of brown clay in applied decoration. Of late fifteenth- or early sixteenth-century date green-glazed jugs are found parallel with those of England and green-glazed dishes moulded in relief and an admirable type with *sgraffiato* decoration are both associated with Beauvaisis.

This early lead-glazed pottery is essentially similar not only to the finer sixteenth-century wares developed from it but also to the unpretentious peasant pottery of more recent date which has continued to be made, especially in Northern France, almost to the present day.

Faïence tiles and other wares painted in green and purple (or black) were made in late-medieval times, probably under Spanish or Italian influence.

The above medieval wares were the immediate fore-runners of the finer sixteenth-century pottery of La Chapelle-des-Pots, Avignon and Beauvaisis, which in turn supplied the medium used by Bernard Palissy for his work in coloured glazes. The famous sixteenth-century *'faïences Henri Deux'* of Saint-Porchaire are an isolated phenomenon, without effect on the history of French pottery and equally free from all outside influences in pottery technique.

The sixteenth-century maiolica wares of Brou, Rouen, Nîmes, Lyon and Nevers are almost indistinguishable from their Italian prototypes, but in the seventeenth century Nevers produced entirely distinct and beautiful wares in both maiolica colours and the well-known deep blue ground polychrome type.

About 1680 Rouen introduced a new traditional faïence decorated mainly in blue which had a great formative influence in French faïence over a long period. Paris, Saint-Cloud, Lille, Saint-Armand-les-Eaux, Leroy's Marseilles factory and even Strasbourg all being followers of Rouen in this phase. During the middle of the eighteenth century Rouen again set the fashion with rich polychrome wares in Chinese and Rococo styles, this time to be followed by Sinceny, Quimper, Samadet and Moulins.

In the late seventeenth century the factory at Moustiers introduced a novel style, again in blue only, of pictorial panels exquisitely painted on great dishes and plates giving place about 1735–40 to new styles in which yellow, green and manganese were employed. Moustiers wares prompted the foundation of many other factories, and their styles were frankly adopted at Varages, Lyon, Montpellier, Ardus, Montauban, Goult and Auvillar in the south, whilst farther to the north the decorations employed at Clermont-Ferrand,

Limoges and Bordeaux were obviously indebted to Moustiers.

About the middle of the eighteenth century Paul Hannong's factory at Strasbourg began producing wares painted with enamel colours as on porcelain; this practice was quickly taken up at Niderviller, Marseilles, Rouen and Moustiers and the ideal of porcelain decoration was of course the inspiration of all this enamel-painting, and the fashionable material was definitely imitated at Sceaux and Aprey. With the general use of enamel colours the more virile high-temperature colours went out of fashion except in the commoner—virtually peasant—pottery of the smaller centres whose characteristic productions date from the later part of the eighteenth century and the early nineteenth century.

The cream-coloured and white earthenware of Staffordshire quickly found imitators in France, and table-wares in lead-glazed *faïence fine* (as it is called in France) were made at Lunéville, Bellevue, Saint-Clément, Niderviller, Paris, Orléans and many other factories.

At Sarreguemines various types of glazed pottery and stoneware, and at Apt a beautiful marbled ware, were all inspired by Staffordshire.

Distinct from the English material is the soft white *'terre de pipe'*, used for biscuit figures at Lunéville, Bellevue and Saint-Clément as early as 1748.

French porcelain falls historically into three groups. The earliest comprises the incomparable soft-pastes, and dates from the first making of porcelain at Rouen in 1673 and the rise of the Saint-Cloud factory towards the end of the seventeenth century; it includes the best work also of Chantilly and Mennecy (after 1730) and the earliest Vincennes (founded 1738), and ends with the establishment of the rigorous Vincennes-Sèvres monopoly about the middle of the eighteenth century.

The orders prohibiting rival factories were issued in 1745, 1752, 1759–60, and 1766, when the French potters were again authorized within certain limits to make porcelain, which was thenceforward to bear a mark registered with the police. Further orders, more or less ineffective, were issued in 1769, 1779, 1784 and 1787.

Though rival porcelain-making by no means ceased altogether, the monopoly orders were to some extent effective over the whole of the second period—roughly twenty years from about 1750 onwards—which was precisely that when the best work of the national manufacture was being done.

The third period dates from the breakdown of the monopoly about 1770, when other factories began to make hard-paste with the newly-found French china-clay of Saint-Yrieix. Many of these were in Paris and in several instances under the protection of members of the Royal family. Niderviller, Lunéville and Strasbourg in the east of France are also important, and Marseilles in the south should be named as standing somewhat apart. These hard-paste manufacturers multiplied and are merged as a body in the industrial development of the nineteenth century; concentrated latterly in the kaolin district of Limoges.

The productions of Saint-Cloud, Chantilly, Mennecy, Vincennes and early Sèvres rank among the best porcelain ever made. The later Sèvres, notwithstanding a beautiful material and accomplished workmanship, too often lacks spontaneity, and is laboured and false to the spirit of art. The hard-pastes of the latter part of the eighteenth century are in general without any marked individuality. The fine soft-paste of Tournay (now in Belgium) belongs technically to France, with which Tournay had close cultural connections in the eighteenth century.

25

AIRE (Pas-de-Calais)
  c. 1730–1790
  faïence
  c. 1730–1755
  Prudhomme, Pierre-Joseph
  1755–*c.* 1790
  Dumetz, François

ANGOULÊME (Charente)
  1748–late 19th century   ANGOULEME
  faïence in style of
  Rouen and Nevers

ANNECY (Haute-Savoie)
  1800–1808   ANNECY
  white earthenware

APREY (Haute-Marne)
  c. 1744–*c.* 1860
  faïence
  founded by LALLEMANT, Jacques,
  Baron d'Aprey and Joseph
  Lallemant de Villehaut.
  factory mark in monogram
  together with initials of
  painters, generally on pieces
  made before 1772

  probably mark of
    Jarry, painter

in black or other
enamel colour

rare marks

19th-century mark of
Abel Girard, 1832–1878
old moulds and marks
used during this period

18th-century hard-paste porcelain made here but
unidentified
unglazed red pottery,   APREY
late 19th century   impressed

APT (Vaucluse)
  1728–1852   *'La Bergère dans*
  faïence and English   *l'inquiétude au Départ*
  styled earthenware,   *de son amant à*
  figures and agate wares   *Castelet parmoy*
  founded by   *César Moulin fils*
  César Moulin at Le Castelet   *ex'*

  Veuve Arnoux, late 18th
  century–1802

impressed

ARBOIS (Jura)
  1745–late 18th century   Arbois
  'faïences patriotiques'

         ARBOIS

ARBORAS (Rhône)
  1839–
  hard-paste porcelain

ARRAS (Pas-de-Calais)
  1770–1790   AR   AR
  soft-paste porcelain   crimson   purple
  founded by Joseph-François
  Boussemaert of Lille   AR   AA

  Dlles Delemer, 1771–1790

underglaze blue

AUXERRE (Yonne)
  1799–
  'faïence patriotique'   *Fayence d'Auxerre*
  of Nevers style
  established by   Boutet
  Claude Boutet

AVIGNON (Vaucluse)
  late 16th century–
  lead-glaze earthenware

  Louis Carbonel
  c. 1737   CARBONEL
  faïence   signed
  Moustiers style

AVON (Seine-et-Marne)
  early 17th century–
  lead-glazed earthenware
  in Palissy style

  probably mark of
  'Bertélémy de Blenod'

incised

BAYEUX (Calvados)
  (factory transferred
  from Valognes in 1810)
  hard-paste porcelain

  Joachim Langlois (*d.* 1830)

  Veuve Langlois (1830–1847)

(continued by daughters
until 1849)

Ve L.   V^.L.
         B.X.

François Gosse (1849–1878)

1849–1851

Ve L.   V^e L
Bayeux   B.X.
G   G
              G
              Bayeux

1851–1878

BAYEUX

(BX)   BX

Jules Morlent 1878–
(and descendants
until 1951)

BELLEVILLE (nr. Paris)
branch factory of Jacob Petit, *c.* 1830
(see FONTAINEBLEAU)

BELLEVUE (nr. Toul, Meurthe-et-Moselle)
1758–
faïence and biscuit

*'Bellevue Ban
de Toul'*
incised

Lefrançois

Charles Bayard and
François Boyer, 1771–

faïence fine

BELLVUE
impressed

BLOIS (Loir-et-Cher)
late 19th century
Adrien Thibault
biscuit

A   Y

BOISETTE (Seine-et-Marne)
1732–faïence
1778–*c.* 1792
hard-paste porcelain

Jacques Vermonet
and son

'Manufacture de
S.A.S. Mgr. le Duc
d'Orleans A Boisset'

ß   B.. ß

underglaze blue
and black enamel

BORDEAUX (Gironde)
1711–19th century
faïence
Jacques Hustin
and son

'Fait à la MANUFACTURE
ROYAL DE M. HUSTIN
E. 1750 R.'

Jean-Etienne Monsau
1778–1783

'F. P. Monsau'

'Fait par Monsau 1783'

'Monsau fecit 1779'

1834–
creamware and
soft-paste porcelain
David Johnston

1845–
J. Vieillard

impressed

1781–1787
hard-paste porcelain
Pierre Verneuilh
and nephew Jean

·W·   W

gold or
underglaze blue

1787–1790
Michel Vanier and
Alluard

stencilled in underglaze
blue

1828–
Lahens and Rateau

mark of a Bordeaux
dealer, on Paris or
Limoges wares

'Omont à
bordeaux'
'Omont à box'

BOULOGNE (Pas-de-Calais)
c. 1817–1859
hard-paste porcelain
Haffreingue

H F
o D

red

BOURG-LA-REINE (nr. Paris)   see under MENNECY

CAEN (Calvados)
1797–1806
hard-paste porcelain
from 1799–
Aigmont-Desmares

caen
CAEN
CAEN

CN   CM

reddish brown

**Caen wares sometimes decorated
by Paris enamellers, Halley &
Dastin**

CALAIS (Pas-de-Calais)
1812–
white and creamwares

'Calais'
impressed

CHANTILLY (Oise)
1725–1800
soft-paste porcelain
protected by Louis-Henri
de Bourbon, Prince de
Condé

red enamel and
occasionally black
for the early period,
underglaze blue and
occasionally crimson
for the later period,
other enamel colours
sometimes seen

rare mark

marks of identified
workmen

Chantilly

cabin adrot

Lrille Bonfoy

Bonnefoy

LeJru

incised

name of Château for
which service was
made

villers cotteret

villers Cottereti

1803–1812
hard-paste porcelain
Pigory, Mayor of Chantilly

underglaze blue

Michel-Isaac Aaron
1845–1870

M·A

underglaze blue

Bougon and Chalot
c. 1818

B & C
D.L.V
chatillon
red

CHATILLON (Seine)
c. 1775
hard-paste porcelain

CHÂTRES (sur Cher)
1918–
hard-paste porcelain

Gaston Sailly

CHOISY-LE-ROI (Seine)
c. 1785–
hard-paste porcelain
Clément

1804– earthenware
Paillart
Paillart and Hautin
1824–1836
Hautin and Boulanger
1836–

P & H
CHOISY

H B & Cie
CHOISY
LE ROY

Cie
Choisy le Roy

Ernest Chaplet (*d.* 1909)
artist-potter
stoneware with Chinese-
type glazes

CLERMONT-FERRAND (Puy-de-Dôme)
c. 1730–1743
faïence in Moustiers
style
Perrot and Sèves

Clermont fd
M

c. 1774–c. 1784
Verdier, Donnat and Morel

late 18th century
Perrier and Pierre Launche
'*faïence patriotique*'

6 P

COLMAR (Alsace)
1800–
Charles-Armand Anstett

'*Colmar*'
gold

'*Anstett*'

porcelain and
white earthenware

gold

CREIL (Oise)
c. 1794–1895
English-type earthenware
(factory united with
Montereau early 19th
century

CREIL
impressed

monogram of Stone
early 19th century

printed in red

monogram of Stone,
Coquerel and Legros
d'Anisy, 1807–1849
generally transfer-
printed wares

printed in black

Lebœuf and Milliet
1841–1895

L.M & Cie
impressed

CRÉPY-EN-VALOIS (Oise)
1762–1770
soft-paste porcelain
Gaignepain, Louis-François

crepy
c.p.

incised

DESVRES (Pas-de-Calais)
1732– faïence

CO
4P

1764–
Jean-François Sta

J 3P

in blue

1899– hard-paste porcelain
Manufacture de Fayence d'Art
Gabriel Fourmaintraux

DIJON (Côte-d'Or)
1669–second half of
18th century
faïence in Nevers and
Strasbourg styles

'*Dijon*'

DOUAI (Nord)
1781– English-type
earthenwares
Charles and James Leigh
1781–1784

'*Douai*'
impressed

Houze de l'Aulnoit
& Cie, 1784–*c.* 1830

'*Leigh & Cie*'

Martin Dammann
1799–1804

'*Martin Dammann*'

Halfort, 1804–1807

'HALFORT'

D'UZES (Gard)
1837–
earthenware biscuit
François Pichon

F D
AVZES

black

ÉPINAL (Vosges)
c. 1760–
faïence and creamwares
François Vautrin, under
protection of Stanlislas,
King of Poland
1766– brothers Le Bon

'ÉPINAL'
impressed

ETIOLLES (Seine-et-Oise)
c. 1768– hard-paste porcelain
Jean-Baptiste Monier
Dominique Pellevé

Etiolle
x bre 1770

Pelleve
incised

'MP' Monier and
Pellevé

P   *MP.*
E
Pelleve 1770
incised

FERRIÈRE-LA-PETITE (Nord)
late 18th–first half
of 19th century
white earthenware
and lead-glazed
pottery

'FERRIÈRE LA
PETITE DELANNO
FRÈRES'

FISMES (Marne)
1840–
hard-paste porcelain
Vernon

VP F
VP. F&C

FOECY (Cher)
1802– Klein
hard-paste porcelain

1850–*c.* 1920
C. H. Pillivuyt & Co.
(also at Mehun and
Noirlac)

CP
& Co.

P&F
France

C.H.PILLIVUYT
& Cie Paris

L 5L

Louis Lourioux
late 19th century

PORCELAINE A FEU
·L L·
FOECY(FRANCE)

FONTAINEBLEAU (Seine-et-Marne)
1795–
hard-paste porcelain
Benjamin Jacob
Aaron Smoll

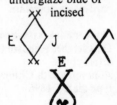

1830–1862
Petit, Jacob and
Mardochée

J. P   JP.
underglaze blue or
incised

1862
E. Jacquemin

1874–
Godebaki & Co.

FRAUENBERG (nr. Sarreguemines)
1760– faïence
Villeroy

F B
monogram in blue

GIEN (nr. Orleans)
1864–
faïence in Rouen &
Italian maiolica
styles

GIEN

GIEY-SUR-AUJON (Haute-Marne)
1809–1840
hard-paste porcelain
F. Guignet

GIF
E Guignet

GOINCOURT (Oise)
1793–
faïence
Michel

L'ITALIENNE

l'Italienne
impressed

HAGUENAU (Alsace)
A branch of the Hannong factory
at Strasbourg, 1741–1781; for marks
see STRASBOURG

HESDIN (Pas-de-Calais)
late 18th–early 19th century
faïence of early
Lambeth and Bristol
type

*'Manufacture
d'Hesdin, 1820'*

ISIGNY (Calvados)
1839–1845
Frédéric Langlois
hard-paste porcelain

Isigny
I.Y.
Isigny

ISIGNY

ISLE D'ELLE (Vendée)
faïence
c. 1740–
Pierre Giraud

'Pierre Giraud 1741'

LA CELLE-BRUÈRE (Cher)
modern
hard-paste porcelain

PORCELAINE
G.D.V
A FEU

LA CHAPPELLE-AUX-POTS (nr. Beauvais)
Delaherche, Auguste (*d.* 1940)
artist-potter
stoneware with Chinese-
type glazes, 1896–

AUGUSTE · DELAHERCHE

LA-CHARITÉ-SUR-LOIRE (Nièvre)
1802–
English-type earthenwares
Francis Warburton
1803–
Le Bault

LA-CHARITÉ
impressed

LA FOREST (Savoie)
1730–1810
faïence in Nevers style

Noel Bouchard

*'La Forest
en Savoye'*

LA ROCHELLE (Charente-Inférieure)
1722–1789
faïence in style of
major French factories
de Bricqueville, 1743–

I.B

Roussencq, 1749–1789

'La Rochelle 1777'

LA SEINIE (Saint-Yrieix, Haute-Vienne)
1774–1856
hard-paste porcelain

LS
red

LA TOUR D'AIGUES (Vaucluse)
1753
faïence and possibly
porcelain after 1773

*'fait à la Tour
Daigues'*

LE HAVRE (Seine-Inférieure)
c. 1780–1810
faïence, white and
creamwares

*'De la Vigne,
D' Yngoville, 1806'*

'DELAVIGNE AU HAVRE'

'L.DELAVIGNE'

'AU HAVRE'
impressed

LE MONTET (Saône et Loire)
19th century
white stoneware

LES ISLETTES (Meuse)
c. 1737–
faïence
François Bernard, 1785

'FABRIQUE DE CIT
BERNARD, AUX
ISLETTES'

LILLE
1696–1802
faïence
Jacques Feburier
Jean Bossu

B
FB *F⁶B B*

Joseph-François Boussemaert
1729–1773

B *B*

Phillippe Auguste Petit
1773–1802

Barthélémy Dorez
1711–*c.* 1820
faïence and soft-paste
porcelain
'F. & B. DOREZ', 1716–

mark commonly found
on modern forgeries

hard-paste porcelain
1784–1817
Leperre–Durot, under
protection of the Dauphin

stencilled in red

in blue

LIMOGES (Haute-Vienne)
1736–
faïence

'*At Limoges le
18 May 1747*'

1771–
hard-paste porcelain

1771–1796
brothers Grellet
(under protection of
the Comte d'Artois)

incised or in colour

in 1784 factory taken over
by King to make white wares
for decoration at Sèvres

incised and blue enamel

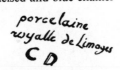

the initials incised
the inscription in red

impressed or incised

19th-century and modern factories:

hard-paste porcelain

Charles Ahrenfeldt
1894–

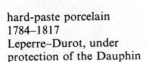

Aluminite, L.

F.R.G.
LIMOGES
FRANCE

LIMOGES
B & Cⁱᵉ
FRANCE

Balleroy, H.-A.

Julien Balleroy & Cie

L. Bernardaud & Cie
1863–

B & CO
LIMOGES
FRANCE

Beulé, Reboisson & Parot

Boisbertrand, Dorat &
　Boisbertrand

J. Boyer

JEAN BOYER

Chabrol frères &
　Poirer

Chaufriasse, Rougérie & Co.

Fontanille & Marraud
1925–

G.D.A.
1798–

FRANCE

J. Granger & Cie

LIMOGES
FRANCE

Guérin-Pouyat-Elite, Ltd.
1841–

LIMOGES
ELITE
FRANCE

LIMOGES
W.G
& Cⁱᵉ
FRANCE

LIMOGES
J.P.
L.
FRANCE

Haviland & Cie
1797–

H & Cᴼ
L

Haviland & Co
Limoges

Robert Haviland &
　C. Parlon, 1924–

Robert Haviland &
　le Tanneur, *c.* 1949–

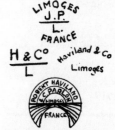

Theodore Haviland
& Co., (*d.* 1919), 1893–

Charles Field Haviland
1878–1891

A. Lanternier & Cie
1855–

La Porcelaine Limousine

M. REDON
BARNY & RIGONI
LIMOGES

F. Legrand & Cie

E. Madesclaire, Jeune

Charles Martin & Duché
1875

Merlin-Lenias

PML
LIMOGES
(FRANCE)

Miautre, Raynaud & Cie

M. R. Cie
LIMOGES

LES ARTISANS
LIMOGES
CÉRAMISTES

Mousset & Cie

George Papault

*GeoRGes
PAPAULT*

Raynaud & Cie
1919–

Rousset & Guillerot

Serpaut

Societé Porcelainière
de Limoges

ANCIENNE FABRIQUE
ROYALE
LIMOGES FRANCE

Jules Teissonnière
1908–

Leon Téxeraud
1923–

LT
LIMOGES
FRANCE

C. Tharaud
1919–

THARAUD

Touze, Lemaitre Frères
& Blancher

T.L.B

LIMOGES

Union Céramique

UC
LIMOGES

FRANCE

Union Limousine
1908–

UL
LIMOCES
FRANCE

A. Vignaud
1911–

Villegoureix, Société
des Porcelaines

V

LIMOGES

LONGWY (Lorraine)
late 18th century–
present
faïence & earthenware

LONGWY
incised or impressed

LORIENT (Morbihan)
1790–1808
hard-paste porcelain

'Porcelaine Lorientaise'

'PL'

Sauvageau

*'Fabriqué dans le
Dept du Morbihan
par Sauvageau à
Lorient'*

LUNÉVILLE (Meuthe-et-Moselle)
1731–19th century
faïence, '*terre de pipe*'
biscuit porcelain and
creamware

Jacques Chambrette
1731–1758

'*Chambrette à
Lunéville*'

Gabriel Chambrette
Charles Loyal
1758–1788

Keller & Guerin
1788–19th century

recent mark

Paul-Louis Cyfflé
modeller of figures and groups in
soft '*terre de pipe*', from 1755 for
Chambrette

Cyfflé's own factory
1766–1777
porcelain
(moulds to Niderviller
and Bellvue, 1780)

impressed

MARANS (Charente-Inférieure)
faïence in Strasbourg style
1740–
monogram of Pierre
Roussencq, founder

transferred to
La Rochelle, 1756

MARSEILLES (Bouches-du-Rhône)
17th century–
faïence

Saint-Jean-du-Désert
1679–18th century

Clérissy, Joseph (*d.* 1685)
(factory remained in
family until at least,
1743)

Fauchier factory
1711–*c.* 1794
Joseph Fauchier
1711–(*d.* 1751)

Joseph Fauchier, II
1751–(*d.* 1789)

Leroy factory
1749–*c.* 1793
Louis Leroy (*d.* 1788)
continued by son,
Antoine (*d.* 1790), then
Jean-Baptiste Sauze

Savy's factory, *c.* 1770
Honoré Savy (*d. c.* 1793)
(previously a
partner to Veuve
  Perrin)

Veuve Perrin factory
c. 1740–*c.* 1795

Claude Perrin, founder
d. 1748, factory
continued by widow
until 1793, then by
son, Joseph

The marks of this
factory are much
copied on forgeries

Robert's factory
c. 1750–at least 1793

Joseph-Gaspard Robert
(hard-paste porcelain
also made from 1773)

marks found on
porcelain

Bonnefoy's factory
1762–at least 1827
Antoine Bonnefoy
(*d.* 1793)
(hard-paste porcelain
also made from 1803)

MARTRES (Haute-Garonne)
second half of 18th century
faïence

'*Fait à Martres 1751*'

MARZY (Nièvre)
1854–
faïence copies of
Rouen and Nevers

ℜ over 'Marzy, Nievre'

Ristori, T. H.

MEHUN-SUR-YÈVRE (Cher)
hard-paste porcelain

La Mehunite

Albert Blot & Cie
modern

MARQUE DE 𝔅 FABRIQUE
DÉPOSER

Pillivuyt & Cie
1853–

PILIVITE

PORCELAINES À FEU PILLIVUYT & CIE MEHUN FRANCE

MEHUN C.P. & CO FRANCE

MENNECY-VILLEROY (Ile-de-France)
1734–1806

soft-paste porcelain, faïence and,
for about last twenty years, creamware
protected by Louis-François de Neufville,
    duc de Villeroy
1734–1748 Paris
1748–1773 Mennecy
1773–1806 Bourg-la-Reine

mark on faïence
    dated 1738

D·V·
blue

early wares in Japanese
    style

·D·V·

~D·V

in red

D·V·
in black

usual marks of the
middle and late period

D·V· blue

DV D,Vf

D,V, ⌀
incised

de Villeroy

de Villeroy
incised

Mennecy mark
including initials of
modeller: Christophe
    Mô, 1767

DV·Mō
incised

Jean Mô, 1767

D V
JMO
incised

possibly Mathieu Simon
1756

mathius
DV
incised

Bourg-la-Reine

B,R. BR
incised   N

marks found on pieces
in Mennecy style but
probably made at
Crépy-en-Valois
    or
Orléans

D,C,O
FS KO
D,C.P m,D
all incised

MONTAUBAN (in Quercy, Tarn-et-Garonne)
1761–early 19th century
(three minor factories)
faïence in Moustiers
style

'*Montauban en
Quercy* 1799'

MONTEREAU (Seine-et-Marne)
1748–19th century
salt-glazed stoneware
and creamware
Mazois, John Hill &
Warburton

MONTEREAU M^AU NO 1

1775–late 19th century
Clark, Shaw & Cie
English-type creamware

'M^AU NO 1'
impressed

MONTREUIL (Seine)
1815–1873
hard-paste porcelain
Tinet

TINET
32
Rue du Bac

Marzolf & Cie
1885–

MOULINS (Allier)
c. 1730–19th century
faïence

a moulins

in red

second half
of 18th century

'Terre de Moulins'

MOUSTIERS (Basses-Alpes)
1679–19th century
faïence

Pierre Clérissy, 1679–1728   Gvizy fchez Clerissy a Moustiers

son, Antoine II, 1728–1736

grandson, Pierre II,
1736–1783
sold to Joseph Fouque
1783–1852

1710–1740

Olerys, Joseph
Laugier, Jean-Baptiste
1738–*c.* 1790

marks attributed to
Olerys & Laugier
with painters' marks

£.S.c

OY   F.P.

I·E·BARON·1752

f   Fi

Joseph Fouque (*d.* 1800)
Jean-François Pelloquin
1749–1852

x J.Fouque

faïence tablewares,
large services and
altar vases

stencilled

Jean-Baptiste Ferrat
1718–1791

berrat moustier

the later wares in
Strasbourg style

Jean-Gaspard Féraud
1779–1792
(continued by
descendants until
1874)

f^d   F^d

later ware
depicted many
contemporary
events

i·BAIOL

Barbaroux
late 18th–early 19th
century

Jean-François Thion
1758–1788

Joseph-Gaspard Guichard
c. 1760

J Fouque Fecit

fouque
A
Moustiers   JHF

P.F.   F

X

FAÇON PORCELAINE
FOUQUE
DE MOUSTIERS

NANCY (Meuthe-et-Moselle)
Gallé, Emile (*b.* 1846, *d.* 1904)
artist-potter
(more renowned
for *l'art nouveau*
glass)

**GALLE
NANCY**

EFG
déposé

NEVERS (Nièvre)
16th century
faïence

IS89
FESI·A·
NEVRS

late 16th century

Agostino Corado
a Nev.ers

probably made by
Dominique Conrade
(*b.* 1630)

elecomrar
A Nevers

mark on group
attributed to
Denis Lefebvre
c. 1629–1649

DLF
1636

probably mark of
Gabriel Cassiat, painter
b. 1708, *d.* 1777

Calliat Pinx

dated 1731

Pierre or Philippe Haly
(sons of François Haly,
d. 1762)

HAly
1762
„hALy„
1772

probably made by
Henri Borne,
d. 1716

H·B
1689
EBorne
1689

J. Boulard, potter

'J. Boulard a Nevers
1622'

Pierre Custode and
family
1632–late 18th century

J:Custodeff

M. Montagnon,
late 19th century

reproductions of
earlier styles
such as *bleu
persan*

NIDERVILLER (or NEIDWILLER or
NIDERWEILER)
faïence, from 1754–
also porcelain from 1765–

Baron Jean-Louis de
Beyerlé, 1754–1770

marks on faïence
and porcelain

in
manganese   in
brown   black

mark found only
on porcelain

in blue

Comte de Custine
1770–1793

blue

brown   black

blue

mark normally found
only on porcelain

blue   brown

stencilled

Claude-François Lanfrey
1793–1827

signature of Lemire,
modeller, 1759–*c.* 1808–

LE MI RE PERE
incised

mark of late 18th-
century figures

NIDERVILLE
impressed in relief
on an applied label

NIDERVILLER
impressed

No·36 F
F No·37

incised

in use from start
of factory

N.
black

late 18th century

Nider
Niderviller
black

M. L. G. Dryander
1827–
earthenwares

NÎMES (Gard)
c. 1548–1620
tin-glazed wares
in Italian manner

Antoine Sigalon, *d.* 1590
(succeeded by nephews)

ORLÉANS (Loiret)
faïence from 17th century–
soft-paste porcelain from 1753–1812

Jean Louis, modeller
c. 1756–1760
Pierre Renault (or Renard)

both incised

mark sometimes attributed
to Orléans, but probably
Chantilly

registered porcelain-mark
(hard-paste from 1770)

both blue

registered porcelain-mark,
also found on '*faïence-fine*'

blue

Benoist Le Brun, 1806–1812

in red with blue dot

on later 'agate' and
marbled earthenware

GRAMMONT
LAINE FABQT
A ORLEANS

ORLEANS
both impressed

Molier-Bardin, late
18th-century porcelain

Barlois and Dabot
c. 1800

B D
Orleans
both stencilled in red

PARIS
    The major Paris factories are first
listed in alphabetical order of name,
followed by a list of later firms
and individuals, in some cases
decorators only.

Barrière de Reuilly, 1779–1785
Henri-Florentin Chanou

CH   C.H

red

Boulevard des Italiens
1830–
Cassé-Mailard
decorators
1845–
Chapelle-Maillard
decorators

red

gold

1830–
Montginot
decorator

gold

Boulevard Montmartre
1840–
Couderc
decorator

red

1806–
Person
decorator

gold

Boulevard Poissonnière
(*see* Petit rue Saint-Gilles)

Boulevard St. Antoine
(*see* Petit rue Saint-Gilles)

Boulevard Saint-Martin
(*see* Rue de Bondy)

Clignacourt, 1771–*c.* 1798
hard-paste porcelain
registered mark 1771–1775

underglaze   gold
blue

monogram of 'Protector'
Louis-Stanislas-Xavier
1775–1793

stencilled in red

'M' for 'Monsieur'

stencilled in red

Moitte, modeller
1791–1798

M

underglaze blue or
other colour

Cour des Fontaines
1800–1840
Bondeux
decorator
Cour-Mandar
1799–
Scheilheimer

Bondeux

Scheilheimer Cours Mandar
No 5

Escalier de Cristal
(*see* Palais Royal)

Faubourg Saint-Antoine
1773–
Morelle
(*see also* rue de la Roquette)

M.A.P

Faubourg Saint-Denis
   1771–*c.* 1828
Pierre Antoine Hannong
1771–1776
hard-paste porcelain

mark registered by
Hannong in 1773

all underglaze blue

mark registered by
Stahn in 1779, 'cp'
For Charles-Philippe,
Comte d'Artois,
protector of factory

CP
stencilled in red
cp
in underglaze blue

C.P.

in red or gold

Marc Schœlcher
c. 1800–*c.* 1810

Schoelcher

in red or other colour

Faubourg Saint-Honoré
(*see* Saint Cloud, rue de la Ville-'Evêque)

Faubourg Saint-Lazare
(*see* Faubourg Saint-Denis)

Galeries du Louvre
1793–
Lagrenée

reddish-brown

Gros Caillou (or Vaugirand-lès-Paris)
Broillet, Jacques-Louis
1765–
hard-paste porcelain

mark registered in 1762

L. B.

Advenier and Lamare
mark registered in 1773

SD

underglaze blue

La Courtille (or rue Fontaine-au-Roy or
   Basse Courtille, faubourg du Temple)
1771–*c.* 1840
hard-paste porcelain

forms of the mark
registered in 1773
by Jean Baptiste
   Locré

underglaze blue

incised

Palais Royal (*see* rue de Charonne)

Passage de l'Opéra
c. 1840
Gailliard, decorator
of porcelain

Gailliard
passage de
l'opéra.

gold

Petite rue Saint-Gilles (*or* Boulevard
   Saint Antoine)
1785–
hard-paste porcelain
François-Maurice Honoré

F. D. HONORÉ

F. M. HONORÉ

R. F. DAGOTY

DAGOTY ET HONORÉ

Pont-aux-Chou
1743–*c.* 1785
Claude-Humbert Gérin
earthenware, salt-glaze
stoneware and creamware

gold

hard-paste porcelain
mark registered by
Mignon in 1777

underglaze blue

Quai de la Cité
1790–1827
dealer and possibly
manufacturer of
hard-paste porcelain

gold

rue Amelot
1784–1825
hard-paste porcelain

La Marre de Villiers
and Montarcy
1784–1786

stencilled in red

Outrequin & Montarcy, 1786–
(under the protection of
Louis Philippe, Duke of
Orléans, 1786–1793)

stencilled in red

mark attributed to rue Amelot

gold or red

period of protection of
the Duke of Orléans

underglaze blue

period of *Restauration*
c. 1820–1825

*Lefevre rue Amelot
a Paris*
gold

rue de Bondy
1780–1829
hard-paste porcelain
Dihl (under protection
of the Duc d'Angoulême)
about 1780–1793

gold

mark registered in 1781,
perhaps Angoulême-Guerhard

gold or
underglaze blue

Guerhard in partnership
from c. 1786

c. 1780–1793

MANUF^RE
de M^OR le Duc
d'Angouleme

both stencilled in red

1817–1829

Dihl.

red or underglaze blue

late 18th–early 19th
century

MANUF^RE
de MM
Guerhard et
Dihl a Paris

stencilled in red

rue des Boulets (*see* rue Amelot)

rue de Charonne
1795–
hard-paste porcelain

Darte *frères*

DARTE
FREKES
A PAKIS

stencilled in red

later in rue de la Roquette,
rue Popincourt, decorating
shop in the Palais Royal,
until 1840 in the rue
Fontaine-au-Roi

rue de Crussol
1789–19th century
hard-paste porcelain
Christopher Potter

'Manufacture du Prince
de Galles'

transferred or leased
to E. Blancheron in
1792

'Potter Blancheron'

mark on biscuit-ware

rue Fontaine-au-Roy (*see* La Courtille)

rue du Petit Carrousel
1774–1800

Charles-Bartélémy Guy
decorator of hard-paste
porcelain

rue Popincourt
1782–c. mid-19th century
hard-paste porcelain

Nast, J.-N.-H.

rue des Récollets
1793–1825
hard-paste porcelain

Desprez, cameos
in Wedgwood style

rue de Reuilly
c. 1774–c. 1787
hard-paste porcelain

Jean-Joseph Lassia

rue de la Roquette
c. 1750–late 18th century
faïence and porcelain

DARTE
Palais Royal
n° 21

stencilled in red

Potter   B
Paris   Potter
86   42

underglaze blue

EB

PB

underglaze blue

E. BLANCHERON
in relief on
applied label

°P
C G
M.^to du Pt
Carousol
Paris

stencilled in red

NAST
a
PARIS

stencilled in red

DESPREZ
Rue DES RECOLLETS
A PARIS

DESPREZ

L.
red

L

in colour or gold

Ollivier, second half of 18th century
faïence

OLLIVIER
A PARIS
impressed

Ollivier a paris.
painted

1773–
hard-paste porcelain
mark registered by
Souroux
(to Rivet in 1784
and later Ollivier)

red   underglaze blue

Vincent Dubois, 1774–1787

underglaze blue

rue Saint-Pierre (*see* rue Amelot)

rue de Temple (*see* rue de Bondy)

rue Thiroux
c. 1775–19th century
hard-paste porcelain

underglaze blue

André-Marie Lebœuf
(protected by Queen
Marie-Antoinette)

A
stencilled in red

1794 Lebœuf & Housel

1797–98 Guy & Housel

1816–1832 Julienne

Rue Thirou
a Paris red

1832–1850 Léveillé

LEVEILLE
Rue 12 THIROUX

1850–1869 Poullain

1869– Léveillé

Minor manufacturers and decorators
mostly 19th century

Allard, at rue de Jour
1825–1828

A. Allard 1825

Bidot, Clement-Amédée
decorator of faïence

AB
black

Bossé, Hélène
19th-century decorator
in Italian maiolica
style

HB
black

Dastin, 1815–
at rue de Bondy
merchant and decorator

DASTIN

Dastin

gold and red

David, Michel
19th-century manufacture

Déroche, 1812–
decorator at rue
Jean-Jacques Rousseau

*Deroche
R.11 Rousseau
Paris*

Deck, Théodore (*b.* 1823, *d.* 1891)
one of the earliest
studio-potters *c.* 1859

FD

H. DECK

H · DECK·

incised, impressed or
transfer-printed

faïence, Chinese-type
glazes
(Director of Sèvres
   1887–1891)

'Decœur'
'E. Decœur'

Decœur, Emile (*b.* 1876)
studio-potter
stoneware
Delaherche, Auguste
(*b.* 1857, *d.* 1940)
studio-potter
stoneware

 ·FD·

incised or impressed

Devers, Joseph
c. 1847
faïence in early
styles

FD
in black

Duban, at rue Coquillère
1800–

Duban
in red

Feuillet, decorator
of hard-paste porcelain
1820–1845, copyist
of Sèvres styles

*Feuillet
2a de la Paix
n° 20*

gold or green

FLEUR·Y

Fleury at rue du
Faubourg Saint-Denis
1803–1835
hard-paste porcelain

Flamen
Fleury
a Paris
gold

Gaugain, 1815–
decorator of hard-
paste porcelain

Gaugain

Gerrier, le, 1850
decorators of hard-
paste porcelain

LE GERRIER
20 R DE LA HARPE
paris

red

Gille, *jeune*
1845–
biscuit-ware

(modeller Charles
Baury)

ℒC

incised

applied blue tablet

Gillet and Brianchon
Patented 'lustre-sheen'
on porcelain and pottery
1857

G.B
BREVETE
PARIS

black

Halley-Lebon, 1800–1812
decorator of hard-
paste porcelain

le bon halley

halley

gold

Honoré & Grouvelle
c. 1834–
hard-paste porcelain

H & C

red

Housset, 1845–1874
decorators of hard-
paste porcelain

MAISON HOUSSET
PARIS
50
FAUB. St HONORE

red

Jeanne, 1827–
decorator of hard-
paste porcelain

Jeanne

gold

Lagrenée *le jeune*
decorator of Paris
porcelain, 1793–1800
(also at Sèvres as
Art Director)

L'agrenée jne

reddish brown

Leofold, J.
manufacturer, modern

Leplé, 1820–
decorator of hard-
paste porcelain

Leplé je
rue du bacq n°19 a Paris
Leplé
je

Manteau, 1807–1811
decorator of hard-paste
porcelain

*Manteau
au
Veuve antique*

gold

Mansard, 1830–
decorator of hard-paste
porcelain

Menard, C. H., mid-
19th century
hard-paste porcelain

C.H.MENARD
Paris
72 rue de Popincourt

Pull, Georges
mid-19th century
imitator of Palissy
wares

PULL

relief, incised or
painted

Renou, 18th century–
1820
decorator of porcelain

Renou

gold

Revil, 1800–
decorator of Paris
porcelain

REVIL
Rue Neuve
des
Capucines

Rihouet, J., 1820–
decorator of Paris
porcelain

Rihouet

gold

Rousseau, F., 1837–1870
maker and decorator
of hard-paste porcelain

*Rousseau
43
Rue Coquillere*

Samson & Co., 7 rue Béranger, 1845–
'*Reproductions of Ancient Works
emanating from the Museums and
from private collections*'

Japanese and Chinese
wares

Persian and Hispano-
Moresque

Limousin enamels, Italian
and Italian wares

Sèvres and terracotta

Meissen

French, Italian, Spanish,
English porcelain,
European enamels

mark found chiefly on
so-called 'Chinese
Lowestoft'
(this mark may well
be that of another
French factory)

Serres, George
studio-potter
(*b.* 1889, *d.* 1956)

Sigel, Victor
hard-paste porcelain
modern

Toy, W. E.
1845–
dealer in porcelain

Iiélès, J.
hard-paste porcelain

POITIERS (Haute-Vienne)
1776–
faïence

    Pierre Pasquier &
    Felix Faulcon

        Morreine,
probably a modeller
of *terre de pipe*

PONSAS-SUR-RHÔNE
   Sorel, A.
   hard-paste porcelain

PONTENX (Landes)
1779–1790
hard-paste porcelain
de Rosly

PREMIÈRES (Côte-d'Or)
1783–
faïence

'PIGNANT GᵛᴱᵀE'
Premières (Côte-d'Or)

stencilled in blue

Lavelle, J.,

19th-century marks

QUIMPER (Finistère)
1690–
faïence

    Pierre-Paul Caussy
    1743–1782

    Hubaudière, Antoine de la
    1782–
    stoneware and faïence
    including *faïences*
       revolutionnaires
    Fougeray, 1872–
    imitation of 18th-
    century faïence

RAMBERVILLERS (Vosges)
1732– faïence
Jacques Chambrette

    Joseph Lacroix and
    descendants 1762–
    19th century
    faïence and creamware   'R'

                'DE MENONVILLE'

RENNES (Ille-et-Vilaine)
16th century, lead-glazed ware

faïence
1748–late 18th century

    Jean-Baptiste-Alexis
    Bourgoin, painter and
    modeller, 1756–

    Michel Derrennes,
    painter at factory started
    in 1749 by Tutrel

    Jean Baron, painter

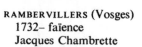

Hirel de Choisy, painter
(later at Sèvres)

Hirel de choisy pen
1767

ROUEN (Seine-Inférieure),
'maiolica' or 'faïence'
in Italian style
c. 1526–c. 1570

Masseot Abaquesne
'MAB'

in blue

inscription on tiles

'à Rouen 1542'

faïence
1644– Nicholas Poirel
1647– Edme Poterat
and son to at
least 1720

late 17th-century
marks found on Rouen
faïence, probably
painters'

signature of Claude
Borne, painter

Pinxit
·1736·
·CB

Dieul, painter
c. 1756

dieulo

Guillibaud factory
c. 1720–1750

Jean Bertin, potter
with father and family
c. 1700–1750

Pierre Heugue, c. 1700
family of potters 1698–
early 19th century

Paul Caussy, son
and grandson, 1707–

Fossé (or Fossey), c. 1740
and widow, potters
1740–at least 1757

Fossé

Michel-Mathieu &
Michel Vallet, potters
1757–

Pierre Mouchard &
family, potters from
c. 1740–

Jean-Marie Levavasseur
and family, potters from
c. 1700–

LE VAVASSEUR
A ROÜEN

Hubert Letellier,
potter from 1781–
(creamware from
1805)

Jean-Nicolas Bellanger
potter from 1800–

NIB

Metterie, 1823–
faïence

D M
A. ROUEN

Amédée Lambert
c. 1827–
faïence

impressed

ROUY (or Amigny-Rouy)
1790–1843
faïence in Strasbourg
style

'ROUY'

RUBELLES (Seine-et-Marne)
1836–
faïence and Palissy-
type earthenware

RUBELLES
S &M

applied tablet

Alexis du Tremblé
1836– *'terre de pipe'*

A DT

incised

RUNGIS (nr. Paris)
19th century
Fortuné de Monestrol
reproductions of
Gubbio (Italian)
lustreware

black

SAINT-AMAND-LES-EAUX (Nord)
faïence, white &
creamwares
1718–1882 (with
possible break from
1793–1818)

Pierre-Joseph Fauquez
(*d.* 1741) in family
until 1793

mark on creamware

all underglaze
blue

soft-paste porcelain
1771–1778
Jean-Baptiste-Joseph
Fauquez

probably F. Bastenaer-
Daudenaert, painter

Maximilien-Joseph
Bettignies
c. 1800–1882
reproductions of
Sèvres and other
early porcelain

red

underglaze blue

SAINT-CLÉMENT (Meurthe-et-Moselle)
faïence and white biscuit
figures of Lunéville

1758– Jacques Chambrette
(*d.* 1758)
1758–1763 Charles Loyal
& Paul-Louis Cyfflé

'SC'
in blue on
early faïence

19th-century mark

'St. Clement'
stencilled in blue

19th-century mark
on figures

'St. Cᵗ'
impressed

SAINT-CLOUD (Seine-et-Oise)
faïence
c. 1670– Pierre Chicaneau
(*d. c.* 1678) widow marries
Henri Trou

in blue

c. 1678–1766
soft-paste porcelain

rare early mark

incised

'sun-face' mark
(always in blue)

usual mark, including
'T' for Henri Trou,
after 1722, when
he was admitted to
the porcelain secret

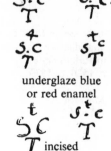

underglaze blue
or red enamel

incised

probably initials and
mark of Chicaneau
and Moreau of the
rue de la Ville-l'Evêque,
a Paris branch of the
St. Cloud factory, *c.* 1722

all in underglaze blue or red enamel

SAINT-GENOU (Indre)
hard-paste porcelain
1930–
'L'Union Française'

SAINT-OMER (Pas-de-Calais)
faïence
1751–end of 18th century

'SO'

Louis Saladin

'A Saint-Omer 1759'

SAINT-PAUL (Oise)
common faïence
late 18th–early 19th century

Michel

'St. Paul'

SAINT-PORCHAIRE (nr. Bressuire)
fine white earthenware
with inlaid decoration
also known as 'Henri Deux'
ware (64 pieces known)
1525–1560

incised

SAINT-SAVIN (Gironde)
faïence
late 18th century

'Man. de Fayence de Boyer à St. Savin'

SAINT-UZE (Drôme)
hard-paste porcelain
1847–
Gustave Revol

SAINT-VALLIER (Drôme)
porcelain & ovenware
1830–
H. Montagne

SAMADET (Landes)
faïence
1732–19th century

Moustiers & Marseilles
styles

 · Samadet 1732

SARREGUEMINES (Lorraine)
c. 1770
creamware, stoneware
and earthenware in
Wedgwood and other
English styles

M. Fabry &
Paul Utzschneider

'Sarguemines'

MAJOLICA
SARREGUEMINES

SCEAUX (Seine)
faïence
c. 1748–19th century
de Bey & Jacques
Chapelle

marks on faïence

OP OP

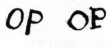

painted

late stencilled marks

Sceaux

sceaux
stencilled

late mark, made for
Château d'Anet

Anet

Sceaux
stencilled

'Sceaux Penthièvre'

·S·P
painted

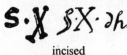
painted

early attempts at soft-paste porcelain
manufacture prevented by Vincennes
monopolies

soft-paste porcelain
marks from about
1763–

incised

anchor of Duc de Penthièvre,
Grand-Admiral de France
protector and patron of
Sceaux from c. 1775

SÈVRES (originally established at Vincennes)
soft-paste porcelain 1738–c. 1800
hard-paste porcelain c. 1770–present

Reigns of Louis XV and Louis XVI
(c. 1745–1793)

marks used before
1753–

blue enamel

underglaze blue   blue enamel

mark with date-letter
for 1753

blue enamel

mark with date-letter
for 1755

blue enamel

mark with date-letter
for 1754

blue enamel

mark with date-letter
for 1781 (crown
generally used on
hard-paste, *c.* 1770–
1793)

blue or red enamel

DATE-LETTERS

letters were used from 1753
until 17th July 1793 to indicate the
year of manufacture, the letter
was either within the 'crossed L's'
or alongside; the mark below, when
present, is usually that of the painter.

Key:/

A	indicates	1753	V	indicates	1774
B	„	1754	X	„	1775
C	„	1755	Y	„	1776
D	„	1756	Z	„	1777
E	„	1757	AA	„	1778
F	„	1758	BB	„	1779
G	„	1759	CC	„	1780
H	„	1760	DD	„	1781
I	„	1761	EE	„	1782
J	„	1762	FF	„	1783
K	„	1763	GG	„	1784
L	„	1764	HH	„	1785
M	„	1765	II	„	1786
N	„	1766	JJ	„	1787
O	„	1767	KK	„	1788
P	„	1768	LL	„	1789
Q	„	1769	MM	„	1790
R	„	1770	NN	„	1791
S	„	1771	OO	„	1792
T	„	1772	PP	„	1793
U	„	1773			(until 17th July)

First Republic (1793–1804)

all in blue

mark of the Consular
period (1803–1804)

M. N^le
Sèvres
— // —

printed in red

First Empire (1804–1814)
1804–1809 (specimen
of 1804)

stencilled in red

1810–1814

printed in red

c. 1810–1820, on cameo-
relief in Wedgwood
style

impressed

KEY TO DATE-LETTERS AND SIGNS
1801–1816

T9 indicates	IX (1801)		8	indicates	1808
X „	X (1802)		9	„	1809
II „	XI (1803)		10	„	1810
			oz	„	1811
„	XII (1804)		dz	„	1812
			tz	„	1813
„	XIII (1805)		qz	„	1814
			qn	„	1815
„	XIV (1806)		sz	„	1816
7 „	1807				

Reign of Louis XVIII (1814–1824)

21 = 1821

printed in blue

22 = 1822

printed in blue

Reign of Charles X (1824–1830)
1824–28
(24 = 1824)   printed in blue

(25 = 1825)   blue

(25 = 1825)   blue

1829–1830 (30 = 1830)	blue	
(30 = 1830)		
Reign of Louis-Philippe (1830–1848)		
(30 = 1830)	blue	
1831–1834 (34 = 1834)	blue or gold	
1834–1845 (1843)	blue or gold	
1845–1848 (48 = 1848)	chrome green	
1845–1848 (1848)	gold or blue	
destination marks added to special pieces ordered by the King	all in red	
Second Republic (1848–1852)		
mark for 1851 (similar marks used until 1899)	chrome green	
decoration mark for 1848	red	

decoration mark for 1849 — red

destination mark — red

Second Empire (1852–1870)

mark indicating revival of soft-paste (1854)

indicating decoration date

destination mark — all in red

Third Republic 1871–onwards

porcelain mark of 1900 and later — chrome green

stoneware mark of 1900 and later — chrome green

mark used on paste invented by Théodore Deck — in relief or printed in underglaze brown

indication of date of gilding (1872) — red

indication of date of decoration (1872) — red

biscuit figures, 1860–1899
(previously unmarked)

SEVRES

impressed

destination mark

red

PEKIN

cancelled mark on
rejected pieces sold
undecorated (1891)

S.91

chrome green
cancelled by a cut
on the wheel

Emile Lessore (*d.* 1876)
painter at Sèvres until
1850

E Lessore

MARKS OF PAINTERS GILDERS and other ARTISTS EMPLOYED AT SÈVRES

$\mathcal{N}$	ALONCLE, François, birds	1758–1781
$\mathcal{J.A}$	ANDRÉ, Jules, landscapes and animals	1843–1869
(house symbol)	ANTHAUME, Jean-Jacques landscapes & animals	1752–1758
$\mathcal{A}$	ARCHELAIS, decorator of *pâte-sur-pâte*	1865–1902
$\mathcal{H}$	ARMAND, P-L-P, flowers and gilding	1746–1788
$\mathcal{A}$	ASSELIN, figures and portraits	1764–1804
(symbol)	AUBERT, *aîné*, flowers	1754–1758
$\mathcal{By}$	BAILLY, *père*, gilder	1753–1767
$=$	BARBET flowers	1751–1758
$\mathcal{B}$	BARBIN, François-Hubert ornaments	1815–1849
$\mathcal{fB}$	BARRAT, *l'oncle*, fruit & flowers	1769–1791
$\mathcal{B}$	BARRE, flowers and ornaments	1773–1774 & 1776–1778
$\mathcal{AB}$	BARRE, Louis Desiré flowers	1844–1881
$\mathcal{B}$	BARRIAT, Charles figures	1848–1883
$\mathcal{GD}$	BAUDOUIN, *père* gilder	1750–1780
$\mathcal{Y}$	BECQUET, flowers	1749–1750 & 1753–1765
$\mathcal{BS}$	BERANGER, Antoine figures	1807–1846

$\dot{c}$	BERTRAND, flowers	1757–1774
(star symbol)	BIENFAIT, Jean-Baptiste gilder and painter	1756–1762
(symbol)	BINET, flowers	1750–1775
	BINET, *Dlle, see* Chanou, Sophie	
$\mathcal{AB}$	BLANCHARD, Alexandre decorator	1878–1901
$\mathcal{B.T}$	BOITEL, Charles-Marie-Pierre gilder	1797–1822
$\mathcal{B}$	BONNUIT, Achile decorator	1858–1894
(bird symbol)	BOUCHER, flowers and garlands	1754–1762
(symbol)	BOUCHET, Jean landscapes	1763–1793
$Pb \cdot \mathcal{PB}$	BOUCOT, P., flowers and birds	1785–1791
$\mathcal{Y}$	BOUILLAT, *fils*, flowers and landscapes	1785–1793
	BOUILLAT, Rachel, *see* Maqueret	
$\mathcal{B}$	BOULANGER, *père* gilder	1754–1784
$\mathcal{\&}$	BOULANGER, *fils* pastorals & children	1778–1781
$\mathcal{AB}$	BOULLEMIER, Antoine-Gabriel gilder	1802–1842
$\mathcal{F.B}$	BOULLEMIER, François-Antoine gilder	1806–1838
$\mathcal{Bh}$	BOULLEMIER, *fils* gilder	1813–1855
$D^n\mathcal{B}$	BOULLEMIER, *Dlle* gilder	1814–1842
$\mathcal{Bn.}$	BULIDON, flowers	1763–1792
$\mathcal{B}$	BULOT, Eugène flowers	1855–1883
MB	BUNEL, *veuve* Marie-Barbe flowers	1778–1816
(symbol)	BUTEUX, *aîné*, Charles figures	1756–1782
$9.$	BUTEUX, *jeune* flowers	1759–1766
$\triangle$	BUTEUX, *fils cadet* flowers and landscapes	1773–1790
$\mathcal{Bx}$	BUTEUX, Théodore	1786–1822
$\mathcal{X}$	CABAU, Eugène-Charles flowers	1847–1885
$\triangle$	CAPELLE, landscapes	1746–1800
$C.\mathcal{P}$	CAPRONNIER, François gilder	1812–1819
(symbol)	CARDIN, flowers	1749–1786
	CARON (signs in full)	1792–1815

5.	CARRIÉ, flowers	1752–1757
C.	CASTEL, landscapes & birds	1772–1797
✱	CATON, figures & pastorals	1749–1798
S	CATRICE, flowers	1757–1774
J.C	CÉLOS, decorator of *pâte-sur-pâte*	1865–1895
ch	CHABRY, *fils*, pastorals	1765–1787
JD	CHANOU, *Dame*, gilder	1779–1800
Sc	CHANOU, *Dame* Sophie (*née* Binet) flowers	1779–1798
Cp	CHAPPUIS, *aîné* flowers & birds	1761–1787
JC.	CHAPPUIS, *jeune* flowers	1772–1777
LC	CHARPENTIER, gilder	1852–1879
J.C.	CHARRIN, *Dlle* Fanny figures	1814–1826
✕	CHAUVEAUX, *aîné* gilder and painter	1753–1788
JH.	CHAUVEAUX, *fils* bouquets	1773–1783
⚭	CHEVALIER, flowers (BOULANGER used similar mark)	1755–1757
Ä ⚓	CHOISY, flowers and ornaments	1770–1812
♫	CHULOT, flowers and emblems	1755–1800
cm	COMMELIN, flowers and garlands	1768–1802
C.C.	CONSTANT, gilder	1803–1840
C.t.	CONSTANTIN, figure subjects	1813–1848
∫	CORNAILLES, Antoine-Toussaint flowers	1755–1800
C C.	COUTURIER, flowers & gilding	1762–1775
DALOU	DALOU, Jules, modeller & sculptor	1879–1887
DAMMOUSE	DAMMOUSE, Pierre-Adolphe modeller & designer	1852–1880
R	d'APOIL, figures	1851–1884
AD	DAVID, Alexandre ornaments	1844–1881
D.F.	DAVIGNON, Jean-François figures	1807–1812
de Gault	DEGAULT, Jean-Marie figures	1808–1817
DF	DELAFOSSE, Denis figures	1804–1815

DP	DEPÈRAIS (or DESPÈRAIS), C. ornaments	1794–1822
DG	DERISCHSWEILER, J-C-G. gilder	1855–1884
Dh	DEUTSCH, ornaments & flowers	1803–1819
CD	DEVELLY, Jean-Charles animals	1813–1848
D.I	DIDIER, Charles-Antoine ornaments	1819–1848
D	DIEU, painter and gilder	1777–1790 1794–1798, 1801–1811
D	DOAT, T-M, sculptor & *pâte-sur-pâte*	1879–1905
K...	DODIN, figures & portraits	1754–1802
DR	DRAND, chinoiseries & gilding	1764–1775 1780
D.C	DROUET, flowers & birds	1785–1825
🌿	DUBOIS, Jean-René flowers	1756–1757
Ac.D	DUCLUZEAU, *Dame* figures	1818–1848
D.y	DUROSEY, C-C-M. gilder	1802–1830
D.	DUSOLLE, flowers	1768–1774
DT	DUTANDA, flowers	1780–1802
CD	DUVELLY, Charles landscapes	1813–1848
⅔	EVANS, birds, butterflies, landscapes	1752–1806
F	FALLOT, birds and ornaments	1773–1790
HF	FARAGUET, figures	1857–1879
E	FICQUENET, flowers & *pâte-sur-pâte*	1864–1881
.·.·	FONTAINE, flowers & ornaments	1752–1775 1778–1807
J	FONTAINE, Jean-Joseph flowers	1825–1857
♡	FONTELLIAU, A., gilder and colour-maker	1753–1754
Y	FOURÈ, flowers	1749 1754–1762
☀	FRITSCH, figures & children	1763–1764
fx.ft	FUMEZ, flowers	1777–1804
Gu	GANEAU, *fils*, gilders	1813–1831
🦋	GAUTIER, figures & landscapes	1787–1791
J.G	GÉLY, J., *pâte-sur-pâte*	1851–1889
G	GENEST, figures	1752–1789

GENIN, flowers	1756–1757
GEORGET, figures	1801–1823
GÉRARD, Claude-Charles pastorals	1771–1804
GÉRARD, *Dame* (*née* Vautrin) flowers	1781–1802
GIRARD, arabesques	1762–1764
GOBERT, figures	1849–1891
GODIN, gilder, painter & ground-layer	1792–1833
GOMERY, birds & flowers	1756–1758
GOUPIL, figures	after 1800
GRÉMONT, *jeune* flowers	1769–1775 1778–1781
GRISON, gilder	1749–1771
GUILLEMAIN, decorator	1864–1885
HALLION, Eugène landscapes	1872–1893
HALLION, François gilder & decorator	1865–1895
HENRION, *aîné*, flowers	1770–1784
HÉRICOURT, flowers	1770–1773 1776–1774
HILEKEN, figures	1769–1774
HOURY, flowers	1754–1755
HUARD, ornaments	1811–1846
HUMBERT, figures	1851–1870
JOYAU, flowers	1766–1775
JUBIN, gilder	1772–1775
JULES André landscapes	1840–1869
KNIPP, *Dame*, flowers & birds	1808–1809 1817–1826
LAMBERT, flowers	1859–1899
LAMPRECHT, figures & animals	1784–1787
LANGLACE, landscapes	1807–1814
LAROCHE (de) flowers	1759–1802
LÉANDRE, children & emblems	1779–1785
LE BEL, *aîné*, figures and flowers	1766–1775

LE BEL, *jeune* flowers	1773–1793
LE BEL, *Dame* flowers	1777–1790 1804–1805
LECOT, gilder & painter	1773–1802
LEDOUX, birds & landscapes	1753–1761
LEGAY, *pâtes-sur-pâtes*	1866–1895
LE GAY, figures, portraits, etc.	1778–1840
LE GRAND, painter & gilder	1776–1817
LE GUAY, *père* E.-A. gilder	1749–1796
LE GUAY, Pierre-André figures	1772–1818
LE GUAY, E.-C. figures	1778–1840
LEVÉ, Denis, flowers & ornaments	1754–1805
LEVÉ, Felix, flowers & chinoiseries	1777–1779
MAQUERET, *Dame*, flowers (*née* Rachel Bouillat)	1796–1820
MASSY, flowers & birds	1779–1803
MAUSSION, figures	1862–1870
MÉREAUD, *aîné*, flowers and borders	1754–1791
MÉREAUD, *jeune* flowers	1756–1779
MERIGOT, ornaments	1845–1892
MEYER, figures	1858–1871
MICAUD, Jacques flowers & ornaments	1757–1810
MICAUD, Pierre-Louis painter & gilder	1795–1834
MICHEL, Ambroise	1772–1780
MILET, Optat decorator	1862–1879
MIREY (or NUREY) gilder	1788–1792
MOIRON, flowers	1790–1791
MONGENOT, flowers	1754–1764
MOREAU, D.-J., gilder	1807–1815
MORIN, military & sea-pieces	1754–1787
MORIOT, figures	after 1800
MUTEL, landscapes & birds	1754–1773

ng.	NICQUET, flowers	1764–1792	XX	ROCHER, figures	1758–1759
	NOËL, figures	1755–1804	N	ROSSET, flowers & landscapes	1753–1795
SD	NOUALHIER, *Dame* flowers	1777–1795	RL	ROUSSELLE, flowers	1758–1774
	NUREY, *see* MIREY		PMR	ROUSSEL, figures	1850–1871
	PAJOU, figures	1751–1759	P.S	SCHILT, Louis-Pierre flowers	1818–1855
P	PARPETTE, flowers	1755–1757 1773–1806	S.h.	SCHRADRE, birds & landscapes	1773–1775 1780–1786
P	PARPETTE, *aînée, Dlle* flowers	1788–1798		SINSSON (or SISSON), N. flowers	1773–1795
P	PARPETTE, *jeune, Dlle* flowers	1794–1798 1801–1817	SS	SINSSON (or SISSON), J. flowers	1795–1846
P.T.	PETIT, *aîné*, gilder	1756–1806	SSp	SINSSON (or SISSON), P. flowers	1818–1848
f	PFEIFFER, flowers	1771–1800	SSl	SINSSON (or SISSON), L. flowers	1830–1847
·P·H·	PHILIPPINE, *aîné* pastorals & children	1778–1791 1802–1825	R	SIOUX, *aîné*, flowers & borders	1752–1792
P.h.	PHILIPPINE, *cadet* flowers & animals	1783–1791 1801–1839	O	SIOUX, *jeune* flowers	1752–1759
pe	PIERRE, *aîné*, gilder	1759–1775	S.H.	SWEBACH, military subjects	1802–1813
pg	PIERRE, *jeune*, Jean-Jacques flowers	1763–1800	◇	TABARY, birds	1754–1755
P.t.	PITHOU, *aîné*, figures	1757–1790		TAILLANDIER, flowers	1753–1790
P.j.	PITHOU, *jeune*, flowers & figures	1760–1795	•••	TANDART, *jeune*, Charles flowers	1756–1760
P	PLINE, decorator	1854–1870	▣	TARDY, flowers	1755–1795
	POUILLOT, flowers	1773–1778	TANAY	TAUNAY	1745–1778
R	POUPART, Achille landscapes	1815–1848	••••	THEODORE, painter & gilder	1765–1779
HP.	PRÉVOST, *aîné*, gilder	1754–1759		THÉVENET, *père*, flowers	1741–1777
·:...	RAUX, *aîné*, flowers	1766–1779	jt	THÉVENET, *fils*, flowers	1752–1758
JR	RÉGNIER, Hyacinthe figures	1825–1863	J.T	TRAGER, Jules, flowers & birds	1847–1873
R	REIGNIER, Ferdinand figures, etc.	1812–1848	T	TROYON, painter & gilder	1801–1817
R	REJOUX, Emile decorator	1858–1893	V	VANDÉ, *père*, gilder	1753–1779
	RENARD, Emile decorator	1852–1882	VD	VANDÉ, P.-J.-B., gilder	1779–1824
ER	RICHARD, Eugène flowers	1833–1872	W	VAVASSEUR, *aîné*, flowers	1753–1770
R	RICHARD, François decorator	1832–1875		VIEILLARD, painter	1752–1790
R	RICHARD, Joseph decorator	1831–1872	⊔	VINCENT, *aîné*, gilder	1753–1758
RB	ROBERT, J.-F. landscapes	1806–1843	2000		
PR	ROBERT, P.-R. ornaments	1813–1832	2000	VINCENT, *jeune*, gilder	1753–1806

W WEYDINGER, Joseph, gilder 1778–1824
and painter

W WEYDINGER, *père*, flowers 1757–1807
and gilding

3V WEYDINGER, Pierre, painter 1781–1816
and gilder

✠ XHROUET, landscapes 1750–1775

1844–1852
N. Moriot
decorator in the style
of Sèvres

sèvres

1866–
Paul Milet & Fils
artist-potters
1941–
Céramique d'Art Milet

SINCENY (Aisne)
1733–1864
faïence

J. B. de Fayard &
Denis-Pierre Pellevé

·S·

early marks, 1733–1775

·Ŝ·   *·S·*

sincheny
all in blue

'second period' marks
1775–1795

à Sinceny

S·c·ÿ   *s·г·y·*

Pierre Bertrand, painter
third quarter 18th century

·B·T

Alexandré Daussy, painter
mid-18th century

·S·
✠ D
all in black

Denis-Pierre Pellevé
1733–1737, director

'S pellevé'

Pierre Jeannot, painter
c. 1740

Ǫ

Joseph Bedeaux, painter
mid-18th century

B

Leopold Malériat, painter
1737–1775

L·m·

Joseph Le Cerf, painter
c. 1773

LJLC
PINXIT 1778

François-Joseph Ghåil
1769

Gℓ

Lecomte and Dantier   'L. et D.'
1824–

Mandois   *'Mandois'*

STRASBOURG (Alsace)
also HAGUENAU
1721–1781
faïence
porcelain from *c.* 1752
(forced to transfer porcelain manufacture
to FRANKENTHAL, Germany in 1755)

1721–1739 Charles-François Hannong
c. 1740–1760 Paul Hannong
1762–1781 Joseph Hannong

painters' marks *c.* 1721–1740:

Nicholas Mittmann

Henri Montoson

Joseph Hannsmann *or*
Jean Hermann

all in blue

mark on Strasbourg   'PH'
porcelain 1752–1755   impressed
(also on FRANKENTHAL)

faïence marks of Paul Hannong (*c.* 1740–1760)
sometimes with a painter's mark

probably Jean Kugelmann
painter

violet   blue and purple

all in blue
blue and green

faïence marks of Joseph Hannong 1762–1781

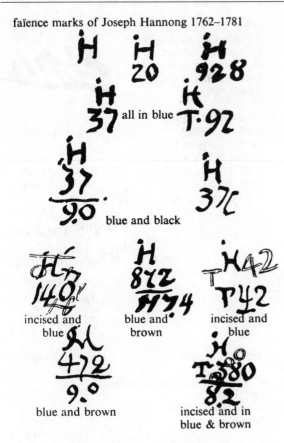

all in blue

blue and black

incised and blue

blue and brown

incised and blue

blue and brown

incised and in blue & brown

marks on Joseph Hannong's porcelain table wares

incised and in blue

incised and in grey

incised and in blue and brown

incised and in blue

incised and in blue and grey

marks on Joseph Hannong's porcelain figures

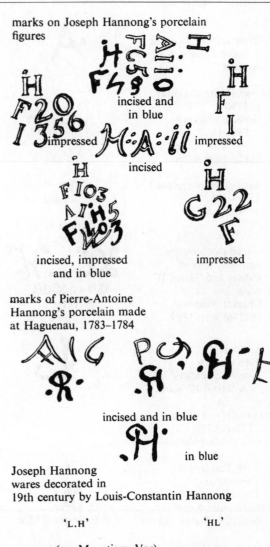

incised and in blue

impressed

impressed

incised

incised, impressed and in blue

impressed

marks of Pierre-Antoine Hannong's porcelain made at Haguenau, 1783–1784

incised and in blue

in blue

Joseph Hannong wares decorated in 19th century by Louis-Constantin Hannong

'L.H'   'HL'

TAVERNES (nr. Moustiers, Var)
1760–1780
faïence
Gaze

G

TOULOUSE (Haute-Garonne)
17th century–1849
lead-glazed earthenware
faïence and creamware

17th-century slipware

'Mathieu de Benque Sieur de Fustinac 1657'

inscription on faïence pilgrim-bottle

'Laurens Basso A Toulouza. Le 14th May 1756'

creamware 1797–
Joseph-Jacques Fouque &
Antoine Arnoux

from 1829 François &
Antoine Fouque with
Arnoux

TOURS (Indre-et-Loire)
c. 1750–
faïence, Mathurin
Epron
1770– Thomas Sailly
1782– Noël Sailly

'*Fait à Tours ce
21 Mars 1782*'

hard-paste porcelain
1776–1783
by Sailly & Son

'A Tours 1782'
incised

'Tours 1778'
in brown

glazed earthenware
reproductions of
Palissy and 'Henri II'
ware
Charles Avisseau
1842–at least 1889

aVisseau
atour
1855

Landais, M.
19th century
copyist of Palissy
& 'Henri II' wares

L

VALENCIENNES (Nord)
1735–c. 1780
unidentified faïence

J.-B- Fauquez &
Lamoninary
1785–1795; 1800–1810
hard-paste porcelain
including biscuit figures

VALENCIEN

underglaze blue

VALENTINE (Haute-Garonne)
faïence and hard-paste
porcelain
Fouque, Arnoux & Cie
1832–1860
(finally closing, after
English owners, in 1890)

A

in red

VALLAURIS
Clément & Jérôme Massier
at Golfe Juan
c. 1870–
artist potters
Lucien Levy, artist
& designer

Clement-Massier
Golfe-Juan.AM

L LEVY

Jerôme Massier
Vallauris

JEROME
MASSIER
VALLAURIS

1946–
Pablo Picasso (b. 1881)
worked at Madoura
workshop in collaboration
with Suzanne & Georges
Ramié, potters

VALOGNES (Manche)
1792– Le Tellier
hard-paste porcelain
1793–1797 Le Masson
1797–1802 Pelouze
1802–1812 Langlois
(then to Bayeux)

PORCELAINE
DE VALOGNES

MANUFACTURE
DE VALOGNES

M^{re}
de
Valognes
L.......

M^{RE} DE
VALOGNES

Mre de Valognes

artist, D. Fontaine

D.F.   P.Fontaine fecit

VAL-SOUS-MEUDON (Seine-et-Oise)
1802–1818
white earthenware
Mittenhoff

1806–1818
Mittenhoff & Mouron

MITTENHOFF
ET MOURON

VARAGES (Var)
faïence in Moustiers
& Marseilles styles
late 17th century–
at least 1800

'*Fait par moi
E. armand à varages
1698*'

V V V

VAUX (nr. Meulan, Seine-et-Oise)
hard-paste porcelain
1769–
Laborde & Hocquart

X X

'HL'

VENDRENNE (Vendée)
1800–
hard-paste porcelain decoration
Marc Lozelet

VIERZON (Cher)
  hard-paste porcelain

1815– Pétry & Rousse
Hache & Pépin-Le-Halleur

H & PL
V

Hache & Julien

H. J & C⁰
V

  all late 19th-century
       marks

A. H & C⁰
V
FRANCE

Rondeleux et Cie
1902–
porcelain for hotel use

Jaquin et Cie
porcelain (modern)

VILLEDIEU-SUR-INDRE
1882–
porcelain
Jean Lang

JL
V
FRANCE

VILLENAUXE-LE-GRANDE
  modern
  Tessier & Cie
  biscuit-ware and
  art-ware

VINCENNES
  soft-paste porcelain (*see under* SÈVRES)

VOISINLIEU (nr. Beauvais)
  salt-glaze stoneware
  1839–*d.* 1856

  Ziegler, Jules-Claude

VRON (Somme)
  1770–
  faïence

'MANUFACTURE DE
VRON 25 AVRIL
DELAHODDE-VERLINGUE
1815'

1815– Delahodde

table-wares & tiles

'VRON'
impressed

'Fabrique de la Vᵉ
Delahodde à Vron'

Germany and Related Areas
(including Bohemia, Moravia and Silesia)

The late-medieval pottery of Germany consists for the greater part of jugs and cups with very little decoration apart from the fifteenth-century decorated wares at Dreihausen. The material was grey, often fired to a stoneware hardness with occasional reddish or brown colouring due to a wash of ferruginous material. The locality of origin of early specimens is often hard to determine though it is certain that Cologne (Köln) and the Rhineland were from early times famous for pottery-making.

Salt-glazed stoneware, which takes rank with the finest German Renaissance art, is indeed among the best pottery ever produced in Europe, and was made from the middle of the sixteenth century at four centres in Rhineland-Cologne, Siegburg, Raeren and the Westerwald; several places in Saxony, Freiburg and Altenburg being important during the seventeenth century; and Kreussen in Bavaria where painted stoneware was developed on the one hand from the Saxon and on the other from the *Hafner*-ware for which the chief Kreussen workers—members of the Vest family—were already famous.

Minor centres were in the Upper Hesse, where a grey and blue ware like that of the Westerwald, with incised decoration, was made in the eighteenth century; brown ware was made at Duingen in Hanover, at Bunzlau in Silesia and at Muskau and Triebel in Upper Lusatia.

The chief merits of the earthenware made by the late fifteenth-, sixteenth- and seventeenth-century German *Hafner* or local stove-makers was in the fine masculine use of green and other coloured glazes, and a rude native strength in design.

Italian-inspired maiolica first made its appearance in Germany during the sixteenth century in the form of panels in large earthenware stoves, followed by a principal and important class of jugs in the form of owls which bear dates ranging from 1540–61. The seventeenth-century faïence doves and blue-and-white faïence made by Lorenz Speckner at Kreussen should also be mentioned.

Whilst the above maiolica wares were probably the work of *Hafner* or other potters, the noble jugs of Hamburg were probably the regular productions of a maiolica-potter.

The great German faïence-industry dating from the latter part of the seventeenth century aimed first of all at reproducing blue-and-white porcelain then being imported from China. The products of Hanau and Frankfurt-am-Main were for long mistaken for Delftware, whilst the early wares of Berlin, Brunswick, Zerbst and many minor factories were of Dutch inspiration.

Contemporary with the rise of Hanau a new development took place in the use of undecorated faïence, chiefly from that factory, by the *Hausmaler* or 'out-side' decorators, the majority of whom worked in Nuremberg.

From about 1715–40, at both Nuremberg and Bayreuth factories, was developed a highly individual Baroque style for the greater part decorated in high-temperature colours. At Ansbach, equally interesting and refined Baroque decoration was invented, side by side with some versions of the Chinese porcelain of the *famille verte* which are chiefly remarkable for their colour.

From about 1740 onwards the wares of Fulda, Höchst, Strasbourg and Kunersberg all begin to show the influence of porcelain, particularly that of Meissen, in painting in enamel colours, and the 'Strasbourg style' of painting on faïence in enamel colours became widely fashionable.

At the head of the minor factories stand those of Thuringia, where at Dorotheenthal and Abtsbessingen were made blue-and-white and high-temperature polychrome faïence in Baroque style equal in quality to that of Bayreuth and Nuremberg.

Imitations of the English cream-coloured earthenware were made at many places in Germany together with black-basaltes and agate-wares in the Wedgwood style.

Soft-paste porcelain was practically never made in Germany (Volkstedt is a negligible example), while the making of hard-paste was fostered at very many of the small independent states of which the country was made up in the eighteenth century.

Bottger's discovery of red stoneware and porcelain in 1708–9 gave the Royal Saxon factory at Meissen (founded in 1710) a lead which it did not lose until the Seven Years' War (1756–63). No other German factory succeeded in making true porcelain until the middle of the century, when within a space of ten years no fewer than six other princedoms had established local manufactories, some of which endured for fifty years or more. But in most, the finest work was done only in the short period of the prince's personal interest and enthusiasm for the affair, generally between 1750–75, when the material was in the height of fashion.

Chief among these later patronized factories were Höchst, Frankenthal, Nymphenburg, Ludwigsburg, Fürstenberg and Berlin, the last having a predominance well into the nineteenth century.

In addition to many minor factories throughout Germany under princely protection, a large number of private factories sprang up towards 1770 in the forest region of Thuringia, but with the exception of Gotha and Kloster-Veilsdorf their productions were coarse, grey in material and of little artistic importance.

The work of the *Hausmaler* on porcelain is of great

interest, especially about 1720–50, and should not be overlooked.

CZECHOSLOVAKIA. Late-medieval wares are ascribed to Loschitz and Brunn in Moravia; the former was a class of stoneware sometimes with graphite-blackened surface, whilst the latter were pottery cups of distinctive form, sometimes decorated with masks on the upper part.

A distinct and important type of peasant maiolica known as '*Habaner*' ware was made from the late sixteenth and seventeenth centuries onwards. Some of the earlier specimens show a striking resemblance to late Italian maiolica and the seventeenth-century types resemble the contemporary wares of Winterthur in Switzerland, which perhaps had a parallel derivation.

In the early nineteenth century considerable factories making cream-coloured earthenware and lead-glazed earthenware in the English style were conducted at Prague and Kaschau. A number of small manufactories of porcelain sprang up at Schlaggenwald and elsewhere in Bohemia in the early part of the nineteenth century.

ABTSBESSINGEN (Thuringia)
mid-18th century
faïence

fork from the arms of Schwarzburg
and painters' initials

'J. G. Kiel 1756'

probably initials of   'G. F.'
George Fuchs, painter, 1760–1772

AICH (nr. Karlsbad, Bohemia)
c. 1870
hard-paste porcelain
Moehling, M. J.

Anger, A. C. J., c. 1900

impressed

'Epiag', c. 1940
(Erste böhmische Porzellan-
Industrie-Akt. Ges.)

ALEXANDRINENTHAL (nr. Oeslau, Thuringia)
1886–
hard-paste porcelain

Recknagel, Th.

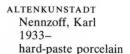

ALTENBURG (Thuringia)
late 18th–early 19th century
earthenware

1794–1806 brothers Döll   A
                 impressed

1806– Mühlberg, Heinrich

ALTENKUNSTADT
Nennzoff, Karl
1933–
hard-paste porcelain

Rothemund, Hager & Co.
20th century
hard-paste porcelain

ALTHALDENSLEBEN (Hanover)
early 19th century
cream-coloured earthenware (1810–)
and porcelain (1826–)

Nathusius, Gottlob, 1810–   N
                       impressed

ALT-ROHLAU (Bohemia)
1811–
cream-coloured earthenware
& hard-paste porcelain
Hasslacher, Benedict
1813–1823

Nowotny, August
1823–1884

Zdekauer, Moritz
c. 1900

1920–1938

M Z

1938–1945

'Epiag', 1885–
(see Aich)
hard-paste porcelain

Gutherz, Oscar & Edgar
1899–
hard-paste porcelain

underglaze green

Manka, Franz
1833–
hard-paste porcelain

Schneider & Co.
1904–
hard-paste porcelain

Porzellanfabrïk Viktoria (Victoria)
Schmidt & Co.
1883–

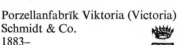

ALTWASSER (Silesia)
1845–
hard-paste porcelain

Tielsch, C. & Co.

AMBERG (Bavaria)
1759–1910
general pottery

1759–, Hetzendörfer, Simon
usual monogram on faïence

1790–, cream-coloured
earthenware and hard-paste
porcelain and reproductions
of Ludwigsburg porcelain models

AMBERG
impressed

ANSBACH (Bavaria)
c. 1710–
faïence, white & cream-
coloured earthenware

rare factory marks:

abbreviation for Onolzbach,
18th-century name for Ansbach

dated 1730

'Ansbach Popp' (after 1769)

mark of Steinlein's cream-
coloured earthenware
1807–1839

'Fay: Porcell:'

painters' marks:

Ripp, Johann Caspar
1710–1712

Oswald, George Christian
1711–1733

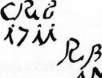

Bontemps, Johann Valentin
c. 1716–1729

Popp, Johann Georg Christoph
1715– (*d.* 1786)

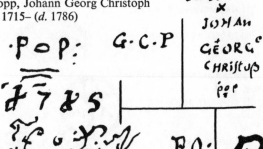

Wackenfeld, Johann Heinrich
1716–1719

Kruckenberger, Christian Imanuel
1718–1730

Uz, Johann Leonhard
1723–1750

Meyerhöfer, Johann Wolfgang
1724–1756

Förster, Johann Leonhard
1732–1744

Hofmann, Georg Nicolaus
1732–1738

Wolf, Joachim Leonhard
1726–1730

Popp, Johann Julius
dated 1749

Rosa, Mathias Carl
1746–1766

hard-paste porcelain
1758–1860 (transferred
to Bruckberg, 1762)

mark before transfer

late marks

all in blue

usually on figures

impressed

ARZBERG (Bavaria)
Auvera, Carl
1884–
hard-paste porcelain

CA

Hutschenreuther, C. M.
1839–
hard-paste porcelain

'Porzellanfabrik Schönwald'
c. 1900–
hard-paste porcelain

Schumann, Carl
1881–
hard-paste porcelain
& decorators

ASCHACH (N. Bavaria)
1829–1860
general pottery

Sattler, Wilhelm & Son

W. S. & S.
impressed
(mark also used
at Bodenbach)

ASCHACH
impressed

AUGSBURG (Swabia)
Hausmalerei ('home-painting')
18th century
Aufenwerth, Johann, (*d.* 1728)
porcelain—*Hausmaler*

iAW

Seuter, Bartholomäus, *b.* 1678,
d. 1754

B.S.

Wald, Anna Elizabeth

"*Augsberg*, 1748
*Künersberg Anna
Elizabeth Wald*"

AUMUND (nr. Vegesack, Bremen
in Hanover)
1751–1761
faïence

Mülhausen, Johann Christoph
Terhellen, Wilhelm
Terhellen, Diederich
1751–1757

M. J. T

Terhellen, D. & W.
1751–1757

D & WT

Erberfeld, Albrecht von
1757–1761

A v E

AUSSIG (Bohemia)
1881–
general pottery
Kindler, Bernhard
Kindler, Paul

P. K.
A.

BADEN-BADEN
1770–
faïence, porcelain &
earthenware

Pfalzer, Zacharias
1770–1778

in underglaze blue
on porcelain

in black or colour
on faïence

Anstett, François-Antoine II
1793, glazed earthenware

AA   AA

BAYREUTH (Bavaria)
c. 1713–
faïence

early marks (before 1728)

Bayreu:

Bäyr-

Ripp, Johann Kaspar
dated 1714

**RiB
1714**

marks of the 'Knöller period'
1728–1744
(G. W. Knöller was proprietor)

BK ·B·K·
all in blue

Hagen, G. A., painter

**B·K
GAH**

mark of Knöller with
that of Johann Clarner
painter

Bayr.K

Jucht, Johann Christoph
painter

B·K·

Parsch, Wolfgang Heinrich
painter

B. K.

Fränkel, Adolf (*d.* 1747)
Schreck, Johann Veit
proprietors, 1745–1747

**W.P.
B.J.S.**

Popp, Johann Albrecht
painter

Pfeiffer & Fränkel (widow)
proprietors, 1747–60

Pfeiffer, Johann Georg
proprietor, 1760–67

Pfeiffer and Johann Martin
Anton Oswald, painter

Hagen, Johann Markus
(*b.* 1737, *d.* 1803), painter

all in blue

Wezel, C. A., 1788–1806
proprietor
faïence & cream-coloured
earthenware

WEZEL
impressed

Steinbach, Johann Henrich
(*d.* 1761), painter

brown & yellow earthenwares:

signature of J. W. G. Wanderer
dated 1724

marks of members of
the Wanderer family

Horn, Johann August
dated 1749

Fiechthorn, Johann Andreas
c. 1745, painter

Metzsch, Johann Friedrich
1735–1751, *Hausmaler*

Meyer, Siegm. Paul
1886–
hard-paste porcelain

BELGERN (nr. Torgau, Saxony)
early 19th century
white earthenware & stoneware

'BELGERN'
impressed

BERLIN (Prussia)
faïence and red earthenware
1678–late 18th century

Funcke, Cornelius
1699–

Lüdicke, Karl Friedrich
1756–1779

'B' 'L'
in monogram

hard-paste porcelain
mid–18th century–present
Wegely, Wilhelm Kaspar
1752–1757

factory mark of 'W', together
with 'Repairers', and
other marks

in blue & impressed

Gotzkowsky, Johann Ernst
1761–1763 (factory sold
to Frederick the Great)

Royal factory, 1763–present

c. 1763–1765 and later

c. 1765–1770

c. 1770–1775

c. 1775–1800

painter's mark added in
overglaze blue enamel
1803–1810
similar stroke in red
enamel added 1821–1823

all in underglaze
blue

the orb added at decorating
stage, 1832–

KPM
printed in blue or red

printed 1837–1844
also impressed on plaques,
'Lithophanies', etc.
1835–1844

KPM

printed in red or brown
a decoration mark, 1823–1832

printed in blue, a factory
mark, 1844–1847

printed in blue
1847–1849

printed in blue
1849–1870

1870–present   printed

Seger, 1882–
hard-paste porcelain

Schumann, A., 1835–

State factory

BERNBURG (Thuringia)
18th century
faïence

Prince Victor Friedrich
of Anhalt-Bernburg
1725–

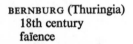

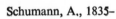

BIELA (nr. Bodenbach, Bohemia)

1882–
Dressler, Julius
general pottery

BLANKENHAIN (Thuringia)

Carstens, C. & E.
first quarter 20th century
hard-paste porcelain

Fasolt & Eichel
1790–
hard-paste porcelain

Krüger, Edmund
1847–
hard-paste porcelain

BOCK-WALLENDORF (Thuringia)

1903–
Fasolt & Stauch
hard-paste porcelain

BODENBACH (Bohemia)

1829–
stonewares

Schiller & Gerbing   S & G

Gerbing, F.   F. G.

Schiller, W., & Sons   W. S. & S.

WEDGWOOD

BONN (Rhineland)

Mehlem, Franz A.
1755–
general pottery

BRAMBACH (Saxony)
Reinhardt, Fritz
Aurnhammer, Alfred
1904–
hard-paste porcelain

BRESLAU (Silesia)
Hausmaler
hard-paste porcelain

Bottengruber, Ignaz
c. 1720–1730 (also at
Vienna

Bressler, Hans Gottlieb von
(d. 1777)
c. 1732–1740

Wolfsburg, Carl Ferdinand von
(*b.* 1692, *d.* 1764)
c. 1729–1748
(also at Vienna)

'*C. F. de Wolfsbourg
pinxit 1729*'

BRUCKBERG (Bavaria), *see* ANSBACH

BRUNSWICK
1707–1807
faïence

Duke Anton Ulrich of
Brunswick, founder

Horn, Heinrich Christoph von
Hantelmann, Werner von
1710–1749

Reichard, Johann Heinrich
Behling, Johann Erich
1749–1756

Duke, Karl, 1756–1773
and later

Rabe & Co., 1773–1776

Chely, Rudolph Anton
1745–1757
factory marks with
painters' marks

usually in
manganese purple

BRÜX (Bohemia)

Spitz, Carl
1896–
general pottery

BUCKAU (Magdeburg)

'Buckau Porzellan Manufaktur'
1832–
general pottery

BURGAU-GÖSCHWITZ (Thuringia)
Selle, Ferdinand
1902–
'Porzellan-Manufaktur-
Burgau'

BÜRGEL (Thuringia)
Fischer, Carl
early 20th century
artist-potter
'Kunstkeram. Werkstätten'

Gebrauer, C.
1892–
'Majolika' wares

BURGGRUB (Bavaria)
Schoenau & Hoffmeister
1901–
'Porzellanfabrik Burggrub'

CADINEN (West Prussia)
'Majolika-Werkstatt
Cadinen'
early 20th century

CASSEL (KASSEL) (Hesse-Nassau)
1680–1788
faïence
probably mark of Johann
Heinrich Koch, 1719–1724

Johann Christoph Gilze,
1724–, 'Hessen-Land'

earthenware
1771–1862

'Steitzische Vasenfabrik
in Cassel'

impressed

hard-paste porcelain
1766–1788
mark of the Hessian lion
'Hessen-Cassel'
(*resembling the Frankenthal
mark, but with double tail*)

CHARLOTTENBRUNN (Silesia)
Schachtel, Joseph
1859–
hard-paste porcelain

J. S.

J. S.
GERMANY

CHODAU (Bohemia)
Portheim & Sohn
1810–
hard-paste porcelain

'von Portheim'

Richter, Felkl & Hahn
1905–
hard-paste porcelain

Haas & Czizek
1905–
hard-paste porcelain
(also at Schlaggenwald)

COBURG (Thuringia)
1738–1786
faïence

Riemann, Albert
1860–
hard-paste porcelain

COLDITZ (Saxony)
1804–
cream-coloured earthernware

COLDITZ
impressed

COLOGNE (KÖLN) (Rhineland)
c. 1770–early 19th century
faïence & hard-paste porcelain

'*Eug. Cremer u. Sohn
in Cöln a. R*'

'*Cremer Nippe*'
impressed

in black   in purple

KÖLN
impressed

CRAILSHEIM (Würtemberg)
c. 1745–19th century
faïence

CREIDLITZ (Bavaria)
Gumtau, Theodor
1906–
hard-paste porcelain

'Porzellanfabrik Creidlitz'

DALLWITZ (Bohemia)
1804–
cream-coloured earthenware

D

DALWITZ

W. W. Lorenz, 1832–

WWL
DALWITZ

DAMM (nr. Aschaffenburg)
1827–
cream-coloured earthenware

mark on reproductions
of Höchst figures

DESSAU (Thuringia)
1807–
dark-brown stoneware

Hunold, Friedemann

'HUNOLD'
impressed

DIRMSTEIN (nr. Worms, Rhineland)
faïence and cream-coloured
earthenware
1778–1788
mark taken from the arms
of the episcopal see of Worms

DOROTHEENTHAL (nr. Arnstadt, Thuringia)
c. 1716–*c.* 1806
faïence

'Augustenburg'

probably Johann Michel
Rasslender, painter

probably Johann Martin
Franz, painter

probably Johann Martin
Meiselbach, painter

an unidentified painter

DRESDEN
(*For 'crossed swords' factory see* MEISSEN)

Hörisch, Christiane
1708–1784
faïence

Villeroy & Boch
1856–
general pottery

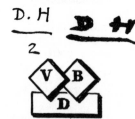

DECORATORS
Donath, decorator in Meissen style
1872–

Dresden

Hamann, decorator in Meissen style
1866–

Hirsch, F., decorator in Meissen style
early 20th century

Klemm, decorator in Meissen style
1869–

Lamm, A., decorator in Meissen style
1887–

dresden

Meyer & Sohn
decorator in Meissen style
late 19th century

Wolfsohn, Helena
1843–

Heufel & Co.
1891–   H
Dresden

Junkersdorf, Franz
early 20th century

DUISDORF (Bonn, Rhineland)

Wittelsberger & Co.
1904–

Porzellan-Fabrik Rhenania

DURLACH (Baden)
1722–1840
faïence & cream-coloured
earthenware

early mark on faïence   'Herzog'

on cream-coloured
earthenware from 1818   'DURLACH'
impressed

DUX (Bohemia)

Eichler, Ed.
1860–
Duxer Porzellan-Manufaktur

EBERSBACH (Saxony)
Neumann, C.
1893–   C.N.
decorator in Meissen style

ECKERNFÖRDE (Schleswig)
1765–1785
faïence
(factory started in
1759 at CRISEBY)

mark attributed to Criseby
under Johann Nicolaus Otte
1765–

probably initials of
Abraham Leihamer
painter, 1764–1768

probably initials of painter,
Johann Cornelius Ewald
1767–1769
(Buchwald was modeller,
potter & director from
1761–1768)

ECKERSREUTH (Bavaria)
Hofmann, Gebr.
modern
hard-paste porcelain

EICHSTATT (or Aichstätt, Middle
Franconia)
1819–
white & cream-coloured
earthenware   EICHSTAETT
impressed

EICHWALD (Bohemia)

Bloch, B.　　　　　　　Eichwald
1871–
general pottery

EISENACH (Saxony)
Sältzer, August
1858–
pottery & reproductions
of antiques

EISENBERG (Thuringia)

Mühlberg
early 19th century
earthenware

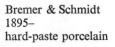

Bremer & Schmidt
1895–
hard-paste porcelain

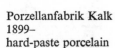

Jäger, Wilhelm
1867–
hard-paste porcelain

Porzellanfabrik Kalk
1899–
hard-paste porcelain

Reinecke, F. A.
1796–
hard-paste porcelain

ELBOGEN (Bohemia)

1815–
Haidinger, Rudolf Eugen
earthenware & hard-
paste porcelain
(Springer & Co., c. 1900)

'Epiag', 1941–
(Erste böhmische
Porzellan-Industrie-
Akt. Ges.)

Kretschmann, Heinrich
hard-paste porcelain, c. 1900

Persch, Adolf
1902–
hard-paste porcelain
(also at Hegewald)

ELGERSBURG (Thuringia)
Arnoldi, C. E. & F.
1808–
hard-paste porcelain

Eichhorn & Bandorf
1895–
general pottery

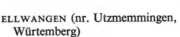

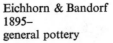

ELLWANGEN (nr. Utzmemmingen,
Würtemberg)
c. 1758–
hard-paste porcelain

rare mark from the
arms of Ellwangen　　underglaze blue

ERBENDORF (Bavaria)
Schrembs, J.
early 20th century

Seltmann, Christian
1923–
hard-paste porcelain

ERFURT (Thuringia)
c. 1717–1792
faïence

rare factory mark
(from the arms of Mayence)

mark of J. J. Wunderlich
painter

mark of Georg Matthäus Schmidt

mark of Johann Andreas or
Christian Andreas Vogel

unidentified painter

FISCHERN (Bohemia)
  Knoll, Carl
  1844–
  general pottery

Karl Knoll
Karlsbad

FLÖRSHEIM (nr. Frankfurt-
  am-Main)
  1765–present
  faïence

F.H. in monogram with
initials of unidentified
painters

probably for '*Chur-Mainz*'
or '*Carthaus-Mainz*'

cream-coloured earthenware
1781–1793
Weingartner, Mathias Joseph

impressed

FRANKENTHAL (Palatinate)
  1755–1799
  hard-paste porcelain

'Paul Hannong', 1755–1756
and perhaps later (also
on Strasbourg porcelain
1753–1754

impressed

'Paul Hannong Frankenthal'
1755–1756 and possibly
until 1759

impressed   *impressed*

from the arms of the
Elector Palatine Karl Theodor
about 1756

in blue   *in blue*

initials of Joseph Hannong
1758–1762

incised

in blue   *impressed*

from the arms of the Palatinate
c. 1756–1759 (*not to be confused
with the two-tailed lion of
Cassel*)

in blue

monogram of 'Joseph-
Adam-Hannong'
1759–1762

in blue

'Carl Theodor, period
1762–1793; 1796

in blue

'Carl Theodor' mark with
that of Adam Bergdoll
1762–1770

in blue

'Carl Theodor' mark with
the last two numerals of
the year of manufacture of
the porcelain, *c.* 1770–1788

in blue

late 'Carl Theodor' mark
c. 1780–1793

in blue

mark of Peter van Recum
potter, 1795–

in blue

marks of Johann Nepomuk
van Recum, potter
1797–1798

in blue

Clair, Adam, 'repairer'
1787–1799 (*also on his
work at Nymphenburg*)

incised

Eger, A. Van, 'repairer'
1770–74

incised

unidentified marks
possibly 'repairers'

incised

Appel, painter
1765–1784

Ael

in enamel colour

Glöckel, painter, 1762–1799

G:MM:

in enamel colour

Gastel, P. Hyacinth
painter (possibly *Hausmaler*)
c. 1765

'*P. Hy. Gastel*'
signature

FRANKFURT-AM-MAIN
1666–*c.* 1772
faïence

unidentified painter, 'J.A.J'

probably the mark of
Balthasar Thau

marks found on
'blue & white' in
Chinese style

FRANKFURT-AN-DER-ODER (Brandenburg)
1763–19th century
faïence and glazed earthenware

Heinrich, Karl
'Frankfort-Heinrich'

FRAUENTHAL (Austria)
Neumann, Ludwig
1920–
hard-paste porcelain

FRAUREUTH (Saxony)
Porzellanfabrik Fraureuth
1865–

FREIBERG (E. Germany)
Risler & Cie.
c. 1870–
hard-paste porcelain

FREIBURG (Saxony)
late 17th century
stoneware

impressed

FREIWALDAU (Bohemia)
Schmidt, H.
1842–
hard-paste porcelain

FRIEDBERG (nr. Augsburg, Bavaria)
1754–1768
faïence

Hackhl, Joseph
'Chur-Bayen'

FRIEDLAND (Bohemia)
Heintschel, Jos. Ed.
1869–
hard-paste porcelain

J E H
F

FULDA (Hesse)
faïence
1741–1758
arms of Fulda and signature
of Adam Friedrich von Löwenfinck

usual form of factory mark

hard-paste porcelain
1764—1790

c. 1765–1780

'Fürstlich-Fuldaisch', 1780–1788
and earlier, so-called '*Heinrich-
marke*' (for Heinrich von Bibra,
Prince-Bishop of Fulda, 1759–1788

'*Adalbertsmarke*' for Adalbert III
von Harstall, Prince-Bishop
from 1788–1803

FÜRSTENBERG (Brunswick)
1753–present
Duke Carl I of Brunswick
hard-paste porcelain

early marks

in blue

late 18th & early 19th century

in blue

'repairers'' marks on early
figures by Feilner

mark used on 'biscuit'
busts and reliefs

impressed

on reproductions of
old models

in blue

modern factory marks

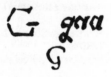

GEHREN (Thuringia)
Porzellanfabrik Günthersfeld
1884–
hard-paste porcelain

GEIERSTHAL (nr. Wallendorf, Thuringia)
Sontag & Söhne
1812–
decorators of porcelain

GERA (Thuringia)
1752–*c.* 1780
faïence

1779–
hard-paste porcelain

GIESSHÜBEL (nr. Carlsbad, Bohemia)
1803–
earthenware and hard-paste porcelain

early mark, 1803–1828

BK
impressed

Benedict Knaute, 1828–

Neuberg-Gieshübl-Fabrik
1846–

N.G.F
impressed

c. 1850

GIESSHÜBEL

GLIENITZ (Silesia)
1753–
faïence and glazed earthenware

Countess Anna Barbara von
Gaschin, 'Gaschin-Glienitz'
1767–*c.* 1780

in brown

cream-coloured and
white earthenware
1830–

GLINITZ
M

Mittelstadt, 1830–1870

G
impressed

GÖGGINGEN (nr. Augsburg)
1748–1752
faïence

usual factory marks

initials of the painter,
H. Simon

marks of Joseph Hackl,
probably after closing of
factory

GÖPPINGEN (Wurtemberg)
1741–1778
faïence
stag's horn from the
arms of Wurtemberg

initials of Johann Mathias
Pliederhauser ('Blieder Hauser')

GOTHA (Thuringia)
1757–
hard-paste porcelain

 R
impressed

c. 1783 and later
'R-g' for Rotberg, founder

c. 1805–

'Gotha'
in blue or enamel
colour

Henneberg, Egidius
1802– *c.* 1830–

mid-19th-century mark
on lithophanies, 'Hennebergsche
Porzellan Manufaktur'

H.P.M.
impressed

Morgenroth & Co.
1866–
hard-paste porcelain

Pfeffer, Fr.
1892–
faïence & porcelain

Simson, Gebr.
1883–
hard-paste porcelain

GRÄFENRODA (Thuringia)
Dornheim, Koch & Fischer
1860–
hard-paste porcelain
& earthenware

GRÄFENTHAL (Thuringia)
Unger, Schneider &
Hutschenreuther, 1861–
hard-paste porcelain

Schneider's Erben, Carl, 1885–

Scheidig, Carl
1906–
hard-paste porcelain

Weiss, Kühnert & Co.
1891–
hard-paste porcelain

GRÄFENTHAL-MEERNACH (Thuringia)
Heinz & Co.
1897–
hard-paste porcelain

GRENZHAUSEN (Rhineland)
stoneware
15th century–

Merkelbach & Wick
1873–

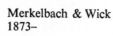

GROSS-STIETEN (Mecklenburg)
c. 1753–
faïence

Chely, Christoph Rudolph
'v.h' for von Hagen, propr.

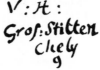

GROSZBREITENBACH (Thuringia)
c. 1778–
hard-paste porcelain

mark as for Limbach
used from 1788–

Bühl & Söhne, 1869–

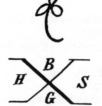

GRÜNLAS (Bohemia)
1911–
hard-paste porcelain

GRÜNSTADT (Rhineland)
1801–present
general pottery

Bordollo and family
1812–*c.* 1880

'Gebrüder Bordollo
Grünstadt'

'GBG'

HAIDA (Bohemia)

Boseck & Co., Carl Fr.
1880–
porcelain decorators

Grohmann, Franz J.
second half 19th century
porcelain decorators

HAINDORF (Bohemia)

Kratzer & Söhne, Josef
1880–
hard-paste porcelain

HAMBURG
c. 1625
faïence

marks presumed to be
those of painters:
c. 1625–1630

c. 1630–1640

c. 1640–1655

HANAU (Frankfurt-am-Main)
1661–1806
faïence

1797–1806
cream-coloured earthenware

marks of early period
(incised marks of throwers,
the others of painters)

Hieronymus von Alphen period
1740–1786

late marks

HILBRINGEN (nr. Trèves, Rhineland)
early 19th century
earthenware   HILBRINGEN
                  impressed

HILDESHEIM (Hanover)
mid-18th century
hard-paste porcelain
decorators & engravers

Busch, Canon of Hildesheim   'Busch'
(*b.* 1704, *d.* 1779), engraver   signature
c. 1748–75

Kratzberg, Canon of Hildesheim
second half of 18th century
engraver

HIRSCHAU (nr. Amberg, Bavaria)
1826–   HIRSCHAU
cream-coloured earthenware   impressed

Dorfner & Cie, Ernst   E. D. & Cie
c. 1850–1875   Hirschau
hard-paste porcelain &
earthenware

HÖCHST (nr. Mayence)
faïence
1746–1758
founded by Adam Friedrich von Löwenfinck

factory marks with
those of painters:
marks of Georg Friedrich
Hess, 1746–1750, or his
son Ignatz, *c.* 1750

Hess, G. F., 1746–1750

Hess, Ignatz, *c.* 1750

Zeschinger, Johannes
c. 1750

Ludwig, Adam
c. 1749–1758

probably Joseph Philipp
Dannhofer, 1747–1751

probably Pressel
c. 1750

unusual forms of
the factory mark

unidentified painters:

hard-paste porcelain
c. 1750–1796
wheel-mark versions of
the Mayence armorial device,
1750–*c.* 1765   in red

inaccurate version of
the above

in crimson

Charlot, Lothar, painter
1748

in purple   in red

rare marks

incised   impressed

1762–1796

underglaze blue

c. 1765–1774

underglaze blue

probably mark of Simon
Feilner, 1750–53

incised

'repairers' marks

all incised

Löwenfinck, Adam Friedrich
von, *b.* 1714, *d.* 1754, painter,
also at Bayreuth, Meissen,   'F.v.L.'
Ansbach, Fulda, Weissenau,
Haguenau   'v. Löwenf. peint'

'de Löwenfincken
pinx'

HOF-MOSCHENDORF (Bavaria)
Reinecke, Otto
1878–
hard-paste porcelain

HOHENBERG (Bavaria)
Hutschenreuther, Carl Magnus
1814–
hard-paste porcelain

HOHENSTEIN (nr. Teplitz)
1822–
earthenware

**HOHENSTEIN
TEPLITZ**

Hufsky, Carl
1822–1834

CH
impressed

Hufsky, Vincent
1834–

V.H
impressed

Bloch, B.
1822–

BB
impressed

HORN (Bohemia)
Wehinger & Co., H., 1905–
hard-paste porcelain & decorators

HORNBERG (Baden)
Schwarzwälder Steingutfabrik
1906–
earthenware   Hornberg

HUBERTUSBURG (Saxony)
1770–1848
Tännich, Johann Samuel Friedrich

H.
7

marks on earthenware:
'*Königliche sächsische*
Steingut-Fabrik Hubertusburg'

K.S.ST.F.
H

K.S.ST.F
Hubertusburg

Wedgwood
all impressed

Weigel and Messerschmidt
1840–1850   'W & M'

HÜTTENSTEINACH (Thuringia)
Swaine & Co. ·
1854–
hard-paste porcelain

Schoenau, Gebr.
1865–
hard-paste porcelain

△
H

Gebr. Schoenau, Swaine & Co.
early 20th century
hard-paste porcelain

ILMENAU (Thuringia)
1777–
hard-paste porcelain

Griener, Gotthelf
1788–1792

Nonne, Christian
1792–1808

Nonne & Roesch
1808–

N & R

Abicht & Co.
1875–
earthenware

Fischer, Arno
1907–
hard-paste porcelain

Galluba & Hofmann
1888–
hard-paste porcelain

Metzler, Gebr., & Ortloff
1875–
hard-paste porcelain

Weise, L.
early 20th century
earthenware figures

ITZEHOE (Holstein)
c. 1802–
faïence

Stemmann, Heinrich

JEVER (Oldenburg)
1760–1776

faïence

Tännich, Johann Friedrich Samuel
1760–1763

'K' for unidentified painter

JOKES (Bohemia)
Menzl, Jos. Th.
1897–
hard-paste porcelain

KAHLA (Thuringia)
Porzellanfabrik Kahla
1844–
hard-paste porcelain

Lehmann, C.A., & Sohn
1899–
hard-paste porcelain

KARLSBAD (Bohemia)
Knoll, Carl
1844–
general pottery

Karl Knoll
Karlsbad

KARLSRUHE (Baden)
1901–
general pottery

Grossherzogliche Keramische
Manufaktur

Grossherzogliche Majolika-
Manufaktur

KASSEL *see* CASSEL

KATZHÜTTE (Thuringia)
1762–

Hertwig & Co., 1864–
hard-paste porcelain

KELLINGHUSEN (Holstein)
18th century–
faïence

Carsten Behren's factory
1763–1782

Joachim Moeller
1785–1795

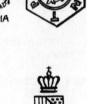

Dr. Sebastian Grauer
1795–1820

K·H
———
D'r G'

c. 1800–

K·H·
———
P·A

KELSTERBACH (Hesse Darmstadt)
faïence & cream-coloured earthenware
1758–*c.* 1823

early faïence mark,
'Königstädten', or
'Kelsterbach'

K

hard-paste porcelain
1761–1768 }
1789–*c.* 1802 }
marks used 1766–1768
and 1789–1802

HD　Ð

in blue
or manganese

porcelain mark, rare
before 1789

in blue or
impressed on
cream-coloured
earthenware

HD

probably mark of Seefried
repairer & modeller

's'
incised

Johann Andreas Gunther
repairer

'G'
incised

KIEL (Holstein)
1763–1788
faïence

Kiel

probably factory of Kleffel
1762–1763

Kleffel

mark of Tännich and
Kleffel (painter)

Kiel
T
—
K

mark of Tännich and
Christopherson (painter)

K
—
T
—
C

mark of Buchwald and
Leihamer (painter)

K
—
B
—
TL

mark of Buchwald and
Koch (painter)

K
—
B.
—
K

mark of Buchwald and
Abraham Leihamer (painter)

K
—
B Dir.t
—
A·L·69

Kieler Kunst-Keramik
first quarter 20th century

KIRCHENLAMITZ (Bavaria)
Schaller, Oscar, & Co.
1917–
hard-paste porcelain

Bavaria

Wächter, Rudolf
early 20th century–
hard-paste porcelain

KLOSTERLE (Bohemia)
1793–
porcelain & earthenware
1794–1803

K

1804–1830

K

1808–1830

HK

1830–

TK
impressed

Thun'sche Porzellanfabrik
c. 1895–

green underglaze

KLOSTER-VEILSDORF (Thuringia)
1760–present
hard-paste porcelain

CV.　V

usual factory-marks
1760–1797

V　V

rare and early mark
including the arms of
Saxony, before 1765

C V

monogram mark to
imitate Meissen

V

1797 onwards, also used
from 1788 at Limbach,
Ilmenau & Groszbreitenbach

incised mark on Italian
Comedy figures

E Z
B

modern factory marks

KLOSTER VESSRA (Saxony)
Porzellanfabrik Kloster Vessra
1892–
hard-paste porcelain

KÖLN *see* COLOGNE

KÖNIGSBERG (East Prussia)
1772–1811
faïence and lead-glazed
wares

'Hofrath Ehrenreich'
1778–1787   impressed & painted

lead-glazed wares   K
1780–1811   impressed

wares in Wedgwood style
1775–1785   *'frères Collin*
Collin, Paul Heinrich   *à Königsberg'*

KÖNIGSZELT (Silesia)
Porzellanfabrik Königszelt
1860–
hard-paste porcelain

KÖNITZ (Thuringia)
Metzel, Gebr.
1909–
hard-paste porcelain

KÖPPELSDORF (Thuringia)
Hering, Julius, & Sohn
1893–
hard-paste porcelain

Heubach, Ernst
Marseille, Armand
1887–
hard-paste porcelain

'Vereinigte Köppelsdorfer
Porzellanfabriken'

KÖPPELSDORF-NORD
Schoenau, Gebr., Swaine & Co.
1854–   *see* HÜTTENSTEINACH

KRANICHFELD (Saxony)
1903–
hard-paste porcelain

Kranichfelder Porzellan-
Manufaktur

KREUSSEN (nr. Bayreuth)
16th century–
stoneware

'House-marks' of members
of the Vest family

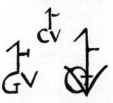

faïence
early 17th century
Lorenz Speckner, dated 1618

'Johann Georg Herzog von
Sachsen', Duke and Elector
of Saxony

KRONACH (Bavaria)
Pech, R. & E.
1830–
porcelain figures

Goebel, M. L.
1895–
hard-paste porcelain

Porzellanfabrik Ph. Rosenthal
& Co.
1897–
general pottery

Stockhardt & Schmidt-Eckert
1897–
hard-paste porcelain
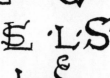

KRUMMENNAAB (Bavaria)
Illinger & Co.
1931–
hard-paste porcelain

Lange, Hermann
1934–
hard-paste porcelain

Mannl, W.
1892–
hard-paste porcelain
& decorator

KÜNERSBERG (nr. Memmingen)
1745–c. 1790
faïence

monogram of Conradi;
on piece dated 1745

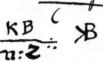

KÜPS (Bavaria)
Ohnemüller & Ulrich
1890–
hard-paste porcelain

Küps

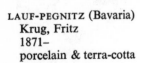

Edelstein Porzellanfabrik
1932–
hard-paste porcelain

Edelstein

BAVARIA

LAIM (nr. Munich, Bavaria)
1797–
earthenware

Fab. Laim
impressed

LANGEWIESEN (Thuringia)
Schlegelmilch, Oscar
1892–
hard-paste porcelain

LAUF-PEGNITZ (Bavaria)
Krug, Fritz
1871–
porcelain & terra-cotta

LEIPZIG (Saxony)
Zenari, Oscar
1901–
decorator of hard-paste
porcelain

LESUM (nr. Bremen)
1755–present
faïence & earthenware

Johann Christoph Vielstich, founder

factory mark with that
of painter Grote

factory-mark with
unidentified painter

LETTIN (Saxony)
1858–
hard-paste porcelain

Baensch, Heinrich

LICHTE (Thuringia)
Heubach, Gebr.
1820–
hard-paste porcelain

LIMBACH (Thuringia)
1772–
hard-paste porcelain

1772–1788

1772–1788, in imitation
of 'Marcolini' Meissen

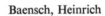

marks of Greiner 1778–,
also used at Kloster-Veilsdorf, 1797–;
Groszbreitenbach, 1788–;
and probably Ilmenau, c. 1786–1792

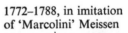

Haag, Johann Jakob Heinrich
factory painter & *Hausmaler*
1767–c. 1800

Heinrich Haag

Haag, Johann Friedrich
factory painter & *Hausmaler*
1767–c. 1800

J:Haag.

Porzellanfabrik Limbach

LIPPELSDORF (Thuringia)
Wagner & Apel
1877–
hard-paste porcelain

LUBAU (Bohemia)
'Alp'
1941–
hard-paste porcelain

Martin, Gebr.
1874–
hard-paste porcelain

G.M. MG

LUBENZ (Bohemia)
Reinl, H., 1846–

HR

LUDWIGSBURG (Wurtemberg)
faïence
1757–1824
(very similar marks on
Niderviller & Brunswick)

cream-coloured earthenware
1776–1824

hard-paste porcelain
1756–1824
Charles Eugene,
Duke of Wurtemberg
1758–1793

in blue, also rarely in red

1758–1793
common about 1770

in blue

stag's horns from the arms
of Wurtemberg, last quarter
of the 18th and early 19th century

mark with stag's horns
c. 1780

Duke Ludwig, 1793–1795

King Friedrich ('Friedrich Rex')
1806–1816

both painted in red or gold,
or impressed

LOUISBOURG

in black

King Wilhelm
1816–1824

red, gold
or
impressed

probably Jean-Jacob,
Louis, 'chief-repairer'
1762–1772

incised

'repairers' F. N. Schmauch
and 'Garnier' (?)

incised

Heinzenmann, J. G.
1760–1789
painter

HM

red or other enamel colour

Sausenhofer, D. C.
1760–1802
painter

red or other enamel colour

Grothe, J. J.
c. 1765–
painter

red or other enamel colour

1760–1770
generally on figures

all the above marks have been
used in modern times by the
Wurttembergische Porzellan-
Manufaktur, Schorndorf,
generally with the letters 'W.P.M.' below

modern Ludwigsburg
factory, 1948–

MÄBENDORF (Saxony)
Matthes & Ebel
1883–
hard-paste porcelain

MAGDEBURG (Hanover)
faïence
1754–1786

'Magdeburg Fabric'

Guichard, Johann Philipp

cream-coloured
earthenware, 1786–1839

M GUISCHARD
impressed

earthenware, 1799–

SCHUCHARD Mg M
H S
impressed

Schuchard, Georg
1806–1865

Bauer, A., 1865–

MANNHEIM (Baden)
Rheinische Porzellanfabrik
1900–

Bensinger, Fritz
c. 1925–
porcelain decorator

MARKTLEUTHEN (Bavaria)
Winterling, Heinrich
1903–
hard-paste porcelain

HW
ML
BAVARIA

MARKTREDWITZ (Bavaria)
Jaeger & Co., 1872–
hard-paste porcelain

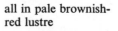

Thomas, F.
1903–
hard-paste porcelain

Neukirchner, Franz
1916–
hard-paste porcelain

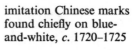

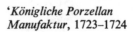

MAYENCE
early 19th century–
cream-coloured
earthenware

MZ MAINZ
impressed

MAYERHÖFEN (Bohemia)

Gebr. Benedikt

Benedikt, Gebr.
1884–
hard-paste porcelain

Britannia Porcelain Works
Moser Bros., 1890–
hard-paste porcelain
& decorators

MEISSEN (nr. Dresden, Saxony)
1710–present
hard-paste porcelain

marks found on Böttger's
red stoneware
c. 1710–1720 or later

impressed

B C Î Ì3

incised

about 1724–

impressed

porcelain decorated
at Augsburg,
c. 1730–1735

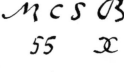

all in pale brownish-
red lustre

imitation Chinese marks
found chiefly on blue-
and-white, *c.* 1720–1725

all in underglaze blue

so-called 'caduceus-
mark', from *c.* 1723

in
underglaze blue

*'Königliche Porzellan
Manufaktur*, 1723–1724

*'Königliche Porzellan
Fabrik'*, 1723–1724

'*Meissner Porzellan
Manufaktur*', 1723–1724

M. P. M

all in underglaze blue

crossed-swords mark
adopted 1724

in blue or black enamel

early examples of crossed-
swords mark
c. 1724–1725

underglaze blue

1725–1763

underglaze blue

c. 1725–1745, with
unexplained numerals

26
underglaze blue & gilt

on blue-and-white
wares, *c.* 1725

underglaze blue

type of
'Dot Period', mark in
c. 1740

underglaze blue

'Dot Period', *c.* 1763–
1774

underglaze blue

'Marcolini Period'
1774–1814

underglaze
blue

biscuit-ware
after *c.* 1780

impressed

c. 1814–1818

c. 1818

c. 1818–1924 ('1710' and
'1910' were written on
either side of mark of
all important products
during 1910)

since 1924

cipher (for 'Augustus Rex')
of King Augustus II of
Poland, generally 1725–1730.
Common on forgeries

all in underglaze blue

rare mark probably only
in 1733 for Frederick
Augustus II

underglaze blue

c. 1725–1730

in gold

Examples of palace marks:

'*Königliche Hof-Conditorei*'
(Royal Confectionery or Pantry)

K . H . C .

'*Königliche Hof-Conditorei
Warschau*' (same at Warsaw)

K . H . C . W .

in red, black or other
enamel colours

'*Churfürstliche Hof-Conditorei*'
(Electoral Court Confectionery)   C.H.C

'*Königliche-churfürstliche-
Polnische Conditorei*'   K.C.P.C.

'*Königliche Hof-Kuche*'
(Court-Kitchen)   K.H.K

unidentified palace mark
c. 1725

B . P . J .
Dresden.
underglaze blue

unidentified 'repairers'
or indications of body
compositions

all incised

rare mark, *c.* 1730–1750 (?)

impressed

painters' marks

ΛD₀   XI

both underglaze blue

inventory mark on Meissen
porcelain in (or from) the
Royal Collection at the
JOHANNEUM

N = 2)4
W

engraved on the wheel
and coloured black

factory cancellation
marks on wares sold
in the white or as
imperfect specimens
about 1760

impressed numerals are generally
mould numbers referring to an
inventory begun in 1763

Dietrich, Christian Wilhelm Ernst
(Art-Director at Meissen, 1764–
1770) mark when painter   'CWED in 1730'

Häuer (or Hoyer), Bonaventura
Gottlieb, painter, 1724–

'B. G. H. Ping'
signed

Herold (or Höroldt) Johann
Gregor, Art-director

*'Johan Gregorius
Höroldt inven:
Meissen den 22
Janu. ano* 1727'

Herold (or Heroldt), Christian
Friedrich, painter, 1725–1777

*'C. F. Herold invt.
et fecit
a Meissē* 1750: *d.
12 Sept'*

Hunger, Christoph Conrad,
gilder and enameller at
Meissen, *c.* 1715–1717
(also at Vienna, Venice,
Rörstrand, Copenhagen,
Stockholm, St. Petersburg)

Hünger. F.
. ℈ .

Kaendler, Johann Joachim
Modellmeister, 1733–1775

'J. J. Kaendler'
signed

Busch, August Otto Ernst
von dem, engraver of
Meissen and Fürstenberg
porcelain, 1748–1775

'Busch'

*'Busch, fecit
Himmelthuer* 1768'

Ferner, F. J. (*Hausmaler*)
on out-dated blue-and-
white Meissen

'Ferner inve'

Teichert, Ernst
1884–
general pottery

MEISSEN

MERKELSGRÜN (Bohemia)
Karlsbader Kaolin-
Industrie-Gesellschaft
1881–
hard-paste porcelain

METTLACH (Rhineland)
1809–
glazed earthenware

J. F. Boch & Buschmann

BB
in blue

Boch Buschmann
à Mettlach
impressed

Villeroy & Boch, 1842–

MITTERTEICH (Bavaria)
Emanuel, Max, & Co.
early 20th century
hard-paste porcelain
& decorators

MOSANIC

Porzellanfabrik Mitterteich
1917–
hard-paste porcelain

Rieber, Josef, & Co.
1868–
hard-paste porcelain

MOSBACH (Baden)
1770–
faïence & cream-coloured
earthenware

'Carl Theodor', also
claimed as Frankenthal

'Mosbach-Tännich'

'Tännich'

Carl Friedrich of Baden
after 1806

probably Mosbach
after 1806

cream-coloured earthenware
after 1818   M   'MOSBACH'
                                  impressed

MÜNDEN (Hanover)
1737–1854
faïence and glazed
earthenware

mark of von Hanstein
1737–1793

including a painter's
mark

painter's mark

NEUHALDENSLEBEN (Saxony)
Hubbe, Gebr.
1875–
earthenware

Carstens, C. & E.
1904–
earthenware

Uffrecht, J., & Co.
1855–
earthenware

    U. & C.

NEUSTADT (Gotha)
Heber & Co.
1900–
hard-paste porcelain

NEUSTADT (Coburg)
Knoch, Gebr.
1887–

NIEDER-SALZBRUNN (Silesia)
Prause, Franz
1899–
hard-paste porcelain

Ohme, Hermann,
1882–
hard-paste porcelain

NUREMBERG (Bavaria)
maiolica
16th century–

probably Reinhard
dated 1526

Hirschvogel-Nickel-
Reinhard factory
second quarter of the
16th century

faïence
1712–*c.* 1840

factory mark after 1750

painters' signs

probably Johann Rossbach
painter, *c.* 1715–

probably Johann Andreas Mark
painter, *c.* 1715–1770

probably J. V. Bontemps
c. 1730–40

Kordenbusch, Andreas, *c.* 1726–
painter, (*d.* 1754)

marks of painter Georg
Friedrich Kordenbusch (*d.* 1763)
and his pupils

Justus Glüer, painter
1722–1723

unknown painter

G. F. Grebner, painter
1717–1730

N. Pössinger, painter
1725–1730

P. C. Schwab, painter
1725–1730

L. F. Marx, probably
after 1750

Seligmann, painter

Hausmaler:

Faber, Johann Ludwig
1678–1693 (also on glass)

Gebhard, Johann Melchior
c. 1720

Helmhack, Abraham
c. 1675–1700

Schaper, Johann
b. 1621; *d.* 1670
(also on glass)

Monogrammist I.C.
(or C.I. or J.C.)
late 17th century (painter
in black enamel)

Monogrammist C.B.
early 18th century

Monogrammist I.H.,
second half of 17th century
(Johann Heel, *b.* 1637,
d. 1709)

Monogrammist M.B.
mid-18th century

Monogrammist M.S.
(probably M. Schmid)
early 18th century

Monogrammist W.R.
(probably Wolf Rössler)
late 17th century

NYMPHENBURG (nr. Munich, Bavaria)
1753–present
hard-paste porcelain

'Bustelli period'
1754–1765

impressed

'Auliczek period'
c. 1765–1780

impressed

rare early mark   incised

c. 1780–1790

impressed

c. 1800   impressed

c. 1810–1850

middle of 19th century

both impressed

c. 1850–1862   impressed

the 'hexagram mark'
1763–1767

another form of the
above mark

marks on coffee-cups
made for the Turkish
market:

'Chur-Bayern'

form of crossed swords

all in blue

initials of Franz Bustelli
1754–1763

F.B

impressed

initials of unknown
workmen

Adam Clair, repairer
1800–1829

AC

all incised

Georg Christoph Lindemann
painter, 1758–1760

GCL
1758

Johann Klein, painter
1765–1771

K.

Franz Jezinger (?) painter
1764 or later

FI

Kajetan Purtscher, painter
1758–1813

· C Pulscher

Inventory marks of the
Court of the Elector
Carl Theodor

C.H.Conditoreij
j7
j77j

C.H.C.   C.H.Z.

C.H
δöchrgaden„j77j.

C.H.Silberkamer
1771
all in enamel colour

Anton Auer, painter
1795–1814

A: A:

Hausmaler:

Amb. j774

Amberg (place of decoration?)

Johann *or* Franz Willand
1756–1758

J. W:

J. A. Huber, 1758–*c.* 1769
gilder

unidentified

unidentified

Staatliche Porzellan-Manufaktur
modern marks

OBERHOHNDORF (Saxony)
Kaestner, Friedrich
1883–
hard-paste porcelain

OBERKOTZAU (Bavaria)
Greiner & Herda
1898–1943
hard-paste porcelain
& decorators

Porzellanfabrik Neuerer K.G.
1943–

OESLAU (Bavaria)
Goebel, Wm.
1879–
hard-paste porcelain

OETTINGEN-SCHRATTENHOFEN (Bavaria)
1735–19th century
faïence, white and
cream-coloured ware

Köhler, Albrecht August
1749–1802

Schnten hofen
Kohler

OFFENBACH (nr. Frankfurt-am-Main)
faïence
1739–early 19th century

OHRDRUF (Thuringia)
Baehr & Proeschild
1871–
hard-paste porcelain

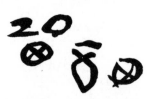

Kestner & Comp
in production 1907
hard-paste porcelain

Kling & Co., C. F.
1836–
hard-paste porcelain

OSNABRÜCK (Hanover)
1727–1731
faïence

OTTWEILER (Rhineland)
hard-paste porcelain
and faïence
1763–1794
glazed earthenware
from 1784–1794

'Nassau-Saarbrucken'
on porcelain vessels

.N S.
underglaze blue
or gold

mark on figure

PASSAU (Bavaria)
1840–
hard-paste porcelain

second half of 19th century
Lenck family

Porzellanfabrik Passau
Dietrich, Philipp
1937–1942

Älteste Volkstedter
Porzellanfabrik

mark used on wares
made from Höchst
moulds

PILSEN (Bohemia)
Schertler, Fr.
1881–
hard-paste porcelain

F. S
P

PIRKENHAMMER (Bohemia)
1802–
hard-paste porcelain

Hölke, Friedrich
List, J. G.

⊢K

Fischer & Reichenbach
1810–1816

F&R

Fischer, Christian
1846–1857

C.F   CF

Fischer & Mieg
1857–

F & M

Pirkenhammer

PLANKENHAMMER (Bavaria)
Porzellanfabrik Plankenhammer
1908–
hard-paste porcelain

PLAUE-ON-HAVEL (Thuringia)
Schierholz, C. G. & Sohn.
1817–
hard-paste porcelain

'Plaue Porzellanmanufaktur'
mark on lithophanies

P.P.M.

POPPELSDORF (Bonn)
1755–present
faïence & general pottery

Wessel, Ludwig
1825–

late 19th century

modern mark

POSCHETZAU (Bohemia)
Maier & Comp
1890–
hard-paste porcelain

M. & C.

PÖSSNECK (Saxony)
Conta & Boehme
1790–
hard-paste porcelain
modern mark

POTSCHAPPEL (Dresden)
Thieme, Carl
1875–

POTSDAM (nr. Berlin)
1739–1800
faïence

Rewend, Christian Friedrich

'POTSDAM-REWEND'

PRAGUE (Czechoslovakia)
1795–
earthenware

1795–1810   P

1810–1862   **Prag**   Prager

Hübel, Joseph Emanuel
1810–1835   Hubel in Prag

Kriegel & Co., 1836–1862   K & C
                         Prag
                 all impressed

PROBSTZELLA (Thuringia)
1886–
Hutschenreuter, H.
hard-paste porcelain

PROSKAU (Silesia)
1763–1850
faïence up to 1793
& earthenware

Count Leopold von Proskau
1763–1769

'Dietrichstein' period
1770–1783

'Leopold' period
1783–1793

Dietrichstein at Weisskirchen
c. 1783

marks on earthenware
1788–1850

PROSKAU
impressed

PR:NO:1(
2
impressed

RAEREN (nr. Aix-la-Chapelle,
      Rhineland)
c. 1565–
stoneware

mark of Jan Emens, c. 1566–1594

Jan Mennicken   'IM 1576'

Mennicken der Alte   'M. der A 1583'

Tilman Wolf   'T. W.'
first half of 17th century
'*Tilman Wolf Kannenbacker*' 'T. W. K.'

Hubert Schiffer, 1880–   'H. S.'

RATIBOR (Silesia)
1794–1828
cream-coloured earthenware
and stoneware

                              R
Joseph Beaumont
      of Leeds   BEAUMONT

Baruch, Salomon   BARUCH
1803–1826   all impressed

RAUENSTEIN (Thuringia)
1783–
hard-paste porcelain

early marks

19th century

modern mark

REHAU (Bavaria)
Hertel, Jacob & Co.
1906–
hard-paste porcelain

Zeh, Scherzer & Co.
1880–
hard-paste porcelain

REICHENBACH (Thuringia)
Carstens, C. & E.
1900–
hard-paste porcelain

REICHMANNSDORF (Thuringia)
Scheidig, Carl
1896–
hard-paste porcelain

RENDSBURG (Holstein)
1764–1818
faïence & earthenware

(faïence ceased in 1772)

Clar, Christian Friedrich
1764–c. 1784

on cream-coloured
earthenware
1772–1818

RHEINSBERG (Brandenburg)
1762–1866
faïence, cream-coloured
and other earthenware

Lüdicke, Karl Friedrich
'Rheinsberg-Lüdicke'

REN. I.

RF

L. R. B. G

on earthenware and
'black basaltes' from
1786

R

both impressed

ROSCHÜTZ (Saxony)
Roschützer Porzellanfabrik
Unger & Schilde
1811–
hard-paste porcelain

RÖSLAU (Bavaria)
Winterling, Gebr.
1906–
hard-paste porcelain

RUDOLSTADT (Thuringia)
faïence
1720–1791
(for porcelain see
also *Volkstedt*)

early mark

Bohne, Ernst
1854–
hard-paste porcelain

Münch, Wilhelm, & Zapf
1905–
hard-paste porcelain
& 'majolika'

New York & Rudolstadt
Pottery Co.
1882–
general pottery

Weithase, C. K.
c. 1928–
porcelain & glass
decorator

SAALFELD (Thuringia)
1718–1719
faïence

SCHAALA (Thuringia)
Voigt, Hermann
1872–
hard & soft-paste porcelain

SCHATZLAR (Bohemia)
Porzellanfabrik Schatzlar
Pohl, Theodor
1878–
hard-paste porcelain

SCHAUBERG (Bavaria)
Greiner, G., & Co.
1807–
hard-paste porcelain

SCHEIBE (Thuringia)
Kister, A. W. F.
1838–
hard-paste porcelain
in Meissen style

SCHIRNDING (Bavaria)
Reichel, Lorenz
1902–
hard-paste porcelain
& decorator

SCHLACKENWERTH (Bohemia)
Pfeiffer & Löwenstein
1873–
hard-paste porcelain

SCHLAGGENWALD (Bohemia)
c. 1793–
hard-paste porcelain

early 19th century

Lippert & Haas
1832–1846

'Saalfeld d.18
Marzi anno
1718 f'

K.P.M.
×

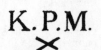

s

Schlaggenwald

SCHLAGGENWALD

Haas & Czjzek
1867–1888

Haas & Czjzek
in
Schlaggenwald

modern

Sommer & Matschak
1904–
hard-paste porcelain

S.M

SCHLESWIG
1755–1814
faïence

SLℑℳℐG

rare marks

Schleswig

probably Johann Leihamer
painter, *c.* 1758

$\frac{S}{L}$

Otte & Lücke
1755–1756

$\frac{S}{L}$

factory mark with that
of Conrade Bade, painter
1764–1791

$\frac{S}{C\beta}$

factory mark with that
of Boerre Odewald
painter, 1761–1765

$\frac{S}{B'O}$

factory mark with
unidentified painter

$\frac{S}{R}{F \cdot M}$

SCHLIERBACH (Prussia)
Wächtersbach Steingutfabrik
1832–
earthenware

SCHMIEDEBERG (Silesia)
Pohl, Gebr.
1871–
hard-paste porcelain

P

GP.

SCHMIEDEFELD (Saxony)
Schmidt, Sebastian
1857–
hard-paste porcelain

SCHNEY (Bavaria)
Liebmann, E.
c. 1783–early 20th century
hard-paste porcelain

SCHNEY
impressed

$\times$ S

SCHÖNWALD (Bavaria)
Müller, E. & A.
1904–
hard-paste porcelain

M. P. M.

Porzellanfabrik Schönwald
1879–
hard-paste porcelain

Camag
BAVARIA

J.N.M.

Alt Schönwald

SCHORNDORF
Bauer & Pfeiffer
1904–
hard-paste porcelain

Württembergische Porzellan-Manufaktur

WPM

L
WPM

WR
WPM

R
WPM

SCHRAMBERG (Wurtemberg)
1820–
white & cream-coloured
earthenware

SCHRAMBERG
impressed

Schramberger Majolika-
Fabrik
early 20th century

SCHREZHEIM (nr. Ellwangen, Wurtemberg)
1752–
faïence

usual factory mark with
unexplained additions

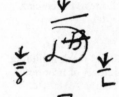

common painter's (?) mark

SCHWARZA-SAALBAHN (Thuringia)
Müller, E. & A.
1890–
hard-paste porcelain

SCHWARZENBACH (Bavaria)
Kronester, J., & Co.
1904–
hard-paste porcelain

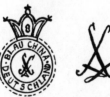

Schaller, Oscar, & Co.
1882–
hard-paste porcelain

SCHWARZENHAMMER (Bavaria)
Schumann & Schreider
1905–
hard-paste porcelain

SCHWERIN (Mecklenburg)
1753–
faïence
Apfelstädt, Johann Adam
(*d.* 1771)

'Apfelstädt-Schwerin'
and painter's mark

SELB (Bavaria)
Gräf & Krippner
early 19th century

Heinrich & Co.
1904–
porcelain & decorators

Hutschenreuther, Lorenz
1856–
hard-paste porcelain

Müller, Paul
1890–
absorbed by above firm
in 1917

P. M. S.

Krautheim & Adelberg
1884–
decorator

89

Rosenthal, Ph., & Co.
1879–
hard-paste porcelain

Zeidler, Jacob, & Co.
1866–
hard-paste porcelain

J. Z. & CO.

SITZENDORF (Thuringia)
Voigt, Alfred,
1850–
hard-paste porcelain

Sitzendorfer Porzellan-
Manufaktur

SORAU (Brandenburg)
Carstens, C. & E.
1918–
hard-paste porcelain

Porzellanfabrik Sorau
1888–
hard-paste porcelain

STADTLENGSFELD (Thuringia)
Porzellanfabrik Stadtlengsfeld
1889–
hard-paste porcelain

STANOWITZ (Silesia)
Striegauer Porzellanfabrik
(formerly C. Walter & Comp.
1873–)

St. P. M.

STOCKELSDORF (nr. Lübeck)
1771–19th century
faïence

'Stockelsdorff-Buchwald-
Abraham Leihamer'
modeller & painter
1772–1774

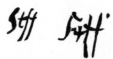

probably initials of painters
also found on similar marks:

Johann Leihamer   'JL'

J. A. G. Adler   'A'

D. N. O. Seritz   'S'

C. T. F. Kreutzfeldt   'C'

STRALSUND (Pomerania)
c. 1755–1792
faïence

Johann Eberhardt
Ludwig Ehrenreich
1766–

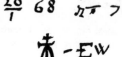

usual mark including
initials of proprietor,
painter, date, etc.

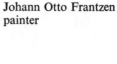

including mark of
Johann Otto Frantzen
painter

Christian Adam Dettloff
painter

STRIEGAU (Silesia)
c. 1600
earthenware

wares made in imitation
of Roman *'terra sigillata'*

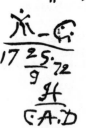

impressed

90

SUHL (Prussia)
Schlegelmilch, Erdmann
1861–
hard-paste porcelain

Schlegelmilch, Reinhold
1869–
hard-paste porcelain

TANNOWA (Bohemia)
c. 1813–1880
faïence & porcelain

Tannawa   *Tannowa*

TAUBENBACH (Thuringia)
Moritz, Carl
1848–
hard-paste porcelain

TEINITZ (Bohemia)
1801–1866
earthenware

Count Wrtby
1801–1839

impressed

F. L. Welby, 1839–

impressed

TELTOW (Prussia)
1904–
hard-paste porcelain

Berliner Porzellan-
Manufaktur
Schomburg & Co.

TETTAU (Franconia)
1794–
hard-paste porcelain

Porzellanfabrik Tettau

TIEFENFURT (Silesia)
Donath, P.
1808–
hard-paste porcelain

Steinmann, K.
1868–1932
hard-paste porcelain

Tuppack, Carl Hans
1808–
hard-paste porcelain

TILLOWITZ (Silesia)

Degotschon, Johann   'T'   'TbF'
1804–
faïence & earthenware   'Tillowitz'

TISCHENREUTH (Bavaria)
Porzellanfabrik Tischenreuth
1838–
hard-paste porcelain

TRIPTIS (Thuringia)
Porzellanfabrik Triptis
1891–
hard-paste porcelain

TURN (Bohemia)
Alexandra Porcelain-Works
Wahliss, Ernst
1894–
general pottery

**'Amphora' Porzellanfabrik
Riessner & Kessel
1894–
general pottery**

**Dachsel, Paul
1904–
art-pottery**

**Strnact jun., Josef
1881–
earthenware**

UHLSTÄDT (Thuringia)
Alberti, Carl
1837–
hard-paste porcelain

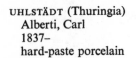

UNTERKÖDITZ (Thuringia)
Möller & Dippe
1846–
generally pottery

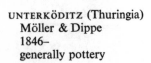

VAUDREVANGE *see* WALLERFANGEN

VILLINGEN (Baden)
Glatz, J.
1870–
'Majolika' wares

VOHENSTRAUSS (Bavaria)
Seltmann, Johann
1901–
hard-paste porcelain

VOLKSTEDT (Thuringia)
c. 1760–
soft and hard-paste procelain

Macheleid, Georg Heinrich
1760–1767
mark on soft-paste
including the hay-fork
from the Schwarzburg
arms *c.* 1760

hard-paste marks
1760–1799

mark used after the
protest of Meissen
in 1787

Greiner & Holzapfel
1799–1817 or later

Älteste Volkstedter Porzellanfabrik
(formerly Triebner)

modern marks

Ackermann & Fritze
1908–
hard-paste porcelain

Beyer & Boch, decorating
from 1853, manufacturing
from 1890

Eckert, Richard, & Co.
1895–
hard-paste porcelain

WALDSASSEN (Bavaria)

    Gareis, Kühnl & Cie.
1899–
hard-paste porcelain

Ens, Karl
1900–
hard-paste porcelain

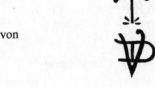

Bareuther & Co.
1866–
hard-paste porcelain

Dornis, Christian von
1905–
general pottery

WALLENDORF (Thuringia)
1764–
hard-paste porcelain

imitation Meissen mark
before 1778

probably after 1778

 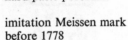

Müller & Co.
1907–
hard-paste porcelain

Kaempfe & Heubach
late 19th century

WALLERFANGEN (Saar Basin)
1789–
cream-coloured earthenware   VV

Schäfer & Vater
1890–
hard-paste porcelain
& decorators

Villeroy & Boch   Vaudrevange

both impressed

WALDENBURG (Silesia)
Krister, Carl
1831–
general pottery

KPM
in green

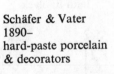

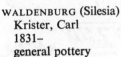

WALDERSHOF (Bavaria)
Haviland, Johann
1907–
hard-paste porcelain

WEIDEN (Bavaria)
Bauscher Gebr.
Porzellanfabrik Weiden
1881–

Bauscher
Weiden

JHW.
Bavaria

Seltmann, Christian
1911–
hard-paste porcelain

WEILBURG (Hesse)
1797–
glazed earthenware

H
impressed

1813–

'W. J. WIMPF'

WEINGARTEN (Baden)
Wolfinger, R.
Porzellanfabrik Weingarten
1882–
hard-paste porcelain

P. W.

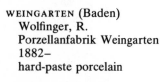

WEISSWASSER (Silesia)
Schweig, August
1895–
hard-paste porcelain

WERDAU (Saxony)
Fraureuth
1865–
hard-paste porcelain

WIERSBIE (Silesia)
1775–1783
faïence

W

WIESBADEN (Nassau)
faïence and cream-
coloured earthenware
1770–1795

'Wiesbaden-Dreste'

'Nassau-Usingen'

Dienst, Wilhelm
1770–
general pottery

Erlemann, Fr.
1893–
earthenware

WRISBERGHOLZEN (Hanover)
1735–1834
faïence
factory mark with that
of painter

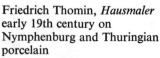

WUNSIEDEL (Bavaria)
Retsch & Co.
1890–
hard-paste porcelain

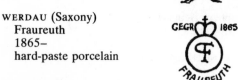

WÜRZBURG (Lower Franconia)
hard-paste porcelain
c. 1775–1780

'Johann Caspar Geyger'

Friedrich Thomin, *Hausmaler*
early 19th century on
Nymphenburg and Thuringian
porcelain

W B

W
both in black

ZELL (Baden)
Schmider, Georg
1820–
hard-paste porcelain

Lenz, J. F.
1846–1867
hard-paste porcelain

ZELL

ZERBST (Anhalt)
1720–1768
1793–1861
faïence

factory mark

probably Christian
Langendorf, artist
1722–1723

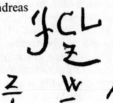

Langendorf, Christian Andreas
(son), artist
1761–1782

1793–1861　　　　　ZERBST
　　　　　　　　　　impressed

Sandkuhl, late 18th century　LS
　　　　　　　　　　　　　　Z

ZEVEN (Hanover)
　Zevener Porzellanfabrik
　Carstens, C. & E.
　early 20th century–

ZWICKAUER (Saxony)

Kaestner, Friedrich *see* OBERHOHNDORF

Zwickauer Porzellanfabrik
early 20th century
hard-paste porcelain

Great Britain and Ireland

The English late-medieval wares are not only of great artistic interest, but historically important as the direct ancestors of the Staffordshire wares. Little is known of the places of their production, the finer specimens perhaps being made in monasteries, and though of coarse materials the jugs and pitchers are often of great beauty of form with simple but effective decoration.

In the fifteenth and sixteenth centuries smaller neater jugs appear with a rich copper-green glaze together with a hard red pottery with dark brown or black glaze sometimes decorated with trailed white slip or with applied pads of white clay.

A rare and distinct class of sixteenth-century English pottery comprises cisterns, stove-tiles and candle-brackets finely moulded in relief and covered with a green or yellow glaze.

English pottery tradition before the industrial period was rooted in the medieval use of lead-glazed earthenware. The sixteenth-century Cistercian pottery was the immediate forerunner of the Tickenhall and Staffordshire slip-wares, and the tradition of the last in turn gave vitality to the 'Astbury' and 'Whieldon' wares made in the same district in the eighteenth century.

The impulse towards refinement, which had been inspired by the Elers brothers (who made fine red wares in the Chinese style) and by the vogue of porcelain, also led to the making of a fine white salt-glazed stoneware in Staffordshire, where the industrializing process was finally carried through by Josiah Wedgwood. His cream-coloured ware was immediately imitated at numerous neighbouring potteries as well as at Leeds, Liverpool, Bristol, Swansea, Sunderland, Newcastle, Portobello and elsewhere, quickly securing a world-wide market.

Aside from the main English tradition are the decorative stonewares of Wedgwood, products of the neo-Classical enthusiasm.

Tin-glazed ware, largely inspired by Italian, Dutch and Chinese models, was made at London, Bristol, Liverpool, Dublin and Glasgow, but had little effect on the main current of the English tradition as represented by the wares of Staffordshire, where delftware (as this is called) was never made. English delftware was painted in high-temperature colours; overglaze enamels were used only on very rare examples and were probably the work of Dutch independent enamellers.

The seventeenth-century stoneware of Fulham, inspired at first by the Rhenish and Chinese wares, produced the isolated phenomenon of Dwight's admirable figures; that of Nottingham, though typically English, was of minor importance, reflecting latterly something of the Staffordshire style.

English porcelain of the eighteenth century is remarkable for its variety of composition. Soft-pastes of French type were made at Chelsea, Derby and Longton Hall; soapstone pastes at Worcester, Caughley and Liverpool; and hard-paste at Plymouth and Bristol. From about 1750 onwards for several decades Derby was a most productive factory and a large proportion of the surviving English porcelain figures were made there. At Bow the use of bone-ash from 1747 heralded the type of porcelain which towards the end of the eighteenth century became and still remains the English standard body; this last was a hybrid porcelain in which some part of the kaolin was replaced by bone-ash. At Nantgarw and Swansea a belated soft-paste was made in the period 1813–22.

None of the factories enjoyed royal or princely protection or subsidy and most were short-lived. Chelsea, and possibly Worcester, alone reached the standard set by the chief manufacturers of France or the many establishments supported by the rulers of small states in Germany; the porcelain of the first-named, however, ranks with the best ever made in Europe. The unsophisticated charm of Bow and Lowestoft is of a different order and typically English.

The ceramic art of the nineteenth century suffered no less than others from misdirected effort and mistaken enthusiasms. While the early part of the century lived largely on the artistic capital of the preceding period, the later part was chiefly occupied with the deliberate revival of former styles.

Yet in spite of unfavourable conditions the native genius of the English potters did succeed in producing wares which are both beautiful and of permanent value: the simple 'cottage china' and lustre wares of the New Hall type and its kindred earthenware; Worcester, Derby, Spode, Coalport and other porcelains which were its opulent contemporaries and successors; the charming blue-printed ware; and the entirely English brown stonewares of the Midlands and Lambeth. A singular use of glazed Parian is to be noted in the wares of Belleek in Co. Fermanagh, Ireland, where a pottery was started in 1863. Vases in naturalistic shell-forms were especially characteristic.

At the end of the century the revival of handicraft makes its appearance with De Morgan and the Martin Brothers, heralding the studio pottery of the present day.

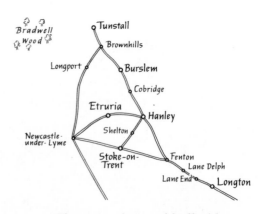

The pottery district of Staffordshire

Greenock
Glasgow Edinburgh
Fife

Newcastle
Sunderland

Belfast

Co. Fermanagh

Dublin

Leeds Hull
Swinton
Liverpool Castleford
Chesterfield
Stoke Nottingham
Caughley Derby
Coalport STAFFS Yarmouth
Birmingham Lowestoft
Worcester Ipswich
Gloucester Castle Felixstowe
Hedingham
Swansea Chelmsford
Bristol London
West Malling
Marlborough Wrotham
Barnstaple Salisbury
Honiton Poole
Plymouth
St Ives
Truro

ENGLAND

AMESBURY (Wiltshire)
Zillwood, W., late 18th–
early 19th centuries
pottery

W.Z.
incised

ASHBY-DE-LA-ZOUCH
(Leicestershire)
Thompson, J., *c.* 1815–56
general pottery

JOSEPH THOMPSON
WOODEN BOX
POTTERY
DERBYSHIRE
impressed
and other printed marks

Wilson & Proudman
Coleorton Pottery
1835–42, general pottery

WILSON &
PROUDMAN
impressed

ASHTEAD (Surrey)
Ashtead Potters Ltd.
1926–36, earthenware

AYLBURTON (Gloucestershire)
Leach, Margaret, 1946–56
Taena Community, 1951–56
and Upton St. Leonards, Glos.
where L. A. Groves also
used mark. Studio-pottery

impressed

BARNSTAPLE (Devon)
Baron, W. L., 1899–1939
Rolle Quay Pottery
earthenware

BARON. BARNSTAPLE
incised

Brannam, Ltd., C. H.
Litchdon Pottery, 1879–
earthenwares

C. H. BRANNAM
BARUM
incised

as from 1913–

C. H. BRANNAM LTD.
impressed

printed or impressed, 1929–

impressed, 1930–

C. H. BRANNAM
BARUM DEVON

BELPER (Derbyshire)
Belper Pottery 1809–34
stonewares
(transferred to Denby 1834)

BELPER
impressed

BENTHALL (Salop)
Pierce & Co., W., *c.* 1800–18
earthenwares

W. PIERCE & CO.

Salopian Art Pottery Co.
1882–*c.* 1912 earthenwares

SALOPIAN
impressed

BILLINGHAM (Cleveland) and
elsewhere
Dunn, Constance, 1924–
studio-pottery

incised

BIRKENHEAD (Merseyside)
Della Robbia Co. Ltd.
earthenwares, *c.* 1894–1901

top initial that of decorator

DELLA ROBBIA
impressed or incised

BISHOPS WALTHAM
(Hampshire)
Bishops Waltham Pottery
decorative earthenwares
only from 1866–7 in
Greek revival form

BISHOPS
WALTHAM
printed

BOURNEMOUTH (Dorset)
Purbeck Pottery Ltd.
stoneware, Dec. 1965–

printed marks

Purbeck
Pottery
England

BOVEY TRACEY (Devon)
Bovey Tracey Pottery Co.
earthenwares, 1842–94
Bovey Pottery Co. Ltd.
1894–1957
also
'Blue Waters Pottery'
c. 1954–57

B.T.P. CO.
printed or impressed

c. 1937–49   1949–56

Devonshire Potteries Ltd.
earthenwares. 1947–
also
'Trentham Art Wares'
1959–

TRENTHAM
ART WARE

Ehlers, A. W. G.
Lowerdown Cross, 1946–55
studio-potter

incised or painted

Leach, David, 1956–
(also at St. Ives *c.* 1932–56)
'LD' for Lowerdown
Pottery

LD
impressed

BOW (London)
(Stratford High St., Essex)
c. 1747– *c.* 1776
soft-paste porcelain
  early marks, *c.* 1750

presumably 'repairers'
marks 1750–60

incised

incised

impressed **B**

probably mark of
'repairer'
Mr. Tebo (Thibaud?)
marks on blue-painted
wares 1750–70

impressed

underglaze blue

on figures and other late pieces
and
'anchor and dagger'
period, *c.* 1762–76

⚓ †   ⚔

in red   in underglaze
           blue and red

in red   **I A**

         in underglaze blue

B ✗   ❋

in underglaze   in underglaze
blue and red   blue

C   ⦂

on blue-and-white
cups, in underglaze
blue   in underglaze blue

BRADFORD (W. Yorkshire)
Booth, Frederick, *c.* 1881
earthenware

F.B.

BRAMPTON (Derbyshire)
Knowles & Son, Matthew
stonewares, *c.* 1835–1911

KNOWLES

Oldfield & Co., *c.* 1838–88
earthenware

J. OLDFIELD

OLDFIELD & CO.
impressed
J.P. LTD.
impressed or printed
from 1907

Pearson Ltd., James
Oldfield and London
Potteries, stonewares
19th century—1939
1920–

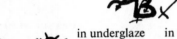

BRAUNTON (N. Devon)
Braunton Pottery Co. Ltd.
earthenwares, 1910–
  mark of *c.* 1947–
(moved or finished by 1972)

printed or impressed

BRISTOL (Avon)
(Lund & Miller's factory)
soft-paste (soapstone)
porcelain 1748–52, then
transferred to Worcester

BRISTOL
BRISTOLL
in relief

(Cookworthy & Champion's factory)
hard-past porcelain
1770–81, transferred
from Plymouth

4

early mark during
Cookworthy's
ownership (also used
at Plymouth)

underglaze blue,
blue enamel, red or
gold

X   6

      X

in blue enamel

underglaze blue
and blue enamel

X X   X B

blue
enamel

tin-glazed earthenware
(delftware) *c.* 1650–

mark of John Bowen
painter, apprenticed
1734

yf. 1st : Sept.
1761
Bowen-fecit,
in blue

initials of Michael Edkins
delft-painter and his wife
on plate dated 1760

E
M B
J7 60
in blue

Bristol Pottery
c. 1785–1825
earthenwares

BRISTOL POTTERY
impressed or painted

Coombes, a china-mender
c. 1775–1805
  in pale brown lustre

Coombes
Queen St
Bristol

Fifield, William (*b.* 1777,
d. 1857) painter on
Bristol pottery
c. 1810–55

W.F.
W.F.B.
W. FIFIELD

Pardoe, Thomas (*d.* 1823)
painter at Derby,
Worcester, Cambrian
Pottery, Swansea,
factories, independent
decorator of pottery and
porcelain in Bristol
c. 1809–20

Pardoe
28 Bath St.,
Bristol
Warranted

Pardoe, Bristol
painted

Pardoe, William Henry
(son), decorator at
Cardiff and elsewhere
c. 1820–35

PARDOE, CARDIFF

Patience, Thomas
18th century stoneware

PATIENCE
impressed

Pountney & Allies
Bristol Pottery *c.* 1816–
35, earthenware

P.
P. & A.　P.A.
B.P.

printed, impressed or
painted

P.A.
BRISTOL POTTERY

impressed

Pountney & Goldney
Bristol Pottery, 1836–49

POUNTNEY & GOLDNEY
(or as above)

impressed
Pountney & Co., 1849–
Bristol Victoria Pottery

BRISTOL POTTERY
P. & CO.

1849–89

POUNTNEY & CO.

1889–

POUNTNEY & CO. LTD.

c. 1954–
now Cauldon Bristol
Potteries Ltd.

Powell, William (& Sons)
Temple Gate Pottery
c. 1830–1906, stoneware

impressed *c.* 1830–
Ring, Joseph 1785–
(*d.* 1788), cream
coloured earthenware
continued by partners
until 1812

BRISTOL TEMPLE
GATE POTTERY
RING & CO.
impressed

BROADSTAIRS (Kent)
Broadstairs Pottery Ltd.
stoneware, 1966–
printed mark

BROSELEY (Salop)
Maw & Co. Ltd., 1850–
tiles and art-pottery
from *c.* 1875
c. 1880–

MAW & CO.

FLOREAT MAW
SALOPIA

BRUTON (Somerset)
Goddard Ltd., Elaine
earthenware, 1939–

mark printed label

BURTON-ON-TRENT (Derbyshire)
Bretby Art Pottery, Woodville
Tooth & Ault 1883–87
Tooth & Co. 1887–
earthenwares
　Henry Tooth *c.* 1883–1900

c. 1914–

CLANTA
WARE

Woodward, James
Swadlincote Pottery
'Majolica' earthenware
1859–88

printed or impressed

CASTLE HEDINGHAM (Essex)
Hedingham Art Pottery
Bingham, Edward
1864–1901
reproduction of medieval
and Tudor type wares

incised signature
1864–1901

E. BINGHAM
CASTLE HEDINGAM
ESSEX

applied in relief

early 20th century

ROYAL ESSEX ART
POTTERY WORKS

CASTLEFORD (W. Yorkshire)
Clokie & Masterson
earthenware, 1872–81

C. & M.
CLOKIE &
MASTERSON
printed or impressed

Clokie & Co., 1888–1961
earthenware
(Ltd. after 1940)
printed

Dunderdale & Co., David
Castleford Pottery
c. 1790–1820
earthenware and
stoneware

D.D. & CO.

D.D. & CO.
CASTLEFORD

Gill, William (& Sons)
Providence Pottery
1880–1932

printed

Hartley's (Castleford)
Ltd., Phillips Pottery
c. 1898–1960
stoneware and earthenware;
decorative art-wares
from 1953

HARTROX

Nicholson & Co., Thomas
earthenware, *c.* 1854–71

T.N. & CO.
printed with name
of pattern

Robinson Bros.
Castleford & Allerton
Potteries
stoneware, 1897–1904

R.B.
printed or
impressed

Robinson & Son, John
stoneware, 1905–33

J.R. & S.
impressed

CAUGHLEY (Salop)
Turner, Thomas
c. 1772–1799 (then taken over by John Rose
of Coalport factory)
soft-paste porcelain and
black basaltes
(*see also* BENTHALL)

SALOPIAN
Salopian
impressed

printed or painted in
underglaze blue *c.* 1772–95

$\mathcal{S}$ $\mathcal{S}x$

$\mathcal{S}_o$

printed or painted
c. 1772–95

$\mathbb{C}$ $\mathbb{C}$

printed mark usually
Worcester
open printed crescent
also on Coalport

$\mathbb{C}$ $\mathbb{C}$

printed

Chinese type mark

CHEAM (Surrey)
Clark, Henry, 1869–80
earthenware

HENRY CLARK
CHEAM POTTERY
impressed or incised

CHELSEA (London)
c. 1745–1784 soft-paste porcelain
(1770–84 known as 'Chelsea-Derby'
period under William Duesbury)

rare incised mark on
'triangle' period
1745–*c.* 1749

Chelsea
△
$5 \, tr \, Ll$

usual triangle mark

△
incised

rare mark of 'crown
and trident', 1745–*c.*
1750 in underglaze blue

'raised-anchor' mark
c. 1749–52, latterly
picked out in red

in applied relief

'red-anchor' mark
1752–*c.* 1758
occasionally painted in
blue or purple
c. 1750–56

painted in red

painted in underglaze blue
'gold anchor' mark
c. 1756–69
(also seen on Chelsea-
Derby wares as late
as 1775)

in gold

rare 'repairers' mark
(not Roubiliac)

impressed

Chelsea Pottery, 1952–
(Rawnsley Academy Ltd.)
impressed or
incised, 1952–

CHELSEA POTTERY
incised

Vyse, Charles, 1919–*c.* 63
studio-potter

C.V.   C.V.
CHELSEA

painted mark with
year-date added

CHESTERFIELD (Derbyshire)
Price, Powell & Co. Ltd.
earthenware, 1740–
(Ltd. from 1961)
Now subsidiary of Pearsons of Chesterfield

No registered
trade mark

P. & CO.

Pearson & Co., 1805–
Whittington Moor
Potteries
1805–*c.* 1880

PEARSON & CO.
WHITTINGTON
MOOR
impressed

1880–

from *c.* 1925 renamed as
Pearson & Co. (Chesterfield) Ltd.

Barker Pottery Co.
1887–1957
stoneware
printed or impressed
mark 1928–1957

CHURCH GRESLEY (Derbyshire)
Green & Co. Ltd., T.G.
c. 1864– earthenware
and stoneware
  printed mark c. 1888–

GRESLEY

mark of c. 1930, numerous
other late marks all
include 'T. G. Green
& Co., Ltd.'

GRESLEY
MADE IN
ENGLAND

Products
unmarked

Mason, Cash & Co. Ltd.
Pool Potteries, 1901
domestic earthenware
(Ltd. Co. since 1941)

CLEVEDON (Avon)
Elton, Sir Edmund
Sunflower Pottery
1879–1930

1879–1920

Elton

1920–30

Holland, William Fishley
studio-potter, 1921–
earthenware

I. HOLLAND

Holland, Isabel Fishley
pottery figures, 1929–42

Holland, George Fishley
earthenware, 1955–

CLIFTON JUNCTION
(nr. Manchester)
Pilkington Tile & Pottery
Co. Ltd., earthenwares
and tiles (decorative
pottery, 1897–1938, 1948–57)

P

early incised mark

factory mark, VIII for
1908

VIII

c. 1914–38   'ROYAL LANCASTRIAN'

marks of notable designers:

Lewis F. Day   Walter Crane   C. E. Cundall   R. Joyce

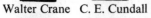

Jessie Jones G. M. Forsyth Gladys Rodgers W. Mycock

COALPORT (Salop)
John Rose, c. 1796–
(transferred to Stoke-on-Trent
c. 1926)
  rare early mark in red

COALBROOKDALE

1815–25 on many wares
decorated in Swansea
style

impressed

c. 1810–25, in underglaze
blue

Coalport

Dale

underglaze blue mark
c. 1810–20

C. B. DALE

marks used from c. 1820

1830–50

JOHN ROSE & CO.
COALBROOKDALE
SHROPSHIRE
c. 1851–61, painted or gilt

c. 1861–75, 'c'
Coalport, 's',
Swansea, 'N', Nantgarw

painted or gilt

printed mark c. 1870–80
incorporating Patent
Office Registration
mark

c. 1875–81, printed or
painted
late marks c. 1881–
'England' added 1891
'Made in England'
c. 1920

COALPORT A.D. 1750

wares made for London
dealer A. B. & R. P.
Daniell c. 1860–1917

large size anchor mark
on Coalport copies of
Chelsea, also on
Continental wares
without 'c'

CODNOR PARK
(Derbyshire)
Burton, William,
c. 1821–32, stoneware

W. BURTON
CODNOR PARK
impressed

CROWBOROUGH (Sussex) & REDHILL (Surrey)
Walford, J. F., 1948–
studio-potter

DARTINGTON (S. Devon)
Trey, Marianne de
studio-potter, 1947–
Shinners Bridge Pottery

incised or painted

Haile, T. S., *c.* 1936–43,
1945–8, studio-potter

impressed

DARTMOUTH (Devon)
Britannia Designs, Ltd.
earthenware, 1959
   mark an applied label
   used from 1971

DENBY (Derbyshire)
Bourne & Son Ltd.,
Joseph, *c.* 1809–
stoneware

BOURNES
WARRANTED

Joseph Bourne, 1833–60
   'Son' added 1850

J. BOURNE & SON
PATENTEES
DENBY POTTERY
NEAR DERBY
impressed

DENHOLME (W. Yorkshire)
Taylor, Nicholas
1893–1909
earthenware

N. Taylor
Denholme
incised

DERBY (Derbyshire)
c. 1750–1848
soft-paste-porcelain
   early marks of Planché
   period *c.* 1750–56

incised

Derby Porcelain Works
1756–1848
   'William Duesbury &
   Co.' *c.* 1760

incised

'N' seen on dishes, etc.
c. 1770–80

incised

'Chelsea-Derby' marks
c. 1770–84

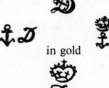

in gold

c. 1770–82, in blue or
purple

incised model numbers
on figures, *c.* 1775–
early 19th century

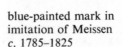

common Derby mark
1782–, incised, purple,
blue or black
c. 1800–25 in red
enamel

mark of Isaac
Farnsworth 'repairer'

mark of Joseph Hill
'repairer'

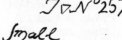

'size' mark

'Duesbury & Kean',
c. 1795
in blue, crimson or purple

blue-painted mark in
imitation of Meissen
c. 1785–1825

Robert Bloor Period

printed in red
c. 1820–40

printed in red
c. 1830–48

mark in imitation of
Sèvres, *c.* 1825–48
in blue enamel

Locker & Co., King Street factory
c. 1849–59

similar marks used also
by:
Stevenson Sharp & Co.
1859–61
'Courtney late Bloor'
1849–63

Stevenson & Hancock
1861–1935, this mark
also used after 1935
when King St. factory
was taken over by Royal Crown Derby
Porcelain Co. Ltd.

Derby Crown Porcelain Co. Ltd. Est. 1876
c. 1878–90, together
with year-mark as
shown in table on next
page

Derby

impressed

printed

Royal Crown Derby Porcelain Co. Ltd.
1890–
printed mark of *c.* 1890
'England' from 1891
'Made in England'
added from *c.* 1920
together with year-
mark

(Part of Royal Doulton Tableware Ltd. from 1973)

TABLE OF DERBY YEAR-MARKS
1882–

1882	1883	1884	1885	1886	1887	1888
1889	1890	1891	1892	1893	1894	1895
1896	1897	1898	1899	1900	1901	1902
1903	1904	1905	1906	1907	1908	1909
1910	1911	1912	1913	1914	1915	1916
1917	1918	1919	1920	1921	1922	1923
1924	1925	1926	1927	1928	1929	1930

1931	1932	1933	1934	1935	1936	1937
1938	1939	1940	1941	1942	1943	1944
I	II	III	IV	V	VI	VII
1945	1946	1947	1948	1949	1950	1951
VIII	IX	X	XI	XII	XIII	etc.

Derby Pot Works
creamwares, *c.* 1750–80

T. RADFORD SC.
DERBY

Thomas Radford,
engraver of prints
found on some
Cockpit Hill wares

RADFORD fecit
DERBY POT WORKS

Potts, W. W.
St. George's Works,
c. 1831–, earthenware
(also at Burslem)

marks indicating
patent printing
processes, 1831 & 1835

DONYATT (Somerset)
Rogers, James, 19th century
(with descendants)
sgraffiato slipwares

Jas Rogers
Maker Octr 10th
1848

impressed on jug
dated 1864

ROGERS & SONS
CROCK STRETT
POTTERY

EAST HENDRED (Oxfordshire)
Thompson, Pauline
studio-potter, 1950–

incised or painted

EAST HORSLEY (Surrey)
Moore, Denis & Michael
Buckland
Green Dene Pottery
1953–
(initials also used)

impressed or painted

ELKESLEY (Nottinghamshire)
Aston, Christopher S.
stoneware, 1968
(moved to Elkesley
from Bawtry in 1971)

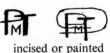

applied label

FARNHAM (Surrey)
Hammond, Henry
studio-potter, 1934–40,
1946–

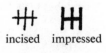

incised   impressed

Harris & Sons, A.
earthenware, 1872
(established in 1864
at Elstead, Surrey)

No special mark
used

Barron, Paul
studio-potter, 1948–

impressed

FELIXSTOWE (Suffolk)
Kemp, Dorothy, 1939–
studio-potter

incised or impressed

FERRYBRIDGE (Yorkshire)
Ferrybridge Pottery, 1792–
known as Knottingley Pottery, 1792–1804

1792–6, *c.* 1801–34   TOMLINSON & CO.
impressed or printed

Wedgwood, Ralph, *c.*   WEDGWOOD & CO.
1796–1801

c. 1804–   FERRYBRIDGE
impressed

Reed & Taylor, *c.* 1843–56   R. & T.   R.T. & CO.
Woolf & Sons, L., *c.*   L.W.   L.W. & S.
1856–83
Poulson, Bros., Ltd.   P.B.   P.BROS
1884–97
Sefton & Brown, *c.*   S.B.
1897–1919

Brown & Sons, T., *c.*   T.B & S.
1919–

FREMINGTON (Devon)   E. B. FISHLEY
Fishley, Edwin Beer   FREMINGTON
1861–1906, earthenware   N. DEVON
incised
no certain
FULHAM (London)   marks
Dwight, John, 1671–
salt-glazed stoneware

De Morgan, William
c. 1872–1907
decorator of earthenwares made to order
from other factories, and own wares
    impressed mark, 1882–
    '& Co.' added after 1888

marks used at Merton Abbey, 1882–88
made own tiles from *c.*
1879, and wares from 1882

impressed or painted
1882–

Sands End Pottery, 1888–97
(period of partnership with
Halsey Ricardo)

1898–1907, partnership with
Frank Iles, Charles & Fred
Passenger at Fulham

decoration continued
until 1911, four years
after De Morgan retired   all impressed

earthenwares were decorated
in De Morgan style at
Mrs. Ida Perrin's studio,
Bushey Heath, 1921–33
by Fred Passenger

Fulham Pottery & Cheavin Filter Co. Ltd.
vases & commercial pottery
1889–present   FULHAM POTTERY
LONDON
1948–   impressed

GATESHEAD (Tyne and Wear)
Durham China Co. Ltd.
general ceramics, 1947–57

printed or impressed

HENLEY-ON-THAMES   'FAMOUS HENLEY CHINA'
(Berkshire)   EST. 1867
Hawkins, John & Son   HAWKINS
china and glass dealers   HENLEY-ON-THAMES
closed about 1935

HEREFORD
Godwin & Hewitt, tiles
1889–1910, mark printed
or impressed

HINDHEAD (Surrey)
Surrey Ceramic Co. Ltd.
Kingswood Pottery
earthenware and
stoneware, 1956–

HONITON (Devon)   THE HONITON
Honiton Art Potteries   LACE ART POTTERY
Ltd., earthenware, *c.*   CO.
1881–, printed or
impressed *c.* 1915

Collard, C., 1918–1947   COLLARD HONITON
printed or impressed   ENGLAND

Hull, N. T. S., 1947–1955   N.T.S. HULL

1947–   HONITON POTTERY
        DEVON

Hull, Norman   NORMAN HULL
Norman Hull Pottery   POTTERY
1947–55

HORNSEA (Humberside)
Hornsea Pottery Co. Ltd.
earthenware, *c.* 1951
   printed or impressed, 1962–

HULL (Humberside)   S.L.
Longbottom, Samuel   impressed
earthenware, late 19th
century, closed 1899

IPSWICH (Suffolk)   W. BALAAM
Balaam, W., 1870–81   ROPE LANE POTTERY
Rope Lane Pottery   IPSWICH
slipwares   impressed

ISLEWORTH (London)   SHORE & CO.
earthenware, *c.* 1760–   S. & CO.
1825, Shore, J.   S. & G.
Shore & Co.   ISLEWORTH
Shore & Goulding
   (*Note:* S. & G. seen on Wedgwood type wares
   are Schiller & Gerbing, Bodenbach, Bohemia.

JACKFIELD (Salop)   CRAVEN & CO.
Craven Dunnill & Co.
Ltd., tiles, 1872–1951   JACKFIELD

KEW (Surrey)
Duckworth, Ruth
studio-potter, 1956–

    painted or incised

KILMINGTON MANOR (Wiltshire)
Pleydell-Bouverie, Katharine
stoneware, 1925–
studio-potter
(also at other addresses)

    incised or stamped

LAMBETH (London)   'Coade Lambeth'
Coade & Sealy, 1769–
1811, artificial stoneware

Doulton & Watts
stoneware and earthenware
c. 1815–1858
   c. 1826–1838
   on early brown salt-
   glazed wares

   c. 1826–1858

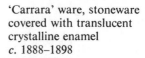

all marks impressed, moulded or incised

Doulton & Co.
Lambeth, *c.* 1858–1956
Burslem, *c.* 1882–
   c. 1869–77, decorated
   coloured wares, year often
   appears in centre after 1872

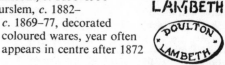

'4D' mark on decorated
salt-glaze

Note: 'England' added
after 1891   *c.* 1877–80   *c.* 1880–1902

mark on mural tiles
c. 1879–1900

on wares decorated with
coloured clays
c. 1887–1900

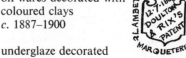

underglaze decorated
earthenware

c. 1872–73

c. 1873–1908

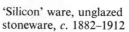

underglaze decorated
earthenware, *c.* 1881–1910

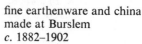

'Carrara' ware, stoneware
covered with translucent
crystalline enamel
c. 1888–1898

'Silicon' ware, unglazed
stoneware, *c.* 1882–1912

fine earthenware and china
made at Burslem
c. 1882–1902

standard impressed mark
c. 1902–22
c. 1927–36

   Lambeth stoneware
   c. 1922–

Burslem factory marks   DOULTON
c. 1882–1902

    DOULTON
    & SLATERS
    PATENT

c. 1900–   ROYAL   ROYAL
DOULTON   DOULTON
FLAMBE   KALON

c. 1960–   ENGLISH
TRANSLUCENT
CHINA

selection of initials used
by Doulton decorators:
Atkins, Elizabeth, *c.* 1876–82   EA
Banks, Eliza, *c.* 1876–84   E∫B
Barlow, Arthur B., 1871–8   AB 3
Barlow, Florence E., *c.* 1873–1909   FEB

Barlow, Hannah B., *c.* 1872–1906   HBB

Barnard, Harry, *c.* 1880–90   B

Butler, Frank A., *c.* 1872–1911   FB

Butterton, Mary, *c.* 1874–94   AB

Capes, Mary, *c.* 1876–83   MC

Dewsberry, David, 1889–1919   D.Dewsberry

Dunn, William, E., *c.* 1883–95   WED

Lee, Frances E., *c.* 1875–90   FEL

Marshall, Mark V., 1879–
1912   M·V·M
Pope, Frank C., 1880–1923   F·C·P

Raby, Edward J., 1892–1911   E.Raby

Rowe, William, 1883–1939   WR

Simeon, Henry, 1894–1936   HS

Simmance, Eliza, *c.* 1873–1928   S

Tinworth, George, 1886–1913   TG

A full list of painters, modellers and designers
shown in *Royal Doulton 1815–1965* by Desmond
Eyles, London, 1965, together with full guides,
etc. to precise dating

Green, Stephen   STEPHEN GREEN
Imperial Pottery   IMPERIAL
stoneware,   POTTERIES
c. 1820–58   LAMBETH

   impressed marks

Stiff, James   J. STIFF
London Pottery, *c.* 1840–
1913 stonewares
   c. 1863   J. STIFF & SONS
          impressed

LANGLEY MILL (Nottingham)
Lovatt & Lovatt, 1895–
stoneware and earthenware
printed or impressed marks
         c. 1900–

      now Langley
     Pottery Ltd. (1967)   *c.* 1900–   *c.* 1931–62

LEEDS (W. Yorkshire)
c. 1770–1881
creamware, earthenware and stoneware

Green Bros., 1770–   LEEDS *POTTERY
                impressed

Humble, Green & Co., 1774–76

Humble, Hartley, Greens   LEEDS POTTERY
& Co., 1776–1780

                 LEEDS *POTTERY

Hartley, Greens & Co.   LEEDS *POTTERY
1781–1830

   1800–1830   LEEDS.POTTERY

     HARTLEY   GREENS & Co   LEEDS*POTTERY
     LEEDS * POTTERY   LEEDS*POTTERY

   all marks impressed

     HARTLEY·GREENS   HARTLEY LEEDS
     LEEDS POTTERY & Co.   HARTLEY GREENS & Co
                  LEEDS * POTTERY

   1780–1810
   impressed or enamelled   LP

Britton & Son, Richard   R.B. & S.
1872–8, earthenware   printed
   initials found on variety
   of transfer-printed wares

Rainforth & Co. 1800–17   RAINFORTH & CO.
Petty's Pottery, 1817–46   PETTYS & CO. LEEDS
earthenware & creamware

         printed or impressed

Burmantofts   BURMANTOFTS
art-pottery, 1882–1904   FAIENCE
   marks impressed   B+F   B

Leeds Fireclay Co. Ltd.   L.
earthenware, *c.* 1904–14   F.C.

decorative wares, made up
until 1914, after which   LEFICO
only commercial & utility
wares were produced   GRANITOFTS

Yates, William, *c.* 1840–76
(retailer only)

YATES
LEEDS
printed or painted

LETCHWORTH
(Hertfordshire)
Cowlishaw, W. H.
1908–14, earthenwares

ICENI WARE
impressed

LIVERPOOL (Merseyside)
Chaffers, Richard, 1743–65
tin-glazed earthenware and soft-paste porcelain
dated example referring
to son:

Christian, Philip
c. 1765–1776

'CHRISTIAN'
impressed

Billinge, Thomas
engraver, *c.* 1760–80

Billinge Sculp
Liverpool

Sadler, John & Green,
Guy, printers only, their
work seen on tiles,
Wedgwood's creamware,
Longton Hall, etc. 1756–1799
Abbey, Richard
engraver and printer
1773–80, potter from 1790
Johnson, Joseph
engraver, second half
18th century

J. Sadler, Liverpool

Green, Liverpool

ABBEY
LIVERPOOL

R. Abbey, sculp.

'I. JOHNSON,
LIVERPOOL'

Herculaneum Pottery
earthenware and procelain
c. 1793–1841
Worthington, Humble
& Holland, 1794–1806

HERCULANEUM

impressed or printed marks, *c.* 1796–1833

1822–41

HERCULANEUM POTTERY
impressed or printed
in blue

Case, Thomas & Mort,
John, 1833–1836

printed, usually in red

Mort & Simpson

'Liver' bird printed or
impressed, *c.* 1836–41

Gibson, John &
Solomon, earthenware
early 19th century

JOHN GIBSON
LIVERPOOL
1813

Prince William Pottery Co.
earthenware, 1953–

'PRINCE WILLIAM'

LONDON
VARIOUS RETAILERS OF POTTERY & PORCELAIN

Allsup, John, 1832–58
printed

JOHN ALLSUP
ST. PAUL'S CHURCH-
YARD, LONDON

Blades, John
c. 1800–30

BLADES LONDON

Bradley & Co., J.
decorators and retailers
c. 1813–20

J. BRADLEY & CO.

Brameld, J. W.
c. 1830–50
partner of
Rockingham Works

I. W. BRAMELD

at various
London addresses

Daniell, A. B. & R. P.
c. 1825–1917
printed mark on wares
of Coalport, etc. made
to order for Daniell's

Dreydel & Co., Henry
late 19th century
mark of wares made
to order both in England
and on Continent

Goode & Co. (Ltd.), Thomas
c. 1860–present
'Ltd' from 1918
now in South Audley St.

Green & Co., J.
1834–42 at St. Paul's
Churchyard, elsewhere
until *c.* 1874

Haines, Batchelor & Co.
1880–90

H.B.
printed

Hales, Hancock &
Goodwin, Ltd., 1922–60
(Hales, Hancock & Co.
Ltd., and Hales Bros.)

H.H. & G. LTD.
printed

Hart & Son
1826–69

H. & S.
printed

Howell & James
c. 1820–1922 (also
retailers of materials
for amateur decorators)

HOWELL & JAMES

Mortlock, J.
1746–*c.* 1930
    many marks used
    including name of such
    manufacturers as
    Mintons

MORTLOCK

MORTLOCKS
OXFORD STREET

Pearce, Alfred B.
1866–1940

ALFRED B. PEARCE
39 LUDGATE HILL
LONDON

Pellatt & Co., Apsley
c. 1789–
(also glass retailers)

APSLEY PELLATT
& CO.

Pellatt & Green
c. 1805–30

PELLATT & GREEN
LONDON

Pellatt & Wood
c. 1870–90

PELLATT & WOOD

Phillips, *c.* 1799–1929
    c. 1858–97
    c. 1897–1906
    c. 1908–29

W. P. & G. PHILLIPS
PHILLIPS & CO.
PHILLIPS LTD.

Walker, William
c. 1795–1800

WALKER MINORIES

MINOR FACTORIES AND STUDIO-POTTERS IN LONDON

Benham, Tony, 1958
    mark written or incised
    with year, studio-potter
    (now at Wateringbury, Kent),

Billington, Dora
studio-potter, 1912–

incised or painted

Briglin Pottery Ltd.
earthenware, 1948–

BRIGLIN
impressed

Dalton, William B.
stoneware and porcelain
studio-potter, 1900–
c. 1955
(In U.S.A. from 1941)

incised or painted

Eeles, David
studio-potter, 1955
Shepherd's Well Pottery
London, then in 1962
to Mosterton, Dorset

D.E.

Fine Arts Porcelain Ltd.
earthenwares, 1948–52

Fry, Roger, Omega
Workshops *c.* 1913–19
studio-potter

Groves, Lavender
studio-potter, 1952–

GROVES

Leach, Jeremy
studio-potter, *c.* 1959

J.L.   J.L.
D.S.

Macbride, Kitty
(Brown & Muntzer)
earthenware figures of
mice. Trade-name:
'The Happy Mice of
Berkeley Square'
1960–

Kitty MacBride
England

Martin Bros. (Robert Wallace, Walter, Edwin
and Charles), studio-potters, stoneware
1873–1914
    1873–5   R. W. Martin fecit

    1873–4   *R W Martin Fulham*

    1874–8   *R W Martin London*

    1878–9   *R W Martin Southall*

SOUTHALL   MARTIN
MARTIN   SOUTHALL
POTTERY   POTTERY

    1879–82   *R W Martin London & Southall*

    1882–   *R W Martin & Brothers London & Southall*

all marks either incised or impressed together
with month and year

Mills, Donald
studio-potter, 1946–55

Donald Mills

Murray, William Staite
studio-potter, 1919–62
in S. Rhodesia from 1940

W. S. MURRAY
(date)
LONDON

Northen & Co., W.
Union Potteries
Lambeth, stoneware
1847–92, '& Co.'
added 1887

W. NORTHEN
POTTER
VAUXHALL
LAMBETH

O'Malley, Peter
studio-potter, 1953–

CHELSEA CHEYNE
(date)
G.P.

Parnell, Gwendolen
studio-potter, 1916–36

Parr, Harry
studio-potter, *c.* 1919–
c. 1948

HY PARR
CHELSEA (date)

Powell, Alfred & Louise
decorators of Wedgwood
earthenwares, *c.* 1904–39

Powell, John
painter and retailer
c. 1810–30

Powell
91, Wimpole St.

Richards, Frances E.
studio-potter, 1922–31
mark incised

Rie, Lucie
studio-potter, *c.* 1938–
mark impressed

Samuel, Audrey
studio-potter, 1949–

A S

Smith & Co., Thomas
stonewares, 1879–93

T. SMITH & CO.
OLD KENT ROAD
LONDON

Stabler, Harold &
Phoebe, earthenware
designers and potters
b. 1872–*d.* 1945 (wife
d. 1955)

Phoebe Stabler
(date)

Stabler (date)

Vergette, Nicholas
studio-potter, 1946–58

Walters, Helen
studio-potter, 1945–
(now Helen Swain,
mark 'HWS')

V. ⋀⋁
✕ HW
65.

1945–53   1953–

White, William J.
Fulham Pottery
stoneware, *c.* 1750–1850

incised dated marks

W.W.
(date)

W. J. WHITE
(date)

LOWER DICKER (Sussex)
U. Clark & Nephews
1843–1946, earthenware
1933–
Dicker Potteries Ltd. 1946–59

U.C. & N.
THE DICKER
SUSSEX
DICKER WARE

LOWESBY (Leicestershire)
Lowesby Pottery
Fowke, Sir Frederick
c. 1835–40
earthenwares

LOWESBY

LOWESTOFT (Suffolk)
soft-paste porcelain
c. 1757– *c.* 1800
decorators numbers,
to approx. 17, painted
on inner wall of foot-
rim, *c.* 1760–75
copies of Worcester
and Meissen marks
c. 1775–1790

1 3 5
7 9 13
X (

Allen, Robert, *b.* 1744, *d.* 1835
decorator at Lowestoft factory
and independent enameller
from *c.* 1800

*Allen
Lowestoft*
painted

MADELEY (Salop)
Randall, Thomas M.
c. 1825–40, decorator of
English and Sèvres porcelain;
with factory at Madeley
for production of soft-paste
imitations of Sèvres

*T MR
Madeley
S*
painted

MALVERN (Worcestershire)
Woods, Richard, *c.* 1850–
retailer only

R. WOODS
printed

MANCHESTER
Sutcliffe & Co., *c.* 1885–1901
decorative tiles

printed or impressed

MANSFIELD
(Nottinghamshire)
Billingsley, William
1799–1802
painter and gilder

BILLINGSLEY
MANFIELD
painted

MEXBOROUGH
(S. Yorkshire)
Emery, James
earthenware, 1837–61

J. EMERY
MEXBRO

incised

Rock Pottery
Reed, James, *c.* 1839–49

REED
impressed

Mexbro Pottery
Reed, John, *c.* 1849–73

Sowter & Co., *c.* 1795–
1804, Mexborough Old
Pottery
marks impressed

SOWTER & CO.
MEXBRO

S. & CO.

Wilkinson & Wardle
Denaby Pottery, 1864–6
earthenware

Wardle & Co., John,
Denaby Pottery
earthenwares (including creamware)
1866–70
    printed mark   JOHN WARDLE & CO.

MIDDLESBROUGH   LINTHORPE
(Cleveland)   impressed
Linthorpe Pottery, 1879–90
earthenware (art-pottery type)

    incised, impressed or   Chr. Dresser
    painted signature of Dresser

    Tooth, Henry, manager   Ħ HT
    1879–1882

Middlesbrough Pottery Co.   M.P. CO.
1834–44
earthenware and   MIDDLESBRO'
creamware   POTTERY CO.

Middlesbrough   M.E. & CO.
Earthenware Co.
1844–52, earthenware
    initials used with various
    printed or impressed marks

      MIDDLESBRO POTTERY
      (with anchor)
Wilson & Co., Isaac   I.W. & CO.
Middlesbrough Pottery   MIDDLESBRO'
1852–87   impressed

MORTLAKE (London)   KISHERE
Mortlake Pottery,
c. 1800–43,   I.K.
Kishere, Joseph   impressed
salt-glazed stoneware

NEW BARNET (Hertfordshire)   D.A.
Arbeid, Dan, 1956–
Abbey Art Centre   ARBEID
studio-potter   painted or impressed
(now at Saffron Walden, Essex)

NEWCASTLE UPON TYNE   DAVIES & CO.
(Tyne and Wear)   impressed
Davies & Co., 1833–51
Tyne Main Pottery
earthenware

Fell, Thomas, 1817–90   FELL
St. Peter's Pottery   impressed
earthenware and creamware
1817–30

    F ⚓   FELL&CO

    impressed

Fell & Co., *c.* 1830–90   F. & CO.
    initials used with   T.F. & CO.
    various marks: T. FELL & CO.

Ford & Patterson   FORD & PATTERSON
Sheriff Hill Pottery   Sheriff Hill
c. 1820–*c.* 1830   Pottery
earthenware   impressed
Jackson & Patterson   J. & P.
1830–45
Maling, Robert   MALING
Ouseburn Pottery   M
1817–59, earthenware   impressed

Maling, C. T.   MALING
Ford Pottery, 1859–90   C. T. MALING
earthenware, often   C.T.M.
with lustre decoration

Maling & Sons, Ltd.
1890–1963
earthenwares, mark of
    c. 1875–1908

    1890–   *c.* 1908   *c.* 1949–63

Patterson & Co.   PATTERSON & CO.
Sheriff Hill Pottery   printed or
1830–1904, earthenware   impressed

Sewell, 1804– *c.* 28   SEWELL
St. Anthony's Pottery, *c.* 1780–1878
earthenware (including creamwares)
1780–1820   ST. ANTHONY'S
Sewell & Donkin   SEWELL & DONKIN
1828–52
Sewell & Co., 1852–78   SEWELL & CO.
      all impressed or printed

Taylor & Co., *c.* 1820–5   TAYLOR & CO.
Tyne Pottery   printed
earthenware

Wallace & Co., J.   WALLACE & CO.
Newcastle or Forth Bank   impressed
Pottery, 1838–93, earthenware

Warburton, John, &   J. WARBURTON
family, Carr's Hill   N. ON TYNE
Pottery, earthenware, *c.* 1750–1817

NEWTON ABBOT (Devon)
Phillips & Co., John
Aller Pottery, 1868–87

ΦΙΛΕΩ ΙΙΊΙΊΟΝ

printed or impressed

Aller Vale Art Potteries
earthenware, 1887–1901

ALLER VALE
impressed

Royal Aller Vale &
Watcombe Pottery Co.
(Torquay) *c.* 1901–62
impressed or printed
1901–

ROYAL ALLER VALE

ROYAL   DEVON
TORQUAY   MOTTO
POTTERY   WARE

Candy & Co. Ltd.
Great Western Potteries
earthenwares, 1882–

CANDY WARE
C
N A

NORTH SHIELDS
(Tyne and Wear)
Carr, John
earthenware, *c.* 1845–1900

J. CARR & CO.

NOTTINGHAM
(Nottinghamshire)
Lockett, William
stoneware, *c.* 1740–80

'Wm. and Ann Lockett,
1755'

OXFORD (Oxfordshire)
Blackman, Audrey
studio-potter, 1949–
'Astbury-type' figures

A. BLACKMAN

OXSHOTT (Surrey)
Oxshott Pottery, 1919
Wren, Henry, *c.* 1919–47

HW   *hw*

Wren, Denise, *c.* 1919–

DKW

Wren, Rosemary, *c.* 1945–
(Now at Hittisleigh, Exeter.)

OXSHOTT

PAIGNTON (Devon)
Barn Pottery, Ltd.
earthenware, 1964

Trade-name 'Barn' ware

PINXTON (Derbyshire)
Pinxton Works, *c.* 1796–1813
John Coke, William Billingsley
soft-paste porcelain
(Billingsley, *c.* 1796–93)
(Cutts, *c.* 1803–1813)

marks found on late
pieces

in red   in purple
from arms of Coke

PLYMOUTH (Devon)
Plymouth Porcelain Works
Cookworthy, William
hard-paste porcelain, 1768–70
(transferred to Bristol in 1770)
workman's mark also seen
on Bow, Worcester, Bristol
and Wedgwood

underglaze blue,
blue enamel,
red or gold

T°

Plymouth Pottery Co. Ltd.
earthenware, 1856–63

P.P. COY.L
STONE CHINA

POOLE (Dorset)
Carter & Co.
earthenware, 1873–1921

CARTER & CO.
CARTER POOLE

Carter, Stabler & Adams
1921–
'Ltd.' added 1925
1956–
1963– Poole Pottery Ltd.

POOLE
ENGLAND

printed

PRAZE (Cornwall)
Crowan Pottery, 1946–62
Davis, Harry & May
studio-potters

impressed

PRESTBURY (Cheshire)
Nowell, C. D., *c.* 1946–59
studio-potter
(at Disley *c.* 1946–51)

PRESTBURY
WN
(date)

PRESTWOOD (Buckinghamshire)
Newland, William
studio-potter, 1948–

Casson, Michael & Sheila
studio-potters, 1953–
Sheila Casson, 1951–59

CM   M
w
s

RAINHAM (Kent)
Upchurch Pottery, 1913–61
Baker, W. & J.
'Seeby', name of agent
1945–61

UPCHURCH

UPCHURCH
SEEBY

Rainham Pottery Ltd.
earthenware, 1948–
Wilson, Alfred, now
E. J. Baker

Rainham
impressed or painted

RAMSBURY (Wiltshire)
Holdsworth Potteries
Holdsworth, Peter, 1945–

READING (Berkshire)
Collier Ltd., S. & E.
terracotta, *c.* 1848–1957

REDRUTH (Cornwall)
Foster's Pottery Co.
earthenware, 1949–

FOSTER'S
POTTERY
REDRUTH

stamped mark

RICHMOND (Surrey)
Sykes, Steven, 1948–55
studio-potter

Steven Sykes
(signature)

ROCKINGHAM (Yorkshire)
Rockingham Works
(nr. Swinton) earthenware
c. 1750–1842 (porcelain
also made from about 1826)
c. 1778–87

BINGLEY
impressed

Brameld & Co., 1806–42

BRAMELD
impressed

c. 1826–30   ROCKINGHAM ROCKINHGAM
               WORKS,   BRAMELD
               BRAMELD

c. 1830–42   ROYAL
                      ROCKINGHAM
                        WORKS
                       BRAMELD

'griffin-mark', *c.* 1826–30
from crest of Earl Fitzwilliam,
Marquis of Rockingham

from *c.* 1830–42
'Royal' added to title
of factory
mark in red *c.* 1826–30, puce 1830–42
'Manufacturer to the King' added to mark
in 1830–37 (William IV)

Baguley, Alfred & Isaac
Rockingham Works
decorator only of
porcelain in Rockingham
style, *c.* 1842–65 (Mexborough)
c. 1865–91

'Griffin mark'
with
'Baguley'

printed

ROLVENDEN (Kent)
Watson, Dorothy
Bridge Pottery 1921–

impressed or printed

ROTHERHAM (S. Yorkshire)
Holmes Pottery, 1870–87
Jackson & Co., J.
earthenware
Shaw & Sons, Ltd., G.
1887–1948

J.J. & CO.

J. & CO.

G.S. & S.
printed

Northfield Pottery
earthenware
Hawley, W. & G., 1863–8
Hawley Bros Ltd.
1868–1903, 'Ltd'. added 1897

W. & G. HAWLEY

H.B.
HAWLEY BROS.

Northfield Hawley Pottery Co. Ltd.
earthenware, 1903–19

impressed or printed
mark introduced about
1898 by Hawley Bros.

Walker & Son
earthenware, *c.* 1772–

WALKER

RUSTINGTON (Sussex)
Champion, G. H. & E. E.
studio-potters, 1947–

RYE (Sussex)
1869– mark of *c.* 1900
pottery (including tin-glaze)
c. 1869–1920
(Sussex Rustic Ware)
's.a.w.' Sussex Art Ware
c. 1920–39
J. C. Cole & W. V.
Cole, 1947–
    various marks including
    name 'RYE'
Walter V. Cole, 1957–

SUSSEX WARE

RYE

Cadborough Pottery,
1807–71, earthenware

OLD SUSSEX WARE
RYE

Mitchell, William, *c.*
1840–, W. Mitchell &
Sons, 1859–69
Mitchell, F. & H., 1869–71

MITCHELL
M

Iden Pottery, 1961–
Townsend, D. & Wood, J. H.
studio-potters
(moved from Iden to Rye
in 1963)

Everett, Raymond, 1963–
studio-potter

ST. IVES (Cornwall)
Leach, Bernard, 1921–
Leach Pottery marks
studio-pottery
personal marks of B. Leach
(*b.* 1889 *d.* 1979)

Hamada, Shoji
1920–23, 1929–*c.* 30

Leach, Janet, 1956–

Leach, John, *c.* 1950–8
(at Langport, Somerset since 1964)
Marshall, William, 1954–

    LJ   impressed

incised

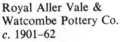

McKenzie, Warren, 1950–2

(at Dartington from 1963–)
mark used at Dartington

Quick, Kenneth, 1945–63
(at St. Ives 1945–*c.* 55 and
1960–63)
mark used at Tregenna Hill Pottery
c. 1955–60

ST. MARY CHURCH (Devon)   WATCOMBE
Watcombe Pottery Co.   TORQUAY
1867–1901
       WATCOMBE
       POTTERY
printed mark, 1875–1901

Royal Aller Vale &   ROYAL
Watcombe Pottery Co.   TORQUAY
c. 1901–62   POTTERY

SALISBURY (Wiltshire)   PAYNE SARUM
Payne, retailer only   printed
c. 1834–41

SMETHWICK   TAYLOR
(nr. Birmingham)   impressed
Ruskin Pottery, 1898–1935
earthenware
Taylor, W. Howson, *c.* 1898–

painted or incised

impressed mark, *c.* 1904–15
with added date

STANMORE (London)   E.C./(date)
Collyer, Ernest & Pamela
studio-potters, 1950–

Collyer-Nash   P.N. (Pamela Nash)

STEDHAM (Sussex)   Ray Marshall
Marshall, Ray   (date)
studio-potter, 1945–
impressed mark   signature

STOCKTON-ON-TEES (Cleveland)
Ainsworth, W. H. & J. H.
1865–1901, earthenware

impressed

Harwood, J.   HARWOOD
Clarence Pottery, 19th   STOCKTON
century earthenware
impressed mark, *c.* 1849–77

Skinner & Co., George   G.S. & CO.
Stafford Pottery   printed
earthenware, *c.* 1855–70

Skinner & Walker   S. & W.
1870–80   QUEEN'S WARE
       STOCKTON

Smith & Co.,   W.S. & CO.   W.S. & CO.
William, *c.* 1825–55   STAFFORD
Stafford Pottery   W.S. & CO'S   POTTERY
      WEDGWOOD

Smith, George F.   G.F.S.
North Shore Pottery
c. 1855–60, earthenware

Smith (Junr), William   W. S. JUNR. & CO.
c. 1845–84   all printed or impressed

STOKE D'ABERTON (Surrey)
Everson, Ronald
porcelain and bone-china
1953
mark in the form of
a dated signature

STOURBRIDGE (West Midlands)
Sunfield Pottery, 1937–
earthenware and stoneware

SUNDERLAND   ATKINSON & CO.
(Tyne and Wear)   impressed or
Southwick Pottery   printed
1788–99, Atkinson & Co., earthenware

Deptford Pottery   COPYRIGHT BALL
1857–1918   BROS.
Ball, William   SUNDERLAND
earthenware, Ball Bros., 1884–

Wear Pottery   J. BRUNTON
Brunton, John   printed
1796–1803, earthenware

South Hylton & DAWSON   I. DAWSON
Ford Potteries
Dawson, John, c. 1799–1864
c. 1799–1848, earthenware
Thomas Dawson & Co.   DAWSON & CO.
c. 1837–48, earthenware
    printed marks   FORD POTTERY   J. DAWSON
                          SOUTH HYLTON

Garrison or   J. PHILLIPS
Sunderland Pottery   SUNDERLAND
earthenware, c. 1807–65   POTTERY
    c. 1807–12

    c. 1813–19   PHILLIPS & CO. DIXON & CO.
                      DIXON, AUSTIN
    c. 1820–26   & CO.
                      DIXON, AUSTIN
    c. 1827–40   PHILLIPS & CO.

    c. 1840–65   DIXON, PHILLIPS
                      & CO.

Wear Pottery, 1803–74   MOORE & CO.
Moore & Co., Samuel   SUNDERLAND
earthenware

North Hylton   MALING
Pottery, 1762–67   impressed
earthenware, Maling, William, 1762–, continued
by family until 1815

Phillips & Co.,   JOHN PHILLIPS
John, 1815–67   HYLTON POT
(Phillips &   WORKS
Maling, 1780–1815)

Southwick Pottery, c. 1800–97
    c. 1800–29   A. SCOTT & CO.
                      SCOTT, SOUTHWICK
    c. 1829–44   A. SCOTT & SONS
                      S. & SONS
    c. 1844–54   S.B. & CO.
                      SCOTT BROTHERS
    c. 1854–97   A. SCOTT & SON
                      S. & S.

Union Pottery   UNION POTTERY
c. 1802   printed

SWADLINCOTE (S. Derbyshire)
Ault, William, 1887–1923
earthenware
    The wares of this
    pottery sometimes
    bear the signature
    of the designer
    Christopher Dresser
    and date from
    1891–6   printed or   printed
                    impressed

Ault & Tunnicliffe Ltd.
1923–37
(*see* Ashby Potter's Guild)

Ault Potteries Ltd., 1937–
(now Pearson & Co., Group)
    marks impressed or printed

SWINTON (Yorkshire)   DON POTTERY
Don Pottery, earthenware
1790–1893
    1800–34   GREEN
                            DON POTTERY
    1820–34, impressed or
    printed

Barker, Samuel, 1834–93
                                BARKER
    '& Son' or '& Sons'   DON POTTERY
    added 1851–93

Bingley & Co., Thomas   BINGLEY
earthenware, 1778–87   impressed

Twigg, Joseph & brothers
Kilnhurst Pottery & Newhill Pottery, c. 1822–81
earthenware
    impressed or   J.T.
    printed, c. 1822–
    impressed, c.   TWIGG
    1822–66   NEWHILL
    impressed, c.   TWIGG
    1839–81   K.P.

TONBRIDGE (Kent)   TONBRIDGE WARE
Slack & Brownlow   printed or impressed
earthenware, c. 1928–34

TORQUAY (Devon)
Torquay Terra-Cotta Co. Ltd.
Dr. Gillow, 1875–1909
earthenware figures, busts, etc.

                    impressed or printed

TRING (Hertfordshire)
Pendley Pottery, 1949–
Fieldhouse, Murray
studio-potter (now at
Northfields Studio)   incised or printed

TRURO (Cornwall)   LAKE'S CORNISH
Chapel Hill Pottery   POTTERY TRURO
1872–, Lake & Son Ltd.,   printed or impressed
W. H., earthenware

WAREHAM (Dorset)   SIBLEY POTTERY LTD
Sibley Pottery Ltd.,   DORSET
1922–62, earthenware   ENGLAND
and stoneware   impressed or printed

WATTISFIELD (Suffolk)
Watson Potteries Ltd., Henry
earthenware and stoneware
c. 1800–; mark of about
1948, early wares unmarked

WELWYN GARDEN CITY (Hertfordshire)
Coper, Hans, 1947–
studio-potter

WENFORD BRIDGE (nr. Bodmin, Cornwall)
Wenford Bridge Pottery
c. 1939–42; 1949–
impressed mark
(*see also* WINCHCOMBE)

WESTON-SUPER-MARE (Avon)
Matthews, John
terra-cotta, 1870–88
impressed mark with
Royal Arms

JOHN MATTHEWS
LATE PHILLIPS
ROYAL POTTERY
WESTON-SUPER-MARE

WHITTINGTON (Derbyshire)
Walton Pottery Co. Ltd.
1946–56
Gordon, William
salt-glazed stoneware

WINCANTON Somerset)
Ireson, Nathaniel
c. 1730–50
tin-glazed earthenware

IRESON
WINCANTON

WINCHCOMBE (Gloucestershire)
c. 1926–39
Cardew, Michael A.
also at Wenford Bridge
c. 1939–42
studio-potter

mark impressed

Finch, Raymond, 1939–
studio-potter, impressed
mark used from c. 1926

WITHERNSEA (Humberside)
Eastgate Potteries, Ltd.
earthenware, 1955–

EASTGATE
ENGLAND
(on a gate)

WOODVILLE (Derbyshire)
Ashby Potters' Guild
earthenware, 1909–22

impressed

Mansfield Bros., Ltd.
Art Pottery Works, c. 1890–
1957

M.B.
impressed

WORCESTER (Worcestershire)
Worcester Porcelain Factory
1751 (Lund & Miller's Bristol factory
est. 1748, taken over in 1752)
soft-paste porcelain (soapstone)

workmen's marks
in underglaze blue

'open' crescent on painted
wares, 1755–83

crescent mark with
crossed-hatched lines
on printed wares

in underglaze blue

any crescents in gilt or enamel colour
probably indicate outside decorator or
reproduction
on painted and printed
wares

painted in blue

marks on wares decorated
with 'Japan patterns'
c. 1760–75

in blue

'fretted square' mark
usually on heavily decorated
wares with scale-blue ground
c. 1755–75 (frequently seen
on reproductions)

in blue

Worcester imitation of Meissen
crossed-swords mark
c. 1760–70

in blue

printed numerals disguised as Chinese
characters, numbers 1–9, until recent
excavations at Worcester factory site these were
thought to be marks of Caughley (Salop)

'Flight' period, 1783–92
'small crescent', 1783–92

mark in blue, 1783–92

mark in blue, 1788–92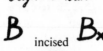

'Flight & Barr' period 1792–1807

F. & B.

'Barr', *c.* 1792–1807

B   incised   **B**x

'Barr Flight & Barr' period 1807–13

B F B
impressed

Barr, Flight & Barr	BARR, FLIGHT
Worcester	& BARR
Flight & Barr	ROYAL PORCELAIN
Coventry Street,	WORKS
London	WORCESTER
Manufacturers to their	LONDON HOUSE
Majesties and	NO. 1
Royal Family	COVENTRY STREET

'Flight, Barr & Barr' period 1813–40

F B B
impressed

(factory taken over by Chamberlains, 1840–52)

Kerr & Binns, 1852–62

Kerr & Binns, '54' = 1854
mark on outstanding
examples, including decorator's
initials (bottom left)

standard mark, printed or
impressed, *c.* 1852–62
Note: crown added
in 1862

'Worcester Royal Porcelain Company Ltd.'
(Royal Worcester) 1862–present

standard mark, 1862–present
early version, with 'C'
in centre replacing crescent
in Kerr & Binn's version
numbers below = last 2 years
of date

From 1867 a letter indicating the year of
manufacture was printed under the factory mark
according to the following table:

A	1867	G	1872	M	1877	T	1882	Y	1887
B	'1868	H	1873	N	1878	U	1883	Z	1888
C	1869	I	1874	P	1879	V	1884	O	1889
D	1870	K	1875	R	1880	W	1885		
E	1871	L	1876	S	1881	X	1886		

'a' in Old English script in 1890; date letter
omitted in 1891.
'Royal Worcester England' written around mark
from 1891, after which, dots, stars and other
letters and forms were added to the mark each
year as listed below until 1963 when the year in
full is added.

1892, dot to left of crown, 1893 dot either side of
crown; dots were then added to either side of
crown until 1915, thus:

1894	3 dots	1900	9 dots	1906	15 dots	1912	21 dots
1895	4 dots	1901	10 dots	1907	16 dots	1913	22 dots
1896	5 dots	1902	11 dots	1908	17 dots	1914	23 dots
1897	6 dots	1903	12 dots	1909	18 dots	1915	24 dots
1898	7 dots	1904	13 dots	1910	19 dots		
1899	8 dots	1905	14 dots	1911	20 dots		

In 1916 the dots alongside the crown were
replaced by a star under the mark, dots were then
added to either side of this star until 1927:

1916	1 star.	1922 star & 6 dots
1917	star & 1 dot	1923 star & 7 dots
1918	star & 2 dots	1924 star & 8 dots
1919	star & 3 dots	1925 star & 9 dots
1920	star & 4 dots	1926 star & 10 dots
1921	star & 5 dots	1927 star & 11 dots

then as follows:

1928 □   1929 ◇   1930 ÷

1931 ∞   1932 ∞∞   1933 ∞∞·

further dots were then added to three interlaced
circles as follows:

1934 circles & 2 dots	1938 circles & 6 dots
1935 circles & 3 dots	1939 circles & 7 dots
1936 circles & 4 dots	1940 circles & 8 dots
1937 circles & 5 dots	1941 circles & 9 dots

from 1941 to 1948 inclusive there were no changes in
the year-mark

1949 V	1953 W and 3 dots
1950 W	1954 W and 4 dots
1951 W and 1 dot	1955 W and 5 dots
1952 W and 2 dots	

1956 R in place of W   1960 R and 10 dots
     with 6 dots   1961 R and 11 dots
1957 R and 7 dots   1962 R and 12 dots
1958 R and 8 dots   1963 R and 13 dots
1959 R and 9 dots

From 1963 all new patterns have the year in full.

(*By courtesy of the Worcester Royal Porcelain Co. Ltd.*)

Hancock, Robert, *b.* 1730, *d.* 1817
engraver of transfer-prints
c. 1756–65

        RH . Worcester

(Hancock associated with   initials of Hancock
Turner of Caughley in   and rebus of Richard
1776)   Holdship on prints

Chamberlain, *c.* 1786–1852
decorators from *c.* 1786–*c.* 1790, then
manufacturers of soft-paste porcelain
    c. 1790–1810

        *Chamberlains
         Worcs No 276*
           in red

written or printed   *Chamberlain's*
c. 1811–40   *Worcester,*
(under crown)   *& 155*
               New Bond Street
               London,
               Royal Porcelain
               Manufactory

c. 1814–16   *Chamberlain's*
               Worcester,
               & 63 Piccadilly,
               London

         written or printed

incised, *c.* 1815–25   CHAMBERLAINS
               ROYAL PORCELAIN
               WORCESTER

printed mark under   CHAMBERLAIN & CO.
crown, *c.* 1840–5   WORCESTER
('& Co.' from this   155 New Bond St.
date)   & No. 1
               COVENTRY ST.
               LONDON

written or printed   CHAMBERLAIN & CO.
c. 1846–50   WORCESTER

impressed or printed   CHAMBERLAINS
c. 1847–50

---

printed *c.* 1850–52

(then Kerr & Binns, p. 86)

Doe and Rogers   Doe & Rogers
c. 1820–40   Worcester
porcelain decorators

Grainger, Wood & Co.   Grainger Wood & Co.
c. 1801–12, porcelain   Worcester, Warranted
rare mark

Grainger, Lee & Co.   Grainger, Lee & Co.
c. 1812–*c.* 39   Worcester
porcelain   painted

    c. 1820–30 painted   New China Works
               Worcester
    c. 1812–30 painted   Royal China Works
               Worcester

Grainger, George   GEO. GRAINGER
c. 1839–1902   CHINA WORKS
porcelain   WORCESTER
   painted or printed mark
   c. 1839–60
   '& Co.' added *c.* 1850   G. GRAINGER & CO.
               WORCESTER

's.P.' for 'Semi-   G.G. & CO.   S.P.
Porcelain', *c.*   S.P.   G.G.W.
1850–   impressed or printed
initials included in   G.W.
printed marks, 1850–60
1850–89   G. & CO. W.

printed mark on copies   GRAINGER & CO.
of 'Dr. Wall' period wares   WORCESTER
c. 1860–80
printed or impressed
c. 1870–89

c. 1889–1902 ('England'
added in 1891)

letters added under mark to indicate year of
manufacture from 1891–1902:

A 1891	D 1894	G 1897	J 1900
B 1892	E 1895	H 1898	K 1901
C 1893	F 1896	I 1899	L 1902

George Grainger & Co. was taken over by
Worcester Royal Porcelain Co. Ltd. in 1889 and
closed down in 1902.

Hadley & Sons, James
porcelain and earthenware
1896–1905

   signature on work   incised or impressed
modelled by Hadley for
Worcester Royal Porcelain Co.
c. 1875–94
printed or impressed
1896–97

1897–1902
impressed

FINE ART
HADLEY'S
TERRA-COTTA

printed mark 1897–1902
(centre ribbon omitted
from 1900)

printed mark, 1902–5

Locke & Co., porcelain   LOCKE & CO.
1895–1904   WORCESTER

   'globe-mark', *c.* 1895–1904
   'Ltd,' added in *c.* 1900

Sparks, George, *c.*   Sparks Worcester
1836–54, decorator of   written mark
Worcester and Coalport porcelain

WROTHAM (Kent)   I.G.
Greene, John
slipware potter, *c.* 1670

Hubble, Nicholas   N.H.
slipware potter, second
half of 17th century

Ifield, Thomas, Henry   T.I.
& John   H.I.   I.I.
slipware potters whose
   initials are found on wares
   dating from *c.* 1620–75

Livermore, John   I.L.
(*d.* 1658) slipware potter
wares dated from 1612–49

Richardson, George   G.R.
slipware potter, wares
dated from 1642–77   all above slip-trailed

Wells, Reginald   WELLS
(1877–1951)   incised
studio-potter

c. 1909   COLDRUM
                       WROTHAM
c. 1910–24 (at   COLDRUM
Chelsea)   CHELSEA

c. 1910   R. F. WELLS

c. 1918–51   SOON
(at Storrington,   impressed or incised
Sussex, *c.* 1925–51)

YARMOUTH (Norfolk)
   Absolon, William, 1784–1815
   independent enameller of
   the wares of various
   earthenwares and glass   painted in brown

STAFFORDSHIRE

Since the early seventeenth century the area in,
and around, Stoke in Staffordshire has been the
centre of the English ceramic industry.
Manufacture was first confined to earthenwares,
but later included salt-glazed stonewares,
jasperwares, bone-china and the mass of various
hybrid pottery and porcelain bodies introduced
about 1800 and later. The smaller pottery towns
are today grouped together to form
Stoke-on-Trent.

   In this section of the book, the various
Staffordshire potters are listed alphabetically
under the names of the towns in which they
potted.

   Many of the more recent factories have often
changed their mark many times and the following
general aids to dating are often sufficient to serve as
a guide.

   Few serious collectors seek pieces which
include 'ENGLAND' in the mark, for this
implies the piece was made in, or after, 1891 in
order to comply with the American McKinley
Tariff, which called for the country of origin to
be marked on imported wares. The term 'MADE
IN ENGLAND' suggests a date of about 1920.

   The mass of blue-printed earthenwares are
difficult to attribute if unmarked. Many have just a
Royal Arms as a mark; this is a sure indication of
a 19th-century date, whereas often similar marks,
or 'back-stamps', include the name of the design
and the initials of the potter. These initials may
well be included in the index at end of the book.
Versions of the Royal Arms used after 1837 lack
the small inescutcheon on the quartered shield
which is present on arms previous to this date.

   In addition to factory marks, many wares will be
found to bear the well-known 'diamond' or
'lozenge'-mark (see Appendix A, page 172).

This mark was applied by either printing, impressing, or applying as a relief medallion and indicates that the design of the form or decoration had been registered with the London Patent Office and was protected against 'piracy' for a period of three years. If the numbers and letters in the four corners of this 'diamond-mark' can be accurately read, the reader should consult the key diagrams and tables on page 172 to check the day, month and year the design was initially registered between 1842 and 1883. After this year wares bear only a registered number (e.g. Rd. 12345), which can be dated to the year, up until 1909.

Appendix B (pages 173–201) is an abbreviated copy of the Class IV (pottery, porcelain, etc.) Index, giving the name and whereabouts of the firms registering ceramic designs between 1842 and 1883. This list is reproduced with the kind permission of the Public Record Office.

BILSTON (Staffs., now West Midlands)
Myatt Pottery Co., *c.* 1850–94
earthenware, mark of 1880

MYATT

BURSLEM (Staffs. now West Midlands)
Albert Potteries Ltd.
earthenware, 1946–54

printed or impressed

Allman, Broughton & Co.
earthenware, 1861–8

A.B. & CO.
printed or impressed

Baggaley, Jacob
earthenware, 1880–6

J.B.
impressed

Bagshaw & Meir
earthenware, 1802–8

B. & M.
printed or impressed

Ball, Izaac
slipware, *c.* 1700

I.B.

Bancroft & Bennett
earthenware, 1846–50

Barker & Son
earthenware, *c.* 1850–60

B. & S.
printed
BARKER & SON
printed or impressed

Barker, Sutton & Till
earthenware, 1834–43

B.S. & T.

Bates, Elliott & Co.
general ceramics, 1870–5

B.E. & CO.

Bates, Gildea & Walker
general ceramics, 1878–81

B.G. & W.
printed

Bates, Walker & Co.
general ceramics, 1875–78

B.W. & CO.
printed

Bathwell & Goodfellow
earthenware, 1818–23
(also Tunstall 1820–2)

BATHWELL &
GOODFELLOW
impressed

Beech, James
earthenware, 1877–89
Swan Bank Works (also
at Tunstall)

J.B.
printed

Blackhurst & Bourne
earthenware, 1880–92

B. & B.
printed

Blackhurst & Tunnicliffe
earthenware, *c.* 1879

B. & T.
printed

Bodley & Co.
earthenware, 1865

Bodley & Co., E. F.
earthenware, *c.* 1862–81

E.F.B. & CO.

SCOTIA POTTERY

BODLEY
Bodley & Son
bone-china, 1874–5

B. & SON
printed

Bodley, E. J. D.
general ceramics, 1875–92

E.J.D.B.
printed,
impressed or as
monogram

Bodley & Harrold
Scotia Pottery
1863–5, earthenware

B. & H.
Bodley & Harrold
printed

Boote, Ltd., T. & R.
Waterloo Pottery
general ceramics and
tiles, 1842–*c.* 1966

T. & R.B.   T.B. & S.

T. & R. BOOTE
printed or impressed

printed mark
1890–1906
'England' added
from 1891

Booth & Co., Thomas
(also at Tunstall)
earthenware, 1868–72

T.B. & CO.
printed

Bridgwood & Clarke
(also at Tunstall)
earthenware, 1857–64

BRIDGWOOD &
CLARKE
impressed
B. & C.   B. & C.
BURSLEM
printed

Brown & Steventon, Ltd.
earthenware, 1900–23

B. & S.
printed
'sun-face' mark
from 1920–

printed or impressed

Buckley, Heath & Co.
earthenware, 1885–90

Buckley, Wood & Co.
earthenware, 1875–85

B.W. & CO.
printed or impressed

Burgess, Henry
earthenware, 1864–92

H.B.
impressed or printed
under Royal Arms

Burgess & Leigh
earthenware, *c.* 1862–

B. & L.
impressed or printed

'Ltd.' added to marks
from *c.* 1919, large
variety of printed
marks from 1880,
'England' added from
1891

printed

monogram mark
1862–

impressed or printed

Burslem Pottery Co. Ltd.
earthenware, 1894–1933

printed

ENGLAND

Burslem School of Art
earthenware, figures, etc.
in 'Astbury' style
1935–41

impressed

Clarke & Co., Edward
earthenware, *c.* 1880–87
(also at Tunstall, *c.* 1865–
77, and Longport, *c.*
1878–80)

EDWARD CLARKE

EDWARD CLARKE &
CO.
printed

Clowes, William
general ceramics
c. 1783–96

W. CLOWES
impressed

Collinson & Co.,
Charles, earthenware
1851–73

C. COLLINSON & CO.
printed

Cooper & Co., J.
earthenware, 1922–5
printed or impressed
in circle

J. COOPER & CO.
ENGLAND
DUCAL WORKS

Cooper Pottery, Susie
('Ltd.' from *c.* 1961)
general ceramics
c. 1930–

CROWN WORKS
BURSLEM
ENGLAND

printed mark, 1932–

Cooper China Ltd., Susie
(also at Longton, *c.* 1950–9)
china, *c.* 1959–
Member of the
Wedgwood Group

Cork & Edge
earthenware
1846–60

C. & E.
printed with a
variety of designs

Cork, Edge & Malkin
earthenware, 1860–71

C.E. & M.
printed with varying
'backstamps' often
including pattern-name

Dale, John
'Staffordshire
figures', early 19th century

J. DALE
BURSLEM

I. DALE
BURSLEM

Daniel & Cork
earthenware, 1867–9

DANIEL & CORK
printed

Davison & Son, Ltd.
earthenware
c. 1898–1952

mark of 1948–

printed

Dean, S. W.
earthenware, 1904–10

printed mark

Deans (1910) Ltd.
earthenware, 1910–19
printed mark

DEANS (1910) LTD.
BURSLEM
ENGLAND

Doulton & Co.
earthenware and
porcelain, *c.* 1882
(Doulton Fine China Ltd.
from 1955 and Royal
Doulton Tableware Ltd., 1973–)

see under
LAMBETH
for major
marks

impressed name of
new material from
1960

ENGLISH
TRANSLUCENT
CHINA

Duke & Nephews, Sir James
various hybrid porcelains
c. 1860–3

impressed hand

Dunn, Bennett & Co.
earthenware, 1875–
('Ltd.' added from 1907–)
(now Royal Doulton Group)
marks 1875–1907

D.B. & CO.
printed

printed mark, 1937–

DUNN BENNETT & CO. LTD
BURSLEM
ENGLAND

added to mark on
'Ironstone' from 1955–

'Vitreous Ironstone'

Edge, Malkin & Co.
earthenware, 1871–1903

E.M. & CO.

'LTD.' added from 1899

E.M. & CO.
B
printed

Edwards & Son, James
various pottery, 1851–82

J.E. & S.

'Dale Hall', Burslem

EDWARDS
D.H.
printed or impressed

Edwards, James & Thomas
earthenware, 1839–41

J. & T.E.

printed or impressed

J. & T. EDWARDS
B

Ellgreave Pottery Co. Ltd.
earthenware, 1921–
(Wood & Sons Ltd.)
  and other fully
  named marks

'Lottie Rhead Ware'

'Heatmaster'

Elton & Co. Ltd., J. F.
earthenware, 1901–1910
(also in monogram)

J.F.E. CO. LTD.
BURSLEM
printed or impressed

Emery, Francis J.
earthenware, *c.* 1878–93

F. J. EMERY
printed

Evans & Booth
earthenware, 1856–69

E. & B.
printed

Ford & Co., Samuel
earthenware, 1898–1939
(*see* Smith & Ford)

'F. & CO.' alternative to
'S. & F.'

printed

c. 1936–9

'Samford Ware'

Ford & Riley
earthenware, 1882–93

F. & R.
B

Ford & Sons ('Ltd.'
added 1908),
earthenware, *c.* 1893–1938

F. & S.
B

also 'CROWN
FORD', 'NEWCRAFT'

F. & SONS, LTD.
printed

Ford & Sons (Crownford)
earthenware, 1938–

printed, 1961–

Gibson & Sons, Ltd.
earthenware, 1885–

G. & S. LTD.
B

Gibson & Sons, Ltd.
'Harvey Pottery'
  printed, *c.* 1904–9

'Royal Harvey', *c.* 1950–5
  large variety of fully named marks, 1909–

Gildea & Walker, 1881–5
earthenware

c. 1881–5:
$$\frac{4}{82} = \text{APRIL, 1882}$$

Gildea, James
earthenware, 1885–8

printed mark includes
a pattern-name

Godwin, B. C.
earthenware, *c.* 1851–

B.C.G.
printed

Godwin, Thomas &
Benjamin, general
ceramics, *c.* 1809–34

T. & B.G.
T.B.G.
printed

Godwin, Thomas earthenware, 1834–54	THOS GODWIN BURSLEM STONE CHINA
Godwin, Rowley & Co. earthenware, 1828–31	G.R. & CO. printed
Hall & Sons, John earthenware, 1814–32 *c.* 1822–32	I. HALL　　HALL I. HALL & SONS impressed or printed
Hammersley & Son, Ralph earthenware, 1860–1905 '& Son' added 1884–	R.H. R.H. & S. printed
Hancock, Whittingham & Co., earthenware, 1863–72	H.W. & CO. printed
Harding, Joseph earthenware, 1850–1	J. HARDING printed
Harrison & Phillips earthenware, 1914–15	H. & P. BURSLEM printed
Heath & Son earthenware, *c.* 1800	HEATH & SON impressed
Heath, John general ceramics, 1809–23	HEATH impressed
Heath, Thomas earthenware, 1812–35	T. HEATH impressed or printed
Heath & Blackhurst & Co. earthenware, 1859–77	H. & B. H.B. & CO.
Heath & Greatbatch earthenware, 1891–3	H. & G. B printed or impressed
Hill Pottery Co. Ltd. general ceramics, *c.* 1861–7	J.S.H. printed (also as monogram)
Hobson, Charles earthenware, 1865–80 's' added 1873–5	C.H. C.H. & S. impressed or printed
Hobson, G. & J. earthenware, 1883–1901	HOBSON'S printed

Hobson, George
earthenware, 1901–23
　printed or impressed

Holdcroft & Co., Peter earthenware, 1846–52	P.H. & CO. printed
Holdcroft, Hill & Mellor earthenware 1860–70	H.H. & M. printed
Hollinshead & Griffiths earthenware, 1890–1909	CHELSEA ART POTTERY H. & G. BURSLEM

　　mark includes lion and crown

Holmes, Plant & Maydew earthenware, 1876–85	H.P. & M. printed
Hope & Carter earthenware, 1862–80	H. & C. printed
Hughes, Thomas earthenware, 1860–94	THOMAS HUGHES IRONSTONE CHINA impressed
Hughes & Son Ltd., Thomas general ceramics 1895–1957	THOS. HUGHES & SON ENGLAND
Hulme & Sons, Henry earthenware, 1906–32 (mark previously used by Wood & Hulme)	W. & H. B

Hulme, William
earthenware, 1891–1941

printed
1891–1936

printed or impressed 1936–41	ALPHA WARE H ENGLAND
Jackson, Job & John earthenware, 1831–5	J. & J. JACKSON JACKSON'S WARRANTED impressed or printed
Johnson, Ltd., Samuel earthenware, 1887–1931 'Ltd.' 1912– 'BRITANNIA POTTERY' 1916–31	S.J. 　　　　S.J.B. S.J. LTD. printed
Jones, George earthenware, *c.* 1854	GEORGE JONES
Keeling & Co. Ltd. earthenware, 1886–1936	K. & CO. K. & CO. B.

'England' usually added
from 1891
'Losol Ware', *c.* 1912–

all
printed

Kennedy, William Sadler
earthenware, 1843–54

W. S. KENNEDY
impressed or printed

Kennedy & Macintyre
earthenware, 1854–60

W. S. KENNEDY
& J. MACINTYRE
impressed or printed

Kensington Pottery Ltd.
c. 1937–
(also at Hanley 1922–37)
now Price & Kensington Potteries Ltd.

Kent (Porcelains) Ltd., William
earthenware 1944–62

King & Barrett, Ltd.
general pottery, 1898–40

K. & B.
impressed or printed

Lakin & Poole
pottery and figures, *c.* 1791–5

LAKIN & POOLE

L. & P.
BURSLEM
impressed

Leighton Pottery Ltd.
earthenware, 1940–54

'ROYAL LEIGHTON WARE'

Machin & Potts
general ceramics
1833–7
colour-print patent 1835

MACHIN & POTTS

MACHIN & POTTS
PATENT

Machin & Thomas
earthenware, *c.* 1831–2

M. & T.
printed

Macintyre & Co. Ltd.,
James, earthenware, *c.*
1860–1928, '& Co.' from
1867– (continued with
industrial wares only)

MACINTYRE
J. MACINTYRE
J.M. & CO.
printed or impressed

Maddock & Seddon
earthenware, *c.* 1839–42

M. & S.

Maddock, John
earthenware, 1842–55
(not to be confused with
'M' for Minton)

M
printed

Maddock & Sons (Ltd.)
general pottery, 1855–
specialist hotel-ware
'Ltd.' added 1896–

various fully named
marks, and
'ROYAL VITREOUS'
'ROYAL IVORY'

'IVORY WARE'
'EMBASSY'

Malkin, Frederick
earthenware, 1891–1905

printed, *c.* 1900–5

Malkin, Samuel
slip-wares, early 18th century

S.M.
moulded in
relief

Mayer, Thomas, John
& Joseph, general
ceramics, 1843–55

T. J. & J. MAYER
printed

Mellor, Taylor & Co.
earthenware, *c.* 1880–1904

'ROYAL IRONSTONE CHINA'

printed or impressed
with name of firm

'SEMI PORCELAIN'

Mellor, Venables & Co.
general ceramics, 1834–51

MELLOR, VENABLES
& CO.

M.V. & CO.
printed or impressed

Midwinter Ltd., W. R.
earthenwares, 1910–
added numbers indicate
month and year
(now Wedgwood Group)

various fully named
marks with:
'PORCELON'
'STYLECRAFT'

Moorcroft Ltd., W.
earthenware, 1913–

MOORCROFT
BURSLEM

signature of William
Moorcroft (*d.* 1945)

mark of Walter Moorcroft
(son)

Morgan, Wood & Co.
earthenware, 1860–70

M.W. & CO.
printed
(at times with bee)

Mountford, A. J.
earthenware, 1897–1901

BURSLEM
printed

New Wharf Pottery Co.
earthenware, 1878–94

N.W.P.CO.
B
printed

Newport Pottery Co. Ltd.
earthenware, 1920–
(now Wedgwood group)

various fully named
marks

c. 1938–66

'Clarice Cliff'

Parrott & Co. Ltd.
earthenware, 1921
(manufacture ceased *c.* 1962)

Phillips & Son, Thomas
earthenware, *c.* 1845–6

T. PHILLIPS & SON
BURSLEM
printed or impressed

Pinder, Thomas
earthenware, 1849–51

PINDER BURSLEM
printed or impressed

Pinder, Bourne & Hope
earthenware, 1851–62

P.B. & H.
printed

Pinder, Bourne & Co.
earthenware, 1862–82
(taken over by Doultons
in 1878, but name unchanged
until 1882)

P.B. & CO.

Plant Bros. Crown Pottery
porcelain, 1889–1906
(at Longton from 1898)

Plant, Enoch
earthenware, 1898–1905
(such crowns are a
common form of mark)

printed or impressed

Poole, J. E.
earthenware, *c.* 1796–
early 19th century

POOLE
impressed

Price Bros.
earthenware, 1896–1903

Price Bros. (Burslem) Ltd.
earthenware, 1903–61

printed
'star-mark', as above
until 1910

trade-names:
'PALM ATHLO'
'ATHLO WARE'
'MATTONA WARE'

Price & Kensington
Potteries Ltd.
earthenware, 1962–

PRICE
KENSINGTON
printed within wreath

Radford Handcraft
Pottery, earthenware
1933–48

G. RADFORD
BURSLEM
printed signature

Riley, John & Richard
general ceramics, 1802–28

J. & R. RILEY

marks painted,
printed or impressed

RILEY'S
SEMI-CHINA

Robinson, Joseph
earthenware, 1876–98

J.R.
B
printed or impressed

Roddy & Co., E.
earthenware, 1925–8

STAFFORDSHIRE
RODDY
WARE

Sadler & Sons, Ltd.
James, earthenware
1899–
impressed or printed
from 1937–

ENGLAND
J.S.S.B.
impressed

SADLER
BURSLEM
ENGLAND

Simpson, Ralph
slipwares, 1651–*c.* 1724
name slip-trailed on front
of large chargers

RALPH SIMPSON
slip-trailed

Simpson, John
slipwares, first half of
18th century

JOHN SIMPSON
I.S.
slip-trailed

Smith & Co., Ambrose
earthenware, *c.* 1784–6

A.S. & CO.
impressed or printed

Smith & Ford
earthenware, 1895–8
printed (*see also*
Samuel Ford)

Stanyer, A.
earthenware, *c.* 1916–41

A.S.   A.S.
B   ENG.
ENG.   B
impressed

Steel, Daniel
1790–1824
earthenwares and
'Wedgwood-type' stonewares

STEEL
impressed

Stubbs, Joseph
earthenwares, *c.* 1822–35

JOSEPH STUBBS
LONGPORT
impressed or printed

Stubbs & Kent
earthenware, *c.* 1828–30
mark impressed or
printed

Sudlow & Sons, Ltd., R.
earthenware, 1893–
(Part of Howard Pottery
Co. Shelton from 1965)

full-name marks
impressed or printed
from *c.* 1920–

Till & Sons, Thomas
earthenware, *c.* 1850–1928

1861–

'Globe-mark' from 1880
'Tillson' ware, *c.* 1922–8

Tundley, Rhodes &
Proctor, earthenware
1873–83, then:

T.R. & P.
printed

Rhodes & Proctor
1883–5, earthenware

R. & P.
printed

Venables & Baines
earthenware, *c.* 1851–3

VENABLES &
BAINES

Venables & Co.
earthenware, *c.* 1853–5

J. VENABLES
& CO.
printed or impressed

Vernon & Son, James
earthenware, 1860–80
1875–

J.V.

J.V. & Son

J.V. & S.   J.V. junr.

Wade & Son, Ltd.,
George, earthenware
1922–,
1936–

1947–

WADE
Figures

Wade & Co.
earthenware, 1887–1927

WADES

W. & CO.
B

Wade, Heath & Co., Ltd.
earthenware
1927–

WADES
(with lion)

c. 1934–

WADEHEATH
ORCADIA
WARE

c. 1934–

WADEHEATH
(with lion)

Trade-names: 'Flaxman Ware', 'ROYAL
VICTORIA'

Walley, John
earthenware, 1850–67

J. WALLEY
J. WALLEY'S
WARE
printed or impressed

Walton, John
earthenware groups and
figures, *c.* 1818–35

impressed on raised
scroll

Wedgwood & Sons, Ltd.
Josiah, general ceramics, 1759–
very rare incised initials or
signature, *c.* 1760
rare, *c.* 1759–69
c. 1759

'J.W.'

wedgwood   WEDGWOOD

WEDGWOOD

Wedgwood & Bentley
partnership, 1769–80
concerned only with
the manufacture of
ornamental neo-classical
wares

WEDGWOOD
& BENTLEY

WEDGWOOD
& BENTLEY
ETRURIA

impressed on cameos, etc.
impressed or raised mark

W. & B.

c. 1780–98

Wedgwood

rare impressed mark
c. 1790
printed on bone-china
c. 1812–22

WEDGWOOD & SONS

WEDGWOOD
red, blue or gold

rare printed mark on
stone-china, *c.* 1827–61

WEDGWOOD'S
STONE CHINA

impressed mark *c.* 1840–5

WEDGWOOD
ETRURIA

impressed on 'pearlware'
c. 1840–68

PEARL

as above, post–1868

P

From 1860 the Wedgwood factory in addition to their
usual name-mark, adopted a system of date-marking
consisting of three letters side by side: the first indicates
the month, the second a potter's mark and the third
the year of manufacture. As from 1907 the first letter,
which had hitherto denoted the month of manufacture,
was replaced by a number indicating the cycle of year
marks in use; previously there was no indication
whether the piece was made in the first second, or third
cycle.

This system was further changed in 1930 when the
cycle number was replaced by the chronological number
of the month, e.g.: January = 1, February = 2, etc.,
and the initial which had previously indicated the year
was now replaced by the last two years of the actual
date of manufacture.

Examples:

Month	Potter	Year	
Y	O	R	May, 1863
L	O	E	July, 1902
Cycle	Potter	Year	
3	O	N	1911
4	O	A	1924

Month	Potter	Year	
3	O	32	March, 1932
11	O	48	November, 1948

Monthly marks indicated by the first letter from
1860–1864:

January	J	April	A	July	V	October O
February	F	May	Y	August	W	November N
March	M	June	T	September	S	December D

1865–1907:

January	J	April	A	July	L	October O
February	F	May	M	August	W	November N
March	R	June	T	September	S	December D

First cycle of year-marks:

O	1860	R	1863	U	1866	X	1869
P	1861	S	1864	V	1867	Y	1870
Q	1862	T	1865	W	1868	Z	1871

Second cycle of year-marks:

A	1872	H	1879	O	1886	V	1893
B	1873	I	1880	P	1887	W	1894
C	1874	J	1881	Q	1888	X	1895
D	1875	K	1882	R	1889	Y	1896
E	1876	L	1883	S	1890	Z	1897
F	1877	M	1884	T	1891		
G	1878	N	1885	U	1892		

Note: 'ENGLAND' added to mark from 1891
Third cycle of year-marks:

A	1898	H	1905	O	1912	V	1919
B	1899	I	1906	P	1913	W	1920
C	1900	J	1907	Q	1914	X	1921
D	1901	K	1908	R	1915	Y	1922
E	1902	L	1909	S	1916	Z	1923
F	1903	M	1910	T	1917		
G	1904	N	1911	U	1918		

Fourth cycle of year-marks:

A	1924	C	1926	E	1928
B	1925	D	1927	F	1929

the last two years of the date then appear in full.

'Portland Vase' mark printed
on bone-china from *c.* 1878
occasionally seen impressed
on earthenware, *c.* 1891–1900
Note: 'ENGLAND' added
after 1891 'MADE IN

WEDGWOOD
BONE CHINA

MADE IN ENGLAND

ENGLAND' from about 1910
'*Bone China*' added *c.* 1920

printed on creamwares
from *c.* 1940

Lessore, Emile, decorator
c. 1858–76

Thomson, E. G.
decorator, *c.* 1870

E. G. Thomson

Barnard, Harry, decorator
c. 1900

marks on red stonewares
probably Wedgwood
second-half of
18th century

impressed

Whittingham, Ford & Co.
1868–73,
earthenware

W.F. & CO.
printed

Whittingham, Ford & Riley
earthenware, 1876–82

W.F. & R.
printed

Wilkinson, Arthur J.
1885–*c.* 1970, earthenwares
'ROYAL SEMI-PORCELAIN', *c.* 1891–
'ROYAL IRONSTONE CHINA', *c.* 1896–
'IRONSTONE CHINA', *c.* 1910
'Clarice Cliff', *c.* 1930
'Honeyglaze', *c.* 1947
(merged with W. R. Midwinter Ltd., 1964)

many fully named
marks including:

Withinshaw, W. E.
1873–8, general ceramics

W.E.W.
W. E. WITHINSHAW
printed or impressed

Wood, Enoch
c. 1784–*c.* 1790 general
ceramics
    Enoch Wood's marks
can be seen impressed,
moulded or incised

WOOD   E. WOOD
W (***)
E.W.   W.
ENOCH WOOD
SCULPSIT

E. WOOD
SCULPSIT

ENOCH WOOD

Wood & Caldwell
1790–1818, earthenware
especially figures, etc.

WOOD & CALDWELL
impressed

Wood & Sons, Enoch
1818–1846, earthenware
blue-printed wares made
for U.S.A. include the
American eagle in mark

ENOCH WOOD
& SONS
BURSLEM
STAFFORDSHIRE

E. WOOD & SONS
E. &' E. WOOD
BURSLEM

E.W. & S.
E. & E. WOOD
E. & E.W.
all printed

Wood, H. J.
1884–, earthenware
many various fully named marks including:
'Bursley-Ware' *c.* 1930–
'E. Radford' *c.* 1935–
'CHINESE ROSE' *c.* 1960–, etc.

Wood, Isaiah
1710–15, earthenware

ISA WOOD
1712
incised

Wood, John Wedge
1841–4 (also at Tunstall
1845–60)

W.W.
impressed
J. WEDGWOOD
printed

Wood, Ralph (Snr.)   R. WOOD   Ra. WOOD
(1715–72), son of same   Ra. WOOD
name (1748–95)   BURSLEM
grandson (1781–1801)   Ralph Wood
  impressed or incised marks
  c. 1770–1801

  rebus of trees (rare)
  c. 1770–90

Wood & Son
1865–, earthenware, etc.
  '& Sons', from 1907
  'Ltd.' added *c.* 1910

various fully named
marks from *c.* 1890–

Wood & Co., Thomas
1885–96, earthenwares

T.W. & CO.
printed or impressed

Wood & Sons, Thomas
c. 1896–7, earthenware

T.W. & S.
printed

Wood & Co., W.
1873–1932, earthenware
mark of initials printed in 'Staffordshire
knot', 1880–1915, with crown, 1915–32

W.W. & CO.
printed or impressed

Wood & Baggaley
1870–80, earthenware

W. & B.
printed

Wood & Barker, Ltd.
1897–1903, earthenware

W. & B. Ltd.
printed

Wood & Bowers
1839, earthenware

W. & B.
(can be confused
with Wood & Baggaley)

Wood & Clarke
c. 1871–2, earthenware

W. & C.
printed with 'lion
rampant'

Wood & Hulme
1882–1905, earthenware

W. & H.
B
printed or impressed

Wooldridge & Walley
1898–1901, earthenware

W. & W.
B
printed

COBRIDGE (Staffordshire)

Alcock, John & George
1839–46, earthenware and
  'INDIAN IRONSTONE'

J. & G.A.

J. & G. ALCOCK
COBRIDGE
impressed or printed

Alcock, Junior, John &
Samuel, *c.* 1848–50
earthenware

J. & S. ALCOCK JR.
printed or impressed

Alcock, John
1853–61, earthenware

JOHN ALCOCK
COBRIDGE
printed

Alcock & Co., Henry
1861–1910, earthenware
  fully named mark from
  1880, 'Ltd.' from 1900

H.A. & CO.
printed

Alcock Pottery, The Henry
1910–35, earthenware

fully named
'coat of arms' mark
printed

Alcock & Co., Samuel
c. 1828–53, general ceramics
  (Also at Burslem
  c. 1830–59)
  printed, painted or
  impressed, sometimes
  with Royal Arms or
  bee-hive

SAMUEL ALCOCK & CO.
COBRIDGE
printed or impressed
S.A. & CO.
S. ALCOCK & CO.

Bates & Bennett
1868–95, earthenware

B. & B.
printed or impressed

Birks Brothers & Seddon
1877–86, earthenware

IMPERIAL IRONSTONE
CHINA
BIRKS BROS. & SEDDON
printed below Royal Arms

Blackhurst & Co. Ltd., John
1951–9, earthenware

J. BLACKHURST
ENGLAND

Brownfield, William
1850–91, earthenware (also
porcelain after 1871) much
'parian ware'

W.B.

printed, impressed
or moulded

impressed, often with
crown, from 1860–   **BROWNFIELD**
'S' or '& Son', added 1871
'& Sons', added 1876
printed 'double-globe' mark, 1871–91

Brownfields Guild Pottery   **B.G.P. CO.**
Society Ltd., 1891–1900   impressed
general ceramics
(Brownfield's Pottery Ltd.
c. 1898–1900)

printed monogram

printed within circular
strap device   **BROWNFIELDS**

Cartledge, John   **JOHN CARTLEDGE**
c. 1800, earthenware   rare incised mark
figures

Clews, James & Ralph   **CLEWS WARRANTED**
1818–34, pottery and porcelain **STAFFORDSHIRE**
                               impressed under
                                    crown

impressed mark on
blue-printed wares

Cockson & Chetwynd   **C.C. & CO.**
1867–75, earthenware

                               COCKSON &
                               CHETWYND
                               printed

Cockson & Seddon   **IMPERIAL IRONSTONE**
1875–7, earthenware   **CHINA**
                               COCKSON & SEDDON
                               printed under Royal
                                    Arms

Crystal Porcelain Pottery   **C.P.P. CO.**
Co. Ltd., 1882–6   printed or impressed
pottery and porcelain
  (dove sometimes
  included in mark)

Daniel, John   **JOHN DANIEL**
c. 1770–*c.* 86, earthenware incised

Dillon, Francis   **DILLON**
1834–43, earthenware   impressed

                               F.D.
                               printed with various
                                 back-stamps

Furnival & Co., Jacob   **J.F. & CO.**
c. 1845–70, earthenware   printed

Furnival & Sons, Thomas
1871–90, earthenware
  various 'T. F. & Sons'
  monograms

Furnivals (Ltd.)   **FURNIVALS**
1890–1968, earthenware   **ENGLAND**
  'Ltd.' added *c.* 1895

c. 1905–13
(Taken over by Barratt's
of Staffordshire in 1967,
closed 1968)

1913 date included in   **FURNIVALS**
marks from that year   **(1913)**
                                ENGLAND

Globe Pottery Co. Ltd.   fully-named
1914–, earthenware (now   printed 'globe' marks
Royal Doulton Group)
Godwin, Benjamin E.   **B.G.**
1834–41, earthenware   printed with back-
                                    stamp

Godwin, John & Robert   **J. & R.G.**
1834–66, earthenware   printed

Harding & Cockson   **COBRIDGE**
1834–60, earthenware   **H. & C.**
                               printed

Hughes & Co., Elijah   **E. HUGHES & CO.**
1853–67, earthenware   impressed

Hulme, William
1948–54, earthenware

printed mark

Jones, Elijah   fully named
1831–9, earthenware   impressed mark
                                    or
                               E.J. printed

Jones & Walley   fully named
1841–3, earthenware   impressed or
                               moulded mark
                                    or
                               printed **J. & W.**

Meakin, Henry   **IRONSTONE CHINA**
1873–6, earthenware   **H. MEAKIN**
                               printed with Royal
                                    Arms

North Staffordshire Pottery Co. Ltd.
1940–52, earthenware

trade-mark registered
in 1944

Portland Pottery Ltd.
1946–53, earthenware
('P.P.C.' monogram,
Portland Pottery, Cobridge)

Regal Pottery Co. Ltd.
1925–31, earthenware

Richardson, Albert G.
c. 1920–21

REGAL WARE
A.G.R.
printed

Richardsons (Cobridge) Ltd.
1921–25

REGAL WARE
R(C) LTD.
printed

Robinson, Wood &
Brownfield, 1838–41
earthenware, printed

R.W. & B.

Sant & Vodrey
1887–93, earthenware

S. & V.
COBRIDGE
printed or impressed

Shaw, Ralph
c. 1740–, earthenware

Made by Ralph Shaw
October 31, Cobridge
gate

Simpsons (Potters) Ltd.
1944–, earthenware
including various trade-names:
'Ambassador Ware', 'Solian Ware', 'Loh
Yueh Mei Kuei', 'Vogue', 'Chinastyle',
'Marlborough Old English Ironstone',
'Chanticleer'

fully named marks

Stevenson, Andrew
c. 1816–30, earthenware

STEVENSON
A. STEVENSON

impressed 'ship'
mark could also refer to
following potter

Stevenson, Ralph
c. 1810–32, earthenware

R. STEVENSON

marks impressed

R.S.

Stevenson & Son, Ralph
c. 1832–35, earthenware
marks printed

R.S. & S.

R. STEVENSON
& SON

Stevenson, Alcock &
Williams, earthenware *c.* 1825,
marks printed

STEVENSON
ALCOCK &
WILLIAMS

Stevenson & Williams
c. 1825, earthenware

R.S.W.

marks printed

STEVENSON & WILLIAMS

Viking Pottery Co.
1950–63, general ceramics

Walley, Edward
1845–56, general ceramics
marks impressed or printed

E. WALLEY

W.

Warburton, John
c. 1802–25, earthenwares
and stonewares

WARBURTON
impressed

Warburton, Peter
c. 1802–12, general ceramics

c. 1810–12

WARBURTON'S
PATENT
printed or written
under crown

Warburton, Peter & Francis
1795–1802, earthenware

marks impressed

P. & F.W.

P. & F.
WARBURTON

Wood, Son & Co.
1869–79, earthenware

WOOD, SON & CO.
printed under
Royal Arms

Wood & Brownfield
c. 1838–50, earthenware

W. & B.
impressed or printed

Wood & Hawthorne
1882–7, earthenware

WOOD &
HAWTHORNE
printed under Royal
Arms

FENTON (Staffordshire)

Bailey Potteries, Ltd.
1935–40, earthenware

BEWLEY POTTERY
MADE IN ENGLAND
printed

Baker & Co., W.
1839–1932, earthenware

W. BAKER & CO.
printed or impressed

printed or impressed
'Ltd.' added 1893

BAKER & CO.

Barkers & Kent
1889–1941, earthenware
'Ltd.' added 1898

B. & K.
B. & K.L.
printed or impressed

Beardmore & Co., Frank
1903–14, earthenware
  impressed on printed mark

  printed mark

F.B. & CO.
F

Bourne, Charles
1817–30, porcelain

C.B.
(pattern no.)

Bowker, Arthur
1948–58, porcelain

  mark printed under crown

STAFFORDSHIRE
FINE BONE CHINA
OF
ARTHUR BOWKER

Brain & Co. Ltd.
1903–67
porcelain

HARJIAN
ENGLAND

1905–
(now Coalport
a division of
the Wedgwood
Group at
Foley Works)

E.B. & CO.
F.
impressed or
printed within
Staffordshire
knot

(Coalport China Ltd., taken over by
E. Brain & Co. Ltd. in 1958)

British Art Pottery Co. (Fenton) Ltd.
1920–6, porcelain

  mark printed or impressed

Broadhurst & Sons, James
c. 1862–, earthenware
  printed in mark, 1862–70

J.B.

  printed in mark, 1870–1922
  'Ltd.' added 1922

J.B. & S.

Challinor & Co., E.
1853–62, earthenware

E. CHALLINOR & CO.
printed

Challinor, E. & C.
1862–91, earthenware

E. & C.C.

E. & C. CHALLINOR
FENTON
printed

Challinor, C. & Co.
1892–6, earthenware

C. CHALLINOR & CO.
ENGLAND

Clulow & Co.
c. 1802, earthenware

CLULOW & CO.
FENTON

Crown Staffordshire Porcelain Co. Ltd.
1889–, porcelain
(renamed Crown Staffordshire China Co. Ltd. in
1948)

printed 1889–1912
(Wedgwood China Div.
from 1973)
  printed marks of from
  1906, this firm makes
  bone-china reproductions
  of Chelsea 'raised-
  anchor' birds

'STAFFORDSHIRE'
with a crown within
wreath

Edge, Barker & Co.
1835–6, earthenware

E.B. & CO.
printed

Edge, Barker & Barker
1836–40, earthenware

E.B. & B.
printed

Edwards, John
1847–1900, general ceramics
  '& Co.' added *c.* 1873–9
  named marks including
  'PORCELAINE DE TERRE' or
  'WARRANTED IRONSTONE CHINA'
  from *c.* 1880–1900

J.E.

J.E. & CO.
PORCELAINE
IRONSTONE

Elkin, Knight & Co.
1822–6, earthenware
  marks impressed or
  printed

E.K. & CO.

ELKIN KNIGHT
& CO.

Elkin, Knight & Bridgwood
c. 1827–40, earthenware
and porcelain

E.K.B.
printed

Forester & Sons, Thomas
1883–1959, earthenware

T.F. & S.

  'Ltd.' added, 1891–
  'Phoenix China', 1912–

Forester & Hulme
1887–93, earthenware

F. & H.
printed under bee

Hulme & Christie
1893–1902, earthenware
  mark printed with a dove

H. & C.
F

Garner, Robert
late 18th century, earthenware

R.G.
moulded

Gimson & Co., Wallis
1884–90, earthenware

WALLIS GIMSON &
CO.
printed under beehive

Ginder & Co., Samuel·
1811–43, earthenware

S. Ginder & Co.
printed

Greatbatch, William
c. 1760– *c*, 1780, modeller
potter and engraver of
transfer-prints

GREATBATCH
printed

Green, Thomas
1847–59, general
ceramics

T. GREEN
FENTON POTTERIES
printed

Green & Co., M.
1859–76, general ceramics

M. GREEN & CO.
printed

Green, T. A. & S.
1876–89, china

T.A. & S.G.
initials printed in
'Staffordshire knot'

From 1889 this firm became known as
'Crown Staffordshire Porcelain Co.'

Greenwood, S.
late 18th century
black basaltes

S. GREENWOOD
rare impressed mark

Hines Bros.
1886–1907, earthenware

H.B.
impressed

HINES BROS.
printed

Hoods, Ltd.
c. 1919–, earthenware
(firm now closed)

H. LTD.
printed

Hughes & Co., E.
1889–1953, porcelain
impressed mark, 1889–98

H

impressed or printed
1898–1905

H.F.

printed mark
c. 1908–12

various 'globe' marks
from 1912–41

1940 firm retitled Hughes (Fenton) Ltd.

Hulme & Christie
1893–1902, earthenware
(Christie & Beardmore
1902–3)

H. & C.
F
printed with dove

Jones, A. G., Harley-
1907–34, earthenware
and porcelain
initials printed with
various trade-names:
'FENTONIA WARE', 'PARAMOUNT',
'WILTON WARE'

H.J.

A.G.H.J.

Kirkby & Co., William
1879–85, general ceramics

W.K. & CO.

'K. & Co.', also used in
monogram form

K. & CO.
printed or impressed

Knight, Elkin & Co.
1826–46, earthenware

K.E. & CO.

printed initials with
variously designed
backstamps

KNIGHT ELKIN
& CO.

K. & E.

Knight, John King
1846–53, earthenware

J. K. KNIGHT
printed

Knight, Elkin & Bridgwood
c. 1829–40, earthenware
marks printed

K.E. & B.

K.E.B.

Knight, Elkin & Knight
1841–4, earthenware

K.E. & K.
printed

Malkin, Ralph
1863–81, earthenware

R.M.
printed

Malkin & Sons, Ralph
1882–92, earthenware

R.M. & S.
printed

Moore & Co.
1872–92, earthenware

M. & CO.
impressed or printed

Moore, Leason & Co.
1892–6, earthenware

M.L. & CO.
printed in shield
under crown
or initials alone
impressed or printed

Morley, Fox & Co. Ltd.
1906–44, earthenware

M.F. & CO.
printed

c. 1906–

'HOMELEIGHWARE', 1929–

Morley & Co. Ltd., William
1944–57, earthenware

Pratt & Co. (Ltd.), F. & R.
c. 1818–, earthenware

F. & R.P.

PRATT

'Co.' added 1840

F. & R.P. CO.

c. 1847–60

F. & R. PRATT & CO.
FENTON

this firm is known
to have made a great
number of the popular
printed pot-lids and
similarly printed jugs
etc. *c.* 1850

MANUFACTURER'S
TO H.R.H. PRINCE ALBERT

the firm was taken over in *c.* 1925
by Cauldon Potteries Ltd., who continue
original name together with their own

Pratt & Co., John   J.P. & CO. (L.)
1872–8, earthenware   printed

Pratt, Hassall & Gerrard   P.H.G
1822–34, general ceramics   P.H. & G.
     printed

Pratt & Simpson   P. & S.
1878–83, earthenware   printed

Radford (Ltd.), Samuel
1879–1957, porcelain
   'R.S.' monogram from
   about 1880, 'England'
   added 1891

various 'S.R.' monograms
used during this century

Rainbow Pottery Co.   RAINBOW POTTERY
1931–41, earthenware   FENTON
     MADE IN ENGLAND
     printed or impressed

Reeves, James   J.R.   J.R.
   1870–1948, earthenware   F
   printed or impressed   J. REEVES

Rubian Art Pottery Ltd.   L.S. & G.
1906–33, earthenware
   impressed or printed   RUBAY ART WARE
   c. 1926–33

Sterling Pottery Ltd.
1947–53, earthenware

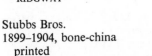

   other marks include:
   'RIDGWAY'   printed

Stubbs Bros.
1899–1904, bone-china
   printed

Victoria Porcelain (Fenton) Ltd.
1949–57, earthenware
   printed

Victoria & Trentham Potteries Ltd.
1957–60, general ceramics
   lion mark as above but includes new name

Wathen & Lichfield   W. & L.
1862–4, earthenware   FENTON

Wathen, James, B.   J.B.W.
1864–9, earthenware   J.B.W.
     F
     printed

Wileman, James & Charles   J. & C.W.
1864–9, general ceramics   J.F. & C.W.
     C.J.W.
   'J. Wileman & Co.'   J.W. & CO.

Wileman, James F.   J.F.W.
1869–92   J. F. WILEMAN

Wileman & Co.
1892–1925
   'SHELLEY' mark used
   from *c.* 1911

Wilson & Sons, J.
1898–1926, bone-china

printed

FOLEY (Staffordshire)
Hawley & Co.   HAWLEY
1842–87, earthenware   HAWLEY & CO.
     impressed

Mayer, John   J.M.
1833–41, earthenware   F
     printed

HANLEY (Staffordshire)
Adams & Co., John   J. ADAMS & CO.
1864–73, earthenwares and   ADAMS & CO.
stonewares, etc.   impressed

Adams & Bromley   A. & B.   A. & B.
1873–86, earthenware   SHELTON
stonewares, etc.   ADAMS & BROMLEY
     printed or impressed

Alcock, Lindley & Bloore (Ltd.)
1919, earthenware
(now Allied English Potteries)
   printed or impressed

Art Pottery Co.   ART POTTERY CO.
1900–11, earthenware   ENGLAND
   printed mark   (with crown)

Ashworth & Bros. (Ltd.)
1862–1970, earthenware   ASHWORTH
   1862–80   impressed
(now Mason's Ironstone
China Co. Ltd.)   A. BROS.
Wedgwood Group from 1973

Ashworth & Bros.
printed *c.* 1862–90
with designs including
pattern names
From 1862 Ashworths used mark similar
to that of Mason's 'Patent Ironstone'
(Mason's Ironstone China
Ltd. from 1968)
'England' added 1891

G.L.A. & BROS.

printed mark from
about 1880

'LUSTROSA' trade-name
1932–

printed on ironstone
c. 1957–

Baddeley, Thomas
1800–34, engraver of
plates for transfer-prints

T. BADDELEY
HANLEY
printed

Baddeley, William
1802–22, 'Wedgwood-
type' ware

EASTWOOD
impressed

Bakewell Bros. Ltd.
1927-43, earthenware

BAKEWELL BROS.
LTD.
printed

Bates, Brown-Westhead
& Moore
1859–61, general ceramics

B.B.W. & M.
printed or impressed

Baxter, John Denton
1823–7, earthenware

I.D.B.
J.D.B.
printed

Bednall & Heath
1879–99, earthenware

B. & H.
printed

Bennett & Co., J.
1896–1900, earthenware

J.B. & CO.
printed or impressed

Bennett (Hanley) Ltd., William
1882–1937
earthenwares

W.B.
H
printed or impressed

Bevington, James & Thomas
1865–78, porcelains

J. & T.B.
impressed

Bevington & Co., John
1869–71, earthenware
printed in backstamp

J.B. & CO.
H

Bevington, John
1872–92, porcelains

This mark was
obviously adopted to
imitate that of Meissen on pieces made in
'Dresden' style

underglaze blue

Bevington, Thomas
1877–91, general ceramics

T.B.

printed

Birch & Whitehead
c. 1796, 'Wedgwood type'
wares

B. & W.
impressed

Bishop & Stonier
1891–1939, general
ceramics

B. & S.
printed or impressed

printed marks
1891–
'England' added
on fully named
marks from *c.* 1899–

1936–9

BISHOP
ENGLAND

Blue John Pottery Ltd.
1939, earthenware

various 'Blue John'
printed marks

Booth, G. R.
1829–44, earthenware
'& Co.' added *c.* 1839
impressed mark

PUBLISHED BY
G. R. BOOTH & CO.
HANLEY
STAFFORDSHIRE

Booth & Colcloughs Ltd.
1948–54, general ceramics
(see Ridgway Potteries Ltd.)
also trade-names:
'Blue Mist', 'Malvern Chinaware'
and 'Royal Swan'

various marks
including
name

Bourne, Samuel
early 18th century
pottery figures

S. BOURNE
impressed

Bournemouth Pottery Co.
(Bournemouth, 1945–52)
Hanley 1952–, earthenware

BOURNEMOUTH
POTTERY
ENGLAND

Boyle, Zachariah | BOYLE
1823–50, general ceramics
'& S.' added from 1828 | Z.B.   Z.B. & S.

Brown-Westhead, Moore & Co. | B.W.M.
1862–1904
general ceramics | B.W.M. & CO.

           printed or impressed

impressed | T. C. BROWN WESTHEAD-MOORE & CO.

printed or impressed
1891–

later marks include
initials & 'CAULDON'

Bullers Ltd. | BULLERS MADE
c. 1937–55, earthenware | IN ENGLAND
          painted

Bullock & Co., A. | A.B. & CO. H.
1895–1915, earthenware | A.B. & CO.
       printed or impressed

Burgess, Thomas
1903–17, earthenware
(mark of Harrop & Burgess
was continued)

       printed or impressed

Burton, Samuel & John | S. & J.B.
1832–45, earthenware | impressed on
       applied tablet

Cauldon Ltd. | CAULDON
1905–20, general ceramics | ENGLAND
      printed under crown

marks previously used by Ridgway
and Brown—Westhead, Moore & Co., used
with addition of 'CAULDON'

Cauldon Potteries, Ltd. | ROYAL CAULDON
1920–62, general ceramics | ENGLAND
           EST. 1774
similar printed marks used from 1930–62,
when factory was taken over by
Pountney & Co. Ltd. of Bristol (now
Cauldon Bristol Potteries Ltd., Redruth, Cornwall)

Ceramic Art Co. Ltd. | THE CERAMIC ART
1892–1903, decorators | CO. LTD. HANLEY
        STAFFORDSHIRE
          ENGLAND
          printed

Clementson, Joseph | J.C.
c. 1839–64, earthenware | J. CLEMENTSON
        printed

Clementson Bros. | CLEMENTSON BROS.
1865–1916, earthenware | with Royal Arms
and stoneware
   printed 1867–80
   various fully named printed marks with
   phoenix from 1870–
   'Ltd.' added 1910

           CLEMENTSON BROS.
printed, 1913–16 | ENGLAND
         under crown

Clementson, Young & Jameson | C.Y. & J.
1844, earthenware

Clementson & Young | CLEMENTSON &
1845–7, earthenware | YOUNG
      impressed or printed

Coalbrook Potteries | COALBROOK
1937–, decorative wares | MADE IN
   printed– | ENGLAND

Coopers Art Pottery Co. | ART POTTERY CO.
c. 1912–58, earthenware | ENGLAND
         with crown

Cotton, Ltd., Elijah | various fully-
1880–, earthenware | named marks
   Trade-names: 'NELSON WARE', *c.* 1913–;
   'LORD NELSON WARE', 1956–

Creyke & Sons, G. M. | G.M.C.
1920–48, earthenware | printed or impressed
   initials also used in
   monogram form
   Trade-name 'BROADWAY'
   c. 1935–

Davenport, Banks & Co. | D.B. & CO.
1860–73, earthenware

          DAVENPORT
impressed or printed | BANKS & CO.
marks | ETRURIA

Davenport, Beck & Co. | D.B. & CO.
1873–80, earthenware

Davis, J. Heath | J. H. DAVIS
1881–91, earthenware | HANLEY

Diamond Pottery Co. Ltd. | D.P. CO.
1908–35, earthenware | D.P. CO. LTD.
         printed

Dimmock (Junr.) & Co., Thomas | D.
1828–59, earthenware

impressed or printed
'double D' monogram

Dimmock & Co., J.
1862–1904, earthenware

J.D. & CO.

firm taken over by
W. D. Cliff in *c.* 1878–
'Cliff' used in varying
forms *c.* 1878–1904

CLIFF
ENGLAND

written on ribbon
under 'lion rampant'

ALBION WORKS
printed

Dudson, James
1838–88, earthenware
(this firm made many
'Spaniels' and 'Rockingham-type' dogs)

DUDSON
impressed

Dudson, J. T.
1888–98, earthenwares
and stonewares
  'England' added 1891

J. DUDSON

J. DUDSON
ENGLAND
impressed

Dudson Bros., Ltd.
1898–, earthenwares and
stonewares

DUDSON ENGLAND

  printed mark, 1936–45

Dudson, Wilcox & Till, Ltd.
1902–26, earthenware
  printed or impressed,
  figure of Britannia also
  used within double-ring
  with full name of firm

Dura Porcelain Co. Ltd.
1919–21, porcelain

  printed mark

Ellis, Unwin & Mountford
1860–61, earthenware

E.U. & M.
printed

Fancies Fayre Pottery
c. 1946, earthenware
  Trade-name 'KNICK
  KNACKS'
(now Bairstow & Co.)

STAFFORDSHIRE
F.F.
ENGLAND
printed or impressed

Fenton & Sons, Alfred
1887–1901, general
ceramics

A.F. & S.
impressed or printed
(also written within
circular crowned strap)

Fletcher, Thomas
c. 1786–1810, printer and
decorator

T. FLETCHER
SHELTON

Ford, Charles
1874–1904, porcelain

impressed
or printed

'Swan' mark, impressed
or printed, *c.* 1900–4

Ford, T. & C.
1854–71, earthenware
impressed or printed
marks

T. & C.F.

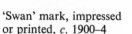

Ford, Thomas
1871–4, porcelain

  numerals indicate
  month and year, e.g.
  JULY, 1872

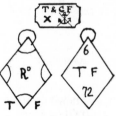

impressed or printed

Ford & Pointon Ltd.
1917–36, porcelain
(absorbed by Cauldon
c. 1921)

Furnival, Jacob & Thomas
c. 1843, earthenware

J. & T.F.
printed under
Royal Arms

Furnival & Co., Thomas
c. 1844–6, earthenware

T.F. & CO.
printed

Futura Art Pottery Ltd.
1947–56, earthenware

FUTURA
ART POTTERY LTD.
printed

Gelson Bros.
1867–76, earthenware

GELSON BROS.
HANLEY
printed

Glass, John
c. 1784–1838, earthenware
and stoneware

GLASS HANLEY
J. GLASS HANLEY
impressed

Glass, Joseph
c. 1700, slipwares

JOSEPH GLASS

Goldscheider (Staffordshire) Pottery Ltd.
1946–59, figures in
pottery and porcelain

printed

Gray & Co. Ltd., A. E.
1912–61, earthenware
(known as 'Portmeirion
Potteries Ltd.' from 1962)
moved to Stoke in 1934

various printed marks
depicting ships with
factory name

  printed mark
  1934–61

Grimwade Bros.
1886–1900, earthenware

G. Bros.
on star within
circle

Grimwades Ltd.
1900–, earthenware
printed mark, *c.* 1900–

STOKE POTTERY

many various fully named marks including
name or trade-name:
'WINTON' *c.* 1906, 'RUBIAN ART' *c.* 1906–,
'VITRO HOTEL WARE' *c.* 1930, 'ROYAL
WINTON IVORY' *c.* 1930, 'ATLAS' *c.* 1934–9

Hackwood & Co.
1807–27, earthenware and
stoneware

H. & CO.
HACKWOOD & CO.
impressed

Hackwood, William
1827–43, earthenware
impressed or printed

W.H.
HACKWOOD
printed or impressed

Hackwood & Keeling
1835–6, earthenware

H. & K.
printed

Hall, Samuel
c. 1840–56, earthenware

HALL
impressed

Hall & Read
1883–8, earthenware
'H. & R.' also probably
used

HALL & READ
HANLEY
printed

Hammersley, J. & R.
1877–1917, general ceramics

J.R.H.
printed

Hanley Porcelain Co.
1892–99, porcelain

printed

Hanley China Co.
1899–1901, porcelain
printed

H
C C°.
in knot

Harrop & Burgess
1894–1903, earthenware

printed

Heath, J.
c. 1770–1800, earthenware

I.H.

HEATH
impressed

Heath, Joshua
c. 1740, earthenware

JOSHUA HEATH
incised

Hollins, T. J. & R.
c. 1818–22, earthenware

T.J. & R. HOLLINS
impressed

Johnson Bros. (Hanley) Ltd.
1883–, earthenware
impressed or printed
name with various
coat-of-arms, crowns
etc.
(now part of Wedgwood Group)

JOHNSON BROS.
ENGLAND

Johnson Bros
England.

Jones & Son
c. 1826–8, earthenware

JONES & SON
printed

Keeling, Joseph
c. 1802–8, earthenware and
stoneware

JOSEPH KEELING
impressed

Keeling & Co., Samuel
1840–50, earthenware

S.K. & CO.

S. KEELING & CO.
printed

Keeling, Toft & Co.
1805–26, stonewares
in Wedgwood style

KEELING & TOFT

KEELING, TOFT & CO.
impressed

Kensington Fine Art Pottery Co.
1892–9, earthenware

printed or impressed

Lancaster & Sons
1900–44, earthenware
'& Sons' & 'Ltd.' added
c. 1906
c. 1920–

'ROYALL & LANSAN' 1930–
'BRITISH CROWN WARE', *c.* 1935–
'CROWN DRESDEN WARE', *c.* 1935–

L. & SONS LTD.
HANLEY. ENG.

c. 1934–44

LANCASTERS LTD.
HANLEY. ENGLAND

Lancaster & Sandland Ltd.
1944–1968, earthenware

BRITISH
CROWN WARE

many various printed
marks including name
'SANDLAND'

CROWN DRESDEN WARE

SANDLAND
STAFFORDSHIRE
ENGLAND

Langdale Pottery Co. Ltd.
1947–58, earthenware
printed

Langdale
MADE IN ENGLAND

Lear, Samuel
1877–86, general ceramics

LEAR
impressed

Livesley, Powell & Co.
1851–66, earthenware
and stoneware

LIVESLEY POWELL
& CO.
L.P. & CO.
impressed or printed

Powell & Bishop
1867–1878, general
ceramics

P. & B.
POWELL & BISHOP
printed or impressed

Powell, Bishop & Stonier
1878–91, general
ceramics

P.B. & S.
printed or impressed

'Chinaman' mark first
registered 1880, but
continued by Bishop
& Stonier

Bishop & Stonier
1891–1939, general ceramics
full name printed in
various designs, 1899–1936
'Bishop' only used 1936–9

B. & S.

BISHOP & STONIER

Lloyd, J. & R.
c. 1834–52, 'Staffordshire
figures'

LLOYD SHELTON
impressed

Lockett, Baguley &
Cooper, 1855–60, porcelain

LOCKETT BAGULEY
& COOPER

Lockitt, William H.
1901–19, earthenware
'DURA-WARE' 1913–19

W.H.L.
H
printed in crescent

Mann & Co.
1858–60, general ceramics

MANN & CO.
HANLEY
printed

Manzoni, Carlo
c. 1895–8, studio-pottery

incised mark including
date

Mason's Ironstone China Ltd.
earthenware, March 1968
(from March 1974 name changed
to: Mason's Ironstone, a Division
of Josiah Wedgwood & Sons Ltd.)
printed marks

Mayer, Elijah
c. 1790–1804, various
Wedgwood-type wares

E. MAYER
impressed

Mayer & Son, Elijah
1805–34
Wedgwood-type wares

E. MAYER & SON
impressed or printed

Mayer & Co., Joseph
c. 1822–33, earthenware

JOSEPH MAYER & CO.
HANLEY

MAYER & CO.

Meakin, Charles
1883–9, earthenware

CHARLES MEAKIN
HANLEY
under Royal Arms

Meakin (Ltd.), J. & G.
1851–, earthenwares
(now part of Wedgwood
Group)
1890–

J. & G. MEAKIN
impressed or printed

'ENGLAND' added from
1891
'Sun-face' marks from
1912–
'PASTEL VITRESOL'
'STUDIO WARE' and 'SOUTH
SEAS' recent trade-names

printed

Meigh, Job
c. 1805–34, earthenware
'Son' added c. 1812

MEIGH
impressed
OLD HALL
impressed or printed
J.M. & S.

Meigh, Charles
1835–49, earthenware and
stonewares

CHARLES MEIGH
impressed
C.M.
printed with device
and pattern name

printed or impressed marks of various
bodies and styles of decoration include:
'Indian Stone China', 'French China',
'Improved Stone China', 'Enamel Porcelain'

Meigh, Son & Pankhurst,
Charles, 1850–51, earthenware

C.M.S. & P.
printed

Meigh & Son, Charles
1851–61, earthenware

C.M. & S.

many of the marks
used by this firm
include the Royal
Arms

M. & S.

C. MEIGH & SON

MEIGH'S
CHINA

printed or impressed

OPAQUE
PORCELAIN

Old Hall Earthenware Co Ltd.
1861–86

printed   O.H.E.C.

printed or impressed   O.H.E.C.(L.)

mark registered in 1884 and
continued by Old Hall
Porcelain Works Ltd.
printed

Old Hall Porcelain Works
Ltd., 1886–1902, general
ceramics   (as above)

Mills, Henry   H. MILLS
c. 1892, earthenware   printed

Moore & Co.   M. & CO.
1898–1903, earthenware   printed with name
of pattern

Morley & Co., Francis   F.M.
1845–58, earthenware

late form of Masons'   F.M. & CO.
Ironstone mark used
from 1845   F. MORLEY & CO.
printed with many
various backstamps

Morley & Ashworth   M. & A.
1859–62, earthenware   MORLEY &
impressed or printed   ASHWORTH
with pattern name   HANLEY

Neale & Co., James   N   NEALE
c. 1776–c. 86, all manner   I. NEALE
of wares in Wedgwood   I. NEALE. HANLEY
style
'& Co.' added c. 1778   NEALE & CO.
impressed

Neale & Bailey   NEALE & BAILEY
c. 1790–1814, earthenware   printed or impressed

Neale, Harrison & Co.   N.H. & CO.
1875–85, general ceramics   printed

Neale & Palmer   NEALE & PALMER
c. 1769–76, earthenwares   impressed
in Wedgwood style

Neale & Wilson   NEALE & WILSON
c. 1784–95, earthenware
and Wedgwood-type wares   NEALE & CO.
impressed

New Hall Porcelain Works
1781–1835, hard-paste
porcelain 1781–c. 1812
bone-china, c. 1812–35

printed on bone-china

New Hall Pottery Co. Ltd.
1899–1956, earthenware

printed, c. 1930–51

New Pearl Pottery Co. Ltd.   PEARL POTTERY CO.
1936–41, earthenware,   printed
'Royal Bourbon Ware'

Palmer, Humphrey   PALMER
c. 1760–78, earthenware
and Wedgwood-type
stonewares

impressed

Pankhurst & Co., J. W.   J.W.P.
1850–82, earthenware
'& Co.' added c. 1852   J. W. PANKHURST

Pearl Pottery Co. Ltd.
1894–1936, earthenware
1894–1912

PP

printed or impressed

printed in various
forms, 1912–36   P.P. CO. LTD.

Physick & Cooper   P. & C.
1899–1900, earthenware   over crown

Art Pottery Co.   ART POTTERY CO.
1900–11, earthenware   over crown

Coopers Art Pottery Co.   printed as above
c. 1912–58, earthenware

Podmore China Co.   'P.C. CO.' monogram
1921–41, porcelain   under crown

Pointon & Co. Ltd.   POINTONS
1883–1916, porcelain   STOKE-ON-TRENT
printed with coat-
of-arms

Poole, Richard   R. POOLE
1790–5, earthenware   impressed

Ratcliffe, William   R
c. 1831–40, earthenware   HACKWOOD
printed or impressed

printed in underglaze blue

Ridgway, Job   R   J.R.
c. 1802–8, earthenware   printed
(J.R. also used by
John Ridgway)

Ridgway & Sons, Job   RIDGWAY & SONS
c. 1808–14, earthenware   impressed or printed

Ridgway, John & William   J.W.R.   J. & W.R.
1814–c. 1830   J. & W. RIDGWAY
printed or impressed

Ridgway & Co., John   JOHN RIDGWAY
c. 1830–55, general ceramics   J.R.
JHN RIDGWAY
printed or impressed   I. RIDGWAY
marks usually including   '& CO.'
name of pattern   added c. 1841

Ridgway, Bates & Co., J.   J.R.B. & CO.
1856–58, general ceramics   printed

Bates, Brown-Westhead   B.B.W. & M.
& Moore, 1859–61   printed or impressed
general ceramics

Brown-Westhead, Moore & Co.
1862–1904, general ceramics   *see* p. 135
then
Cauldon Ltd.
1905–20, general ceramics   *see* p. 135
then
Cauldon Potteries Ltd.
1920–62, general ceramics   *see* p. 135

Ridgway & Robey   RIDGWAY & ROBEY
c. 1837–9, figures   HANLEY
marks very rare   STAFFORDSHIRE
POTTERIES

Ridgway, Morley, Wear   R.M.W. & CO.
& Co., 1836–42   RIDGWAY, MORLEY
earthenware   WEAR & CO.
printed

Ridgway & Morley   R. & M.
1842–44, earthenware   RIDGWAY & MORLEY
printed

Ridgway & Abington   E. RIDGWAY & ABINGTON
c. 1835–60, earthenware   HANLEY
impressed

Ridgway, Son & Co.,   W.R.S. & CO.
William, c. 1838–48   W. RIDGWAY, SON
& CO. HANLEY
printed

Ridgway, Sparks & Ridgway   R.S.R.
1873–79, earthenware   also printed in
'Staffordshire knot'

Ridgways   
1879–20
mark of 1880–

'RIDGWAYS' and 'ENGLAND' in various
marks from c. 1905–20
RIDGWAYS (BEDFORD WORKS) LTD.
1920–52, earthenware
'RIDGWAYS' and/or 'BEDFORD' in variety
of marks used from 1920–52
This firm became 'Ridgway & Adderley Ltd.'
in 1952, Ridgway, Adderley, Booths &
Colcloughs Ltd.' from 1955 and in same year
'Ridgway Potteries Ltd.'
(part of Allied English Potteries, Ltd.
from 1952, now Royal Doulton Group)
name of American firm,   JONROTH
John R. Roth & Co.   J.H.R. & CO. monogram
seen on some Ridgway   printed
exports, c. 1930–56

Rigby & Stevenson   R. & S.
1894–1954, earthenware   printed

Rivers, William   RIVERS
c. 1818–22, earthenware   impressed

Robinson & Wood   R. & W.
1832–6, earthenware   printed

Salt, Ralph   'SALT'
c. 1820–46, earthenware   impressed on scroll

Sandlands & Colley, Ltd.   full name &
1907–1910, general   'S.C.' monogram
ceramics   printed under crown

Scrivener & Co., R. G.   R.G.S.
1870–83, general ceramics

printed or impressed   R.G.S.
& CO.

Sherwin & Cotton
1877–30, tiles
impressed

Shorthose & Co.   SHORTHOSE & CO.
c. 1817–1822   written
impressed or printed

Shorthose & Heath
c. 1795–1815, earthenware

SHORTHOSE &
HEATH
impressed or printed

Shorthose, John
1807–23, earthenware

S

impressed marks

SHORTHOSE

Sneyd & Hill
c. 1845, earthenware
printed

SNEYD & HILL
HANLEY
STAFFORDSHIRE
POTTERIES

Sneyd, Thomas
1846–7, earthenware

T. SNEYD
HANLEY
impressed

Stevenson, William
c. 1802, earthenware
rare impressed mark

W. STEVENSON
HANLEY

Studio Szeiler, Ltd.
c. 1951–, earthenware

printed or impressed

Swinnertons Ltd.
1906–71, earthenware
(Allied English Potteries)
Ltd.), mark printed
    c. 1906–17, later marks all include
    full name of firm

SWINNERTONS
HANLEY

Sylvan Pottery Ltd.
1946–, earthenware

    'B' included in mark
    prior to 1948

Taylor, George
c. 1784–1811, earthenware

G. TAYLOR
GEO. TAYLOR
impressed or incised

Taylor, Tunnicliffe & Co.
1868–, general ceramics
(now electrical &
industrial wares only)

T.T.
T.T. & CO.
printed

Thomas & Co., Uriah
1888–1905, earthenware

printed or impressed

Toft, James (*b.* 1673)
Ralph (*b.* 1638),
Thomas (*d.* 1689), slipware

James Toft
Ralph Toft
Thomas Toft

Unwin, Mountford &
Taylor, *c.* 1864, earthenware

U.M. & T.
printed

Unwin, Holmes &
Worthington, *c.* 1865–8
earthenware

U.H. & W.
printed

Upper Hanley Pottery Co.
c. 1895–1902, then at
Cobridge until 1910
earthenware
    'Ltd.' from 1900

U.H.P. CO.
ENGLAND

impressed or printed

Wardle & Co.
1871–1910, earthenware
Wardle Art Pottery Co. Ltd.
1910–1935, earthenware

WARDLE
impressed

    printed, *c.* 1885–90

    printed, *c.* 1890–1935

Wardle & Ash
1859–62, earthenware

W. & A.
impressed

Weatherby & Sons, Ltd.
1891–, earthenware
    c. 1925–

J.H.W. & SONS

FALCON WARE

    c. 1936–, (trade-name)

WEATHERBY WARE
printed

Wellington Pottery Co.
1899–1901, earthenware

printed or impressed

Westminster Pottery Ltd.
1948–56, earthenware

    1952–, (trade-name)

CASTLECLIFFE WARE

Whittaker & Co.
1886–92, earthenware

W. & CO.
printed

Whittaker, Heath & Co.
1892–8, earthenware

W.H. & CO.
printed

Wilson, Robert
1795–1801, earthenware

WILSON

    impressed marks

Wilson, David
c. 1802–18, general ceramics

WILSON
impressed

Winkle & Wood
1885–90, earthenware

printed

Worthington & Harrop
1856–73, earthenware

W. & H.
printed

Wulstan Pottery Co. Ltd.
c. 1940–58, earthenware

printed

Yates, John
c. 1784–1835, earthenware

J.Y.
printed or impressed

LANE DELPH (Staffordshire)
Edge, William & Samuel
1841–8, earthenware

W. & S.E.
printed

Harrison, George
c. 1790–5, earthenware

G. Harrison
impressed

Mason, William
c. 1811–24, earthenware

W. MASON
printed

Mason, Miles
c. 1792–1816, porcelain
marks impressed c. 1800–16

M. MASON
MILES MASON

printed mark on
chinoiserie patterns

Mason, G. M. & C. J.
1813–29, earthenware
(ironstone)

G.M. & C.J. MASON

G. & C.J.M.

impressed marks
c. 1813–25

MASON'S PATENT
IRONSTONE CHINA

patented in 1813

PATENT IRONSTONE
CHINA

standard mark of
c. 1820, continued by
Ashworth (c. 1862)
'Mason's Ironstone China
Ltd.' from 1968–
(a Division of Josiah
Wedgwood & Sons Ltd., 1974)

printed mark with
pattern number c. 1825–

FENTON
STONE WORKS
C.J.M. & CO.
GRANITE CHINA

Mason & Co., Charles
James, 1829–45
earthenware, (ironstone)
printed

printed

c. 1840–

'MASON'S CAMBRIAN ARGIL',
'MASON'S BANDANA WARE'
impressed or printed
c. 1825–40

Mason, Charles James
c. 1845–8, earthenware
(ironstone), also at
Longton, 1851–4

C.J. MASON & CO.
LANE DELPH

printed

Morley & Co., Francis
1845–58, earthenware
(Hanley)

F.M.
F.M. & CO.
F. MORLEY & CO.

Morley & Ashworth
1859–62, earthenware
(Hanley)

M. & A.
impressed or printed

Myatt, late 18th- early
19th centuries
earthenware

MYATT
impressed

Pratt, William
c. 1780–99, earthenware

PRATT

LANE END (Staffordshire)
Abbott, Andrew
c. 1781–3, earthenware

ABBOTT POTTER
impressed

Abbott & Mist
1787–1810, earthenware

ABBOTT & MIST
impressed or painted

Aynsley, John
1780–1809, engraver of
prints for earthenwares

'J. Aynsley Lane End'
printed

Barker, John, Richard &
William, c. 1800
earthenware

BARKER
impressed

Batkin, Walker & Broadhurst
1840–5, earthenware

B.W. & B.
printed

Booth & Sons
1830–5, earthenware

BOOTH & SONS
impressed

Bott & Co.
c. 1810–11, earthenware

BOTT & CO.
impressed

Carey, Thomas & John
c. 1823–42, earthenware

CAREYS
impressed or
printed with anchor

Chesworth & Robinson
1825–40, earthenware
    C. & R.
    printed

Chetham & Woolley
1796–1810, earthenware
    CHETHAM &
    WOOLLEY
    LANE END
    incised

Cyples, Joseph
c. 1784–1840
(initials of various
potters in this family
rarely used)
    CYPLES

    I. CYPLES
    impressed

Deakin & Son
1833–41, earthenware
printed mark

Everard, Glover &
Colclough, *c.* 1847–
general ceramics
    E.G. & C.
    printed

Floyd, Benjamin
c. 1843, earthenware
    B.F.
    printed

Goodwin, Bridgwood &
Orton, 1827–9
earthenware
    G.B.O.
    G.B. & O.

Goodwin, Bridgwood & Harris
1829–31, earthenware
    G.B.H.

Goodwins & Harris
c. 1831–8, earthenware
    GOODWINS &
    HARRIS
    printed

Griffiths, Beardmore &
Birks, 1830, earthenware
    G.B. & B.
    printed

Harley, Thomas
1802–8, earthenware

printed or written
    HARLEY
    T. HARLEY
    impressed

    T. HARLEY
    LANE END

Harvey, Bailey & Co.
1833–5, earthenware
    H.B. & CO.
    printed

Heathcote & Co., Charles
1818–24, earthenware
    C. HEATHCOTE & CO.
    printed

Hilditch & Son
1822–30, general ceramics

printed in various
surrounds

Hulme & Sons, John
c. 1828–30, earthenware
    HULME & SONS
    printed

Lockett, J. & G.
c. 1802–5, earthenware
    J. & G. LOCKETT
    impressed

Lockett, John
1821–58, earthenware
    J. LOCKETT
    impressed

Lockett & Co., J.
c. 1812–89, earthenware
(also at Longton 1882–
1960, and 1960– Burslem)
    J. LOCKETT & CO.
    impressed
    or
    printed

Lockett & Hulme
1822–6, earthenware
    L. & H.
    L.E.
    printed

Mayer & Newbold
c. 1817–33, general ceramics

    M. & N.

marks painted or
printed
    MAY^R & NEWB^D

Plant, Benjamin
c. 1780–1820, earthenware
marks incised

Plant, Thomas
1825–50, earthenware

    painted

Ray, George, modeller
early 19th century
    G. RAY
    Lane End

Turner, John (also
entered under Longton)
c. 1762–1806, earthenware
and porcelain
early impressed marks
    TURNER
    I. TURNER

printed or impressed
from 1784 after Turner
was potter to the
Prince of Wales

    TURNER

impressed, *c.* 1780–6
1803–6
    TURNER & CO.

painted on earthenwares
1800–5
    Turner's Patent

Turner & Abbott
c. 1783–7 (Abbott
probably only agent)
earthenwares and
stoneware in Wedgwood
style

TURNER & ABBOTT
impressed

LONGPORT (Staffordshire)

Bodley & Son, E. F.
1881–98, earthenware

E.F.B. & SON

   trade-mark, 1883–98

Bourne, Edward
1790–1811, earthenware

E. BOURNE
impressed

Corn, W. & E.
1864–1904, earthenware
(also at Burslem c. 1864–
1904, nearly all marks
   are late and include 'ENGLAND' (post-1891)

W. & E.C.

W.E.C.

Davenport & Co., W.
c. 1793–1887, general
ceramics; 1798–1815

Davenport

c. 1815–60
   'Davenport' or 'DAVENPORT'
   is impressed with or
   without anchor

DAVENPORT

   marks on 'Stone-China'
   c. 1815–30

19th-century mark to
about 1860, including
last two numerals of
year
   anchor mark alone c. 1820–40

many printed wares of 1820–60 bear
name of pattern and 'DAVENPORT'

printed on porcelain
c. 1815–
three numerals denote month and last
two numerals of year made
'Manufacturers of China to His Majesty
and the Royal Family' on porcelain
c. 1830–37

DAVENPORT
LONGPORT

impressed c. 1850–70

DAVENPORT
PATENT

printed in underglaze blue
c. 1850–70
(sometimes in enamel
colours prior to 1830)

This mark was used
from c. 1830–45 in puce
and from c. 1870–87
in red

DAVENPORT
LONGPORT
STAFFORDSHIRE
printed under crown

printed on earthenware
c. 1881–7

DAVENPORTS LTD.

Liddle, Elliott & Son
1862–71, general
ceramics

L.E. & S.
impressed or printed

Mayer & Elliott
1858–61, earthenware
   number of month and
   last two numerals of year

printed

   impressed, e.g. $\frac{6}{59}$ = June, 1859

Phillips, Edward & George
1822–34, earthenware

PHILLIPS
LONGPORT

   printed marks

E. & G.P.

Phillips, George
1834–48, earthenware
   name with or without knot,
   sometimes 'Longport' also

PHILLIPS

Rogers, John & George
c. 1784–1814, earthenware

ROGERS

   impressed marks

J.R.
L.

Rogers & Son, John
c. 1814–36, earthenware

as above and

J.R.S.
ROGERS & SON

Smith, Ltd., W. T. H.
1898–1905, earthenware

W.T.H. SMITH & CO.
LONGPORT
printed with 'globe'

Wood & Son (Longport)
Ltd., 1928–, earthenware
   'ROYAL BRADWELL
   ART WARE' trade-name

ARTHUR WOOD
full name printed in
variety of marks

Wood, Arthur
1904–28, earthenware
   mark impressed or
   printed

A.W.
L
ENGLAND

LONGTON (Staffordshire)

Adams & Co. Harvey
1870–85, general ceramics

H.A. & CO.
over crown
printed

Adams & Cooper
1850–77, porcelain

A. & C.
printed

Adderleys Ltd.
1906–, general ceramics

printed mark 1906–26
many other marks all
including full name of firm

Adderley, J. Fellows
1901–5, porcelain

J.F.A.

printed marks

Adderley, William Alsager
1876–1905

W.A.A.

W.A.A. & CO.

and 'sailing-ship' trade-
mark as above

Adderley Floral China Works
1945– bone-china
decorative wares
    printed mark
(Royal Doulton Group
from 1973)

Aldridge & Co.
1919–49, earthenware

ALDRIDGE & CO.
LONGTON
impressed

Allerton & Sons, Charles
1859–1942, general
ceramics
    printed or impressed
    marks, *c.* 1890–1942
Many other fully named
marks also used

C.A. & SONS

CHAS. ALLERTON &
SONS
ENGLAND

Alton China Co. Ltd.
1950–7, bone-china

ALTON
BONE CHINA
printed

Amison, Charles
1889–1962, porcelain
    impressed initials, 1889–

C.A.
L.

printed mark of 1906–30
'& Co.' added 1916
'& Co. Ltd.', 1930

further late marks include
'Stanley' and 'Staffordshire
Floral Bone China'

Anchor Porcelain Co. Ltd.
1901–18, porcelain
    impressed marks

A.P. CO.

A.P. CO. L.

impressed or printed
'anchor-mark', 1901–15
'ROYAL WESTMINSTER CHINA' printed
with 'A.P. CO. L.', 1915–18

Anton Potteries, Ltd., Jon
ironstone, 1974–
(pottery established
c. 1874, 'Crown Clarence'
from *c.* 1953–1971
Jon Anton Potteries
1971–74)

mark on bone-china

Aristocrat Florals & Fancies
1958–, bone-china decorative
wares (Wedgwood Group
from 1973)

Asbury & Co.
1875–1925, general ceramics
    printed marks

ASBURY
LONGTON

A. & CO.

Avon Art Pottery
1930–69, earthenware
    recent mark, printed
(seemingly merged with
Elektra Porcelain Co., 1962)

Aynsley & Co., H.
1873–, earthenware
    'Ltd.' added 1932
    late marks include
    name in full

H.A. & CO.
L.

Aynsley & Sons, John   AYNSLEY
1864–, porcelain   impressed
    various later marks include full name and
    'ENGLAND' added from 1891
(now Aynsley China Ltd.–Waterford Glass Co.
Ltd.)

Baddeley, William   EASTWOOD
1802–22, earthenware   impressed
(Wedgwood-type)

Baggerley & Ball   B. & B.
1822–36, earthenware   L.
    printed in blue
    within oval frame

Bailey & Sons, William
1912–14, earthenware
    printed mark

Bailey & Batkin   BAILEY & BATKIN
1814–*c*. 27, earthenware
including lustreware
    marks impressed or moulded   B. & B.

Bailey & Harvey   BAILEY & HARVEY
1834–5, earthenware   impressed
including lustre

Balfour China Co. Ltd.   BALFOUR
1947–52, bone-china   ROYAL CROWN
(then known as: POTTERY
Trentham Bone China   printed with crown
Ltd.)

Barker Bros. Ltd.   B.B.
1876–, general ceramics   impressed
    large variety of other printed marks
    including such trade-names as:
    MEIR CHINA, MEIR WARE, TUDOR WARE
    and ROYAL TUDOR WARE
(Alfred Clough Ltd.)

Barlow & Son Ltd., T. W.   B. B. & S.
1882–1940, earthenware   rare impressed
                   marks
    marks used from about 1928 include
    'CORONATION WARE'

Barlow, Thomas   B.
1849–1882, general ceramics   impressed

Barlows (Longton) Ltd.   B. Ltd.
1920–52, earthenware   impressed
    later marks include 'MELBAR WARE'

Baxter, Rowley & Tams   B.R. & T.
1882–5, porcelain   impressed

Beardmore & Edwards   B. & E.
1856–8, earthenware   printed

Bentley & Co. Ltd., G. L.   G.L.B. & CO.
1898–1912, porcelain   LONGTON
    'Ltd.' added from 1904

Beswick & Son   B. & S.
1916–30, porcelain   printed or impressed
    'ALDWYCH CHINA', trade-name also used by
    Bridgett & Bates, former prop's.

Beswick Ltd., John   BESWICK
1936–, earthenware   ENGLAND
(Royal Doulton Group 1973)   printed

Blackhurst & Hulme   B. & H.
1890–1932, porcelain
    early mark of printed
    initials, later full   THE BELGRAVE
    mark used from *c*. 1914   CHINA
                       B. & H.
                       L
                    ENGLAND

Blair & Co.
1880–1930, porcelain
    'Ltd.' added *c*. 1912
    (LONGTON) added *c*. 1923
    early impressed 'B'
    up until about 1900
    'BLAIRS CHINA, ENGLAND'
    impressed or printed
    c. 1900–
    printed mark of *c*. 1900–

Blyth Porcelain Co. Ltd.   B.P. CO. LTD.
c. 1905–35, porcelain   printed in
    'DIAMOND CHINA'   varying forms
    also used from *c*. 1913

Blyth Pottery (Longton) Ltd.
earthenware (taken over by John Tams Ltd.
in April, 1973 and no longer trading on own
account)

Boulton & Co.   B. & CO.   B. & CO.
1892–1902, porcelain   L
           printed or impressed

Bradbury, Anderson & Bettany   B.A. & B.
1844–52, general ceramics   printed

Bradley, F. D.   BRADLEY
1876–96, porcelain   impressed

Bradleys (Longton) Ltd.   BRADLEYS
1922–41, porcelain   LONGTON
    mark printed with crown   MADE IN
                       ENGLAND

Bridgett & Bates
1882–1915, porcelain
'ALDWYCH CHINA' trade-name from *c.* 1912

B. & B.
impressed or printed

Bridgett, Bates & Beech
1875–82
printed or impressed mark

Bridgwood & Son Ltd.,
Sampson, 1805–, earthenware
(porcelain until *c.* 1887)

BRIDGWOOD & SON

impressed or printed marks
from *c.* 1850–

S. BRIDGWOOD & SON

S.B. & S.

other various printed marks include
full name of firm or initials

'Parisian Granite' mark
c. 1870–, printed

Britannia China Company
1895–1906, porcelain

B.C. CO.
impressed

other fully-named marks
also used
1904–6

printed or impressed

British Anchor Pottery Co. Ltd.
1884–, earthenware
(from 1971, Hostess Tableware Ltd.)
printed or impressed
1884–*c.* 1913

other various marks include full
names and such trade-names as:
REGENCY, MONTMARTRE, RICHMOND,
HOSTESS and TRIANON

British Pottery Ltd.
c. 1930–, agents only

B.P. LTD.
printed

Brough & Blackhurst
1872–95, earthenware

BROUGH &
BLACKHURST
printed or impressed

Burgess Bros.
1922–39, earthenware
'Burgess Ware' also
used

"BURCRAFT"
BURGESS BROS.
MADE IN ENGLAND
printed

Capper & Wood
1895–1904, earthenware

C. & W.
printed or impressed

Cara China Co.
1945–, porcelain

CARA CHINA
printed

Cartlidge & Co., F.
1889–1904, porcelain
'& Co.' added *c.* 1892

F.C.
F.C. & CO.
printed or impressed

Cartwright & Edwards, Ltd.
c. 1857–
(Alfred Clough Ltd.)
printed mark of 1912–
'Ltd.' added *c.* 1926–
trade-names of 'Norville'
& 'Baronian' ware used
with 'C. & E.' from *c.* 1930–

C. & E.
printed or impressed

Chapman & Sons, David
1889–1906, porcelain
'Atlas' mark of 1889–1906

Chapmans Longton Ltd.
1916–*c.* '67 porcelain
printed 1916–30
(now Paragon China Ltd.)
various other marks including trade-names of:
'ROYAL STANDARD' and 'ROYAL
MAYFAIR', (from 1973 part of Royal Doulton
Group)

STANDARD CHINA
crown
ENGLAND

Chetham
1810–34, earthenware
'& Son' added 1818

CHETHAM
impressed

Chetham, Jonathan Lowe
1841–62, earthenware

J.L.C.
printed

Chetham, J. R. & F.
1846–69, earthenware

J.R. & F.C.
printed

Chetham & Robinson
1822–37, earthenware

C. & R.
printed

Chew, John
1903–4, porcelain

J.C.
L
impressed

Clare China Co. Ltd.
1951–, decorators
printed mark, possibly
taken over by Taylor &
Kent

BONE CHINA
CLARE
MADE IN ENGLAND
with crown

Clough's Royal Art
Pottery, 1961–69
earthenware
mark also used by
Alfred Clough Ltd.
(Royal Art Pottery), 1951–61
Transferred to Alfred Clough, Ltd., Longton
under name of Barker Bros. Ltd. in 1968

'ROYAL ART POTTERY'
ENGLAND
with crown
printed

Coggins & Hill
1892–8, porcelain

C. & H.
printed or impressed

Colclough & Co. R.S. monogram
1887–1928, general ceramics
  printed marks 'ROYAL STANLEY WARE'

Colclough, H. J. H.J.C.
1897–1937, general ceramics L
  various marks including 'H.J.C.' and/or
  'VALE CHINA'

Colclough China Ltd. Colclough
1937–48, porcelain GENUINE
  BONE CHINA
  late printed marks MADE IN ENGLAND

Collingwood Bros. Ltd. COLLINGWOOD
1887–1957, porcelain early impressed mark

  initials used with crown C.B.
  c. 1887–1912 L
  later marks fully named

Collingwood & Greatbatch
1870–1887, porcelain

  printed or impressed
  (crown also used C. & G.
  alone)

Cone Ltd., Thomas T.C. T.C.
1892–c. 1967 L LONGTON
earthenware printed or impressed
  mark of 1892–1912
(moved to Meir in 1964)
  printed 1912–35 T.C. monogram
  'Alma Ware' 1935–
  'ROYAL ALMA' 1946–68

Conway Pottery Co. Ltd. CONWAY
1930–, earthenware POTTERY
  mark printed from 1945– ENGLAND

Cooke & Hulse COOKE & HULSE
1835–55, porcelain printed

Cooper & Dethick C. & D.
1876–88, earthenware printed

Co-operative Wholesale Society Ltd.
1922, porcelain and
from 1946 also earthenware
  printed mark on porcelain
  from c. 1946, also
  'Clarence Bone-China'

  'Crown Clarence'
  earthenware from 1946–
  also 'Balmoral'
  (from 1971–, Jon Anton Ltd.)

J. H. Cope & Co. Ltd. C. & CO.
1887–1947, porcelain impressed or printed

  printed with 'back-stamps' J.H.C. & CO.
  from c. 1900
  'WELLINGTON CHINA' with crown c. 1906–
  'WELLINGTON CHINA' and profile of Duke
  c. 1924–1947

Cotton & Barlow C. & B.
1850–5, earthenware printed

Cyples & Barker CYPLES & BARKER
1846–7, earthenware impressed

Day, George STAFFORDSHIRE
1882–9, earthenware
  printed mark

Day & Pratt DAY & PRATT
1887–8, porcelain printed or impressed

Decoro Pottery Co. TUSCAN
1933–49, earthenware DECORO
  various fully-named POTTERY
  printed marks

Denton China (Longton) Ltd. DENTON
1945–, porcelain CHINA
(Aynsley China Ltd.)

Dewes & Copestake D. & C.
1894–1915, earthenware L
  various printed marks
  including initials

Diane Pottery Co. DIANE
1960–, now closed POTTERY
porcelain LONGTON
  various printed marks STAFFORDSHIRE
  with full name

Dinky Art Pottery Co. Ltd. MADE IN
1931–47, earthenware DINKY WARE
  printed mark ENGLAND

Dixon & Co., R. F. various marks
1916–29, ceramic retailers include 'D.C.'
and importers for Dixon & Co.

Dresden Floral Porcelain Co. Ltd.
1945–56, porcelain
  printed mark

Dresden Porcelain Co. D.P. CO. D.P. CO.
1896–1904, porcelain L

  printed or impressed

printed mark 1896–1903

Edwards & Brown E. & B.
1882–1933, porcelain L
impressed or printed mark 1882–1933
'E. & B.L.' with 'DUCHESS CHINA', 1910–33

Elektra Porcelain Co Ltd.
1924–71, earthenware
printed mark of 1924–
(now Allied English Potteries)
similar mark 'VULCAN WARE' c. 1940–

Elkin, Samuel S.E.
1856–64, earthenware printed

Elkin & Newbon E. & N.
c. 1844–5, earthenware

Fell & Co., J. T. EMBOSA WARE
1923–57, earthenware
MADE BY CYPLES
printed or impressed OLD POTTERY
1793

Finney & Sons Ltd., A. T. DUCHESS
1947, porcelain BONE CHINA
trade-name in a variety printed
of styles

Flacket, Toft & Robinson F.T. & R.
1857–8, earthenware printed

Floral China Co. Ltd.
1940–51, porcelain
printed mark

Forester & Co., Thomas
1888–, earthenware
printed mark

Forester & Sons, Thomas T.F. & S.
1883–1959, general ceramics
'Ltd.' added 1891
printed, 1891–1912
later marks include
'PHOENIX CHINA'

Gallimore, Robert R.G.
1831–40, earthenware impressed

Gallimore & Co. Ltd. G. & CO.
1906–34, earthenware L
mark impressed or printed

Gladstone China (Longton) GLADSTONE
Ltd., 1939–1952, BONE CHINA
porcelain
printed mark until MADE IN ENGLAND
1961 after firm became: various marks with
Gladstone China 'Gladstone Bone China'
1952–, porcelain

Green & Clay
1888–91, earthenware
printed or impressed

Grove & Stark G. & S.
1871–85, earthenware printed
printed or impressed
'G.S.' impressed GROVE & STARK
monogram also used LONGTON

Hallam & Day H. & D.
1880–85, earthenware printed, often with
Royal Arms

Hammersley & Co. H. & C. H. & CO.
1887–1932, porcelain
(Hammersley & Co., Longton) Ltd. H. & Co
from 1932–present
crown mark used without
initials, 1887–1912 CHINA
many various fully named marks from 1912–
(now Carborundum Group)

Hammersley & Asbury H. & A.
1872–5, earthenware printed, sometimes
with 'Prince of Wales'
feathers

Hampson & Broadhurst H. & B.
1847–53, earthenware printed

Harvey, C. & W. K. C. & W.K.H.
1835–53, general ceramics
name also printed with
Royal Arms and 'REAL HARVEY
IRONSTONE CHINA' printed

Hawley, Webberley & Co.
1895–1902, earthenware
printed mark

Hewitt & Leadbeater
1907–19, porcelain
then Hewitt Bros. until
c. 1926 printed

Hibbert & Boughey H. & B.
1889, general ceramics printed with crown

Hill & Co.
1898–1920, porcelain

H. & CO.
impressed or printed

Holdcroft, Joseph
1865–1940, general ceramics
(Holdcrofts Ltd., c. 1906–
later Cartwright & Edwards Ltd.)
mark of 'H.J.' monogram on globe from
1890–1939

printed or
impressed
1865–1906

Holland & Green
1853–82, earthenware

H. & G.
LATE HARVEY
printed or impressed

Holmes & Son
1898–1903, earthenware
other marks include
full name

H. & S.
LONGTON
impressed or printed

Hostess Tableware

Hostess Tableware
Thomas Poole &
Gladstone China Ltd.
'Royal Stafford' and
'Hostess' bone-china
and 'Hostess' ironstone
1971–

FINE BONE CHINA
STAFFS, ENGLAND

& other full marks

Hudden, John Thomas
1859–1885, earthenware

J.T.H.
J.T. HUDDEN
printed

Hudson, William
1889–1941, porcelain
printed mark 1892–1912
other later marks
include 'SUTHERLAND
CHINA'

W.H.
printed

Hudson & Middleton, Ltd.
1941–, porcelain
various late marks
include 'SUTHERLAND'
and 'H.M.' with lion

Hulse & Adderley
1869–75, general
ceramics
printed mark as
used later by
W. A. Adderley & Co.

H. & A.

Hulse, Nixon & Adderley
1853–68, earthenware

H.N. & A.
printed

Jackson & Gosling
1866–1968, porcelain
'Ltd.' added c. 1930
variety of marks including trade-name of
'Grosvenor China'

J. & G.   J. & G.
L
impressed or printed

Jones (Longton) Ltd., A. E.
1905–46, earthenware
printed or impressed
c. 1908–36
other 'Palissy' mark continued by
Palissy Pottery, Ltd., now a subsidiary of
Royal Worcester, Ltd.

PALISSY
ENGLAND

Jones & Co., Frederick
1865–86, earthenware

F. JONES LONGTON
impressed or printed

Jones & Sons, A. B.
1900–, porcelain
(A. B. Jones from 1876)
large variety of marks including
initials, full name and/or trade-name of
'GRAFTON' or 'ROYAL GRAFTON'
(acquired in 1966 by Crown House Glass Ltd.)

A.B.J. & S.
A.B.J. & SONS
A.B. JONES & SONS

Jones, Shepherd & Co.
1867–8, earthenware

J.S. & CO.
printed

Jones, Josiah Ellis
1868–72, earthenware

J.E.J.
or full name
printed

Kent, James
1897–, general ceramics
'Ltd.' added 1913
printed mark of
1897–1915
various shield or 'globe' marks with full name
or J.K.L. or J.K., from 1897–present, when
'Old Foley' is used

JAMES KENT
ENGLAND
with Royal Arms &
'ROYAL SEMI CHINA'

Lawrence (Longton) Ltd., Thomas
1892–1964, earthenware
printed or impressed
marks include name
'Falcon Ware'

Leadbeater, Edwin
1920–24, porcelain
printed or impressed mark

Ledgar, Thomas P.
1900–5, general ceramics
impressed or printed mark

T.P.L.

Lockett & Sons, John
1828–35, earthenware

J. LOCKETT & SONS
impressed

Longton New Art Pottery Co. KELSBORO'
Ltd., 1932–66, earthenware   WARE
    various printed marks

Longton Porcelain Co. Ltd.   L.P. CO.
1892–1908, porcelains   monogram

Longton Pottery Co. Ltd.   L.P. CO. LTD.
1946–55, earthenware   printed

Lowe, William
1874–1930, porcelain

                    printed or impressed
    also full name or initials with trade-names
    'ROYAL SYDNEY WARE', 'COURT CHINA'

Lowe, Ratcliffe & Co.
1882–92, earthenware
    printed or impressed

Mackee, Andrew   A.M.
1892–1906, general ceramics   L.
                    impressed or printed

Malkin, Walker & Hulse   M.W. & H.
1858–64, earthenware   printed

Martin, Shaw & Cope   MARTIN SHAW
c. 1815–24, general ceramics   & COPE
                           IMPROVED CHINA
                                printed

Mason, Holt & Co.   M.H. & CO.
1857–84, porcelain   printed or impressed

Massey, Wildblood & Co.   M.W. & CO.
1887–9, porcelain   printed

Matthews & Clark   M. & C.
c. 1902–6, general ceramics   L.
    printed mark in frame

Mayer & Sherratt   M. & S.
1906–41, porcelain   L.
                            under crown
    also other printed marks including trade-name
    of 'MELBA CHINA'

McNeal & Co. Ltd.
1894–1906, earthenware
    printed

Middleton & Co., J. H.
1889–1941, porcelain
    various printed marks
    with trade-name of
    'DELPHINE'

Moore Bros.   MOORE
1872–1905, porcelain   printed or impressed

    'Bros.' added 1872–1905   MOORE BROS.

    printed from c. 1880   MOORE (with globe)

    printed mark, 1902–5
Bernard Moore
continued at Stoke
until 1915

Morris, Thomas
1892–1941, porcelain

    early printed mark, from
    c. 1912 trade-name of
    'CROWN CHELSEA CHINA' used

New Chelsea Porcelain Co. Ltd.
    from 1913 many marks used
    including anchor and
    'Chelsea', 'New Chelsea'
    or 'Royal Chelsea'

New Chelsea China Co. Ltd.
1951–61, porcelain

New Park Potteries Ltd.   N.P.P. LTD.
1935–57, earthenware   NEW PARK
    initials or factory-   POTTERIES
    name printed in   LONGTON
    varying frames   NEW PARK

Osborne China Co. Ltd.   'Osborne China'
1909–40, porcelain   with torch

Palissy Pottery Ltd.
1946–, earthenware
(subsidiary of Royal
Worcester Ltd.)

    variety of printed marks include,
    'Palissy Pottery' or 'Palissy Ware', etc.

Paragon China Ltd.
1920–, porcelain
    large variety of marks
    include 'Royal Arms'
    and 'Paragon'
(now an Allied English
Potteries Ltd. company)

Pattison, J.
c. 1818–30, earthenware

JOHN PATTISON
incised

Plant, Benjamin
c. 1780–1820, earthenware

B Plant Lane End.
incised

Plant & Co., R. H.
1881–98, porcelain

'R.H.P. & CO.'
in knot under a
winged crown

Plant, Ltd., R. H. & S. L.
c. 1898–1970, porcelain
numerals under
mark indicate last
two numerals of year
made. From 1973:

'TUSCAN CHINA'
trade-name in
many various
forms
'WEDGWOOD–ROYAL
TUSCAN DIVISION'

Plant & Sons, R.
1895–1901, earthenware

P. & S.
L
printed

Poole, Thomas
1880–1952, general ceramics

impressed or printed
crown, 1880–1912
(common mark)
early form of 'ROYAL
STAFFORD CHINA' used
from 1912–

Poole & Unwin
1871–6, earthenware

P. & U.
printed or impressed

Proctor & Co., J. H.
1857–84, earthenware

WARRANTED
P
printed or impressed
under crown

Procter, John
1843–6, earthenware

J.P.
L
printed or impressed

Procter & Co. Ltd., G.
1891–1940, porcelain
with or without 'L'
for Longton
'GLADSTONE CHINA'
from 1924–40

G.P. & CO.
L
printed

trade-name

printed

Ratcliffe & Co.
1891–1914, earthenware

Redfern & Drakeford Ltd.
1892–1933, porcelain
printed or impressed
mark, 'BALMORAL
CHINA' added in
1909–33

Regency China Ltd.
1953–, porcelain

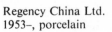

Reid & Co.
1913–46, porcelain

'PARK PLACE CHINA'
c. 1913–24

'ROSLYN CHINA'
c. 1924–46
(*see* Roslyn China)

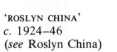

all printed

Riddle & Bryan
c. 1835–40, earthenware

RIDDLE & BRYAN
Longton
printed

Robinson, W. H.
1901–4, porcelain
printed mark in
circle under crown

W.H. ROBINSON
LONGTON
BALTIMORE CHINA

Robinson & Son
1881–1903, porcelain

R. & S.
L.

'Foley' is a name
used by several potters

FOLEY CHINA

Roper & Meredith
1913–24, earthenware

R. & M.
LONGTON

Rosina China Co. Ltd.
1941–
various marks with
trade-names 'Rosina'
or 'Queen's' China

Roslyn China
1946–63, porcelain
printed mark also
used by Reid & Co.

FINE
BONE
Roslyn China
MADE IN
ENGLAND

Rowley & Newton Ltd.
1896–1901, general ceramics
'R. & N.' often with lion 'rampant'

R. & N.
printed or impressed

Royal Albert Ltd.
(Royal Doulton Tableware
Ltd.) Ltd. added 1970
bone-china
  'Royal Albert' previously
  used by Thomas C.
  Wild & Sons Ltd.

ROYAL ALBERT
Bone China
ENGLAND

printed

Royal Albion China Co.
1921–48, porcelain
  printed marks

ROYAL ALBION CHINA
L
ENGLAND
with crown

Royal Grafton Bone China
(A. B. Jones & Sons, Ltd.
part of Crown Lynn Potteries
Group, N.Z. from 1971–)
bone-china from 1959–

Royal Stafford China
1952–, porcelain
  printed marks

variety of marks
with
'ROYAL STAFFORD'

Royal Tuscan
bone-china, *c.* 1962–
(Division of Wedgwood
Group from 1966)

Salisbury Crown China Co.
(Salisbury China Co. from
1949)
c. 1927–61, porcelain

  printed mark of *c.* 1952

Salt & Nixon, Ltd.
1901–34, porcelain
  various marks with initials
  & 'SALON CHINA'

S. & N.
L

printed

Shaw & Sons (Longton) Ltd., John
1931–63, general ceramics

  printed mark of *c.* 1949
  various other marks
  include 'Burlington'

Shaw & Copestake
1901–, earthenware
  various printed or impressed
  marks with trade-name of 'SYLVAC'

Shelley Potteries, Ltd.
1925–67, porcelain
(now Royal Albert Ltd.)
  various printed marks
  with 'SHELLEY' (Royal Doulton Group)

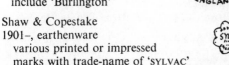

Shepherd & Co., Alfred
1864–70, earthenware

A. SHEPHERD & CO.
printed

Shore & Co., J.
1887–1905, porcelain

J.S. & CO.
printed

Shore, Coggins & Holt
1905–10, general ceramics
  initials printed under
  crown

S.C.H.
L
ENGLAND

Shore & Coggins
1911–*c.* 67, porcelain
  mark of *c.* 1930, other
  marks include trade-name
  'Bell China' (now Royal Doulton Group)

Smith, Sampson
c. 1846–1963, general
ceramics
  's.s.' monogram used in a variety of
  marks during this century and 'WETLEY
  CHINA' or 'OLD ROYAL CHINA'

S.S.
impressed

Stanley & Lambert
c. 1850–4, earthenware

S. & L.
printed

Stanley Pottery Ltd.
1928–31, general ceramics

  same printed marks as
  used by Colclough & Co.

Star China Co.
1900–19, porcelain

S.C. CO.
printed with crown
or star with
'THE PARAGON CHINA'

Stevenson, Spencer & Co. Ltd.
1948–60, porcelain
  fully named marks
  with 'WILLOW' or
  'ROYAL STUART'

SPENCER
STEVENSON
ENGLAND
BONE CHINA

Sutherland & Sons, Danial
1865–75, general
ceramics

S. & S.
impressed or
printed

Swift & Elkin
1840–3, earthenware

S. & E.
printed

Tams, John
c. 1875–, earthenware
  printed marks

J.T.
(or as monogram)

J. Tams

'& Son' added 1903–12   J.T. & S.
'LTD.' from 1912, with trade-marks:
'NANKIN WARE', 'ELEPHANT BRAND',
'TAMS REGENT' and 'CHININE'

Tams & Lowe
1865–74, earthenware

T. & L.
printed

Taylor & Kent
1867–, porcelain

T. & K.
L
printed or impressed
variety of named or initialled marks
with 'KENT' or 'ELIZABETHAN'

Thorley China Ltd.
1940–70, decorative
porcelain
(last six years in Fenton)

THORLEY CHINA
LTD.
printed under crown

Tomkinson & Billington
1868–70, earthenware

T. & B.
printed

Townsend, George
c. 1850–64, earthenware

G. TOWNSEND
printed

Trentham Bone China Ltd.
1952–7, porcelain
printed

Turner, John
c. 1762–1806, Wedgwood-
type earthenwares and
stonewares

TURNER
impressed

printed or impressed
from 1784

TURNER.

impressed c. 1780–6,
1803–6
painted mark on
'ironstone' type ware
1800–5

TURNER & CO.

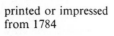

Turner & Abbott
c. 1783–7, Wedgwood-
type wares

TURNER & ABBOTT
impressed

Universal Pottery (Longton) Ltd.
1949–62, general ceramics
variety of printed marks
with 'Universal Ware'

Unwin, Joseph
1877–1926, earthenware
figures, etc.

UNWIN
moulded in
relief

Wagstaff & Brunt
1880–1927, general
ceramics

W. & B.
LONGTON
printed

Wain & Sons, Ltd., H. A.
1946–, earthenware

Waine & Co., Charles
1891–1920, porcelain
printed, 1891–1913
'Ltd.' from 1913

C.W.
or as monogram

Walker & Carter
1866–72, earthenware
(at Stoke 1872–89)

W. & C.
printed

Walton, J. H.
1912–21, porcelain

printed or impressed

Warrilow, George
1887–1940, porcelain
'& S.' or '& Sons'
and 'Ltd.' added
from 1928

G.W.

G.W. & S.

G.W. & S. LTD.

Wayte & Ridge
c. 1864, general
ceramics & figures

W. & R.
L
printed

Wedgwood & Co. Ltd., H.F.
c. 1954–9, general
ceramics

H.F.W. & CO. LTD.
ISLINGTON
printed

Wild Bros.
1904–27, porcelain

J.S.W.
or in monogram
W. Bros.

Wild & Co., Thomas C.
1896–1904
printed or impressed

T.W. & CO.

T.C.W. with crown

Wild, Thomas C.
1905–17, porcelain
printed mark, 1905–7

Wild & Sons (Ltd.), Thomas C.
1917–c. 72, porcelain
various printed marks
with trade-name
'Royal Albert', now Royal Doulton Group

Wild & Adams
1909–27, earthenware
'Ltd.' from 1923
various marks with 'ROYAL CROWN'

W. & A.
printed or impressed

Wildblood, Richard Vernon
1887–8, porcelain

printed

Wildblood & Heath
1889–99, porcelain
printed

Wildblood, Heath & Sons
1899–1927, porcelain

'Ltd.' added from 1915

Williamson & Sons, H. M.
c. 1879–1941, porcelain

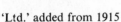

various marks of 'W. & Sons',
'H.M.W.' or 'Heathcote
China'
printed mark of c. 1908–

Winterton Pottery (Longton)   'WINTERTON'
Ltd., 1927–54, earthenware   printed over crown

'Bluestone Ware'

Wood & Co., J. B.
1897–1926, earthenware

late printed or impressed
mark

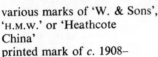

Woolley, Richard   WOOLLEY
1809–14, earthenware   impressed

Yale & Barker   Y. & B.
1841–53, earthenware   printed

LONGTON HALL (Staffordshire)
c. 1749–60, porcelain
rare marks painted in
underglaze blue

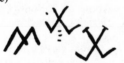

MIDDLEPORT (Staffordshire)   FIVE TOWNS CHINA
Five Towns China Co. Ltd.   CO. LTD.
1957–67, porcelain   ENGLAND
name with various
printed marks

SHELTON (Staffordshire)   ASTBURY
Astbury, mid-18th   incised or impressed
century, earthenware

Astbury, Richard Meir   R.M.A.
1790–, earthenware   impressed

Baddeley, John & Edward   B
1784–1806, earthenware   I.E.B.
impressed initials
then: I.E.B.
    W

Hicks & Meigh   HICKS & MEIGH
1806–22, earthenware   impressed or
and 'Ironstone'   printed
then:
Hicks, Meigh & Johnson   H.M.J.
1822–35, earthenware
and 'Ironstone'   H.M. & J.
    printed with
    Royal Arms

then:

Ridgway, Morley, Wear &   R.M.W. & CO.
Co., 1836–42, earthenware

    RIDGWAY, MORLEY
    WEAR & CO.
then: printed
Ridgway & Morley   R. & M.
1842–44
various printed marks   RIDGWAY & MORLEY
(backstamps) with
names of pattern

Baddeley, Ralph & John   BADDELEY
1750–95, earthenware
marks impressed   R. & J.
    BADDELEY

Bairstow & Co., P. E.   Fancies
1954–. earthenware   Fayre
and porcelain   England

Bentley, Wear & Bourne   BENTLEY, WEAR
1815–23, decorators   & BOURNE
printed mark
(Bentley & Wear 1823–
33)

Birch, Edmund John   BIRCH
1796–1814, Wedgwood-
type wares   E.I.B.
    impressed

Birch & Whitehead   B. & W.
1796, Wedgwood-type   impressed

Cockson & Harding   C. & H.
1856–62, earthenware
marks printed or   C. & H.
impressed   LATE HACKWOOD

Cutts, James   J. CUTTS
c. 1834–70, engraver   signature on
and designer   prints

Dakin, Thomas   THOMAS DAKIN
early 18th century   sliptrailed
earthenware

Hackwood & Son, Wm.
1846–9, earthenware

W.H.
HACKWOOD
printed

Harding, W. J.
1862–72, earthenware

W. & J.H.
printed

Hicks & Meigh
1806–22, earthenware
 'Stone-China' & Royal
 Arms also used

HICKS & MEIGH
impressed or
painted

Hicks, Meigh & Johnson
1822–35, earthenware
 'Stone-China' and
 Royal Arms also used

H.M.J.

H.M. & J.
printed

Hollins, Samuel
c. 1784–1813

S. HOLLINS

'Wedgwood-type' ware

HOLLINS
impressed

Hollins, T. & J.
c. 1795–1820, earthenware

T. & J. HOLLINS
impressed

Howard Pottery Co.
1925–, earthenware
 printed mark of 1925–

Keeling, Charles
1822–5, earthenware

C.K.
printed

Meir John
late 17th – early 18th-
centuries, slipware

JOHN MEIR
sliptrailed

Meir, Richard
late 17th – early 18th-
centuries, slipware

RICHARD MEIR
sliptrailed

Phillips, Edward
1855–62, earthenware
 printed mark

EDWARD PHILLIPS
SHELTON
STAFFORDSHIRE

Read & Clementson
1833–5, earthenware

R. & C.
printed

Read, Clementson &
Anderson
c. 1836, earthenware

R.C. & A.
printed

Ridgway, John & William
1814–1830, general
ceramics

J.W.R.
J. & W.R.
J. & W. RIDGWAY
printed or impressed

Ridgway, William
c. 1830–54, earthenware
(also at Hanley from
c. 1838–48)
 '& Co.' added c. 1834
 'QUARTZ CHINA' used
 from c. 1830–50

W. RIDGWAY

W.R.
printed or impressed

W.R. & CO.

Tittensor, Charles
c. 1815–23, earthenware
including figures

TITTENSOR
impressed or
printed

Twemlow, John
1795–7, earthenware
and stoneware

J.T.

rare initials

Washington Pottery Ltd.
1946–, earthenware
(now Washington Pottery
(Staffordshire) Ltd.)

Worthington & Green
1844–64, earthenware
and Parianware

WORTHINGTON
&
GREEN
impressed

STOKE (Staffordshire)
Alton Towers Handcraft
Pottery (Staffs.) Ltd.
1953–, earthenware

printed or impressed

Arkinstall & Sons (Ltd.)
1904–24, bone-china

A. & S.
printed, 1904–12

 trade-marks on
souvenir wares 1904–
24
(under various other
firms from 1908)

ARCADIAN

ARCADIAN CHINA

printed marks

Atlas China Co. Ltd.
1906–10, china
(name revived by
Grimwades Ltd. 1930–6)

'ATLAS CHINA' with
figure supporting
globe
printed

Baifield Productions Ltd.
(S. Fielding & Co. Ltd., Crown
Devon Group), 1963–

Bennett & Co., George
1894–1902, earthenware

G.B. & CO.
impressed or printed

Bilton (1912) Ltd.
1900–, earthenware
current mark, printed
(now Biltons Tableware Ltd.)

Birks & Co., L. A.
1896–1900, general
ceramics

BIRKS
impressed

B. & CO.

Birks, Rawlins & Co. (Ltd.)
1900–33, bone-china
other marks include
trade-names of:
SAVOY CHINA
CARLTON CHINA

printed

Blakeney Art Pottery
earthenware, 1968–
'Flow Blue Victoria'
printed ware, Kent
Staffordshire figures
and floral art containers.
M. J. Bailey & S. K. Bailey
Note the lion and harp
in coat-of-arms are in
reverse positions to the
authentic version

printed
backstamps in
blue

Similar Royal
Arms mark used,
with 'Romantic'
pattern

IRONSTONE
STAFFORDSHIRE
ENGLAND

IRONSTONE
STAFFORDSHIRE
ENGLAND

printed backstamp
in brown 'M.J.B.'
(Michael J. Bailey)

similar backstamp
used with:
FLO BLUE
T.M. STAFFORDSHIRE
ENGLAND

FLO BLUE
T.M. STAFFORDSHIRE
ENGLAND

Booth & Son, Ephraim
c. 1795, earthenware

E.B. & S.
impressed

Booth, Hugh
1784–9, earthenware
including creamware

H. BOOTH
impressed

Carlton Ware Ltd.
1958–, earthenware
(Arthur Wood & Son Group)

Carlton Ware

modern printed mark

Ceramic Art Co. (1905)
Ltd., 1905–19, earthenware

C.A. & CO. LTD.
printed or impressed

Close & Co.
1855–64, earthenware

CLOSE & CO. LATE
W. ADAMS & SONS
STOKE-UPON-TRENT
printed or impressed

Copeland & Garrett
Copeland, W. T., etc.
(*see under* Spode)

Coronation Pottery Co.
1903–54, earthenware

'Ltd.' from 1947

CORONATION POTTERY
COMPANY LTD.

B

MADE IN ENGLAND
printed or impressed

Crown China Crafts Ltd.
1946–58, general ceramics
printed mark

Daniel, H. & R.
1820–41, pottery and
porcelain
fully named printed
marks also used

H. & R. Daniel

H. Daniels & Sons

written marks

Dorothy Ann Floral China
bone-china floral
jewellery, 1946

STOKE ON TRENT
ENGLAND

Empire Porcelain Co.
1896–1967, earthenware
printed mark, 1896–1912
(1958–67, Qualcast Group)

EMPIRE
ENGLAND *Shelton Ivory*

late printed or impressed marks

Era Art Pottery Co.
1930–47, earthenware

printed mark, 1936–

Featherstone Potteries
1949–50, earthenware
marks impressed or
printed

F.P.

F.N.P.

Fielding & Co., S.
1879–, earthenwares
(part of Crown Devon
Group)

FIELDING
impressed

S.F. & CO.
(over crown and
lion)
printed

'Crown Devon' trade-
mark from *c.* 1930

date-mark:
10th March 1954

FIELDING
10 M 54

Floyd & Sons, R.
1907–30, earthenware

printed or impressed

Folch, Stephen
1820–30, earthenware

FOLCH'S GENUINE
STONE CHINA
impressed

Goss, W. H.
1858–1944, pottery and
porcelain

W.H.G.

printed mark from
c. 1862

W.H. GOSS

W.H. GOSS.

Greta Pottery
1938–41, earthenware

G
P
printed or painted

Hamilton, Robert
1811–26, earthenware

HAMILTON
STOKE
impressed or printed

Hancock & Co., F.
1899–1900, earthenware
printed mark

Hancock, B. & S.
1876–81, earthenware

B. & S.H.
printed

Hancock & Sons, Sampson
1858–1937, earthenware
(at Tunstall prior
to 1870)

S.H.

S. HANCOCK
printed

printed 1891–1935

S.H. & S.

S.H. & SONS

printed 1900–12
From 1935–37:
S. Hancock & Sons
(Potters) Ltd.

Hancock & Whittingham
1873–9, earthenware

H. & W.
printed

Heath, Job
early 18th century
earthenware

JOB HEATH
sliptrailed

Jones, George
1861–1951, general ceramics

'& Sons', added on
crescent from 1873

in relief, impressed
or printed

Keys & Mountford
1850–7, 'Parian' ware

K. & M.

S. KEYS
& MOUNTFORD
impressed

Kirkham, William
1862–92, earthenware

W. KIRKHAM
impressed

Kirkhams Ltd.
1946–61, earthenware
(now Portmeiron
Potteries Ltd.)

Mayer, Thomas
1836–8, earthenware
(last three years at
Longport)

T. MAYER
T. MAYER, STOKE
printed

Meigh, W. & R.
1894–9, earthenware
printed mark

Minton
1793–, general ceramics
(Royal Doulton Group from 1973)
Sèvres-type mark used
on porcelain *c.* 1800–30
sometimes with
pattern number

in blue enamel

printed mark with
'M', 1822–1836

printed 1822–36

'M. & B.' for Minton &
Boyle partnership
1836–41, printed

'M. & Co.' Minton &
Co., 1841–73

'M. & H.', Minton &
Hollins partnership
1845–68

1862–71, 's' added   MINTON
in 1873   impressed

printed 1860–*c.* 69

impressed for 'BEST   B.B.
BODY' mid-19th century

'Globe-mark', 1863–72
'S' added to Minton
in 1871

impressed mark with   18
year 1875, used from   MINTON
1868–80   75

printed mark from 1873
'England' added from
1891, and 'Made in
England' about 1910

impressed or moulded   MINTONS
c. 1890–1910   ENGLAND

'Globe-mark', *c.* 1912–50

standard factory mark
adopted in 1951

'Ermine' mark used
from *c.* 1850 to identify
wares that had been
dipped in a soft-glaze
on which painting was
to be applied

relief mark of *c.* 1847–8
on 'Summerly's Art
Manufacturers' made
by Minton

Solon, Marc Louis, 1870–1904
decorator

signature on 'Henri Deux'   TOFT
reproductions
Mussill, W. (*d.* 1906)   W. Mussill
decorator in 1870s

YEARLY MARKS OF MINTONS LTD.
1842–1942

✳	△	☐	✕	▱
1842	1843	1844	1845	1846
⌣	—	⨯	♣	∴
1847	1848	1849	1850	1851
V	⌒	∽	✳	♀
1852	1853	1854	1855	1856
◇	⋔	⊁	⅄	⋏
1857	1858	1859	1860	1861
ⵣ	⬥	Z	⩘	ⵝ
1862	1863	1864	1865	1866

Date-marks (year symbols):

1867	1868	1869	1870	1871
1872	1873	1874	1875	1876
1877	1878	1879	1880	1881
1882	1883	1884	1885	1886
1887	1888	1889	1890	1891
1892	1893	1894	1895	1896
1897	1898	1899	1900	1901
1902	1903	1904	1905	1906
1907	1908	1909	1910	1911
1912	1913	1914	1915	1916
1917	1918	1919	1920	1921
1922	1923	1924	1925	1926
1927	1928	1929	1930	1931
1932	1933	1934	1935	1936
1937	1938	1939	1940	1941
		1942		

At the commencement of 1943 the system of yearly date-marks that had operated from 1842 was discontinued, being replaced by figures denoting the year of production, preceded by a number allocated to the actual maker of the article, Number one was given to the factory's leading plate-maker, and plates he produces today have stamped in the clay 1–76, the last two digits representing the year.

Moore, Bernard
1905–15, art-pottery and porcelain, with *flambé* glazes

painted

painted or printed

BERNARD BMOORE

Mountford, G. T.
1888–98, earthenware

G.T.M.
STOKE
printed

Mountford, John
1857–9, 'Parian' ware

J. MOUNTFORD
STOKE
incised signature

Myott, Son & Co. Ltd.
1898–, earthenware (now subsidiary of Interpace Corporation) (later Cobridge and Hanley)

late marks fully named

1898–1902

c. 1900–

Ollivant Potteries Ltd.
1948–54, earthenware

O.P.

O.P.L.

printed marks, usually together with pattern

OLLIVANT

Plant & Co., J.
1893–1900, earthenware
printed mark

STOKE POTTERY

Portmeirion Potteries Ltd.
1962–, earthenware

printed mark

PORTMEIRION
POTTERY
STOKE-ON-TRENT
MADE IN ENGLAND

Ridgway Potteries Ltd.
1955, earthenware (an Allied English Potteries Ltd., company)

Est 1792
RIDGWAY
Made in England

RIDGWAY
IRONSTONE
ENGLAND
REGD. TRADE MARK
732990

BONE CHINA
AS
Colclough
MADE IN ENGLAND

BOOTHS

contemporary marks (1972)

Robinson & Leadbeater
1864–1924, 'Parian' ware and bone-china
'Ltd.' added to marks from c. 1905

(R & L)
impressed

Ruscoe, William
c. 1920– (to Exeter in
1944)
   full year-date added
   to initials from c. 1925

incised or painted

Shorter & Son, Ltd.
(member of Crown Devon
Group), 1905–
earthenware

late printed mark

Smith, James
1898–1924, general ceramics

JAMES SMITH

printed or impressed

printed

Spode, Josiah (b. 1733–
d. 1797) 1770–
earthenware
(Copeland & Garrett
from 1833)

Spode   SPODE
impressed or
in blue

   c. 1784–1805

SPODE   S
impressed

painted marks with
pattern numbers, c. 1790–
1820
   c. 1805–

SPODE
printed

mark on stone-china
in black c. 1805–15, in
blue c. 1815–30

Stone China
printed

painted

'Spode Stone China'

impressed 1810–15

printed c. 1805–33

N.S.

Spode's
Imperial

printed in puce enamel
on felspar porcelain
c. 1815–27

Spode
felspar
porcelain

painted, impressed
or printed c. 1797
to 1816

SPODE, SON
& COPELAND

Copeland & Garrett
1833–47, general ceramics

C. & G.
painted or printed

printed in blue, with
name of pattern, c. 1833–
47

COPELAND &
GARRETT

printed c. 1833–47

COPELAND & GARRETT
NEW
JAPAN STONE

Copeland & Sons, Ltd.,
W. T., 1847–
   impressed or printed
   c. 1847–67

COPELAND, LATE
SPODE

printed on Parian figures
c. 1847–55

COPELAND'S
PORCELAIN
STATUARY

printed, 1850–67

printed, c. 1847–51

COPELAND

printed, 1851–85

COPELAND

impressed on earthenware
1850–67

printed on porcelain
c. 1891–

SPODE
COPELANDS CHINA
ENGLAND

printed in various
colours on 'New Stone'
of this century

present-day mark

Spode
ENGLAND

Alcock, S., decorator
c. 1890–

S. Alcock

Hürten, C. F., designer
1859–1897

C.F.H.

Steele & Wood
1875–1892, tiles

printed or impressed

Tittensor, Jacob
1780–95, earthenware

Jacob Tittensor
signature

Turner, Hassall & Peake
1865–9, general ceramics

T.H.P.

printed or impressed

Turner & Wood
1880–8, general ceramics

TURNER & WOOD
STOKE
impressed

Wiltshaw & Robinson Ltd.
1890–1957, general
ceramics
printed mark, 1894–
various marks include
trade-mark 'CARLTON
WARE'

Winkle & Co., F.
1890–1931, earthenware

F.W. & CO.
ENGLAND

printed or impressed
marks, 1890–1910
'Ltd.' added in 1911

F. WINKLE & CO.

printed, 1890–1925

misleading mark used
by Winkle & Co., 1908–25
(the wares of the
18th-century potter,
Thomas Whieldon, were
not marked)

Wolfe, Thomas
1784–1800, earthenware
and later, c. 1811–18

WOLFE
impressed

Wolfe & Hamilton
c. 1800–11, earthenware

WOLFE & HAMILTON
STOKE
impressed or painted

TUNSTALL (Staffordshire)
Adams & Sons (Potters)
Ltd., William,

impressed, 1769–1800
(on creamware)

ADAMS & CO.

---

impressed, 1787–1864

on blue-printed wares
1804–40

ADAMS

impressed on earthenware
1810–25

impressed mark c. 1815

W. ADAMS & CO.

W. Adams & Sons
1819–64, printed
impressed on Parian
ware, 1845–64
printed, mid-19th century

W.A. & S.

ADAMS

W. ADAMS

printed as 'back-stamp'
with name of pattern
1893–1917. 'ENGLAND'
added in 1891

W.A. & CO.

printed from 1879–

printed from 1896–
with varying names
of ceramic bodies
used, e.g. TITIAN
WARE, IMPERIAL
STONE WARE, etc.

impressed on Wedgwood-
type jasperwares
1896 with confusing
establishment date

ADAMS
ESTBD 1657
TUNSTALL
ENGLAND

printed mark, 1914–40

late impressed or
printed mark

late printed mark
c. 1950–

W. Adams & Sons
England
under crown

Adams, Benjamin
c. 1800–20, earthenware
and stoneware

B. ADAMS

impressed

Adams, W. & T.
1866–92, earthenware
  printed mark

W. & T. ADAMS
TUNSTALL
under coat-of-arms

Beech & Hancock
1857–76, earthenware

B. & H.
printed

Blackhurst, Jabez
1872–83, earthenware

JABEZ BLACKHURST
printed

Booth & Son, Thomas
1872–6, earthenware

T.B. & S.
printed

Booth, Thomas, G.
1876–83, earthenware
  name of pattern on strap

Booth, T. G. & F.
1883–91, earthenware

T.G. & F.B.
printed

Booth (Limited)
1891–1948, earthenware
  printed, 1891–1906

painted or printed on
earthenware reproductions
of Worcester porcelain, 1905–

variety of marks used with 'Silicon China'
from about 1906. 'England' sometimes included

late mark of 1930–48

Boulton, Machin & Tennant
1889–99, earthenware

mark printed or impressed

Bourne, Nixon & Co.
1828–30, earthenware
  mark impressed

BOURNE NIXON
& CO.

printed initials included
in backstamp

B.N. & CO.

Bowers & Co., G. F.
1842–68, pottery &
  porcelain
  other printed or
  impressed marks
  include full name

G.F. B.B.T.
printed

Breeze & Son, John
1805–12, pottery & porcelain
(other potters of this
name were operating from
late 18th century to *c.* 1826)

BREEZE
incised or
painted

British Pottery Ltd.
1920–26, earthenware

mark printed

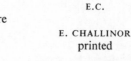

Brougham & Mayer
1853–5, earthenware

BROUGHAM &
MAYER
printed

Brownhills Pottery Co.
1872–96, earthenware

B.P. CO.
printed or impressed

printed marks of
c. 1880–96

Butterfield, W. & J.
1854–61, earthenware

W. & J.B.
printed

Challinor, Edward
1842–67, earthenware

E.C.

E. CHALLINOR
printed

Christie & Beardmore
1902–3, earthenware

C.B.

C.B.
F.

printed initials with
various backstamps

Clews & Co. Ltd., George
1906–61, earthenware
  printed 'globe' mark from
  1906, other marks all
  include full name

Clive, J. H.
1802–11, earthenware

CLIVE
impressed

Clive, Stephen
1875–80, earthenware

S.C.

S.C. & CO.
printed

Colley & Co. Ltd., A.
1909–14, earthenware
  mark printed or impressed

Cumberlidge & Humphreys
1886–9; 1893–5
earthenware
  marks printed or impressed

C. & M.

C. & M.
TUNSTALL

Dean & Sons, Ltd., T.
1879–1947, earthenware
  printed 1896–1947

1937–47

Eardley & Hammersley
1862–6, earthenware

E. & H.
printed

Edge & Grocott
c. 1830, earthenware
figures

EDGE & GROCOTT

Elsmore & Forster
1853–71, general ceramics

ELSMORE & FORSTER
printed with
variety of backstamps

Elsmore & Son, T.
1872–87, earthenware

ELSMORE & SON
ENGLAND

Emberton, William
1851–69, earthenware

W.E.
printed

Emberton, T. I. & J.
1869–82, earthenware

T.I. & J.E.
printed

Ford, Challinor & Co.
1865–80, earthenware

F.C.   F.C. & CO.
initials used with
various printed
marks

Gater & Co., Thomas
1885–94 (at Burslem)
earthenware

G.H. & CO.
later printed initials

Gater, Hall & Co.
1895–1943, earthenware
  printed mark of 1914–

printed mark from 1914–
(firm moved to Burslem
in 1907). Taken over
by:
Barratt's of Staffordshire
1943–. Some former
  marks continued:

  other marks include
  full name of Barratt's.
  'Delphatic' from 1957
(Barratt's now member of the manufacturing
division of G.U.S. Ltd.)

CORONA

CROWN
CORONA

G.H & CO
ENGLAND

Gem Pottery Ltd.
1961–, earthenware
  printed mark

printed

Goodfellow, Thomas
1828–59, earthenware

T. GOODFELLOW
printed

Grenville Pottery Ltd.
1946–, earthenware

Grindley & Co. Ltd., W. H.
1880–, earthenware
  printed mark to 1914
  ('England' included from 1891)
  printed from 1914–25
  'Ltd.' included from 1925
  other marks include full
  name of firm

  modern printed mark

(W. H. Grindley & Co.
now a subsidiary of
Alfred Clough Ltd.)

Grindley Hotel Ware Co. Ltd.
1908–, earthenware
  mark printed from c. 1946–

GRINDLEY HOTEL WARE
ENGLAND
VITRIFIED

Hall, Ralph
1822–49, earthenware
  printed in backstamp
  1822–41

R. HALL

  c. 1836

R. HALL & SON

  1841–49

R. HALL & CO.

R.H. & CO.

Heath & Co., Joseph
1828–41, earthenware

J. HEATH
printed

Heath, Joseph
1845–53, earthenware
  Note: the letter 'J' is
  often printed as 'I'

J. HEATH & CO.
printed
J.H. & CO.
printed

Holland, John
1852–4, earthenware

J. HOLLAND
printed

Hollingshead & Kirkham
1870–1956, earthenware
1870–1900

H. & K.   H. & K.
          TUNSTALL
printed or impressed

  mark of 1890 after
  take-over of Wedgwood
  & Co.

H. & K.
LATE WEDGWOOD
impressed

  printed mark, 1900–24

  later marks all include
  name or initials of
  firm

Ingleby & Co., Thomas
c. 1834–5, earthenware

T.I. & CO.
printed

Keele Street Pottery Co. K.S.P.
1915–, earthenware
  other later printed marks include full name

Keeling, Anthony & Enoch A. & E. KEELING
c. 1795–1811, general ceramics

A.E. KEELING

Kirkland & Co. (Etruria) K. & CO.
1892–, earthenware
  printed on various K. & CO.
  backstamps E
  other various printed marks include full name
  of Kirkland & Co. or K. & Co./E.

'Kirklands (Etruria Ltd.)'
from c. 1938, printed
'Kirklands (Staffordshire)
Ltd.' from c. 1947

Knapper & Blackhurst KNAPPER AND
1867–71, earthenware BLACKHURST
  impressed or printed
(1883–8 at Burslem)
  initials also probably used K. & B.

Lingard Webster & Co. Ltd.
1900–, earthenware

  impressed or printed from
  c. 1946–

Maudesley & Co., J. STONE WARE
1862–4, earthenware J.M. & CO.
  (J.M. & Co. was also
  used by other firms)

Mayer & Maudesley M. & M.
1837–8, earthenware printed

Meakin Ltd., Alfred ALFRED MEAKIN
1875–, earthenware impressed or printed
  'Ltd.' added in 1897 ALFRED MEAKIN
  and omitted from c. 1930 LTD.
  early mark c. 1875–97

Firm re-named 'Alfred
Meakin (Tunstall) Ltd.'
in c. 1913

  printed mark from c. 1891
  when the word 'ENGLAND'
  was added

  later marks include 'M. IRONSTONE'
  'BLEU DE ROI', 'GLO-WHITE' and
  'TRADITIONAL IRONSTONE, LEEDS'

Meir, John J.M. I.M.
c. 1812–36, earthenware printed

Meir & Son, John J.M. & S.
1837–97, earthenware I.M. & S.
  initials used in various J.M. & SON
  printed or impressed
  marks
  Date codes sometimes J. MEIR & SON
  used e.g. 9 : Sept. 1875
       $\overline{75}$ MEIR & SON

Pitcairns Ltd.
1895–1901, earthenware
  printed mark

Podmore, Walker & Co. P.W. & CO.
1834–59, earthenware printed in various
  backstamps

Podmore, Walker & P.W. & W.
Wedgwood, c. 1856–9
  various printed marks WEDGWOOD
  included the confusing
  name of 'Wedgwood' WEDGWOOD & CO.
  Enoch Wedgwood being
  a partner. Name of firm changed to
  Wedgwood & Co. in c. 1860

Rathbone, Smith & Co. R.S. & CO.
1883–97, earthenware printed
then:
Smith & Binnall
1897–1900, earthenware
  printed
then:

Soho Pottery, Ltd.
1901–6, earthenware
(1906–44 at Cobridge)

  other later marks include full name of
  firm and various trade-names, e.g.
  'SOLIAN WARE', 'AMBASSADOR WARE',
  'QUEENS GREEN', 'CHANTICLEER' and
  'HOMESTEAD', etc.
then:
Simpsons (Potters) Ltd.
1944–, earthenware
(at Cobridge)

Simpsons (Potters) Ltd. of Cobridge continue
to use many of the Soho Pottery Ltd.
trade-names plus 'MARLBOROUGH',
'Ironstone' and 'CHINASTYLE'
e.g.

Rathbone & Co., T.
1898–1923, earthenware

late printed mark:

T.R. & CO.
TUNSTALL

Richardson, Albert G.
1915–34, earthenware
(moved to Cobridge
in *c.* 1934)
  various printed marks including trade-
name of 'Crown Ducal'

A.G.R. & Co. Ltd.
printed

Salt Bros.
1897–1904, earthenware
(then 'taken-over' by
T. Till & Sons of
Burslem)

SALT BROS.
TUNSTALL
ENGLAND
printed or impressed

Selman, J. & W.
c. 1864–65, earthenware
figures

SELMAN
impressed

Shaw, Anthony
1851–1900, earthenware

ANTHONY SHAW

A. SHAW   A. SHAW
              BURSLEM

  '& Son' added to
mark in *c.* 1882–*c.* 98

SHAWS   SHAW
             BURSLEM

  '& Son' replaced by
  '& Co.' from *c.* 1898
Shaws taken over by A. J. Wilkinson Ltd.
in *c.* 1900

Simpson, William
late 17th- early 18th-
century, slip-trailed earthenware
(this name is also recorded at other
pottery towns in Staffs.)

WILLIAM SIMPSON
in slip-trailing

Smith, Theophilus
1790–*c.* 97, earthenware

T. SMITH
impressed

Smith & Binnall
1897–1900, earthenware

(*see* Rathbone,
Smith & Co.,
Tunstall)

Soho Pottery Ltd.
1901–6, earthenware

(*see* Rathbone,
Smith & Co.,
Tunstall)

Summerbank Pottery Ltd.
1952–, earthenware
(now Summerbank Pottery
(1970) Ltd.)

SUMMERBANK
printed

COOPERCRAFT
MADE IN
ENGLAND

Tunnicliff, Michael
1828–41, earthenware toys
and figures

TUNNICLIFF
TUNSTALL

Turner, Goddard & Co.
1867–74, earthenware
  'ROYAL PATENT
IRONSTONE'

TURNER, GODDARD
& CO.
printed

Turner & Tomkinson
1860–72, earthenware

  printed in various marks

TURNER &
TOMKINSON

T. & T.

Turner & Sons, G. W.
1873–95, earthenware

  various forms of
initials used in a
variety of backstamps
sometimes in the form
of a Royal Arms
'England' added in
1891

TURNERS

G.W.T. & SONS

G.W.T.S.

G.W.T. & S.

G.T. & S.

Walker, Thomas
1845–51, earthenware
  various printed
backstamps include
name

T. WALKER

THOS. WALKER

Wedgwood & Co.
(Enoch Wedgwood
(Tunstall) Ltd. from 1965)
  printed mark from *c.* 1862

'Ltd.' added from 1900

WEDGWOOD & CO.
impressed

  variety of printed marks used with the
following trade-names: 'IMPERIAL
PORCELAIN', 'WACOLWARE', 'WACOL
IMPERIAL', 'EVERWARE', 'ROYAL
TUNSTALL' and 'VITRILAIN'. From 1965
renamed Enoch Wedgwood (Tunstall) Ltd.
also producing former patterns of
Furnivals, 'Quail', 'Old Chelsea' and
'Denmark'

Wood & Challinor
1828–43, earthenware

W. & C.
printed

Wood, Challinor & Co.
c. 1860–64, earthenware

W.C. & CO.
printed

Wood & Pigott
1869–71, earthenware

W. & P.
printed

Wooliscroft, George
1851–3: 1860–4
earthenware

G. WOOLISCROFT
or
G. WOOLLISCROFT

ISLE OF WIGHT

FRESHWATER (I.o.W.)
Island Pottery Studio
Lester, Joe
earthenware, 1956–
'Freshwater' sometimes
added to mark

printed or impressed

WHIPPINGHAM (I.o.W.)
Isle of Wight Pottery
Saunders, S. E., *c.* 1930–40
earthenware
(same monogram used at
Carisbrooke Pottery Works, Newport, 1929–32)

CHANNEL ISLANDS

GUERNSEY (Channel Islands)
The Guernsey Pottery Ltd.
red-ware, studio-pottery
1961–

JERSEY (Channel Islands)
Jersey Pottery Ltd., 1946–
earthenware

JERSEY POTTERY
C.I.
painted

1946–
impressed or printed marks

1951

ISLE OF MAN

Isle of Man Potteries, Ltd.
earthenware, 1963–

Isle of Man
Pottery
Handmade

NORTHERN IRELAND

PORTADOWN (Co. Armagh)
Wade (Ireland) Ltd., 1947–
porcelain, industrial
and artware
(subsidiary of Wade
Potteries, Ltd.)

printed

SCOTLAND

AIRTH (Central Region)
Dunmore Pottery Co.
1903–11, earthenware
c. 1860–1903
(Dunmore Pottery)

PETER GARDNER
DUNMORE POTTERY
DUNMORE
impressed

BO'NESS (Central Region)
McNay & Sons, Charles W.
earthenware, 1887–1958
'Dalmeny' trade-name

stick-on labels

Marshall & Co. Ltd., John
earthenware, 1854–99
'Ltd.' added in 1897

JOHN MARSHALL &
CO.
printed

COATBRIDGE (Strathclyde)
Crest Ceramics (Scotland)
earthenware souvenirs,
etc.

DUNOON (Strathclyde)
West Highland Pottery Co. Ltd.
earthenware, 1961–
trade-names: 'Flow' ware,
'Argyll', 'Cowal'
printed

EDINBURGH (Lothian)
Millar, John, 1840–82
retailer only

JOHN MILLAR
printed

GLASGOW (Strathclyde)
Bayley, Murray & Co.
earthenware, 1875–
1900 (Saracen
Pottery Co. from *c.* 1884)

B.M. & CO.
SARACEN POTTERY
printed or impressed

Bell, J. & M. P., 1842–1928
(Ltd. from 1881), general pottery

initials used in various printed
or impressed marks
c. 1842–60
c. 1850–70

J.B
J. & M. P. B & CO.

Britannia Pottery Co. Ltd.
earthenware, 1920–35
'HIAWATHA' trade-name
from *c.* 1925

printed

Campbellfield Pottery Co. Ltd.
earthenware, 1850–1905
'Ltd.' added *c.* 1884

C.P. CO.

printed or impressed
marks

CAMPBELLFIELD

C.P. CO. LTD.

printed mark of *c.* 1884–
c. 1905
or,
'SPRINGBURN' with thistle

Cochran & Fleming
earthenware, 1896–
1920

C. & F.

C. & F.
G

ROYAL
IRONSTONE CHINA

printed

PORCELAIN OPAQUE
GLASGOW. BRITAIN
FLEMING

COCHRAN & FLEMING
GLASGOW BRITAIN
printed

Cochran & Co., R.
general ceramics
1846–1896

R.C. & CO.
impressed

Geddes & Son, John
earthenware and porcelain
c. 1806–27
'& Son' added in 1824

JOHN GEDDES
Verreville
Pottery
printed

Govancroft Potteries Ltd.
pottery, 1913–
trade-names: 'Croft',
'Hamilton', 'Lunar'
1913–49

CROWN   GOVAN
printed or impressed

printed 1949–

Grosvenor & Son, F.
pottery, *c.* 1869–1926

printed mark from 1879

Kennedy & Sons Ltd., Henry
stoneware, 1866–1929

Lockhart & Arthur
earthenware, 1855–64
marks impressed or
printed

L. & A.

LOCKHART &
ARTHUR

Lockhart & Co., David
earthenware, 1865–98

D.L. & CO.
printed

Lockhart & Sons Ltd., David
earthenware, 1898–1953
printed in backstamps

D.L. & SONS

Murray & Co. Ltd., W. F.
pottery, 1870–98
mark impressed or
printed

Nautilus Porcelain Co.
porcelain, 1896–1913
printed mark

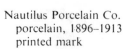

North British Pottery
earthenware, 1869–75

J.M. CO.

printed marks   J.M. & CO.   I.M. & CO.

Port Dundas Pottery Co. Ltd.
stoneware, *c.* 1850–1932

PORT DUNDAS
GLASGOW POTTERY

impressed or printed

Possil Pottery Co.
general ceramics
1898–1901

printed

'Star Pottery'
stoneware and 'majolica'
1880–1907

impressed or printed

Thomson & Sons, John
c. 1816– late 19th century
'& Sons' added *c.* 1866

J.T.
ANNFIELD

J.T. & SONS
GLASGOW

Williamson, John
pottery, 1844–94

WELLINGTON
POTTERY

marks impressed or
printed

WILLIAMSON
WELLINGTON
POTTERY

GREENOCK (Strathclyde)
Clyde Pottery Co. Ltd.
earthenware, *c.* 1815–
1903
'Ltd.' used *c.* 1857–63

CLYDE

G.C.P. CO.

GREENOCK
impressed or printed

Greenock Pottery
earthenware, *c.* 1820–
60

GREENOCK
POTTERY

mark impressed or
printed

Shirley & Co., Thomas
earthenware, *c.* 1840–57

T.S. & COY.

T.S. & C.
impressed

INVERDRUIE (Highland Region)
Castlewynd Studios, Ltd.
earthenware and stoneware
trade-names, 'Castlewynd'
'Aviemore'
Started Edinburgh 1950
moved to Gifford 1954
(Castlewynd Studios
(Highland China) 1974
at Fort William)

printed

KIRKCALDY (Lothian)
Heron & Son, Robert
earthenware, *c.* 1850–
1929
Date of 1820 in mark
is that of an earlier
pottery taken over by Heron

R.H. & S.

printed

Methven & Sons, David
19th century–*c.* 1930
earthenware

D.M. & S.

METHVEN

D. METHVEN & SONS

NORTH BERWICK
(Lothian)
Tantallon Ceramics
earthenware, 1962–

Tantallon
Ceramics
NORTH BERWICK

PAISLEY (Strathclyde)
Brown & Co., Robert
earthenware, 1876–1933

BROWN PAISLEY

printed or impressed

PORTOBELLO (nr. Edinburgh, Lothian)
Buchan & Co. Ltd., A. W.
stoneware, 1867
trade-name: 'Thistle'
printed mark from 1949–

Gray & Sons, Ltd., W. A.
pottery, *c.* 1857–1931
'& Sons' from 1870, 'Ltd.'
from 1926

W.A. GRAY
printed

Milne Cornwall & Co.
stoneware, *c.* 1830–40

MILNE CORNWALL
& CO.
impressed

Rathbone & Co., Thomas
earthenware, *c.* 1810–45

T.R. & CO.

marks printed or
impressed

T. RATHBONE
P

Scott Brothers
earthenware, *c.* 1786–96

SCOTT BROTHERS

SCOTT BROS.   SCOTT
                P.B.

marks impressed

PRESTONPANS (Lothian)
Fowler, Thompson & Co.
earthenware, *c.* 1820–40

FOWLER THOMPSON
& CO.
printed or impressed

Gordon's Pottery
earthenware, 18th century–
1832
initials in printed
backstamps

GORDON
impressed

G.G.

Watson's Pottery
earthenware, *c.* 1750–
1840

WATSON
impressed

mark of *c.* 1800–40

WATSON & CO.
printed

WALES

CARDIFF AND SWANSEA
(Glamorgan)
Primavesi & Son, F.
retailers of earthenware
c. 1850–1915 ('& Son'
added *c.* 1860)

F. PRIMAVESI & SON
CARDIFF
Full name in a
variety of marks

CARDIGAN (Dyfed)
Cardigan Potteries
earthenware, *c.* 1875–90
printed mark

CARDIGAN
POTTERIES
WOODWARD & CO.
CARDIGAN

CREIGIAU (nr. Cardiff)
Creigiau Pottery, 1947–
Southcliffe, R. G. & Co. Ltd.
earthenware in copper
lustre traditional style

'Creigiau'

LLANDUDNO (Gwynedd)
Cambrian Ceramic Co. Ltd.
(formerly Cambrian Pottery
Co. Ltd.), earthenware
1958–

CAMBRIAN
STUDIO
WARE
impressed or printed

LLANELLY (Dyfed)
Guest & Dewsbury
earthenware, 1877–1927
printed initials in
backstamps

G. & D.L.

G.D.

L

South Wales Pottery
earthenware, *c.* 1839–58
Chambers & Co.
c. 1839–54
Coombs & Holland
c. 1854–58

CHAMBERS
LLANELLY

S.W.P.

printed or impressed

NANTGARW (Glamorgan)
Nantgarw China Works
porcelain, 1813–14; 1817–22
Billingsley, William &
Walker, Samuel
'C.W.' stands for 'China
Works' (transferred to
Swansea in 1814 until
1817)

**NANT-GARW
C.W.**
impressed
(painted and stencilled
marks used, but
also found on later
copies)

SWANSEA (Glamorgan)
Swansea Pottery, Cambrian Pottery
c. 1783–1870, earthenwares
c. 1783–, mark impressed

SWANSEA

CAMBRIAN POTTERY

impressed or printed
marks, *c.* 1783–1810

CAMBRIA

impressed or printed
marks, *c.* 1811–17

DILLWYN & CO.
SWANSEA

D. & CO.

impressed from *c.* 1817–24   BEVINGTON & CO.

printed from *c.* 1847–50

impressed, *c.* 1847–50

CYMRO
STONE CHINA

impressed, *c.* 1824–50

DILLWYN

Evans, David & Glasson
pottery, *c.* 1850–62
impressed or printed

Evans, D. J. & Co.
pottery, *c.* 1862–70

D.J. EVANS & CO.

EVANS & CO.

printed, *c.* 1862–70

Swansea porcelain
impressed marks, 1814–22

SWANSEA

printed or written in red
enamel
impressed, sometimes
with 'SWANSEA'

SWANSEA

Swansea

DILLWYN & CO.

rare impressed mark
of *c.* 1820

BEVINGTON & CO.

Baker, Bevans & Irwin
Glamorgan Pottery
earthenware, 1813–38

BAKER BEVANS
& IRWIN
printed or impressed

example of printed mark

The name of Pellatt & Green, retailers
of St. Paul's Church Yard, London, is
sometimes seen on Welsh wares of *c.* 1805–30

Calland & Co., John F.
Landore Pottery
earthenware, 1852–56

C. & CO.

CALLAND SWANSEA

Vodrey's Pottery
earthenware, 1872–*c.* 85

VODREY DUBLIN
POTTERY

impressed

YNYSMEDW (nr. Swansea)
Ynysmedw Pottery
earthenware, *c.* 1850–70

Y.M.P.   Y.P.

impressed

LIMERICK
Stritch, John, *c.* 1760
tin-glazed earthenware

Made by John Stritch
Limerick, 4th June 1761

inscription on plate

IRELAND

BELLEEK (Co. Fermanagh)
porcelain, 1863–
McBirney, David &
Armstrong, Robert

BELLEEK
CO. FERMANAGH

FERMANAGH
POTTERY
impressed

impressed or printed
mark of 1863–80

early version of usual
mark, 1863–91

post-1891 version
includes 'Ireland'
and 'Co. Fermanagh'
to comply with the
McKinley Tariff Act

printed

CORK
Carrigaline Pottery Ltd.
earthenware, 1928–

CARRIG WARE
CARRIGALINE
POTTERY

printed marks

DUBLIN
Chambers, John, *c.* 1730–
c. 1745
tin-glazed earthenware
inscription painted on
plate

Delamain, Captain Henry (*d.* 1757)
1752–*c.* 1771

Donovan & Son, John
decorator of English
pottery and porcelain
c. 1770–1829

'DONOVAN' impressed on
wares made to order

DONOVAN

*DONOVAN
DUBLIN*
painted

Patent Office Registration Mark

From 1842 until 1883 many manufacturers' wares are marked with the following 'diamond-mark', which is an indication that the design was registered with the British Patent Office; ceramics and glass are Classes IV and III, as indicated in the topmost section of the mark, and gave copyright protection for a period of three years (see Appendix B and Preface, page vii).

The date of the 'diamond-mark' only indicates the time of registration, but a popular form of decoration was often produced for far longer than the three years. Printed marks usually refer to the applied pattern, whereas impressed or moulded applied versions are more likely to relate to the form of the ware.

When checking date to determine the name of the manufacturer it will sometimes be the case that the design was registered by retailers, wholesalers or even foreign manufacturers.

'Diamond-marks' impressed into bone-china can often be more accurately read when held before a strong artificial light.

Example of ceramic design registered on 23rd May 1842

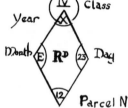

Index to letters for each year and month from 1842 to 1867:

Years

1842 X	1849 S	1856 L	1863 G
1843 H	1850 V	1857 K	1864 N
1844 C	1851 P	1858 B	1865 W
1845 A	1852 D	1859 M	1866 Q
1846 I	1853 Y	1860 Z	1867 T
1847 F	1854 J	1861 R	
1848 U	1855 E	1862 O	

Months

January	C	July	I
February	G	August	R } For September 1857
March	W	September	D } query letter R used
April	H	October	B } from 1st–19th Sept.
May	E	November	K } For December 1860
June	M	December	A } query letter K used.

Index to letters for each year and month from 1868 to 1883:

Example of ceramic design, registered on 6th January 1868

Years

1868 X	1872 I	1876 V	1880 J
1869 H	1873 F	1877 P	1881 E
1870 C	1874 U	1878 D	1882 L
1871 A	1875 S	1879 Y	1883 K

Months

Jan.	C	April H	July I	Oct. B
Feb.	G	May E	Aug. R	Nov. K
Mar.	W	June M	Sept. D	Dec. A

For Registration marks brought in with W for the year, see below:

From 1st to 6th March, 1878, the following Registration Mark was issued:

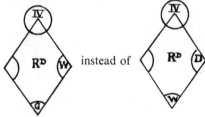

instead of

From 1884 this method of dating registrations ceased and the designs were numbered consecutively in the following manner: 'Rd. 12345' or 'Rd. No. 12345'. The following table gives a guide up until 1910 to the range of numbers used within a year:

Registered in January		Registered in January	
1	1884	291241	1897
19734	1885	311658	1898
40480	1886	331707	1899
64520	1887	351202	1900
90483	1888	368154	1901
116648	1889	385500	1902
141273	1890	402500	1903
163767	1891	420000	1904
185713	1892	447000	1905
205240	1893	471000	1906
224720	1894	494000	1907
246975	1895	519500	1908
268392	1896	550000	1909

Information concerning the work of the full members of the Craftsmen Potters Association (modern studio-potters) is well provided by an excellent directory, *Potters*, where the full particulars, including the mark and an illustration of the ware of the potters, are given. This directory may be obtained from the Craftsmen Potters Shop, William Blake House, Marshall Street, London, W.1.

The part of the Class IV Design Index in the Public Record Office that relates to pottery and porcelain is included in Appendix B, pages 173–201.

Index of Names and Dates of Manufacturers, Retailers, Wholesalers and others who registered designs from 1842 to 1883

(See Appendix A, page 172, and Introduction, page 5)

Date	Parcel No.	Patent No.	Factory, Retailer Wholesaler, etc	Place
1842				
Sept 22	1	1694	James Dixon & Sons	Sheffield
Nov 2	1	2152	Joseph Wolstenholme	Sheffield
3	1	2163	idem	Sheffield
26	3	2503–4	Henry Hunt	London
Dec 2	3	2599–00	Joseph Clementson	Shelton
30	2	3346	James Edwards	Burslem
1843				
Jan 24	2	4296–7	John Ridgway & Co.	Shelton
Feb 3	4	4462	T. Woodfield	London
21	1	5266–70	Samuel Alcock & Co.	Burslem
Mar 21	5	5993–4	Josiah Wedgwood & Sons	Etruria
31	6	6266	Samuel Alcock & Co.	Burslem
May 2	4	6978	Josiah Wedgwood & Sons	Etruria
5	1	7037	W. S. Kennedy	Burslem
11	2	7074	idem	Burslem
13	4	7122	Jones & Walley	Cobridge
June 14	5	7503–5	Samuel Alcock & Co.	Burslem
Aug 30	8	9678–80	James Edwards	Burslem
Oct 6	2	10370	idem	Burslem
Nov 10	3	11292	Minton & Co.	Stoke
28	5	11690	Thos. Dimmock & Co.	Shelton
Dec 14	10	12331	G. F. Bowers & Co.	Tunstall
1844				
Feb 15	9	16264–5	Samuel Alcock & Co.	Burslem
20	4	16374–5	idem	Burslem
Mar 1	6	16687	Hamilton & Moore	Longton
5	3	16831	Mellor, Venables & Co.	Burslem
7	4	16871	J. & T. Lockett	Lane End
Apr 3	3	17566–72	Thos. Edwards	Burslem
11	4	17714	Hilditch & Hopwood	Lane End
May 7	4	18207	Thos. Dimmock & Co.	Shelton
June 29	3	19182	idem	Shelton
July 20	5	19977–9	John Ridgway & Co.	Shelton
30	2	20332–4	Herbert Minton & Co.	Stoke
Aug 15	3	20779	King, Knight & Elkin	Stoke
21	7	21069–73	Herbert Minton & Co.	Stoke
Sept 9	7	21450	Cyples, Barlow & Cyples	Lane End
19	4	21700–1	Jn. Ridgeway & Co.	Shelton
21	2	21715	Henry Hunt	London
30	7	21960	Charles Meigh	Hanley
Oct 14	2	22158	Copeland & Garrett	Stoke
17	3	22192	Clementson, Young & Jameson	Shelton
30	4	22394–6	Herbert Minton & Co.	Stoke
Nov 6	4	22424	idem	Stoke
11	5	22490	James Edwards	Burslem
13	4	22499–500	John Ridgway & Co.	Shelton
22	4	22834	Thos. Dimmock & Co.	Shelton
26	3	22883	Ray & Wynne	Longton
Dec 2	3	22919–20	Copeland & Garrett	Stoke
7	4	23207–10	Thos. Edwards	Burslem
16	6	23593	Willm. Ridgway, Son & Co.	Hanley
24	2	23843	John Meir & Son	Tunstall
1845				
Jan 11	6	24846	George Phillips	Longport
15	2	24996	Clementson, Young & Jameson	Shelton
21	6	25199	T. J. & J. Mayer	Longport
27	5	25273	John Rose & Co.	Coalport
Feb 26	5	26532–3	W. S. Kennedy	Burslem
27	3	26543	George Phillips	Longport
Mar 5	1	26608	Copeland & Garrett	Stoke
6	5	26617	Herbert Minton & Co.	Stoke
17	10	26939	idem	Stoke
20	1	26949	idem	Stoke
31	4	27034	Thos. Pearce	London
Apr 10	1	27202	idem	London
25	2	27350	Copeland & Garrett	Stoke
26	1	27352	George Pearce	London
26	3	27354	T. & R. Boote, Walley & Jones	Burslem, Cobridge and Hanley
30	2	27383	Jacob Furnival & Co.	Cobridge
May 8	2	27451	Herbert Minton & Co.	Stoke
10	3	27482	Walley & T. & R. Boote	Cobridge and Burslem
31	1	27800	Francis Morley	Shelton
June 19	1	28150	George Phillips	Longport
26	3	28296	Minton & Co.	Stoke
July 5	1	28668–71	George Phillips	Longport
5	2	28672	Enoch Wood	Burslem
26	1	29173	William Adams & Sons	Stoke
Aug 28	3	29993	Joseph Clementson	Shelton
Sept 4	3	30161–3	Copeland & Garrett	Stoke
11	2	30286	Thos. Phillips & Son	Burslem
19	1	30383	Minton & Co.	Stoke
Oct 6	1	30543–4	H. Minton & Co.	Stoke
21	1	30699	Copeland & Garrett	Stoke
22	2	30701	Clementson & Young	Shelton
Nov 15	2	31128	Bayley & Ball	Longton
22	2	31329	Minton & Co.	Stoke
Dec 4	4	31670–3	John Ridgway	Shelton
27	2	32553	James Edwards	Burslem
29	2	32555	Joseph Clementson	Shelton
30	3	32601	Furnival & Clark	Hanley
1846				
Jan 7	2	32698	Joseph Clementson	Shelton
24	2	33319	Jacob Furnival & Co.	Cobridge
Feb 26	5	34031	T. J. & J. Mayer	Longport
Mar 2	4	34108	Minton & Co.	Stoke
11	2	34281–5	W. S. Kennedy	Burslem
Apr 7	1	34564–66	idem	Burslem
17	3	34684	Copeland & Garrett	Stoke
May 21	3	35030–1	H. Minton & Co.	Stoke
26	2	35116–7	idem	Stoke
June 6	1	35219	W. Chamberlain & Co.	Worcester

Date	Parcel No.	Patent No.	Factory, Retailer Wholesaler, etc	Place	Date	Parcel No.	Patent No.	Factory, Retailer Wholesaler, etc	Place
26	2	35777	H. Minton & Co.	Stoke	Oct 1	4	46130	Thos. Peake	Tunstall
30	3	35795	John Goodwin	Longton	2	5	46192–4	John Ridgway & Co.	Shelton
July 11	1	36047	J. K. Knight	Longton	4	3	46232	H. Minton & Co.	Stoke
16	1	36167	Ridgway, Son & Co.	Hanley	8	4	46265	John Wedge Wood	Tunstall
17	1	36263	John Ridgway & Co.	Shelton	13	1	46299	W. T. Copeland	Stoke
21	1	36278	F. Morley & Co.	Shelton	23	2	46516–8	H. Minton & Co.	Stoke
Aug 1	2	36447–8	Josiah Wedgwood & Sons	Etruria	27	1	46529	John Ridgway & Co.	Shelton
3	1	36450	idem	Etruria	Nov 11	4	46886	H. Minton & Co.	Stoke
3	2	36451–2	H. Minton & Co.	Stoke	23	4	47183	J. Wedgwood & Co.	Etruria
Sept 3	2	37170	G. Phillips	Longport	Dec 1	2	47417–20	John Rose & Co.	Coalport
3	3	37171–2	F. Morley & Co.	Shelton	10	3	47562–3	Minton & Co. & John Bell	Stoke
14	4	37254	Copeland & Garrett	Stoke	15	4	48130	Minton & Co.	Stoke
26	2	37419–21	John Ridgway & Co.	Shelton					
29	3	37586	T. J. & J. Mayer	Longport	**1848**				
Oct 26	1	37806	F. Morley & Co.	Shelton	Jan 1	4	48540–2	Barker & Till	Burslem
26	5	37864	J. Edwards	Burslem	6	4	48717	Geo. Grainger	Worcester
Nov 3	1	37935	Ridgway & Abington	Hanley	18	2	49040	W. T. Copeland	Stoke
5	2	37986	G. Phillips	Longport	Feb 11	3	49780–1	H. Minton & Co.	Stoke
12	3	38068	C. Meigh	Hanley	29	12	50473	Minton & Co.	Stoke
16	2	38113	H. Minton & Co.	Stoke	Mar 4	4	50549	Minton & Co.	Stoke
21	2	38291–2	Thos. Furnival & Co.	Hanley	7	1	50635–6	Ridgway & Abington	Hanley
Dec 3	4	38606	Ridgway & Abington	Hanley	14	2	50798	W. T. Copeland	Stoke
4	2	38610	H. Minton & Co.	Stoke	15	2	50803	idem	Stoke
10	3	38786	Joseph Clementson	Shelton	20	7	50994	Wood & Brownfield	Cobridge
14	3	39480	James Edwards	Burslem	27	8	51185–91	J. & S. Alcock Jnr.	Cobridge
14	4	39481	Minton & Co.	Stoke	Apr 15	4	51542	John Ridgway & Co.	Shelton
16	1	39519	John Goodwin	Longton	17	6	51599	Frederick Harrison	London
17	2	39544–5	Copeland & Garrett	Stoke	22	3	51661	Josiah Wedgwood & Sons	Etruria
26	5	39614	Henry Hunt	London	27	4	51763	idem	Etruria
29	2	39703	Edward Challinor	Tunstall	28	5	51768	Giovanni Franchi	London
31	3	39746	Josiah Wedgwood & Sons	Etruria	May 30	3	52162	Thos. Peake	Tunstall
					June 20	4	52402	G. F. Bowers & Co.	Tunstall
1847					30	2	52529	W. T. Copeland	Stoke
Jan 9	4	40104–5	John Ridgway & Co.	Shelton	30	3	52530	Ridgway & Abington	Hanley
9	7	40110	Copeland & Garrett	Stoke	Aug 10	3	53782	Geo. Grainger	Worcester
Feb 2	7	41213	T. & R. Boote	Burslem	16	8	53876	Thos. Pinder	Burslem
8	5	41266–7	T. J. & J. Mayer	Longton	23	2	54018	John Wedge Wood	Tunstall
15	4	41459–60	Copeland & Garrett	Stoke	26	2	54067	John Meir & Son	Tunstall
Mar 17	2	42044	John Wedge Wood	Tunstall	Sept 15	3	54438	W. T. Copeland	Stoke
17	6	42047–8	John Ridgway & Co.	Shelton	18	4	54487	Charles Meigh	Hanley
22	2	42233	Bailey & Ball	Longton	25	4	54578–9	Giovanni Franchi	London
23	7	42279	Herbert Minton & Co.	Stoke	30	7	54662	John Ridgway & Co.	Shelton
30	1	42363	James Edwards	Burslem	Oct 17	3	54901	T. & R. Boote	Burslem
Apr 3	6	42435	Samuel Alcock & Co.	Burslem	Nov 4	2	55174	W. T. Copeland	Stoke
27	1	42804	idem	Burslem	13	4	55337	idem	Stoke
May 12	4	43154	Copeland & Garrett	Stoke	21	5	55456–7	Minton & Co.	Stoke
14	1	43170–1	Herbert Minton & Co.	Stoke	27	2	55766	John Ridgway & Co.	Shelton
June 11	2	43536	James Edwards	Burslem	Dec 16	3	56631–3	James Edwards	Burslem
11	6	43557	Joseph Alexander	Norwich	28	2	56845	John Ridgway	Shelton
21	5	43728	John Rose & Co.	Coalport					
25	2	43780	James Edwards	Burslem	**1849**				
July 5	5	43916–7	Mellor, Venables & Co.	Burslem	Jan 3	2	56978	William Adams & Sons	Stoke
15	1	44014–5	idem	Burslem	20	2	57506–8	W. Davenport & Co.	Longport
16	5	44036–9	James Edwards	Burslem	Feb 2	4	58069	Mellor, Venables & Co.	Burslem
27	3	44398	T. J. & J. Mayer	Longport	16	5	58461	Minton & Co.	Stoke
Aug 3	3	44872	John Rose & Co.	Coalport	16	11	58474	Ridgway & Abington	Hanley
16	2	45088	James Edwards	Burslem	26	2	58578	John Rose & Co.	Coalport
17	2	45091–2	W. T. Copeland	Stoke	Mar 13	2	58874	Joseph Clementson	Shelton
19	3	45175	H. Minton & Co.	Stoke	26	5	59232	Minton & Co.	Stoke
26	2	45367	James Edwards	Burslem	27	2	59245	Cope & Edwards	Longton
Sept 9	3	45730	William Taylor Copeland	Stoke	31	2	59286	John Ridgway & Co.	Shelton
16	3	45822	idem	Stoke	Apr 2	5	59308	Podmore, Walker & Co.	Tunstall
25	5	45992	John Wedge Wood	Tunstall	10	4	59400	W. T. Copeland	Stoke

Date	Parcel No.	Patent No.	Factory, Retailer Wholesaler, etc	Place	Date	Parcel No.	Patent No.	Factory, Retailer Wholesaler, etc	Place
16	6	59571	C. J. Mason	Longton	11	6	78312	W. S. Kennedy	Burslem
May 24	1	60081	Mr. Wedge Wood	Tunstall	14	7	78398–401	J. & M. P. Bell & Co.	Glasgow
June 7	3	60265	T. J. & J. Mayer	Longport	26	3	78634	E. Walley	Cobridge
July 16	2	61347	Ridgway & Abington	Hanley	May 30	4	79085	W. T. Copeland	Stoke
Aug 11	4	61865	W. T. Copeland	Stoke	June 7	4	79164	J. Ridgway & Co.	Shelton
15	2	61986	H. Minton & Co.	Stoke	11	2	79183	W. T. Copeland	Stoke
17	2	62003	W. T. Copeland	Stoke	11	3	79184	Ralph Scragg	Hanley
27	5	62316	Mellor, Venables & Co.	Burslem	19	5	79300	W. T. Copeland	Stoke
Sept 14	6	62498	F. & R. Pratt & Co.	Fenton	July 10	3	79588	R. Britton & Co.	Leeds
28	6	62690–4	J. Ridgway	Shelton	14	3	79684	W. T. Copeland	Stoke
Oct 10	2	62883	idem	Shelton	21	7	79750–3	T. & R. Boote	Burslem
12	4	62914	Minton & Co.	Stoke	24	2	79782	Thos. Till & Son	Burslem
26	5	63267	J. Hollinshead	Shelton	26	3	79802	C. Collinson & Co.	Burslem
Nov 8	6	63490	John Cliff Quince	London	Aug 16	2	80184	Ridgway & Abington	Hanley
9	4	63523	W. T. Copeland	Stoke	Sept 2	4	80365	T. J. & J. Mayer	Longport
17	2	63718	Minton & Co.	Stoke	19	3	80629–30	T. & R. Boote	Burslem
22	2	64319	W. T. Copeland	Stoke	29	4	80815–16	James Edwards	Burslem
30	5	64627	John Rose & Co.	Coalport	30	3	80826	idem	Burslem
Dec 6	3	64739	W. T. Copeland	Stoke	Oct 1	1	80827	W. T. Copeland	Stoke
15	4	64982	T. J. & J. Mayer	Longport	7	3	80887	Chamberlain & Co.	Worcester
					10	4	80910–1	W. Brownfield	Cobridge
1850					10	6	80913	T. & R. Boote	Burslem
Jan 3	1	65884	W. Davenport & Co.	Longport	14	4	80980	Thos. Till & Son	Burslem
14	4	66266–7	J. Ridgway	Shelton	16	4	80989	W. Brownfield	Cobridge
26	6	66862	G. Grainger	Worcester	17	3	80997	George Bowden Sander	London
Feb 13	1	67398	idem	Worcester	21	3	81057	Wm. Ridgway	Shelton
13	3	67413	J. & M. P. Bell & Co.	Glasgow	Nov 1	5	81225–6	Geo. B. Sander	London
27	4	67783	G. Grainger	Worcester	10	4	81492	Ralph Scragg	Hanley
Mar 9	3	67987	W. T. Copeland	Stoke	12	6	81510–12	Minton & Co.	Stoke
30	9	68489	John Rose & Co.	Coalport	13	2	81518	Charles Meigh & Son	Hanley
Apr 4	4	68623	T. J. & J. Mayer	Longport	14	4	81558	Geo. B. Sander	London
8	1	68720	J. Clementson	Shelton	Dec 2	2	81815	T. J. & J. Mayer	Burslem
13	7	68797	Minton & Co.	Stoke	4	3	81843–4	Minton & Co.	Stoke
18	11	68959	John Rose & Co.	Coalport	5	5	81864	John Ridgway & Co.	Shelton
24	3	69142	William Pierce	London	8	8	81960	W. T. Copeland	Stoke
25	3	69149	Minton & Co.	Stoke	15	6	82052	Geo. B. Sander	London
June 4	1	69679	J. & M. P. Bell & Co.	Glasgow	**1852**				
5	3	69685	Barker & Son	Burslem	Jan 27	1	83342	W. & G. Harding	Burslem
21	4	69884	E. Walley	Cobridge	Feb 17	1	83826	Venables & Baines	Burslem
July 2	2	70088	T. J. & J. Mayer	Longport	Mar 4	2	84133–4	Wm. Brownfield	Cobridge
16	5	70364	C. & W. K. Harvey	Longton	13	3	84239	Wm. Ridgway	Shelton
Sept 9	5	71843	Thomas Till	Burslem	22	7	84385	Ralph Scragg	Hanley
16	8	71952	J. & M. P. Bell & Co.	Glasgow	24	3	84406	James Edwards	Burslem
16	9	71953–4	J. Ridgway	Shelton	24	4	84407	Minton & Co.	Stoke
19	2	71989	W. T. Copeland	Stoke	25	1	84410	John Milner	Cobridge
21	1	72057	Mellor, Venables & Co.	Burslem	26	3	84471	J. & M. P. Bell & Co.	Glasgow
Oct 9	2	72395–6	Minton & Co.	Stoke	Apr 1	4	84541	Thos. Till & Son	Burslem
17	6	72544	W. T. Copeland	Stoke	8	4	84615	idem	Burslem
Nov 4	4	73327	J. Wedgwood & Sons	Etruria	21	4	84837	George Ray	Longton
20	7	73693	F. Morley & Co.	Shelton	May 5	5	85001–2	J. M. Blashfield	London
22	3	73719	John Rose & Co.	Coalport	6	5	85008	Geo. Bowden Sander	London
Dec 5	3	74138	F. Morley & Co.	Shelton	7	2	85010–3	J. M. Blashfield	London
19	5	74785	John Rose & Co.	Coalport	14	5	85081	W. T. Copeland	Stoke
19	6	74786	T. J. & J. Mayer	Longport	18	1	85102	Minton & Co.	Stoke
20	6	75148	W. T. Copeland	Stoke	June 1	2	85224–5	J. M. Blashfield	London
					5	5	85248	Minton & Co.	Stoke
1851					14	4	85354	W. T. Copeland	Stoke
Jan 20	4	75883–4	James Green	London	21	2	85404	J. & T. Lockett	Longton
Feb 10	9	76664	William Brownfield	Cobridge	July 5	3	85619	J. Pankhurst & Co.	Hanley
Mar 17	13	77481–91	J. Ridgway & Co.	Shelton	23	3	85803–4	Minton & Co.	Stoke
31	4	77986	J. & M. P. Bell & Co.	Glasgow	Aug 4	3	86070–1	W. T. Copeland	Stoke
Apr 9	2	78268	Thos. Till & Son	Burslem	13	5	86126	Thos. Till & Son	Burslem
11	4	78309–10	J. & M. P. Bell & Co.	Glasgow	25	4	86318	Chas. Meigh & Son	Hanley

Date	Parcel No.	Patent No.	Factory, Retailer Wholesaler, etc	Place	Date	Parcel No.	Patent No.	Factory, Retailer Wholesaler, etc	Place
25	5	86319	Geo. Bowden Sander	London	**1854**				
Sept 3	7	86473	Minton & Co.	Stoke	Jan 10	4	94326	W. & G. Harding	Burslem
15	5	86649	Thos. Till & Son	Burslem	13	1	94343–4	Deaville & Baddeley	Hanley
16	1	86657	Minton & Co.	Stoke	14	3	94632	Samuel Moore & Co.	Sunderlnd
24	1	86815	idem	Stoke	21	3	94727	J. & M. P. Bell & Co.	Glasgow
27	3	86857	Warburton & Britton	Leeds	30	4	94815	Samuel Alcock & Co.	Burslem
Oct 1	6	86931	W. T. Copeland	Stoke	Feb 23	3	95163	W. T. Copeland	Stoke
7	5	87040	Ralph Scragg	Hanley	Mar 11	4	95275	Samuel Alcock & Co.	Burslem
23	4	87219	Davenports & Co.	Longport	20	1	95388	Thos. Till & Son	Burslem
25	2	87228	Wm. Brownfield	Cobridge	22	2	95397	James Edwards & Son	Longport
30	3	87464	Marple, Turner & Co.	Hanley	24	3	95420	Minton & Co.	Stoke
Nov 4	5	87541	John Holland	Tunstall	27	3	95448	Geo. Baguley	Hanley
11	3	87633	Minton & Co.	Stoke	27	6	95451	J. Deaville	Hanley
22	3	87883	J. Pankhurst & J. Dimmock	Hanley	31	1	95469	Holland & Green	Longton
					Apr 1	4	95510	Wm. Brownfield	Cobridge
25	4	88037	Keys & Mountford	Stoke	4	3	95523	Woollard & Hattersley	Cambdge
Dec 16	4	88350	John Rose & Co.	Coalport	5	3	95542	Ralph Scragg	Hanley
27	1	88693	Warburton & Britton	Leeds	6	3	95553	Samuel Alcock & Co.	Burslem
					10	3	95575	J. Deaville	Hanley
1853					10	4	95576	Samuel Alcock & Co.	Burslem
Jan 3	3	88808–9	W. T. Copeland	Stoke	11	5	95587–8	Pearson, Farrall & Meakin	Shelton
12	6	88978	Thos. Goodfellow	Tunstall					
14	3	88987	Davenports & Co.	Longport	15	1	95611	Geo. Baguley	Hanley
18	2	89050	idem	Longport	21	3	95646	Warburton & Britton	Leeds
Feb 4	9	89469	J. Pankhurst & J. Dimmock	Hanley	May 4	3	95733	John Ridgway & Co.	Shelton
					8	5	95751	Wm. Brownfield	Cobridge
10	2	89626	Geo. Wooliscroft	Tunstall	June 3	2	96003	Thos. Till & Son	Burslem
11	6	89646	Thos. Worthington & J. Green	Shelton	9	2	96039	Chas. Meigh & Son	Hanley
					21	5	96085–6	T. & R. Boote	Burslem
12	3	89661–3	Minton & Co.	Stoke	July 18	4	96296	idem	Burslem
17	4	89722–3	W. S. Kennedy & Co.	Burslem	18	4	96298	Alcock & Co.	Burslem
26	5	89958	W. T. Copeland	Stoke	Sept 5	3	96773	Samuel Alcock & Co.	Burslem
Mar 10	2	90253	J. & M. P. Bell & Co.	Glasgow	12	2	96826	W. T. Copeland	Stoke
17	5	90360	J. W. Pankhurst & Co.	Hanley	Oct 2	3	96980	Wm. Brownfield	Cobridge
19	2	90372	Minton & Co.	Stoke	6	4	97141	Davenports & Co.	Longport
Apr 4	6	90610	John Rose & Co.	Coalport	9	4	97160	T. J. & J. Mayer	Longport
23	2	90876	Wm. Adams & Sons	Stoke	31	2	97508	Geo. Ray	Longton
May 7	5	91121–4	John Alcock	Cobridge	Nov 10	5	97659	John Ridgway & Co.	Shelton
June 7	3	91329	Geo. Wood & Co.	Shelton	Dec 27	3	98640	Samuel Alcock & Co.	Burslem
14	2	91405–6	Livesley, Powell & Co.	Hanley	27	4	98641	Pankhurst & Dimmock	Hanley
22	3	91469	Pankhurst & Dimmock	Hanley	29	1	98648	F. & R. Pratt & Co.	Fenton
24	3	91487	Geo. Wooliscroft	Tunstall					
24	11	91512–3	Ridgway & Co.	Shelton	**1855**				
July 18	4	91737	John Edwards	Longton	Jan 4	2	98696	Worthington & Green	Shelton
20	2	91749–50	J. H. Baddeley	Shelton	6	4	98786	Samuel Alcock & Co.	Burslem
Aug 8	1	92001	Anthony Shaw	Tunstall	15	2	99042	Pinder, Bourne & Hope	Burslem
10	2	92018	Holland & Green	Longton	15	4	99051	Brougham & Mayer	Tunstall
Sept 3	2	92340	T. & R. Boote	Burslem	19	3	99086	Pankhurst & Dimmock	Hanley
6	3	92364	F. Morley & Co.	Shelton	30	1	99188	John Edwards	Longton
21	2	92631–2	James Edwards	Burslem	Feb 3	4	99231	J. & M. P. Bell & Co.	Glasgow
Oct 5	2	92768–70	Venables, Mann & Co.	Burslem	5	7	99282	Coomb(e)s & Holland	Llanelly
10	3	92859	Barrow & Co.	Fenton	7	2	99310	John Alcock	Cobridge
11	5	92864	Ralph Scragg	Hanley	17	3	99394	Pratt & Co.	Fenton
12	3	92867	James Edwards	Burslem	26	3	99488	Lockett, Baguley & Cooper	Shelton
12	4	92868–9	Livesley, Powell & Co.	Hanley					
19	4	92952	Minton & Co.	Stoke	28	4	99528	J. Ridgway & Co.	Shelton
22	1	93008–9	T. J. & J. Mayer	Longport	Mar 1	5	99538–40	Minton & Co.	Stoke
Nov 24	2	93438–9	Thos. Till & Son	Burslem	5	3	99579	Elsmore & Forster	Tunstall
26	2	93452	W. T. Copeland	Stoke	13	4	99653	Warburton & Britton	Leeds
30	5	93483	Wm. Adams & Sons	Stoke	17	1	99679	Wm. Baker	Fenton
Dec 6	4	93536	J. Alcock	Cobridge	Apr 7	4	99814	W. T. Copeland	Stoke
24	3	93706–7	Samuel Moore & Co.	Sunderlnd	17	4	99876	Stephen Hughes & Son	Burslem
24	4	93708	J. Alcock	Cobridge	26	1	99972–4	Wm. Brownfield	Cobridge

Date	Parcel No.	Patent No.	Factory, Retailer Wholesaler, etc	Place	Date	Parcel No.	Patent No.	Factory, Retailer Wholesaler, etc	Place
28	7	100008	Venables, Mann & Co.	Burslem	Feb 4	5	108854–5	John Meir & Son	Tunstall
May 10	5	100094	Beech, Hancock & Co.	Burslem	9	4	108930	Minton & Co.	Stoke
14	3	100116	Minton & Co.	Stoke	17	3	109063	idem	Stoke
June 7	4	100246–7	John Alcock	Cobridge	23	9	109180	Podmore, Walker & Co.	Hanley
11	3	100299	Saml. Alcock & Co.	Burslem	Mar 20	4	109427	John Alcock	Cobridge
July 4	5	100624	J. Thompson	Staffs.	Apr 16	1	109738	John Alcock	Cobridge
24	1	100816	Chas. Meigh & Son	Hanley	29	1	109810	W. T. Copeland	Stoke
Aug 6	1	101019	James Dudson	Shelton	June 5	3	110096–7	Wm. Brownfield	Cobridge
8	5	101026	J. Edwards & Son	Longport	19	1	110160	W. T. Copeland	Stoke
11	1	101082	Geo. Grainger & Co.	Worcester	19	2	110161	Wilkinson & Rickhuss	Hanley
20	3	101127	Thos. Ford	Shelton	25	1	110247	J. & M. P. Bell & Co.	Glasgow
27	2	101229–31	Barrow & Co.	Fenton	July 30	2	110780	Ridgway, Bates & Co.	Shelton
Sept 27	4	101623–4	Saml. Bevington & Son	Shelton	Aug 4	5	110806	Taylor, Pears & Co.	Fenton
Oct 3	2	101681	Geo. Mayor & Co.	London	11	3	110862	Kerr & Binns	Worcester
3	3	101682	Minton & Co.	Stoke	Sept 7	2	111105	W. T. Copeland	Stoke
17	8	101932	John Williamson	Glasgow	Oct 3	3	111495–6	Doulton & Watts	London
25	3	102325	D. Chetwynd	Cobridge	5	5	111515–6	idem	London
29	6	102355	G. W. Reade	Burslem	14	1	111585	Ridgway & Abington	Hanley
Nov 1	3	102415	Josiah Wedgwood & Sons	Etruria	17	1	111642	Mayer Bros. & Elliott	Longport
22	4	102744	J. & M. P. Bell & Co.	Glasgow	17	2	111643–4	T. & R. Boote	Burslem
28	3	102785	Wm. Brownfield	Cobridge	22	1	111677	Pratt & Co.	Fenton
1856					Nov 3	3	111831–2	Maw & Co.	Broseley
Jan 5	3	103103	J. Edwards	Longton	28	2	112263	Kerr & Binns	Worcester
15	4	103404	James Pankhurst & Co.	Hanley	Dec 4	4	112350	Minton & Co.	Stoke
23	3	103506	J. Roberts	Kent (Upnor)	9	2	112354	Wm. Brownfield	Cobridge
23	4	103507	Minton & Co.	Stoke	**1858**				
31	4	103616	Josiah Wedgwood & Sons	Etruria	Jan 29	3	112875	Cockson & Harding	Hanley
Mar 11	1	104078	Davenports & Co.	Longport	29	4	112876	E. & W. Walley	Cobridge
12	3	104090	Pratt & Co.	Fenton	Mar 25	2	113290	Kerr & Binns	Worcester
Apr 7	2	104313–16	A. Shaw	Tunstall	Apr 9	2	113387	idem	Worcester
7	3	104317	J. & M. P. Bell & Co.	Glasgow	17	4	113456	Ridgway & Abington	Hanley
18	2	104392	Wm. Beech	Burslem	22	5	113565	T. & R. Boote	Burslem
18	3	104393	Ralph Scragg	Hanley	30	5	113631	Minton & Co.	Stoke
18	6	104396	E. Walley	Cobridge	May 6	4	113668	J. Edwards	Longton
18	7	104397	Ridgway & Abington	Hanley	25	4	113864	A. Shaw	Burslem
30	3	104602–3	Wm. Brownfield	Cobridge	31	1	113900	Holland & Green	Longton
May 8	2	104694	Minton & Co.	Stoke	31	4	113903	Wm. Adams	Tunstall
22	1	104762	idem	Stoke	June 2	1	113905–6	Wm. Brownfield	Cobridge
June 13	3	105059	Chas. Meigh & Son	Hanley	23	6	114048	Samuel Alcock & Co.	Burslem
28	3	105223	Worthington & Green	Hanley	July 13	2	114214	Mayer & Elliott	Longport
30	7	105258	J. Clementson	Shelton	29	4	114532	Samuel Alcock & Co.	Burslem
July 28	3	105492	E. Challinor	Tunstall	Aug 24	2	114763	Wm. Brownfield	Cobridge
30	5	105702	J. Edwards & Son	Longport	Sept 3	2	115120	Sharpe Bros. & Co.	Swadlncte
Aug 12	2	105871	F. & R. Pratt & Co.	Fenton	6	5	115197	James Edwards	Longport
19	5	105926	idem	Fenton	10	3	115217	John Edwards	Longton
22	4	105955–9	T. & R. Boote	Burslem	10	6	115343	Bridgwood & Clarke	Burslem
Sept 1	3	106161	W. T. Copeland	Stoke	Oct 5	2	115901	Minton & Co.	Stoke
Oct 2	3	106477	H. Baggaley	Hanley	5	3	115902	Wm. Brownfield	Cobridge
16	2	106671–2	Minton & Co.	Stoke	7	1	115953	Ridgway & Abington	Hanley
22	3	106770	W. T. Copeland	Stoke	18	3	116176	Minton & Co.	Stoke
Nov 7	6	106950	F. & R. Pratt & Co.	Fenton	29	2	116468	B. Green	Fenton
14	9	107038	Davenports & Co.	Longport	Nov 3	8	116585	James Stiff	London
27	3	107708	idem	Longport	5	5	116607	Wm. Savage	Winchstr
27	6	107714	Wm. Brownfield	Cobridge	11	2	116737	E. & W. Walley	Cobridge
29	1	107783–5	E. Walley	Cobridge	Dec 8	11	117336–8	T. & R. Boote	Burslem
Dec 11	3	107955	W. T. Copeland	Stoke	8	12	117339	J. Clementson	Hanley
18	2	108052	Mayer & Elliott	Longport	17	6	117443	W. T. Copeland	Stoke
23	4	108105	idem	Longport	23	2	117516	J. Clementson	Hanley
					23	9	117530	W. T. Copeland	Stoke
1857					27	4	117559	J. Clementson	Hanley
Jan 15	5	108605	F. & R. Pratt & Co.	Fenton	**1859**				
26	7	108785	J. Edwards	Longport	Jan 25	4	118119	W. T. Copeland	Stoke
					Feb 2	3	118294	T. & R. Boote	Burslem

Date	Parcel No.	Patent No.	Factory, Retailer Wholesaler, etc	Place		Date	Parcel No.	Patent No.	Factory, Retailer Wholesaler, etc	Place
3	2	118303–4	Davenports & Co.	Longport		Mar 7	7	138861–2	Turner & Tomkinson	Tunstall
8	6	118415	Leveson Hill (Excrs. of)	Stoke		19	3	139053	W. T. Copeland	Stoke
Mar 19	1	118827	Alsop, Downes,			19	4	139054–5	W. H. Kerr & Co.	Worcester
			Spilsbury & Co.	London		Apr 5	3	139360	Pinder, Bourne & Hope	Burslem
21	7	118891	T. & R. Boote	Burslem		6	1	139369–72	Minton, Hollins & Co.	Stoke
29	7	119137	idem	Burslem		12	3	139714–5	Davenports & Co.	Longport
May 7	1	119721–2	E. & W. Walley	Cobridge		18	5	139881	T. & R. Boote	Burslem
10	2	119760	Samuel Alcock & Co.	Burslem		20	6	139945	F. & R. Pratt	Fenton
20	1	119968	Wm. Brownfield	Cobridge		25	2	140200	James Dudson	Hanley
26	1	120096	Lockett, Baguley &			May 3	8	140367	W. T. Copeland	Stoke
			Cooper	Hanley		6	3	140478	The Hill Pottery Co.	Burslem
July 2	2	120560	W. T. Copeland	Stoke		6	5	140480–1	The Old Hall	
Aug 6	7	121140	F. & R. Pratt & Co.	Fenton					Earthenware Co.	Hanley
27	6	121724	Samuel Alcock & Co.	Burslem		9	3	140578–9	Bates, Brown–Westhead	
Sept 1	3	121833	James Edwards & Son	Longport					& Moore	Hanley
Oct 12	4	122959	Wm. Adams	Tunstall		13	7	140679	Minton & Co.	Stoke
14	4	123116	W. T. Copeland	Stoke		14	2	140683	W. H. Kerr & Co.	Worcester
25	1	123389–91	Minton & Co.	Stoke		25	2	141055	idem	Worcester
28	1	123604	Davenports & Co.	Longport		31	3	141114	Cork, Edge & Malkin	Burslem
Nov 2	3	123738–40	Elsmore & Forster	Tunstall		June 4	1	141214	Bates, Brown–Westhead	
5	4	123816	Wm. Brownfield	Cobridge					& Moore	Hanley
17	4	124140–3	Minton & Co.	Stoke		7	5	141288	The Hill Pottery Co.	Burslem
23	4	124274	idem	Stoke		11	2	141326–7	W. T. Copeland	Stoke
Dec 10	5	124653	Josiah Wedgwood & Sons	Etruria		13	6	141369	Minton & Co.	Stoke
14	2	124716	E. & W. Walley	Cobridge		July 4	2	141715	Lockett & Cooper	Hanley
15	3	124725	Minton & Co.	Stoke		5	2	141727	Beech & Hancock	Tunstall
						6	2	141732	Wm. Brownfield	Cobridge
1860						18	4	141869–70	Josiah Wedgwood & Sons	Etruria
Jan 10	4	125365	W. T. Copeland	Stoke		Aug 19	7	142755	T. & R. Boote	Burslem
23	7	125863	Mayer & Elliott	Longport		22	7	142847	Wedgwood & Co.	Tunstall
Feb 14	9	126446–7	W. T. Copeland	Stoke		23	2	142850	G. W. Reade	Cobridge
Mar 1	2	126950	Bates, Brown–Westhead			Sept 6	6	143313	Wm. Brownfield	Cobridge
			& Moore	Hanley		12	6	143400	J. & J. Peake	Newcastle
27	1	127513	idem	Hanley		17	2	143702	W. T. Copeland	Stoke
Apr 5	1	127766	Geo. Grainger & Co.	Worcester		17	7	143769	Wm. Beech	Burslem
12	4	127965	Minton & Co.	Stoke		26	7	144179	John Cliff & Co.	London
May 2	2	128476	John Meir & Son	Tunstall		Oct 10	5	144757	W. H. Kerr & Co.	Worcester
19	9	129129	Lockett, Baguley &			11	3	144767	Mountford & Scarratt	Fenton
			Cooper	Hanley		15	3	144896	Leveson Hill (Excrs of)	Stoke
30	10	129578	Edward Corn	Burslem		18	3	145157	W. T. Copeland	Stoke
June 6	4	129680–2	Wm. Brownfield	Cobridge		24	5	145499	Hulse, Nixon &	
22	2	130106	Minton & Co.	Stoke					Adderley	Longton
28	2	130135	Minton & Co.	Stoke		28	7	145686–7	Bates, Brown–Westhead	
Aug 21	2	131943	John Wedge Wood	Tunstall					& Moore	Hanley
Sept 24	3	133411	Minton & Co.	Stoke		Nov 15	3	146352–4	J. Clementson	Hanley
29	7	133788	idem	Stoke		29	5	146924	Josiah Wedgwood & Sons	Etruria
Oct 13	5	134204	B. Green	Fenton		Dec 4	7	147309–10	Wm. Brownfield	Cobridge
18	4	134519–20	Bates, Brown–Westhead			5	5	147322	Till, Bullock & Smith	Hanley
			& Moore	Hanley		20	7	147820	Lockett & Cooper	Hanley
19	4	134555–7	J. Clementson	Shelton		20	9	147823	Wedgwood & Co.	Tunstall
19	5	134558–9	Holland & Green	Longton						
29	3	134936	Minton & Co.	Stoke		**1862**				
29	9	134968	Wm. Brownfield	Cobridge		Jan 11	5	148517	Wm. Brownfield	Cobridge
Nov 23	9	136032	T. & R. Boote	Burslem		25	3	148870	idem	Cobridge
Dec 3	3	136285–6	Bates, Brown–Westhead			Feb 1	4	149090	Elliot Bros.	Longport
			& Moore	Hanley		10	4	149290	W. H. Kerr & Co.	Worcester
12	3	136643	Bates & Co.	Hanley		10	8	149292	Minton & Co.	Stoke
						27	4	149673–4	James Dudson	Hanley
1861						Mar 1	6	149716	T. & R. Boote	Burslem
Jan 8	6	137217	T. & R. Boote	Burslem		13	6	149938	W. T. Copeland	Stoke
21	7	137529	Wedgwood & Co.	Tunstall		13	7	149939	Wm. Adams	Tunstall
Feb 15	3	138356	J. Furnival & Co.	Cobridge		14	8	149955	J. Knight	Fenton
27	5	138535	James Edwards & Son	Longport		14	9	149956	Wedgwood & Co.	Tunstall

Date	Parcel No.	Patent No.	Factory, Retailer Wholesaler, etc	Place	Date	Parcel No.	Patent No.	Factory, Retailer Wholesaler, etc	Place
14	.10	149957–8	Wm. Brownfield	Cobridge	**1863**				
21	6	150100	Thompson Bros.	Burton-on-Trent	Jan 12	6	159083	Davenport, Banks & Co.	Etruria
					16	2	159123	Minton & Co.	Stoke
22	9	150152	T. & R. Boote	Burslem	16	8	159153	Liddle, Elliot & Sons	Longport
27	1	150241	J. & M. P. Bell & Co.	Glasgow	29	1	159551	Josiah Wedgwood & Sons	Etruria
28	5	150301–3	idem	Glasgow	30	3	159573	T. & R. Boote	Burslem
29	3	150322	Minton & Co.	Stoke	Feb 2	3	159613	Minton & Co.	Stoke
Apr 1	5	150377	Josiah Wedgwood & Sons	Etruria	17	4	159972	T. & R. Boote	Burslem
4	2	150455	Minton & Co.	Stoke	24	5	160110	James Stiff & Sons	London
4	5	150458	J. & T. Furnival	Cobridge	Mar 6	2	160319	G. L. Ashworth & Bros.	Hanley
7	12	150515	Geo. Grainger & Co.	Worcester	13	2	160456	Hope & Carter	Burslem
9	3	150538	The Old Hall Earthenware Co. (Ltd.)	Hanley	13	3	160457	Wilkinson & Sons	Hanley
					20	8	160752	Worthington & Green	Hanley
17	5	151029–30	Thompson Bros.	Burton	20	9	160753–4	John Pratt & Co.	Fenton
24	2	151141	Turner & Tomkinson	Tunstall	21	2	160759	Beech & Hancock	Tunstall
May 1	7	151351	Eardley & Hammersley	Tunstall	21	4	160761	Hulse, Nixon & Adderley	Longton
3	3	151378	G. L. Ashworth Bros.	Hanley					
5	5	151456	John Cliff	London	21	5	160762	James Edwards & Son	Burslem
9	9	151568–9	Brown–Westhead, Moore & Co.	Hanley	23	2	160791–2	Bodley & Harrold	Burslem
					Apr 11	1	161404	J. Macintyre	Burslem
14	3	151672–3	Geo. Jones & Co.	Stoke	23	4	161852	T. C. Brown–Westhead Moore & Co.	Hanley
27	3	151995	E. Challinor	Tunstall					
29	5	152013	J. Furnival & Co.	Cobridge	25	1	161861	Beech & Hancock	Tunstall
June 24	5	152709	T. C. Brown–Westhead, Moore & Co.	Hanley	30	3	162021	Wilkinson & Son	Hanley
July 2	4	152859	Minton & Co.	Stoke	May 4	6	162122	Harding & Cotterill	Burton-on-Trent
4	8	152963	J. Clementson	Hanley	11	3	162261–2	E. Pearson	Cobridge
12	4	153112	idem	Hanley	12	1	162267	Bodley & Harrold	Burslem
14	2	153127	Beech & Hancock	Tunstall	15	10	162304	Harding & Cotterill	Burton-on-Trent
19	6	153366	J. Clementson	Hanley					
31	3	153476	Jones & Ellis	Longton	22	4	162618–9	W. T. Copeland	Stoke
31	4	153477	Minton & Co.	Stoke	26	9	162765	T. C. Brown–Westhead, Moore & Co.	Hanley
Aug 16	5	153821	Richard Edwards	Longport					
16	7	153823	J. H. Baddeley	Hanley	·June 4	5	162976	The Old Hall Earthenware Co. (Ltd.)	Hanley
18	4	153827	Hulse, Nixon & Adderley	Longton	8	15	163188	Minton & Co.	Stoke
					8	16	163189	Wm. Brownfield	Cobridge
19	4	153844	G. L. Ashworth & Bros.	Hanley	July 14	2	164213	Turner & Tomkinson	Tunstall
25	3	154143–4	E. F. Bodley & Co.	Burslem	15	3	164221	H. Venables	Hanley
30	3	154220	Thos. Fell & Co.	Newcastle upon Tyne	20	3	164353	Wm. Brownfield	Cobridge
					24	3	164468–9	W. T. Copeland	Stoke
30	4	154221	T. & R. Boote	Burslem	28	6	164635	Minton & Co.	Stoke
Sept 6	2	154401	Malkin, Walker & Hulse	Longton	Aug 11	3	165045–7	Turner & Tomkinson	Tunstall
11	3	154678	Minton & Co.	Stoke	12	4	165171	Hancock, Whittingham & Co.	Burslem
12	2	154693	Thos. Cooper	Longton					
17	6	154812	Hope & Carter	Burslem	21	1	165317	J. Clementson	Hanley
22	7	155103	Minton & Co.	Stoke	28	5	165448	H. Venables	Hanley
26	1	155220–2	Hope & Carter	Burslem	Sept 7	6	165720	T. & R. Boote	Burslem
Oct 1	7	155263–4	Thos. Fell & Co.	Newcastle upon Tyne	28	4	166439	H. Venables	Hanley
					28	6	166441–2	James Edwards & Son	Longport
					Oct 2	5	166625	H. Venables	Hanley
9	3	155550	Hill Pottery	Burslem	6	5	166775	Thompson Bros.	Burton
15	2	156190	Turner & Tomkinson	Tunstall	14	7	167289	Wm. Brownfield	Cobridge
23	8	156715–7	Wm. Baker & Co.	Fenton	15	2	167299	F. Brewer & Son	Longton
Nov 11	3	157274	E. F. Bodley & Co.	Burslem	17	1	167374	T. & R. Boote	Burslem
19	5	157547	Geo. Wooliscroft	Tunstall	22	5	167536	Eardley & Hammersley	Tunstall
28	4	157907	Minton & Co.	Stoke	24	5	167560	Josiah Wedgwood & Sons	Etruria
Dec 3	5	158052–3	T. C. Brown–Westhead Moore & Co.	Hanley	26	7	167594–5	The Old Hall Earthenware Co. (Ltd.)	Hanley
5	2	158091	Wm. Brownfield	Cobridge	28	8	167715	George Jones & Co.	Stoke
9	5	158221	Thomas Cooper	Hanley	31	3	167761–3	Edmund T. Wood	Tunstall
17	5	158480	The Old Hall Earthenware Co. (Ltd.)	Hanley	Nov 3	5	168132	John Meir & Son	Tunstall
					4	7	168188	T. & R. Boote	Burslem
18	3	158498	Geo. Jones	Stoke	6	1	168234–5	Geo. Jones & Co.	Stoke

Date	Parcel No.	Patent No.	Factory, Retailer Wholesaler, etc	Place	Date	Parcel No.	Patent No.	Factory, Retailer Wholesaler, etc	Place
16	10	168765	Wm. Kirkham	Stoke	19	1	178680–1	Josiah Wedgwood & Sons	Etruria
26	12	169553	Wm. Brownfield	Cobridge	21	1	178693–4	Minton & Co.	Stoke
27	3	169561	Bodley & Harrold	Burslem	22	6	178823–7	Josiah Wedgwood & Sons	Etruria
Dec 2	5	169774	J. W. Pankhurst	Hanley	Oct 4	2	179445	Geo. Jones & Co.	Stoke
2	6	169775	T. & R. Boote	Burslem	12	4	179656	Wm. Brownfield	Cobridge
18	4	170294	F. & R. Pratt & Co.	Fenton	27	4	180444	Evans & Booth	Burslem
23	2	170418	Wm. Brownfield	Cobridge	28	2	180449	The Worcester Royal Porcelain Co. Ltd.	Worcester
30	1	170590	T. C. Brown–Westhead Moore & Co.	Hanley	28	4	180453	Bodley & Harrold	Burslem
					28	9	180483	Minton & Co.	Stoke
1864					29	2	180486	Chas. Collinson & Co.	Burslem
Jan 5	2	170759	Wm. Brownfield	Cobridge	31	3	180569	Cork, Edge & Malkin	Burslem
11	5	170883	Malkin, Walker & Hulse	Longton	Nov 1	7	180695	W. T. Copeland	Stoke
Feb 2	5	171421	Josiah Wedgwood & Sons	Etruria	4	3	180713	Livesley, Powell & Co.	Hanley
5	5	171520	Hope & Carter	Burslem	10	2	181214–5	Elsmore & Forster	Tunstall
6	3	171536	Thos. Goode & Co.	London	10	3	181296	Hope & Carter	Burslem
13	6	171673	W. T. Copeland	Stoke	10	10	181286	Geo. Jones & Co.	Stoke
22	7	171970	Cork, Edge & Malkin	Burslem	24	5	181722	T. C. Brown–Westhead Moore & Co.	Hanley
25	6	172060	Liddle, Elliot & Son	Longport					
29	6	172183	J. & D. Hampson	Longton	29	1	181843	Hope & Carter	Burslem
Mar 3	4	172212	Geo. L. Ashworth & Bros.	Hanley	Dec 9	1	182203	Wm. Kirkham	Stoke
12	5	172559	Cork, Edge & Malkin	Burslem	10	8	182249	Hope & Carter	Burslem
18	1	172648	T. C. Brown–Westhead, Moore & Co.	Hanley	31	6	182699	Geo. Jones & Co.	Stoke
22	3	172815–6	Minton & Co.	Stoke					
23	4	172876	Burgess & Leigh	Burslem	**1865**				
Apr 9	4	173200	Josiah Wedgwood & Sons	Etruria	Jan 6	3	182806	Hope & Carter	Burslem
15	4	173659	Geo. Jones	Stoke	6	4	182807	Minton & Co.	Stoke
18	5	173671	Minton & Co.	Stoke	14	4	183331	Geo. Jones & Co.	Stoke
21	4	173785	T. C. Brown–Westhead Moore & Co.	Hanley	Feb 1	1	183650–2	Minton & Co.	Stoke
21	8	173799	Liddle, Elliot & Son	Longport	2	4	183706–7	Geo. L. Ashworth & Bros.	Hanley
23	11	173996	Geo. L. Ashworth & Bros.	Hanley	13	7	183940	F. & R. Pratt & Co.	Fenton
26	3	174112	Bodley & Harrold	Burslem	14	4	183945	Liddle, Elliot & Son	Longport
27	4	174138	Hope & Carter	Burslem	27	4	184220	Livesley, Powell & Co.	Hanley
29	2	174168	Wm. Brownfield	Cobridge	Mar 31	3	185473	Hope & Carter	Burslem
May 9	3	174424	R. T. Boughton & Co.	Burslem	Apr 1	4	185520	Wm. Brownfield	Cobridge
10	5	174455–8	Geo. Jones & Co.	Stoke	3	4	185613	Minton & Co.	Stoke
11	3	174475	R. H. Grove	Barlaston	22	5	186266	Thos. Till & Sons	Burslem
18	5	174795	Geo. Ray	Longton	22	7	186273	James Edwards & Son	Burslem
21	1	174817	J. & D. Hampson	Longton	26	5	186325	idem	Burslem
June 9	7	175330	Minton & Co.	Stoke	28	4	186349	Hope & Carter	Burslem
16	3	175500	Hope & Carter	Burslem	28	7	186354	Henry Alcock & Co.	Cobridge
30	4	175927	Wm. Brownfield	Cobridge	29	3	186361	The Worcester Royal Porcelain Co. (Ltd.)	Worcester
30	10	175935	The Worcester Royal Porcelain Co. Ltd.	Worcester	May 2	8	186477	Livesley, Powell & Co.	Hanley
July 2	3	175959	Wood & Sale	Hanley	15	2	186841	J. T. Hudden	Longton
9	5	176164	Pinder, Bourne & Co.	Burslem	17	2	186901	Minton & Co.	Stoke
11	8	176235–6	idem	Burslem	June 6	6	187358–9	J. T. Hudden	Longton
18	6	176597	Bodley & Harrold	Burslem	9	4	187403	The Worcester Royal Porcelain Co. (Ltd.)	Worcester
18	7	176598	Evans & Booth	Burslem	13	5	187533	idem	Worcester
19	4	176701	Hope & Carter	Burslem	14	6	187574	The Hill Pottery Co. Ltd.	Burslem
19	8	176706	Wood & Sale	Hanley	15	2	187576	J. T. Hudden	Longton
28	4	176916	Holland & Green	Longton	16	1	187583	Evans & Booth	Burslem
Aug 10	2	177455	James Fellows	W/hmptn	17	5	187633	The Worcester Royal Porcelain Co. (Ltd.)	Worcester
20	10	177912	Geo. Jones & Co.	Stoke	29	2	187847–8	Ed. F. Bodley & Co.	Burslem
26	5	178037	T. C. Brown–Westhead, Moore & Co.	Hanley	30	4	187861	The Hill Pottery Co. Ltd.	Burslem
Sept 6	5	178264	W. T. Copeland	Stoke	July 3	7	187972	T. C. Brown–Westhead, Moore & Co.	Hanley
10	1	178410	Minton & Co.	Stoke	12	3	188167	James Edwards & Son	Burslem
12	2	178433	idem	Stoke	Aug 21	6	189155	J. Furnival & Co.	Cobridge
14	4	178521	Bodley & Harrold	Burslem	23	5	189283	Josiah Wedgwood & Sons	Etruria
16	6	178597–8	Geo. L. Ashworth & Bros.	Hanley	Sept 11	4	189700	R. T. Boughton & Co.	Burslem

Date	Parcel No.	Patent No.	Factory, Retailer Wholesaler, etc	Place	Date	Parcel No.	Patent No.	Factory, Retailer Wholesaler, etc	Place
11	5	189701	Thos. Cooper (Excrs of)	Hanley	**1867**				
14	2	189718	T. C. Brown–Westhead,		Jan 8	5	205372	James Edwards & Son	Burslem
			Moore & Co.	Hanley	17	3	205596	Ed. F. Bodley & Co.	Burslem
18	6	189782	Liddle, Elliot & Son	Longport	23	2	205759	The Worcester Royal	
28	4	190200	Minton & Co.	Stoke				Porcelain Co. (Ltd.)	Worcester
30	4	190656	S. Barker & Son	Swinton	Feb 9	1	206033	Ed. F. Bodley & Co.	Burslem
Oct 13	8	190903	T. C. Brown–Westhead,		23	5	206275	Worthington & Harrop	Hanley
			Moore & Co.	Hanley	Mar 2	7	206422	Josiah Wedgwood & Sons	Etruria
24	4	191292	Edward Johns	Staffs.	4	4	206497	T. C. Brown–Westhead,	
30	4	191407–8	Wm. Brownfield	Cobridge				Moore & Co.	Hanley
Nov 10	4	192236	Pinder Bourne & Co. &		5	6	206517	Powell & Bishop	Hanley
			Anthony Shaw	Burslem	6	4	206522	The Old Hall	
23	10	192793	The Old Hall					Earthenware Co. (Ltd.)	Hanley
			Earthenware Co. Ltd.	Hanley	9	3	206564	John Edwards	Fenton
29	8	192963	James Edwards & Son	Burslem	11	2	206662	Josiah Wedgwood & Sons	Etruria
Dec 2	3	193061	The Worcester Royal		14	1	206718	Davenport Banks & Co.	Etruria
			Porcelain Co. (Ltd.)	Worcester	15	7	206762–6	Wm. Brownfield	Cobridge
23	3	193844	James Dudson	Hanley	18	5	206867–8	Cockson & Chetwynd	
								& Co.	Cobridge
1866					19	5	206881	James Edwards & Son	Burslem
Jan 2	4	194063	Pratt & Co.	Fenton	20	2	206887	Josiah Wedgwood & Sons	Etruria
3	6	194194	J. T. Close & Co.	Stoke	21	10	206971	James Edwards & Son	Burslem
13	2	194450	Ed. F. Bodley & Co.	Burslem	25	3	206994	Josiah Wedgwood & Sons	Etruria
17	4	194537	Burgess & Leigh	Burslem	26	4	207024–5	Minton & Co.	Stoke
24	1	194696	Minton & Co.	Stoke	Apr 3	5	207163	idem	Stoke
31	5	194840	James Edwards & Son	Burslem	4	2	207165	Josiah Wedgwood & Sons	Etruria
Feb 2	7	194949	W. T. Copeland	Stoke	4	9	207201	Elsmore & Forster	Tunstall
Mar 2	2	195644	Ford, Challinor & Co.	Tunstall	17	1	207564	Chas. Hobson	Burslem
10	1	195841	The Old Hall		23	3	207616	Adams, Scrivener & Co.	Longton
			Earthenware Co. (Ltd.)	Hanley	24	2	207636	W. T. Copeland	Stoke
Apr 14	6	196551	Walker & Carter	Longton	May 6	3	207938	J. & M. P. Bell & Co.	Glasgow
14	7	196552–4	Geo. L. Ashworth & Bros.	Hanley	7	4	207977	John Meir & Son	Tunstall
16	8	196619	The Old Hall		8	6	208002	T. C. Brown–Westhead	
			Earthenware Co. (Ltd.)	Hanley				Moore & Co.	Hanley
18	4	196651	James Edwards & Son	Burslem	18	7	208394	Wm. McAdam	Glasgow
20	7	196672–3	Wm. Brownfield	Cobridge	22	6	208434–5	Clementson Bros.	Hanley
May 1	4	196987–8	J. Furnival & Co.	Cobridge	June 6	3	208750	Josiah Wedgwood & Sons	Etruria
25	1	197705–6	Hope & Carter	Burslem	11	6	208819	Clementson Bros.	Hanley
June 4	4	197857	James Broadhurst	Longton	11	7	208820	Cockson, Chetwynd & Co.	Cobridge
12	1	198135–7	John Edwards	Fenton	13	3	208891	W. & J. A. Bailey	Alloa
21	4	198383–4	Pinder, Bourne & Co.	Burslem	21	4	209057	Wm. Brownfield	Cobridge
30	4	198589	Thos. Minshall	Stoke	21	8	209062	E. & D. Chetwynd	Hanley
July 19	5	199186	J. T. Hudden	Longton	24	4	209087	idem	Hanley
25	3	199295	Geo. Jones	Stoke	July 1	7	209290	Joseph Ball	Longton
Aug 17	3	200006	Morgan, Wood & Co.	Burslem	4	5	209362	E. J. Ridgway	Hanley
29	4	200324	Ed. F. Bodley & Co.	Burslem	8	3	209431	Geo. L. Ashworth	
Sept 6	4	200599	F. & R. Pratt & Co.	Fenton				& Bros.	Hanley
13	9	201040	T. & C. Ford	Hanley	12	5	209530	Geo. Jones	Stoke
15	8	201089	Geo. L. Ashworth & Bros.	Hanley	15	2	209556	Josiah Wedgwood & Sons	Etruria
20	8	201495	Anthony Keeling	Tunstall	17	2	209601	E. & D. Chetwynd	Hanley
Oct 8	3	202103–5	Minton & Co.	Stoke	25	3	209726	Hope & Carter	Burslem
13	3	202493	Thos. Furnival	Cobridge	Aug 28	10	210598	The Worcester Royal	
Nov 3	6	203173	Minton & Co.	Stoke				Porcelain Co. Ltd.	Worcester
12	3	203538	W. T. Copeland	Stoke	Sept 16	7	211275	Thos. Goode & Co.	London
14	8	203817	T. C. Brown–Westhead,		17	3	211290	Wedgwood & Co.	Tunstall
			Moore & Co.	Hanley	21	1	211536	Geo. L. Ashworth & Bros.	Hanley
15	4	203912	Geo. Grainger & Co.	Worcester	25	9	211873–4	Powell & Bishop	Hanley
Dec 13	4	204764	Liddle, Elliot & Son	Longport	Oct 2	1	211995	Minton & Co.	Stoke
14	8	204794	Samuel Barker & Son	Swinton	3	5	212054	Thompson Bros.	Burton-on-Trent
15	5	204863	T. C. Brown–Westhead,						
			Moore & Co.	Hanley	3	6	212055	Minton & Co.	Stoke
19	5	205088	John Meir & Son	Tunstall	7	4	212078	idem	Stoke
24	2	205201	J. T. Hudden	Longton	10	1	212194	Thos. Booth	Hanley

Date	Parcel No.	Patent No.	Factory, Retailer Wholesaler, etc	Place
24	5	212765	Ford, Challinor & Co.	Tunstall
26	1	212881	W. T. Copeland & Sons	Stoke
28	4	212956	idem	Stoke
29	3	212964	Josiah Wedgwood & Sons	Etruria
30	3	212974	J. T. Hudden	Longton
31	7	213065	Powell & Bishop	Hanley
Nov 6	7	213430	W. & J. A. Bailey	Alloa
7	4	213436	James Edwards & Son	Burslem
18	9	214000	Ford, Challinor & Co.	Tunstall
Dec 3	3	214618	W. T. Copeland & Sons	Stoke
12	6	214981	F. & R. Pratt & Co.	Fenton
20	3	215085	Josiah Wedgwood & Sons	Etruria
27	1	215314	J. & J. B. Bebbington	Hanley

1868

Date	Parcel No.	Patent No.	Factory, Retailer Wholesaler, etc	Place
Jan 3	1	215481	Minton & Co.	Stoke
7	8	215636	Thompson Bros.	Burton-on-Trent
7	11	215642	Cockson, Chetwynd & Co.	Cobridge
8	5	215674	T. & R. Boote	Burslem
9	7	215698	Taylor, Tunnicliffe & Co.	Hanley
10	2	215705	Cork, Edge & Malkin	Burslem
11	2	215725	Wm. Brownfield	Cobridge
13	2	215735	Geo. L. Ashworth & Bros.	Hanley
16	13	215879	The Old Hall Earthenware Co. (Ltd.)	Hanley
25	3	216186	Hope & Carter	Burslem
30	6	216333	J. Furnival & Co.	Cobridge
31	8	216347	Josiah Wedgwood & Sons	Etruria
31	14	216363	T. & R. Boote	Burslem
Feb 5	4	216451	Adams, Scrivener & Co.	Longton
5	8	216470	E. Hodgkinson	Hanley
10	8	216676–8	Minton & Co.	Stoke
12	1	216699	Josiah Wedgwood & Sons	Etruria
14	10	216821	John Mortlock	London
18	1	216895	Josiah Wedgwood & Sons	Etruria
18	2	216896–7	T. C. Brown–Westhead, Moore & Co.	Hanley
20	9	216988	Minton & Co.	Stoke
25	6	217070	John Rose & Co.	Coalport
27	5	217100	Alcock & Digory	Burslem
28	7	217112	W. & J. A. Bailey	Alloa
Mar 5	12	217208	Thos. Goode & Co.	London
5	15	217212	Minton & Co.	Stoke
25	7	217615	W. T. Copeland & Sons	Stoke
25	8	217616–7	The Worcester Royal Porcelain Co. (Ltd.)	Worcester
26	3	217630	Walker & Carter	Longton
Apr 1	6	217727	Minton & Co.	Stoke
6	6	217938–9	Pinder, Bourne & Co.	Burslem
16	7	218139	Geo. L. Ashworth & Bros.	Hanley
21	6	218285	Beech & Hancock	Tunstall
23	8	218387	R. Hammersley	Tunstall
28	7	218466	T. G. Green	Burton-on-Trent
May 13	1	218664	Adams, Scrivener & Co.	Longton
14	2	218764	Hope & Carter	Burslem
14	6	218773	Philip Brookes	Fenton
26	5	218951	T. C. Brown–Westhead Moore & Co.	Hanley
26	6	218952	Pinder, Bourne & Co.	Burslem
28	3	218967	Holdcroft & Wood	Tunstall
28	5	218969–71	Minton & Co.	Stoke

Date	Parcel No.	Patent No.	Factory, Retailer Wholesaler, etc	Place
28	7	218973	J. & T. Bevington	Hanley
30	4	219042	T. & R. Boote	Burslem
June 8	4	219174	Burgess & Leigh	Burslem
12	5	219316–7	Wm. Brownfield	Cobridge
16	4	219344	W. P. & G. Phillips	London
22	5	219484	Minton & Co.	Stoke
July 10	3	219756	Josiah Wedgwood & Sons	Etruria
16	3	219833	Hackney & Co.	Longton
20	2	219942–3	Hope & Carter	Burslem
24	4	219997	W. T. Copeland & Sons	Stoke
30	6	220183	Adams, Scrivener & Co.	Longton
Aug 1	5	220236–7	T. & R. Boote	Burslem
13	1	220772	Josiah Wedgwood & Sons	Etruria
15	8	220821–4	James Edwards & Son	Burslem
17	2	220828	Ed. F. Bodley & Co.	Burslem
21	2	220906	Ralph Malkin	Fenton
31	7	221124	T. & R. Boote	Burslem
Sept 1	1	221125–6	James Wardle	Hanley
4	6	221203–4	Gelson Bros.	Hanley
5	3	221214	T. C. Brown–Westhead, Moore & Co.	Hanley
5	6	221217–9	McBirney & Armstrong	Belleek
9	4	221311	Hope & Carter	Burslem
9	5	221312	F. Jones & Co.	Longton
9	6	221313	Wedgwood & Co.	Tunstall
9	9	221316	J. & T. Bevington	Hanley
12	3	221521–2	Minton & Co.	Stoke
14	4	221548	Thos. Booth & Co.	Burslem
17	4	221688	T. C. Sambrook & Co.	Burslem
21	4	221814–7	George Ash	Hanley
25	4	221881–2	Minton & Co.	Stoke
25	13	222083–4	T. C. Brown–Westhead, Moore & Co.	Hanley
Oct 8	7	222460	Minton & Co.	Stoke
9	2	222476	J. Holdcroft	Stoke
9	3	222477	Hope & Carter	Burslem
9	5	222482–4	Davenports & Co.	Longport
14	8	222736	Geo. Jones	Stoke
17	4	223063	Minton & Co.	Stoke
21	8	223308	W. P. & G. Phillips	London
22	1	223309	McBirney & Armstrong	Belleek
22	5	223314–5	James Edwards & Son	Burslem
Nov 3	5	223817–8	Minton & Co.	Stoke
3	6	223819	T. C. Brown–Westhead, Moore & Co.	Hanley
6	13	224090	Powell & Bishop	Hanley
9	5	224172	Josiah Wedgwood & Sons	Etruria
16	3	224382	Knapper & Blackhurst	Tunstall
17	1	224389	Moore Bros.	Cobridge
21	5	224539	Minton & Co.	Stoke
24	5	224645	T. C. Brown–Westhead Moore & Co.	Hanley
25	4	224724	Cork, Edge & Malkin	Burslem
Dec 1	4	224953	T. C. Brown–Westhead, Moore & Co.	Hanley
3	5	225073–4	The Worcester Royal Porcelain Co. (Ltd.)	Worcester
11	5	225410	Ed. T. Bodley & Co.	Burslem
12	4	225425	Wm. Brownfield	Cobridge
14	7	225441	Cockson, Chetwynd & Co.	Cobridge
23	5	225734	Minton & Co.	Stoke
23	6	225735	The Worcester Royal Porcelain Co. (Ltd.)	Worcester

Date	Parcel No.	Patent No.	Factory, Retailer Wholesaler, etc	Place	Date	Parcel No.	Patent No.	Factory, Retailer Wholesaler, etc	Place
31	6	225993	Geo. L. Ashworth & Bros.	Hanley	27	4	231256	J. T. Hudden	Longton
31	7	225994	R. Hammersley	Tunstall	Aug 2	6	231504	W. T. Copeland	Stoke
1869					3	5	231602	John Edwards	Fenton
Jan 1	8	226051	Geo. Jones	Stoke	4	4	231613	Tomkinson Bros. & Co.	Hanley
4	4	226098	Minton & Co.	Stoke	11	13	231812	W. P. & G. Phillips & Pearce	London
7	6	226131	Thos. Goode & Co.	London	19	6	232307	W. T. Copeland & Sons	Stoke
21	6	226527–8	Minton & Co.	Stoke	26	6	232474	idem	Stoke
22	5	226570	Gelson Bros.	Hanley	31	6	232586–7	John Pratt & Co.	Lane Delph
22	13	226581	T. C. Brown–Westhead, Moore & Co.	Hanley	31	12	232598	W. T. Copeland & Sons	Stoke
25	3	226625	Worthington & Son	Hanley	Sept 4	3	232822	Minton & Co.	Stoke
28	5	226738	Minton & Co.	Stoke	8	5	232878	W. T. Copeland & Sons	Stoke
28	10	226747–8	George Ash	Hanley	8	6	232879	Pinder, Bourne & Co.	Burslem
Feb 1	7	226910	T. C. Brown–Westhead, Moore & Co.	Hanley	9	3	232890	John Pratt & Co.	Lane Delph
2	4	226928	Geo. Yearsley	Longton	10	4	232903	Minton & Co.	Stoke
9	5	227219	Minton & Co.	Stoke	21	7	233411	Gelson Bros.	Hanley
11	10	227277	Geo. Jones	Stoke	22	10	233527	W. & J. A. Bailey	Alloa
15	1	227307	Thos. Booth & Co.	Burslem	30	8	233864–6	T. C. Brown–Westhead Moore & Co.	Hanley
19	2	227345	Josiah Wedgwood & Sons	Etruria	Oct 1	3	233923–4	Minton & Co.	Stoke
22	6	227403	idem	Etruria	4	6	234016	idem	Stoke
22	11	227409	McBirney & Armstrong	Belleek	14	3	234465	McBirney & Armstrong	Belleek
22	13	227411	Pinder, Bourne & Co.	Burslem	15	6	234486	Geo. Jones	Stoke
27	5	227518	Josiah Wedgwood & Sons	Etruria	23	4	235012	idem	Stoke
Mar 1	8	227556–8	Worthington & Son	Hanley	26	2	235158	James Ellis & Son	Hanley
3	8	227619	Thos. Till & Sons	Burslem	27	5	235168	McBirney & Armstrong	Belleek
6	8	227668	F. Primavesi	Cardiff	29	3	235399–400	Minton & Co.	Stoke
8	6	227696	F. & R. Pratt & Co.	Fenton					
9	1	227743–4	Geo. Jones	Stoke	29	4	235401–2	Powell & Bishop	Hanley
9	3	227746	idem	Stoke	Nov 2	12	235589	Ed. Clarke	Tunstall
10	10	227823	F. Primavesi	Cardiff	3	12	235691	T. C. Brown–Westhead, Moore & Co.	Hanley
24	1	228141	J. F. Wileman	Fenton	8	1	235827–9	McBirney & Armstrong	Belleek
Apr 1	1	228290	Wood & Pigott	Tunstall	8	2	235830	T. C. Brown–Westhead, Moore & Co.	Hanley
2	6	228377	Wm. Brownfield	Cobridge	9	11	235966	Tams & Lowe	Longton
2	7	228378	Minton & Co.	Stoke	10	3	235974	Wm. Brownfield	Cobridge
6	3	228430	Baker & Chetwynd	Burslem	13	5	236184–5	McBirney & Armstrong	Belleek
7	2	228455	Minton & Co.	Stoke	15	8	236203–7	Liddle, Elliot & Son	Longport
7	4	228457	The Worcester Royal Porcelain Co. (Ltd.)	Worcester	18	5	236435	Alcock & Digory	Burslem
12	4	228572	Taylor, Tunnicliffe & Co.	Hanley	19	12	236478	The Worcester Royal Porcelain Co. (Ltd.)	Worcester
12	5	228573	Liddle, Elliot & Son	Longport	20	8	236533	Thos. Goode & Co.	London
20	5	228764	idem	Longport	20	9	236534	John Mortlock	London
28	13	228937	J. & T. Bevington	Hanley	23	1	236585	McBirney & Armstrong	Belleek
May 11	1	229319	Adams, Scrivener & Co.	Longton	24	4	236628	Minton & Co.	Stoke
13	16	229405	James Edwards & Son	Burslem	26	3	236653	idem	Stoke
21	1	229523	Worthington & Son	Hanley	Dec 1	3	236756	Geo. Jones	Stoke
26	4	229627	Thos. Booth	Hanley	3	9	236829	Wm. Brownfield	Cobridge
27	8	229642–4	Davenport & Co.	Longport	17	7	237224	Minton & Co.	Stoke
June 3	6	229837	McBirney & Armstrong	Belleek	18	2	237229	Powell & Bishop	Hanley
8	7	229959	W. P. & G. Phillips & Pearce	London	18	3	237230	McBirney & Armstrong	Belleek
19	5	230183–4	Wm. Brownfield	Cobridge	20	8	237358	George Ash	Hanley
25	4	230429	James Edwards & Son	Burslem	22	7	237500	Geo. Jones	Stoke
26	9	230455	Minton & Co.	Stoke	24	1	237552	Gelson Bros.	Hanley
July 3	9	230707–8	Josiah Wedgwood & Sons	Etruria	28	2	237565	John Pratt & Co.	Lane Delph
6	3	230739	John Meir & Son	Tunstall	31	2	237644	Minton & Co.	Stoke
19	8	231101	James Wardle	Hanley					
20	2	231124	Josiah Wedgwood & Sons	Etruria					
21	6	231153–4	George Ash	Hanley					
23	6	231215	Minton & Co.	Stoke					
24	4	231222	W. T. Copeland & Sons	Stoke					
26	4	231241	Leveson Hill (Excrs of)	Stoke					

Date	Parcel No.	Patent No.	Factory, Retailer Wholesaler, etc	Place	Date	Parcel No.	Patent No.	Factory, Retailer Wholesaler, etc	Place
1870					26	5	241960	Minton & Co.	Stoke
Jan 1	5	237691	T. C. Brown–Westhead, Moore & Co.	Hanley	30	15	242077	Geo. Jones	Stoke
					June 3	8	242154	F. & R. Pratt & Co.	Fenton
3	4	237742	Geo. Jones	Stoke	7	15	242233	Hope & Carter	Burslem
7	9	237899	Pellatt & Co.	London	7	16	242234	Thos. Booth	Hanley
15	12	238147–8	Liddle, Elliot & Son	Longport	9	3	242391	T. C. Brown–Westhead, Moore & Co.	Hanley
27	8	238388	Chas. Hobson	Burslem					
29	3	238436	Minton & Co.	Stoke	10	1	242392–4	Wm. Brownfield	Cobridge
Feb 1	6	238527–8	T. C. Brown–Westhead, Moore & Co.	Hanley	11	3	242439	James Edwards & Son	Burslem
					17	7	242503–8	Minton, Hollins & Co.	Stoke
3	13	238595–6	idem	Hanley	22	1	242634–5	Harvey Adams & Co.	Longton
4	7	238603	Powell & Bishop	Hanley	22	3	242637–8	Minton, Hollins & Co.	Stoke
5	5	238627	Wiltshaw, Wood & Co.	Burslem	22	4	242639	The Worcester Royal Porcelain Co. Ltd.	Worcester
7	6	238628	W. & J. A. Bailey	Alloa					
9	2	238663	Josiah Wedgwood & Sons	Etruria	27	1	242715	Geo. Jones	Stoke
10	8	238688	Minton & Co.	Stoke	July 5	5	242859	Baker & Co.	Fenton
11	12	238761–2	W. P. & G. Phillips & Pearce	London	8	7	243049–50	James Wardle	Hanley
					13	8	243176	James Edwards & Son	Burslem
15	6	238898–9	T. C. Brown–Westhead Moore & Co.	Hanley	14	9	243197–9	Minton, Hollins & Co.	Stoke
					14	10	243200	The Worcester Royal Porcelain Co. Ltd.	Worcester
25	2	239139	Minton & Co.	Stoke					
28	6	239239	idem	Stoke	15	1	243207	W. T. Copeland & Sons	Stoke
Mar 2	4	239304	idem	Stoke	16	2	243235	James Wardle	Hanley
7	6	239422	Chas. Hobson	Burslem	19	6	243352	F. & R. Pratt & Co.	Fenton
8	1	239424–6	Geo. Jones	Stoke	20	5	243368	Thos. Booth	Hanley
10	1	239474	idem	Stoke	21	1	243378	idem	Hanley
10	9	239510	Powell & Bishop	Hanley	22	1	243385	Cork, Edge & Malkin	Burslem
11	8	239528	Leveson Hill (Excrs of)	Stoke	27	1	243480	Beech, Unwin & Co.	Longton
14	4	239548	T. C. Brown–Westhead, Moore & Co.	Hanley	Aug 1	2	243555	R. G. Scrivener & Co.	Hanley
					4	4	243646	James Wardle	Hanley
15	6	239585	Thos. Till & Sons	Burslem	4	5	243647–8	J. Broadhurst	Longton
16	2	239590–1	Minton & Co.	Stoke	9	2	243807	Wm. Brownfield	Cobridge
17	4	239610–1	McBirney & Armstrong	Belleek	22	4	244137–8	T. & R. Boote	Burslem
17	7	239622	The Worcester Royal Porcelain Co. (Ltd.)	Worcester	23	6	244173	Geo. Jones	Stoke
					25	5	244223	T. & R. Boote	Burslem
17	9	239628	J. Mortlock	London	Sept 7	7	244703	Bailey & Cooke	Hanley
18	6	239642	Minton & Co.	Stoke	10	9	244741	Minton & Co.	Stoke
23	9	239793–4	J. Blackshaw & Co.	Stoke	16	5	244961	idem	Stoke
25	4	239968	Hope & Carter	Burslem	19	2	244976	Wm. Brownfield	Cobridge
25	5	239969–70	Minton & Co.	Stoke	27	4	245227	Elsmore, Forster & Co.	Tunstall
26	1	240000–1	idem	Stoke	27	6	245229	W. P. & G. Phillips & D. Pearce	London
26	2	240002	Worthington & Son	Hanley					
28	9	240079	The Old Hall Earthenware Co. Ltd.	Hanley	28	11	245265	Gelson Bros.	Hanley
					Oct 4	7	245463	Joseph Holdcroft	Longton
Apr 7	9	240383	Cork, Edge & Malkin	Burslem	4	8	245464	Minton & Co.	Stoke
7	10	240384–5	Baker & Co.	Fenton	6	4	245604	idem	Stoke
7	11	240386	Harvey Adams & Co.	Longton	6	5	245605	James Broadhurst	Longton
9	1	240458	Minton & Co.	Stoke	7	3	245620	Minton & Co.	Stoke
11	3	240493	The Worcester Royal Porcelain Co. Ltd.	Worcester	8	9	245668	Powell & Bishop	Hanley
					19	2	245985–6	Geo. Jones	Stoke
13	4	240516	Thos. Goode & Co.	London	22	2	246149	Wm. Brownfield	Cobridge
14	7	240570	Minton & Co.	Stoke	25	6	246181	T. C. Brown–Westhead, Moore & Co.	Hanley
May 5	1	241231	James Oldham & Co.	Hanley					
6	5	241264–5	McBirney & Armstrong	Belleek	Nov 4	9	246927	idem	Hanley
10	4	241367–8	George Ash	Hanley	9	8	247047	John Meir & Son	Tunstall
13	8	241474	T. C. Brown–Westhead, Moore & Co.	Hanley	9	9	247048	Pellatt & Co.	London
					10	5	247071–3	Minton & Co.	Stoke
17	7	241544	idem	Hanley	10	10	247079–80	Wm. Brownfield	Cobridge
18	6	241567–8	Bates, Elliott & Co.	Longport	12	3	247248	McBirney & Armstrong	Belleek
21	6	241649	The Old Hall Earthenware Co. Ltd.	Hanley	12	8	247255	Minton, Hollins & Co.	Stoke
					22	3	247944	Geo. Jones	Stoke
21	12	241666	James Edwards & Son	Burslem	24	3	248041	Minton & Co.	Stoke
25	7	241754	idem	Burslem	24	8	248049	Bates, Elliott & Co.	Longport

Date	Parcel No.	Patent No.	Factory, Retailer Wholesaler, etc	Place	Date	Parcel No.	Patent No.	Factory, Retailer Wholesaler, etc	Place
25	1	248051	Minton & Co.	Stoke	9	9	252387	Liddle, Elliott & Co.	Longport
25	2	248052	Turner, Goddard & Co.	Tunstall	11	13	252487	Powell & Bishop	Hanley
26	9	248114–6	T. & R. Boote	Burslem	13	6	252503	Elsmore & Forster	Tunstall
Dec 1	7	248242	Wm. Brownfield	Cobridge	22	9	252709	McBirney & Armstrong	Belleek
2	11	248294	T. C. Brown–Westhead,		24	10	252756	John Meir & Son	Tunstall
			Moore & Co.	Hanley	June 2	4	253017	T. C. Brown–Westhead,	
5	4	248309–15	Minton, Hollins & Co.	Stoke				Moore & Co.	Hanley
16	5	248869	Bates, Elliott & Co.	Longport	7	7	253069	Grove & Stark	Longton
17	11	248899	idem	Longport	16	9	253335	John Twigg	Rother'm
19	9	248953	Harvey, Adams & Co.	Longton	17	3	253339–40	Minton & Co.	Stoke
27	4	249104	James Edwards & Son	Burslem	19	9	253378–9	Pinder, Bourne & Co.	Burslem
					22	1	253472	Thos. Till & Sons	Burslem
1871					23	9	253571	Bates, Elliott & Co.	Longport
Jan 2	2	249235	Gelson Bros.	Hanley	July 4	8	253796–8	W. T. Copeland	Stoke
6	3	249331	Minton & Co.	Stoke	14	6	254013	Taylor, Tunnicliffe & Co.	Hanley
7	8	249356	Bates, Elliott & Co.	Longport	15	2	254030	Thos. Booth	Hanley
9	4	249388–93	McBirney & Armstrong	Belleek	19	2	254074	Ambrose Bevington	Hanley
10	7	249439	Geo. Jones	Stoke	22	8	254130–3	Haviland & Co.	London
11	4	249464	J. Mortlock	London					and
12	7	249479	McBirney & Armstrong	Belleek					Limoges
12	12	249490	Soane & Smith	London	25	12	254239	Bates, Elliott & Co.	Longport
24	4	249811	idem	London	29	6	254344	Hope & Carter	Burslem
26	8	249903–6	Minton, Hollins & Co.	Stoke	Aug 2	3	254429	Robinson & Leadbeater	Stoke
27	9	249927	The Worcester Royal		9	7	254757	Bates, Elliott & Co.	Longport
			Porcelain Co. Ltd.	Worcester	18	10	254899	Pratt & Co.	Fenton
30	2	249972	Gelson Bros.	Hanley	28	5	255267	James Wardle	Hanley
Feb 2	3	250020	James Edwards & Son	Burslem	29	2	255274	Geo. Jones	Stoke
6	5	250168–71	McBirney & Armstrong	Belleek	30	4	255320	Thos. Barlow	Longton
8	9	250231	James Macintyre & Co.	Burslem	31	9	255333	J. H. & J. Davis	Hanley
11	9	250291	T. C. Brown–Westhead,		Sept 15	7	255821	J. Bevington & Co.	Hanley
			Moore & Co.	Hanley	15	10	255825	Thos. Barlow	Longton
13	6	250366	Edge, Malkin & Co.	Burslem	19	2	255849	Minton & Co.	Stoke
13	7	250367	Worthington & Son	Hanley	25	8	256079	T. C. Brown–Westhead,	
13	9	250369	Powell & Bishop	Hanley				Moore & Co.	Hanley
13	10	250370	Ed. F. Bodley & Co.	Burslem	28	5	256215	Thos. Booth & Co.	Tunstall
15	7	250416–8	Powell & Bishop	Hanley	Oct 4	7	256357–60	Minton & Co.	Stoke
17	7	250440–1	Thos. Peake	Tunstall	4	9	256362	Pinder, Bourne & Co.	Burslem
20	2	250478–9	Elsmore & Forster	Tunstall	6	6	256427–9	Moore & Son	Longton
28	8	250657	The Watcombe Terra		9	8	256538	E. J. Ridgway & Son	Hanley
			Cotta Clay Co. Ltd.	Devon	10	3	256582	J. T. Hudden	Longton
Mar 9	4	250865	J. & T. Bevington	Hanley	10	6	256586	T. C. Brown–Westhead,	
14	4	250954	John Pratt & Co.	Lane				Moore & Co.	Hanley
				Delph	11	4	256598	McBirney & Armstrong	Belleek
15	10	251013	Bates, Elliott & Co.	Longport	14	6	256687	Thos. Booth & Co.	Tunstall
27	1	251246	Wm. Brownfield & Son	Cobridge	14	7	256688	Josiah Wedgwood & Sons	Etruria
29	1	251329	Thos. Furnival & Son	Cobridge	14	8	256689	McBirney & Armstrong	Belleek
Apr 4	4	251453	McBirney & Armstrong	Belleek	18	4	256853	Moore & Son	Longton
22	4	251966	John Pratt & Co.	Stoke	19	6	256907	W. T. Copeland & Sons	Stoke
24	4	251988	Josiah Wedgwood & Sons	Etruria	24	3	257126	Robert Cooke	Hanley
26	12	252068	Minton, Hollins & Co.	Stoke	31	5	257258	Minton & Co.	Stoke
27	7	252093–4	Wood & Clarke	Burslem	31	6	257259	Edge, Hill & Palmer	Longton
27	8	252095–7	W. P. & G. Phillips &		Nov 3	4	257364–5	R. G. Scrivener & Co.	Hanley
			Pearce	London	3	5	257366	J. F. Wileman	Fenton
28	1	252128	Wood & Clarke	Burslem	15	4	257728	John Thomson & Sons	Glasgow
29	6	252156	idem	Burslem	23	6	257944–6	Thos. Ford	Hanley
29	7	252157	James Edwards & Son	Burslem	Dec 1	6	258095	Geo. Jones	Stoke
May 1	9	252171–3	T. C. Brown–Westhead,		15	5	258773	Robinson & Leadbeater	Stoke
			Moore & Co.	Hanley	16	7	258816	McBirney & Armstrong	Belleek
2	3	252176	Ambrose Bevington	Hanley	22	6	258949	F. & R. Pratt	Fenton
2	4	252177–80	Wm. Brownfield & Son	Cobridge	23	3	258956–7	Geo. Jones	Stoke
3	4	252188	John Jackson & Co.	Rother'm	29	10	259053	T. C. Brown–Westhead,	
6	1	252258	W. P. & G. Phillips &					Moore & Co.	Hanley
			Pearce	London					

Date	Parcel No.	Patent No.	Factory, Retailer Wholesaler, etc	Place
1872				
Jan 1	5	259076	Moore & Son	Longton
1	6	259077	Edge Malkin & Co.	Burslem
5	3	259264	McBirney & Armstrong	Belleek
6	1	259271	Minton & Co.	Stoke
18	6	259801	The Worcester Royal Porcelain Co. Ltd.	Worcester
20	6	259854	Geo. Jones	Stoke
30	7	260081	W. T. Copeland & Sons	Stoke
Feb 2	2	260187	Moore & Son	Longton
2	11	260240–1	Turner & Tomkinson	Tunstall
3	4	260255–6	Geo. Jones	Stoke
7	3	260297	Ambrose Bevington	Hanley
15	3	260463	Powell & Bishop	Hanley
16	6	260503	McBirney & Armstrong	Belleek
16	7	260504–6	Geo. Jones	Stoke
19	6	260565	Wm. H. Goss	Stoke
20	4	260578	The Worcester Royal Porcelain Co. Ltd.	Worcester
22	3	260640	Minton & Co.	Stoke
Mar 4	3	260868	Geo. Jones	Stoke
4	4	260869–70	Minton & Co.	Stoke
4	6	260872	Minton, Hollins & Co.	Stoke
7	7	260992–3	Harvey, Adams & Co.	Longton
7	10	260998	Bates, Elliott & Co.	Burslem
8	5	261006–8	Minton, Hollins & Co.	Stoke
9	1	261016	McBirney & Armstrong	Belleek
13	8	261120	Minton, Hollins & Co.	Stoke
16	6	261190	Minton & Co.	Stoke
18	6	261207	idem	Stoke
20	10	261325	The Worcester Royal Porcelain Co. Ltd.	Worcester
21	14	261379	R. M. Taylor	Fenton
22	5	261391	J. Holdcroft	Longton
22	8	261394	T. C. Brown–Westhead, Moore & Co.	Hanley
26	3	261453–4	Robinson & Leadbeater	Stoke
26	6	261458	Phillips & Pearce	London
Apr 5	4	261638	Wedgwood & Co.	Tunstall
5	5	261639	Minton & Co.	Stoke
6	1	261646–7	J. Holdcroft	Longton
9	6	261724	T. C. Brown–Westhead, Moore & Co.	Hanley
10	11	261749	Thos. Furnival & Son	Cobridge
17	13	261976	E. J. Ridgway & Son	Hanley
19	5	262013	Minton, Hollins & Co.	Stoke
24	5	262203	John Pratt & Co. Ltd.	Lane Delph
27	9	262354	Moore & Son	Longton
May 2	9	262425–6	Harvey Adams & Co.	Longton
2	11	262428–9	Thos. Furnival & Son	Cobridge
3	9	262471–2	Minton & Co.	Stoke
3	11	262474	Bates, Elliott & Co.	Burslem
6	3	262483–5	Moore & Son	Longton
6	8	262493	Bates, Elliott & Co.	Burslem
6	9	262494–5	Minton, Hollins & Co.	Stoke
10	1	262651	Moore & Son	Longton
11	4	262672	Thos. Booth & Sons	Hanley
27	1	262951	Geo. Jones	Stoke
27	3	262953	Minton, Hollins & Co.	Stoke
29	2	262990	Geo. Jones	Stoke
29	5	262993–4	Geo. Grainger & Co.	Worcester
30	1	262999–3000	Minton & Co.	Stoke
June 3	6	263106	The Watcombe Terra Cotta Clay Co. Ltd.	Devon
5	3	263134	Hope & Carter	Burslem
6	6	263162	Wm. Brownfield & Son	Cobridge
7	4	263191	Minton, Hollins & Co.	Stoke
11	5	263315	Josiah Wedgwood & Sons	Etruria
11	12	263348	W. T. Copeland & Sons	Stoke
18	3	263496–7	Geo. L. Ashworth & Bros.	Hanley
18	4	263498–9	Minton, Hollins & Co.	Stoke
21	7	263541–2	idem	Stoke
22	5	263561	Minton & Co.	Stoke
22	8	263565	Wm. Brownfield & Son	Cobridge
27	1	263771	T. C. Brown–Westhead, Moore & Co.	Hanley
July 2	2	263883–4	Robinson & Leadbeater	Stoke
2	3	263885	Josiah Wedgwood & Sons	Etruria
13	5	264081	Gelson Bros.	Hanley
15	4	264194	Robinson & Leadbeater	Stoke
16	5	264206–7	Minton, Hollins & Co.	Stoke
19	5	264299–303	R. M. Taylor	Fenton
20	3	264306–7	Geo. Jones	Stoke
24	2	264490	W. & T. Adams	Tunstall
29	7	264613	J. Dimmock & Co.	Hanley
31	3	264636–7	Minton & Co.	Stoke
Aug 2	1	264685–6	E. J. Ridgway & Son	Stoke
14	4	265105	T. Booth & Co.	Tunstall
16	1	265167–8	Wm. Brownfield & Sons	Cobridge
19	4	265254	W. E. Cartlidge	Hanley
19	5	265255	W. & J. A. Bailey	Alloa
Sept 2	3	265666	McBirney & Armstrong	Belleek
2	8	265687	Bates, Elliott & Co.	Burslem
12	6	265969	Minton, Hollins & Co.	Stoke
25	9	266628–31	Minton, Hollins & Co.	Stoke
26	2	266633	F. Jones	Longton
26	5	266636	W. E. Cartlidge	Hanley
Oct 7	7	266959	T. C. Brown–Westhead, Moore & Co.	Hanley
11	5	267060–4	Josiah Wedgwood & Sons	Etruria
12	10	267103–4	Bates, Elliott & Co.	Burslem
14	4	267112	Minton, Hollins & Co.	Stoke
17	8	267265	Josiah Wedgwood & Sons	Etruria
18	5	267317–9	Geo. Jones	Stoke
30	2	267523	J. F. Wileman	Fenton
30	5	267527	The Brownhills Pottery	Tunstall
30	9	267534	Maw & Co.	Broseley
Nov 2	6	267588–91	The Worcester Royal Porcelain Co. Ltd.	Worcester
4	3	267618	Geo. Grainger & Co.	Worcester
11	2	267806	W. E. Cartlidge	Hanley
12	4	267839	Minton & Co.	Stoke
14	13	267893–5	Wm. Brownfield & Son	Cobridge
14	14	267896	Moore Bros.	Longton
18	3	267972	Holland & Green	Longton
30	8	268309	Belfield & Co.	Prestonpans
Dec 2	5	268322	T. C. Brown–Westhead, Moore & Co.	Hanley
4	3	268388	John Pratt & Co. Ltd.	Lane Delph
10	2	268724–5	Minton & Co.	Stoke
11	8	268748–9	The Old Hall Earthenware Co. Ltd.	Hanley

Date	Parcel No.	Patent No.	Factory, Retailer Wholesaler, etc	Place	Date	Parcel No.	Patent No.	Factory, Retailer Wholesaler, etc	Place
14	5	268806–7	Wm. Brownfield & Son	Cobridge	27	1	275600	The Worcester Royal Porcelain Co. Ltd.	Worcester
24	1	269197	Cockson & Chetwynd	Cobridge	30	2	275661	T. C. Brown–Westhead, Moore & Co.	Hanley
27	4	269269	John Adams (Excrs of)	Longton	Sept 2	8	275755	Edge, Malkin & Co.	Burslem
27	5	269270	R. G. Scrivener & Co.	Hanley	4	3	275816	Mintons	Stoke
27	8	269275	John Meir & Son	Tunstall	10	7	275994	Powell & Bishop	Hanley
1873					15	3	276151	T. C. Brown–Westhead, Moore & Co.	Hanley
Jan 10	1	269585	Geo. Jones	Stoke	16	4	276159	idem	Hanley
13	4	269621	W. T. Copeland & Sons	Stoke	17	8	276213	The Worcester Royal Porcelain Co. Ltd.	Worcester
14	8	269686	J. Defries	London	19	4	276338	T. C. Brown–Westhead, Moore & Co.	Hanley
15	2	269690	Worthington & Son	Hanley	25	8	276517	Harvey, Adams & Co.	Longton
29	1	269993–70001	Minton, Hollins & Co.	Stoke	25	10	276522	Jane Beech	Burslem
29	2	270002–4	Moore Bros.	Longton	29	2	276566	Wm. Brownfield & Son	Cobridge
Feb 1	1	270042–50	Minton, Hollins & Co.	Stoke	Oct 4	3	276796–8	Moore Bros.	Longton
10	2	270298	W. & J. A. Bailey	Alloa	4	4	276799	Heath & Blackhurst	Burslem
12	4	270354	Bates, Elliott & Co.	Burslem	6	6	276816–7	T. C. Brown–Westhead, Moore & Co.	Hanley
15	1	270385	Minton & Co.	Stoke	11	6	277136	Mintons	Stoke
19	14	270600–1	J. & T. Bevington	Hanley	13	3	277148–9	Geo. Jones	Stoke
25	6	270700	Geo. Jones	Stoke	22	6	277385	Mintons	Stoke
27	4	270751	Thos. Till & Sons	Burslem	Nov 3	3	277844	Hope & Carter	Burslem
27	8	270755	Minton, Hollins & Co.	Stoke	3	4	277845–7	Geo. Jones	Stoke
Mar 6	1	271031–2	Minton & Co.	Stoke	6	6	277969	Wedgwood & Co.	Tunstall
6	9	271057	The Brownhills Pottery Co.	Tunstall	10	7	278169	T. C. Brown–Westhead, Moore & Co.	Hanley
26	6	271561–2	Geo. Jones	Stoke	12	3	278185	Worthington & Son	Hanley
Apr 3	6	271851	Minton & Co.	Stoke	Dec 2	6	278769–70	Taylor, Tunnicliffe & Co.	Hanley
15	4	272091	Taylor, Tunnicliffe & Co.	Hanley	4	6	278821	The Old Hall Earthenware Co. Ltd.	Hanley
19	2	272206	Minton & Co.	Stoke	5	1	278822	Harvey, Adams & Co.	Longton
23	6	272293	Gelson Bros.	Hanley	5	8	278867	Wm. Brownfield & Son	Cobridge
28	5	272364–5	Powell & Bishop	Hanley	10	12	279180	Geo. Jones & Sons	Stoke
29	3	272384–5	Geo. Jones	Stoke	27	7	279437	idem	Stoke
May 3	2	272637	Thos. Till & Sons	Burslem	**1874**				
3	7	272642–6	Wm. Brownfield & Son	Cobridge	Jan 1	3	279476–7	Bates, Elliott & Co.	Burslem
3	8	272647–8	Minton & Co.	Stoke	10	15	279655–6	Davenports & Co.	London (and Longport)
6	2	272662	idem	Stoke	20	3	279938	Powell & Bishop	Hanley
12	8	272835	T. C. Brown–Westhead, Moore & Co.	Hanley	21	7	279964	W. T. Copeland & Sons	Stoke
14	7	272896–7	Moore Bros.	Longton	23	5	280010	John Meir & Son	Tunstall
16	6	272983	Minton, Hollins & Co.	Stoke	30	4	280153–6	Haviland & Co.	Limoges and London
17	4	272988–90	John L. Johnson & Co.	Longton	Feb 9	4	280343	The Worcester Royal Porcelain Co. Ltd.	Worcester
22	5	273089	Worthington & Son	Hanley	9	5	280344	Bodley & Co.	Burslem
26	7	273158–9	Moore Bros.	Longton	11	2	280350	Thos. Booth & Sons	Hanley
26	8	273160	Soane & Smith	London	14	9	280492	Worthington & Son	Hanley
29	4	273246	Worthington & Son	Hanley	19	1	280609	Geo. Jones & Sons	Stoke
29	8	273251	Thos. Ford	Hanley	25	6	280785	Robinson & Leadbeater	Stoke
30	15	273376	T. C. Brown–Westhead, Moore & Co.	Hanley	25	7	280786	Geo. Jones & Sons	Stoke
June 11	4	273662–3	Bates, Elliott & Co.	Burslem	26	7	280802–4	Minton, Hollins & Co.	Stoke
17	3	273736–7	Taylor, Tunnicliffe & Co.	Hanley	Mar 2	1	280853	McBirney & Armstrong	Belleek
19	3	273804	Pinder & Bourne & Co.	Burslem	3	4	280907	Geo. Jones & Sons	Stoke
28	4	274047	Thos. Goode & Co.	London	4	3	280919	Mintons	Stoke
30	3	274054–5	Minton, Hollins & Co.	Stoke	4	8	280925	The Worcester Royal Porcelain Co. Ltd.	Worcester
July 3	9	274162	Minton, Hollins & Co.	Stoke					
4	7	274183	T. C. Brown–Westhead, Moore & Co.	Hanley					
28	2	274663	Chas. Hobson	Burslem					
28	8	274701	John Meir & Sons	Tunstall					
29	3	274704	McBirney & Armstrong	Belleek					
31	1	274725–6	Mintons	Stoke					
Aug 5	2	274804	Baker & Chetwynd	Burslem					
14	10	275050	T. C. Brown–Westhead, Moore & Co.	Hanley					
25	1	275514–5	Geo. Jones	Stoke					

Date	Parcel No.	Patent No.	Factory, Retailer Wholesaler, etc	Place
13	6	281106	J. Dimmock & Co.	Hanley
14	2	281129	Mintons	Stoke
17	5	281190	Powell & Bishop	Hanley
21	5	281301	idem	Hanley
24	4	281319	Mintons	Stoke
27	2	281404	Worthington & Son	Hanley
28	3	281429–30	Geo. Jones & Sons	Stoke
30	1	281437	Worthington & Son	Hanley
Apr 7	4	281639	The Worcester Royal Porcelain Co. Ltd.	Worcester
14	4	281776	A. Bevington	Hanley
15	7	281822	Mintons	Stoke
20	7	281871–80	Minton, Hollins & Co.	Stoke
21	8	281899	Geo. Jones & Sons	Stoke
22	1	281902	Wm. Brownfield & Son	Cobridge
23	8	281954	T. C. Brown–Westhead, Moore & Co.	Hanley
25	2	281984	Geo. Jones & Sons	Stoke
29	7	282088	Ridgway, Sparks & Ridgway	Hanley
29	9	282091	T. Furnival & Son	Cobridge
30	2	282098	Thos. Booth & Sons	Hanley
May 5	3	282134	Bates, Elliott & Co.	Burslem
9	3	282218–9	Geo. Jones & Sons	Stoke
11	2	282249–51	Moore Bros.	Longton
11	3	282252	J. Thomson & Sons	Glasgow
11	4	282253	Holland & Green	Longton
20	11	282497	Bates, Elliott & Co.	Burslem
21	5	282526	Mintons	Stoke
22	8	282555	idem	Stoke
23	4	282567–8	Geo. Jones & Sons	Stoke
June 1	7	282662	The Worcester Royal Porcelain Co. Ltd.	Worcester
6	2	282799–802	Wm. Brownfield & Son	Cobridge
6	5	282806	Chas. Ford	Hanley
16	6	282982	Cockson & Chetwynd	Cobridge
17	7	283041	Edge, Malkin & Co.	Burslem
18	1	283050	Mintons	Stoke
23	3	283201	Williamson & Son	Longton
23	7	283208	The Worcester Royal Porcelain Co. Ltd.	Worcester
25	5	283266–8	Thos. Ford	Hanley
26	4	283275	Pinder, Bourne & Co.	Burslem
July 10	2	283547	Mintons	Stoke
13	6	283570–1	T. C. Brown–Westhead, Moore & Co.	Hanley
27	1	283980	Hulse & Adderley	Longton
30	5	284053	Minton, Hollins & Co.	Stoke
Aug 1	8	284131–5	Mintons	Stoke
1	9	284136	Cockson & Chetwynd	Cobridge
6	7	284204	T. C. Brown–Westhead, Moore & Co.	Hanley
8	2	284254–5	Wm. Brownfield & Son	Cobridge
15	4	284417	Bates, Elliott & Co.	Burlsem
22	6	284562	J. T. Hudden	Longton
28	4	284699–700	Geo. Jones & Sons	Stoke
31	6	284779	T. J. & J. Emberton	Tunstall
Sept 1	3	284791	Thos. Till & Sons	Burslem
3	11	284883	Geo. Adler	Saxony and London

Date	Parcel No.	Patent No.	Factory, Retailer Wholesaler, etc	Place
3	12	284884–5	Cockson & Chetwynd	Cobridge
4	3	284897	Mintons	Stoke
5	4	284916–7	The Worcester Royal Porcelain Co. Ltd.	Worcester
5	7	284920	Furnival & Son	Cobridge
7	3	284936–7	Thos. Booth & Sons	Hanley
10	3	285013	Wm. Brownfield & Son	Cobridge
12	1	285181	Mintons	Stoke
15	2	285281	Geo. Jones & Sons	Stoke
16	7	285304	M. Bucholz	London
17	4	285322	R. Britton & Sons	Leeds
30	4	285776	Wm. Brownfield & Son	Cobridge
Oct 2	5	285826–8	Geo. Grainger & Co.	Worcester
3	4	285841–4	Moore Bros.	Longton
6	3	286000	Mintons	Stoke
6	4	286001	Grove & Stark	Longton
10	4	286134	Mintons	Stoke
12	2	286171	Powell & Bishop	Hanley
17	8	286359–60	Bates, Elliott & Co.	Burslem
21	8	286424	Geo. Jones & Sons	Stoke
24	3	286504–5	Robinson & Leadbeater	Stoke
27	1	286530	George Ash	Hanley
28	9	286563	Pinder, Bourne & Co.	Burslem
Nov 2	3	286715	James Edwards & Son	Burslem
3	4	286720–2	W. & E. Corn	Burslem
6	3	286759	Wm. Brownfield & Son	Cobridge
7	4	286774–80	Thos. Ford	Hanley
10	3	286794	Geo. Jones & Sons	Stoke
12	3	286931	Mintons	Stoke
12	12	286942	Bates, Elliott & Co.	Burslem
20	12	287317	F. & R. Pratt & Co.	Fenton
25	7	287438–9	Minton, Hollins & Co.	Stoke
Dec 1	5	287598	W. T. Copeland & Sons	Stoke
4	6	287638	Thos. Barlow	Longton
5	4	287676	Holmes & Plant	Burslem
7	8	287694–7	T. C. Brown–Westhead, Moore & Co.	Hanley
8	2	287699	Geo. Jones & Sons	Stoke
10	4	287731	Pinder, Bourne & Co.	Burslem
10	11	287752–6	The Worcester Royal Porcelain Co. Ltd.	Worcester
12	3	287776	Geo. Jones & Sons	Stoke
12	5	287785	Port Dundas Pottery Co.	Port Dundas
18	6	287982	Geo. Jones & Sons	Stoke
18	7	287983	Ambrose Bevington	Hanley
18	9	287985	Geo. Grainger & Co.	Worcester
18	11	287990–7	Minton, Hollins & Co.	Stoke
1875				
Jan 2	4	288241–2	T. C. Brown–Westhead, Moore & Co.	Hanley
6	3	288276–8	Minton, Hollins & Co.	Stoke
12	3	288366	The Worcester Royal Porcelain Co. Ltd.	Worcester
16	9	288502	The Brownhills Pottery Co.	Tunstall
18	8	288521	T. C. Brown–Westhead, Moore & Co.	Hanley
20	3	288552	Robinson & Leadbeater	Stoke
20	4	288553–6	Wm. Brownfield & Son	Cobridge
21	2	288682	Geo. Jones & Sons	Stoke
23	9	288755–8	T. C. Brown–Westhead, Moore & Co.	Hanley

Date	Parcel No.	Patent No.	Factory, Retailer Wholesaler, etc	Place
28	5	288830	Mintons	Stoke
29	1	288861-2	Worthington & Son	Hanley
Feb 3	7	288972	Chas. Ford	Hanley
5	5	289076	T. & R. Boote	Burslem
6	2	289083	Moore Bros.	Longton
9	1	289172	Pinder, Bourne & Co.	Burslem
9	2	289173	Geo. Jones & Sons	Stoke
12	6	289280	J. Maddock & Sons	Burslem
15	2	289310	Moore Bros.	Longton
17	7	289334	Mintons	Stoke
23	5	289503	J. Maddock & Sons	Burslem
23	6	289504	Geo. Jones & Sons	Stoke
23	8	289507-8	George Ash	Hanley
24	3	289535	Stephen Clive	Tunstall
Mar 5	2	289769	Wm. Brownfield & Son	Cobridge
12	5	289874-6	Geo. Jones & Sons	Stoke
24	13	290153	Minton, Hollins & Co.	Stoke
24	14	290154-5	T. C. Brown–Westhead, Moore & Co.	Hanley
30	1	290186	Thos. Booth & Sons	Hanley
31	5	290209-10	Wm. Brownfield & Son	Cobridge
Apr 3	7	290259	J. Dimmock & Co.	Hanley
3	9	290261-2	E. F. Bodley & Son	Burslem
7	3	290352	Mintons	Stoke
9	6	290393-4	Wm. Brownfield & Son	Cobridge
10	7	290407-8	Powell & Bishop	Hanley
15	5	290500	R. Malkin	Fenton
17	1	290738	Pinder, Bourne & Co.	Burslem
20	1	290787	J. Dimmock & Co.	Hanley
20	2	290788	Mintons	Stoke
21	5	290812	Stephen Clive	Tunstall
22	3	290841-2	W. P. & G. Phillips	London
22	4	290843-6	Minton, Hollins & Co.	Stoke
May 3	8	290998	Soane & Smith	London
7	7	291109	Geo. Jones & Sons	Stoke
7	8	291110	Burgess & Leigh	Burslem
11	6	291229	Thos. Goode & Co.	London
20	1	291440	Bates, Elliott & Co.	Burslem
20	3	291444	J. Dimmock & Co.	Hanley
22	1	291458	Holland & Green	Longton
26	6	291518-20	T. C. Brown–Westhead, Moore & Co.	Hanley
28	10	291556	Campbellfield Pottery Co.	Glasgow
28	12	291558	J. Mortlock	London
31	8	291568	Geo. Jones & Sons	Stoke
31	18	291611	Ridgway, Sparks & Ridgway	Hanley
June 2	9	291749-51	Minton, Hollins & Co.	Stoke
5	7	291870-1	W. P. & G. Phillips	London
7	3	291882	W. & T. Adams	Tunstall
8	4	291911	The Worcester Royal Porcelain Co. (Ltd.)	Worcester
10	6	292005	Wm. Brownfield & Son	Cobridge
12	5	292034	Chas. Stevenson	Greenock
12	6	292035	Maddock & Gater	Burslem
12	10	292042	Thos. Furnival & Son	Stoke
15	5	292080	Josiah Wedgwood & Sons	Etruria
19	6	292184	Thos. Till & Sons	Burslem
26	2	292367-70	Geo. Jones & Sons	Stoke
July 5	1	292542	Wm. Brownfield & Son	Cobridge
7	8	292579-80	Moore Bros.	Longton
8	5	292620	idem	Longton
20	4	292985	E. J. D. Bodley	Burslem
23	10	293035	T. C. Brown–Westhead, Moore & Co.	Hanley
27	5	293114	F. W. Grove & J. Stark	Longton
28	7	293129	Minton, Hollins & Co.	Stoke
Aug 19	7	293748	F. W. Grove & J. Stark	Longton
28	6	294038-9	W. P. & G. Phillips	London
Sept 2	3	294147	T. Elsmore & Son	Tunstall
13	2	294434-5	Geo. Jones & Sons	Stoke
14	9	294514	Minton, Hollins & Co.	Stoke
18	2	294571-2	Geo. Jones & Sons	Stoke
21	1	294595	R. Cochran & Co.	Glasgow
24	2	294657	H. Aynsley & Co.	Longton
25	3	294662	F. W. Grove & J. Stark	Longton
28	6	294768-9	T. C. Brown–Westhead, Moore & Co.	Hanley
30	4	294825-7	John Edwards	Fenton
Oct 2	6	294906	Josiah Wedgwood & Sons	Etruria
6	4	294936	R. Cooke	Hanley
11	4	295001	Powell & Bishop	Hanley
11	10	295014-5	The Brownhills Pottery Co.	Tunstall
16	8	295131	Burgess, Leigh & Co.	Burslem
28	3	295443	Minton, Hollins & Co.	Stoke
30	9	295473-4	W. P. & G. Phillips	London
Nov 5	3	295551-3	Geo. Jones & Sons	Stoke
8	4	295792-8	Minton, Hollins & Co.	Stoke
8	8	295803	W. T. Copeland & Sons	Stoke
12	1	295908	Geo. Jones & Sons	Stoke
12	2	295909	Burgess, Leigh & Co.	Burslem
13	8	295933	The Worcester Royal Porcelain Co. Ltd.	Worcester
Dec 1	2	296475	Wm. Brownfield & Son	Cobridge
1	9	296508	Gelson Bros.	Hanley
3	4	296531	Geo. Jones & Sons	Stoke
6	8	296644	John Meir & Son	Tunstall
10	3	296770	Mintons	Stoke
11	5	296813	F. W. Grove & J. Stark	Longton
11	8	296818	Soane & Smith	London
13	8	296834-49	Minton, Hollins & Co.	Stoke
15	2	296939-40	Mintons China Works	Stoke
15	3	296941-5	Mintons	Stoke
24	4	297217-8	Chas. Ford	Hanley
24	6	297221	Bates, Walker & Co.	Burslem
29	5	297245	Edge, Malkin & Co.	Burslem
29	6	297246-7	T. C. Brown–Westhead, Moore & Co.	Hanley
30	2	297250	Mintons	Stoke
30	8	297276	Mintons, Hollins & Co.	Stoke
1876				
Jan 4	4	297343	Mintons	Stoke
6	2	297471	Moore Bros.	Longton
11	7	297587	E. J. D. Bodley	Burslem
21	13	297791	Bale & Co.	Etruria
22	6	297809-11	Geo. Jones & Sons	Stoke
22	8	297813	Chas. Ford	Hanley
24	1	297817	Mintons	Stoke
24	4	297845	J. Friedrich	London
24	6	297863-4	Bates, Walker & Co.	Burslem
26	2	297977	Edge, Malkin & Co.	Burslem
26	3	297978	Powell & Bishop	Hanley
28	8	298018	James Edwards & Son	Burslem
29	3	298027-9	Wm. Brownfield & Son	Cobridge
Feb 1	2	298049	idem	Cobridge

Date	Parcel No.	Patent No.	Factory, Retailer Wholesaler, etc	Place	Date	Parcel No.	Patent No.	Factory, Retailer Wholesaler, etc	Place
2	7	298063	Josiah Wedgwood & Sons	Etruria	5	1	301619	Thos. Till & Sons	Burslem
2	12	298069	Ridgway, Sparks & Ridgway	Hanley	5	7	301641	W. T. Copeland & Sons	Stoke
3	5	298077	Powell & Bishop	Hanley	10	3	301877	Thos. Gelson & Co.	Hanley
4	6	298103	Mintons	Stoke	12	2	301926	E. J. D. Bodley	Burslem
4	12	298141–2	The Worcester Royal Porcelain Co. Ltd.	Worcester	18	3	301984	Soane & Smith	London
8	9	298235	Bates, Walker & Co.	Burslem	26	3	302125	Geo. Jones & Sons	Stoke
19	5	298458	Geo. Jones & Sons	Stoke	28	10	302178	Thos. Gelson & Co.	Hanley
21	4	298473	The Worcester Royal Porcelain Co. Ltd.	Worcester	28	11	302179	Powell & Bishop	Hanley
					31	8	302220	G. Grainger & Co.	Worcester
22	3	298480–3	Minton, Hollins & Co.	Stoke	Aug 8	1	302384	Robinson & Chapman	Longton
29	9	298693	J. Dimmock & Co.	Hanley	25	8	302901	F. & R. Pratt & Co.	Fenton
Mar 2	8	298821–4	T. Gelson & Co.	Hanley	Sept 5	5	303289–90	Bates & Walker & Co.	Burslem
2	11	298832	The Brownhills Pottery Co.	Tunstall	6	9	303308	Pinder & Bourne & Co.	Burslem
10	8	299076–8	Minton, Hollins & Co.	Stoke	6	10	303309	Wm. Brownfield & Sons	Cobridge
14	5	299177	T. C. Brown–Westhead, Moore & Co.	Hanley	9	8	303455	Worthington & Son	Hanley
					9	9	303456–7	T. C. Brown–Westhead, Moore & Co.	Hanley
17	5	299236	Mintons	Stoke	11	1	303459	E. J. D. Bodley	Burslem
18	3	299246	Robinson & Chapman	Longton	12	6	303522–3	Geo. Jones & Sons	Stoke
23	8	299366	E. J. D. Bodley	Burslem	18	10	303677	G. L. Ashworth & Bros.	Hanley
24	7	299380	Bates, Walker & Co.	Burslem	20	3	303731–2	Hollinshead & Kirkham	Burslem
28	8	299474	W. E. Withinshaw	Burslem	22	3	303757	Powell & Bishop	Hanley
30	4	299497–9	Geo. Jones & Sons	Stoke	26	5	303853	Hope & Carter	Burslem
Apr 8	6	299773	Bates, Walker & Co.	Burslem	26	10	303918	T. C. Brown–Westhead, Moore & Co.	Hanley
11	4	299819	Thos. Gelson & Co.	Hanley	28	2	303926–7	Moore Bros.	Longton
12	4	299830	Powell & Bishop	Hanley	28	10	303942	Hope & Carter	Burslem
12	11	299852	J. Dimmock & Co.	Hanley	Oct 7	2	304128	Wm. Harrop	Hanley
21	7	300020	Minton, Hollins & Co.	Stoke	7	3	304129–31	Wm. Brownfield & Sons	Cobridge
21	10	300037–8	Furnival & Son	Cobridge	7	4	304132–3	Josiah Wedgwood & Sons	Etruria
22	5	300105	The Worcester Royal Porcelain Co. Ltd.	Worcester	7	6	304144–5	Wm. Adams	Tunstall
					9	1	304149–50	Geo. Jones & Sons	Stoke
27	3	300260	Mintons	Stoke	12	8	304321	Ambrose Bevington	Hanley
May 8	7	300421–3	T. C. Brown–Westhead, Moore & Co.	Hanley	17	4	304376	T. C. Brown–Westhead, Moore & Co.	Hanley
10	3	300463	Geo. Jones & Sons	Stoke	17	9	304383	Wardle & Co.	Hanley
11	9	300491	F. & R. Pratt & Co.	Fenton	19	3	304428	Burgess, Leigh & Co.	Burslem
16	7	300603–4	Mintons	Stoke	20	2	304454–66	Mintons	Stoke
22	3	300682	Moore Bros.	Longton	21	3	304473	Edge, Malkin & Co.	Burslem
22	4	300683–5	Josiah Wedgwood & Sons	Etruria	23	2	304489	Mintons	Stoke
23	7	300734–7	Haviland & Co.	Limoges and London	31	2	304910–4	Wm. Brownfield & Sons	Cobridge
					Nov 1	2	304926	Moore Bros.	Longton
					7	3	305065	Robert Jones	Hanley
24	3	300746	Mintons	Stoke	8	3	305080	Geo. Jones & Sons	Stoke
25	6	300779	Moore Bros.	Longton	8	9	305090	Wm. Brownfield & Sons	Cobridge
29	8	300809–10	Geo. Jones & Sons	Stoke	9	10	305150	Belfield & Co.	Preston-pans
June 3	2	301030	Mintons	Stoke	11	9	305173	Moore Bros.	Longton
3	5	301035–7	E. J. D. Bodley	Burslem	13	3	305181	Mintons	Stoke
7	1	301087	Thos. Gelson & Co.	Hanley	14	2	305189	Josiah Wedgwood & Sons	Etruria
8	4	301099	Mintons	Stoke	14	8	305195	Clementson Bros.	Hanley
9	6	301164	W. T. Copeland & Sons	Stoke	17	3	305222	Banks & Thorley	Hanley
15	1	301254	Henry Meir & Son	Tunstall	18	3	305233	Minton, Hollins & Co.	Stoke
15	9	301267–9	Minton, Hollins & Co.	Stoke	18	7	305264	Minton, Hollins & Co.	Stoke
19	2	301302	Josiah Wedgwood & Sons	Etruria	18	9	305266	The Worcester Royal Porcelain Co. Ltd.	Worcester
19	9	301310	J. Holdcroft	Longton					
21	4	301330	Mintons	Stoke	23	5	305312	Wm. Adams	Tunstall
22	4	301342	Thos. Gelson & Co.	Hanley	24	15	305461–2	Thos. Furnival & Sons	Cobridge
23	5	301402	Mintons	Stoke	28	2	305510	W. Hudson & Son	Longton
26	6	301443–4	Minton, Hollins & Co.	Stoke	29	11	305568	Thos. Furnival & Sons	Cobridge
28	8	301543	J. Aynsley	Longton	Dec 5	2	305684	Wedgwood & Co.	Tunstall
July 1	3	301589–90	Mintons	Stoke	11	2	305829	John Tams	Longton
1	4	301591	John Tams	Longton	12	11	305885	The Campbell Brick & Tile Co.	Stoke
3	2	301596	Ford & Challinor	Tunstall					

Date	Parcel No.	Patent No.	Factory, Retailer Wholesaler, etc	Place
14	1	305934	Harvey Adams & Co.	Longton
14	11	305973	J. Dimmock & Co.	Hanley
18	9	306100	James Beech	Longton
20	7	306184	J. & T. Bevington	Hanley
21	2	306202	F. W. Grove & J. Stark	Longton
23	5	306282	Chas. Ford	Hanley
27	15	306341	The Campbell Brick & Tile Co.	Stoke
28	6	306367	Harvey Adams & Co.	Longton
1877				
Jan 4	10	306564	The Campbellfield Pottery Co.	Glasgow
17	5	306953	The Worcester Royal Porcelain Co. Ltd.	Worcester
20	2	307028	F. W. Grove & J. Stark	Longton
24	10	307213	Wm. Brownfield & Sons	Cobridge
25	6	307236	Wood & Co.	Burslem
25	7	307237–9	Geo. Jones & Sons	Stoke
26	3	307258	Mintons	Stoke
26	4	307259	Powell & Bishop	Hanley
Feb 1	6	307432	James Edwards & Son	Burslem
2	7	307495–7	The Worcester Royal Porcelain Co. Ltd.	Worcester
3	4	307506–7	Minton, Hollins & Co.	Stoke
5	2	307525–7	McBirney & Armstrong	Belleek
7	3	307551	Holland & Green	Longton
7	7	307570–2	Wm. Brownfield & Sons	Cobridge
9	7	307603	Robinson & Co.	Longton
9	11	307613	T. C. Brown–Westhead, Moore & Co.	Hanley
12	3	307646	James Beech	Longton
14	16	307782	The Worcester Royal Porcelain Co. Ltd.	Worcester
15	10	307794	Minton, Hollins & Co.	Stoke
16	9	307866	John Rose & Co.	Coalport
19	2	307877	Wm. Brownfield & Sons	Cobridge
20	8	307892	G. Grainger & Co.	Worcester
21	6	307906	Mintons	Stoke
21	9	307909	W. T. Copeland & Sons	Stoke
24	3	307983	Thos. Hughes	Burslem
27	2	308010	Mintons	Stoke
Mar 1	4	308116–21	Hallam, Johnson & Co.	Longton
8	14	308329	W. T. Copeland & Sons	Stoke
10	7	308357	Geo. Jones & Sons	Stoke
14	9	308493	The Campbell Brick & Tile Co.	Stoke
20	3	308650–2	Clementson Bros.	Hanley
20	8	308662	J. Dimmock & Co.	Hanley
22	14	308718	E. J. D. Bodley	Burslem
24	1	308781–2	Powell & Bishop	Hanley
31	7	308916	E. F. Bodley & Co.	Burslem
Apr 3	1	308918	Powell & Bishop	Hanley
4	5	308932	J. Mortlock	London
5	2	308934	Ford, Challinor & Co.	Tunstall
12	11	309233	J. Dimmock & Co.	Hanley
23	4	309617	John Tams	Longton
26	2	309680	J. & T. Bevington	Hanley
26	7	309696	The Worcester Royal Porcelain Co. Ltd.	Worcester
27	10	309746	John Rose & Co.	Coalport
May 2	2	309818–21	Geo. Jones & Sons	Stoke

Date	Parcel No.	Patent No.	Factory, Retailer Wholesaler, etc	Place
4	13	309917	The Old Hall Earthenware Co. Ltd.	Hanley
5	4	309922	Josiah Wedgwood & Sons	Etruria
12	7	310034	Thos. Furnival & Sons	Cobridge
16	5	310175	Wm. Brownfield & Sons	Cobridge
18	6	310267	Josiah Wedgwood & Sons	Etruria
22	5	310359–61	Wm. Brownfield & Sons	Cobridge
24	8	310448	T. C. Brown–Westhead, Moore & Co.	Hanley
30	13	310556	T. Furnival & Sons	Cobridge
June 1	2	310599	J. & R. Hammersley	Hanley
5	6	310670	E. J. D. Bodley	Burslem
7	1	310709	idem	Burslem
7	2	310710	Joseph Holdcroft	Longton
8	7	310761–4	Minton, Hollins & Co.	Stoke
9	3	310775–6	Baker & Co.	Fenton
13	2	310909	idem	Fenton
15	7	310972	Ridgway, Sparks & Ridgway	Hanley
19	4	311031	Ford & Challinor	Tunstall
19	6	311033	Murray & Co.	Glasgow
22	3	311141	Walker & Carter	Stoke
22	13	311181–6	Steele & Wood	Stoke
22	14	311187	E. F. Bodley & Co.	Burslem
26	11	311366	T. Furnival & Sons	Cobridge
28	9	311423	idem	Cobridge
29	10	311448–9	Sherwin & Cotton	Hanley
July 2	3	311523	W. T. Copeland & Sons	Stoke
6	2	311626	Mintons	Stoke
7	4	311684	Ridge, Meigh & Co.	Longton
9	2	311711	Minton, Hollins & Co.	Stoke
14	2	311883–4	John Tams	Longton
17	9	312019–21	James Edwards & Son	Burslem
20	7	312062–4	Haviland & Co.	London and Limoges
20	15	312113	Taylor, Tunnicliffe & Co.	Hanley
23	2	312125	John Edwards	Fenton
25	5	312187	Ford, Challinor & Co.	Tunstall
26	6	312311–4	Minton, Hollins & Co.	Stoke
31	1	312421	McBirney & Armstrong	Belleek
31	2	312422	Minton & Hollins & Co.	Stoke
Aug 1	4	312434	Holmes, Stonier & Hollinshead	Hanley
3	14	312521	The Campbell Brick & Tile Co.	Stoke
13	5	312909	Haviland & Co.	London and Limoges
15	7	313009	The Campbell Brick & Tile Co.	Stoke
17	11	313080	Ridgway, Sparks & Ridgway	Stoke
18	6	313099–101	Minton, Hollins & Co.	Stoke
18	7	313102	Furnival & Son	Cobridge
23	6	313280	W. Hudson & Son	Longton
25	2	313324	Wm. Wood & Co.	Burslem
25	3	313325–9	Minton, Hollins & Co.	Stoke
28	9	313381	T. C. Brown–Westhead, Moore & Co.	Hanley
Sept 11	3	314046	G. W. Turner & Sons	Tunstall
19	5	314292	Minton, Hollins & Co.	Stoke

Date	Parcel No.	Patent No.	Factory, Retailer Wholesaler, etc	Place
20	3	314385	Josiah Wedgwood & Sons	Etruria
22	7	314470-1	Mintons	Stoke
22	13	314480	Minton, Hollins & Co.	Stoke
25	5	314548	Mintons	Stoke
28	9	314675	J. Holdcroft	Longton
Oct 2	7	314890	Bates, Walker & Co.	Burslem
3	2	314896	Robinson & Leadbeater	Stoke
4	4	314906-7	J. & T. Bevington	Hanley
10	3	315102	John Edwards	Fenton
10	5	315104-5	Wm. Brownfield & Sons	Cobridge
15	2	315271-2	Geo. Jones & Sons	Stoke
16	6	315400-1	Powell & Bishop	Hanley
19	8	315473	Minton, Hollins & Co.	Stoke
19	13	315479	T. C. Brown–Westhead, Moore & Co.	Hanley
24	10	315565	F. W. Grove & J. Stark	Longton
24	14	315574	F. & R. Pratt & Co.	Fenton
30	7	315684	Wedgwood & Co.	Tunstall
31	6	315765	Geo. Jones & Sons	Stoke
Nov 5	4	315918	Powell & Bishop	Hanley
6	11	315954-6	Wm. Brownfield & Sons	Cobridge
7	1	316087-9	E. J. D. Bodley	Burslem
7	·2	316090	Mintons	Stoke
7	10	316101	Pinder, Bourne & Co.	Burslem
9	8	316122	Taylor, Tunnicliffe & Co.	Hanley
15	12	316309	T. C. Brown–Westhead, Moore & Co.	Hanley
20	9	316502	James Edwards & Sons	Burslem
21	8	316526	Davenports & Co.	Longport
22	1	316542-3	The Old Hall Earthenware Co. Ltd.	Hanley
22	13	316560	B. & S. Hancock	Stoke
24	7	316605	J. Dimmock & Co.	Hanley
29	3	316723	J. Holdcroft	Longton
Dec 1	5	316763	J. Holdcroft	Longton
1	6	316764	Oakes, Clare & Chadwick	Burslem
5	2	316842	E. J. D. Bodley	Burslem
6	4	316863	Mintons	Stoke
7	14	316912	J. Unwin	Longton
14	1	317112	J. Dimmock & Co.	Hanley
15	10	317203	The Worcester Royal Porcelain Co. Ltd.	Worcester
21	6	317404	Mintons	Stoke
21	10	317410	T. Furnival & Sons	Cobridge
22	5	317427-8	Wm. Brownfield & Sons	Cobridge
29	6	317494	T. C. Brown–Westhead, Moore & Co.	Hanley

1878

Date	Parcel No.	Patent No.	Factory, Retailer Wholesaler, etc	Place
Jan 3	4	317537-9	Minton, Hollins & Co.	Stoke
9	4	317692-4	The Brownhills Pottery Co.	Tunstall
10	12	317733	J. Mortlock & Co.	London
14	1	317756	J. Maddock & Sons	Burslem
14	2	317757	Cotton & Rigby	Burslem
14	3	317758	Wm. Adams	Tunstall
14	6	317763	Minton, Hollins & Co.	Stoke
15	5	317780	Josiah Wedgwood & Sons	Etruria
18	5	317826	Taylor, Tunnicliffe & Co.	Hanley
22	6	317940	J. Dimmock & Co.	Hanley
24	6	318041	W. T. Copeland & Sons	Stoke
25	9	318107-8	Wm. Brownfield & Sons	Cobridge

Date	Parcel No.	Patent No.	Factory, Retailer Wholesaler, etc	Place
28	11	318141	T. C. Brown–Westhead, Moore & Co.	Hanley
30	3	318158-9	Geo. Jones	Stoke
30	15	318189-90	The Brownhills Pottery Co.	Tunstall
31	1	318210	B. & S. Hancock	Stoke
Feb 1	4	318239	Geo. Jones & Sons	Stoke
1	11	318265-6	Minton, Hollins & Co.	Stoke
1	16	318275-9	The Derby Crown Porcelain Co. Ltd.	Derby
5	5	318397	The Campbell Brick & Tile Co.	Stoke
9	6	318469	J. Dimmock & Co.	Hanley
11	5	318543-4	T. C. Brown–Westhead, Moore & Co.	Hanley
12	5	318556-63	Derby Crown Porcelain Co. Ltd.	Derby
20	6	318800	Minton, Hollins & Co.	Stoke
20	7	318801	The Worcester Royal Porcelain Co. Ltd.	Worcester
21	10	318821	W. E. Cartlidge	Burslem
22	8	318843	The Campbell Brick & Tile Co.	Stoke
28	3	319041	Dunn, Bennett & Co.	Hanley
Mar 5	2	319190	F. W. Grove & J. Stark	Longton
6	5	319201	Minton, Hollins & Co.	Stoke
7	4	319219	John Edwards	Fenton
9	1	319278-9	The Brownhills Pottery Co.	Tunstall
9	8	319293	Moore Bros.	Longton
9	11	319296	Powell & Bishop	Hanley
11	1	319310-1	Taylor, Tunnicliffe & Co.	Hanley
13	1	319370	Mintons	Stoke
13	7	319387	J. & T. Bevington	Hanley
13	10	319394	W. T. Copeland & Sons	Stoke
15	10	319507	John Rose & Co.	Coalport
23	8	319634-6	Derby Crown Porcelain Co. Ltd.	Derby
25	9	319679	F. J. Emery	Burslem
27	6	319725-6	G. W. Turner & Sons	Tunstall
27	15	319867-72	Minton, Hollins & Co.	Stoke
Apr 2	6	320030	Belfield & Co.	Preston-pans
10	4	320281	Mintons	Stoke
13	9	320373	McBirney & Armstrong	Belleek
17	4	320482	Mintons	Stoke
17	14	320568-9	Ridgway, Sparks & Ridgway	Stoke
20	2	320606	Thos. Furnival & Sons	Cobridge
20	6	320616	The Worcester Royal Porcelain Co. Ltd.	Worcester
24	2	320669	Wm. Brownfield & Sons	Cobridge
27	12	320793	McBirney & Armstrong	Belleek
30	7	320874-5	Josiah Wedgwood & Sons	Etruria
May 3	2	321028	Josiah Wedgwood & Sons	Etruria
3	9	321163	Robinson & Leadbeater	Stoke
8	9	321231-2	Bates & Bennett	Cobridge
14	6	321361	Elsmore & Son	Tunstall
17	12	321575	J. Dimmock & Co.	Hanley
20	9	321632-4	Derby Crown Porcelain Co. Ltd.	Derby
21	11	321693	Banks & Thorley	Hanley
23	3	321704	Josiah Wedgwood & Sons	Etruria
23	4	321705	Moore Bros.	Longton
24	2	321726	Josiah Wedgwood & Sons	Etruria

Date	Parcel No.	Patent No.	Factory, Retailer Wholesaler, etc	Place	Date	Parcel No.	Patent No.	Factory, Retailer Wholesaler, etc	Place
27	20	322007	E. J. D. Bodley	Burslem	30	1	327000	Mintons	Stoke
29	9	322039	Minton, Hollins & Co.	Stoke	Oct 2	2	327035	Mintons	Stoke
June 1	5	322130	J. Mortlock & Co.	London	3	8	327110	J. T. Hudden	Longton
4	9	322168	F. Furnival & Sons	Cobridge	4	8	327227	F. & R. Pratt & Co.	Fenton
5	14	322223–4	W. T. Copeland & Sons	Stoke	5	4	327235	Jones Bros. & Co.	W/hmptn
7	1	322309	Geo. Jones & Sons	Stoke	5	13	327271	The Worcester Royal	
8	8	322390	Wm. Wood & Co.	Burslem				Porcelain Co. Ltd.	Worcester
12	10	322471	Harvey Adams & Co.	Longton	8	6	327359	Moore Bros.	Longton
13	2	322476	John Tams	Longton	8	7	327360	Bates, Gildea & Walker	Burslem
13	3	322477	McBirney & Armstrong	Belleek	9	9	327392	Josiah Wedgwood	Etruria
19	7	322597–8	E. F. Bodley & Co.	Burslem	11	8	327556	Minton, Hollins & Co.	Stoke
21	8	322662	Allen & Green	Fenton	14	8	327625–6	W. T. Copeland & Sons	Stoke
27	7	322931–2	Josiah Wedgwood & Sons	Etruria	23	1	328018	The Brownhills Pottery Co.	Tunstall
29	1	322948	Wood, Son & Co.	Cobridge	23	11	328144–5	Pinder & Bourne & Co.	Burslem
July 1	1	322971	Burgess & Leigh	Burslem	24	1	328146	T. Furnival & Sons	Cobridge
3	2	323132	Mintons	Stoke	24	2	328147	J. Dimmock & Co.	Hanley
6	7	323315–20	Joseph Cliff & Sons	Leeds	24	13	328274	The Worcester Royal	
8	6	323396	Josiah Wedgwood & Sons	Etruria				Porcelain Co. Ltd.	Worcester
9	8	323434	Mintons	Stoke	26	4	328320	Wm. Brownfield & Sons	Cobridge
9	9	323435	Josiah Wedgwood & Sons	Etruria	30	3	328436–7	Minton, Hollins & Co.	Stoke
9	10	323436	J. Dimmock & Co.	Hanley	30	5	328439–40	Mintons	Stoke
10	14	323508	Bates & Bennett	Cobridge	Nov 1	3	328620	J. Bevington	Hanley
11	1	323521	Soane & Smith	London	4	1	328699	Edge, Malkin & Co.	Burslem
11	11	323596	W. & J. A. Bailey	Alloa	5	11	328774	H. Burgess	Burslem
12	4	323604	Josiah Wedgwood & Sons	Etruria	5	17	328790–2	E. J. D. Bodley	Burslem
12	13	323626	Samuel Lear	Hanley	6	3	328795	Samuel Lear	Hanley
12	15	323628	T. C. Brown–Westhead,		13	13	329075	John Rose & Co.	Coalport
			Moore & Co.	Hanley	15	1	329108	Craven, Dunnill & Co. Ltd.	Jackfield
15	1	323650–1	Pratt & Simpson	Fenton	15	11	329147	F. & R. Pratt & Co.	Fenton
17	9	323774–5	Wm. Adams	Tunstall	16	5	329157	J. Dimmock & Co.	Hanley
18	2	323778	Ambrose Bevington	Hanley	20	13	329378	Cliff & Tomlin	Leeds
20	1	323847	J. Bevington	Hanley	23	2	329456	E. & C. Challinor	Fenton
20	6	323893	John Meir & Son	Tunstall	26	14	329673	T. & R. Boote	Burslem
20	11	323910–!	E. J. D. Bodley	Burslem	27	9	329709	J. McIntyre & Co.	Burslem
26	3	324177	Josiah Wedgwood & Sons	Etruria	29	14	329782–3	W. & E. Corn	Burslem
30	2	324324	idem	Etruria	Dec 2	7	329901	T. C. Brown–Westhead,	
30	6	324336	Powell, Bishop &					Moore & Co.	Hanley
			Stonier	Hanley	2	8	329902	J. F. Meakin	London
30	12	324347	E. Clarke	Longport	3	9	329922	J. McIntyre & Co.	Burslem
31	8	324383	Mintons	Stoke	4	2	329939	Wm. Brownfield & Sons	Cobridge
31	13	324388	James Edwards & Son	Burslem	6	3	330061	Mintons	Stoke
Aug 6	3	324576	Moore Bros.	Longton	7	2	330097	A. Shaw	Burslem
7	3	324730	Thos. Hughes	Burslem	19	8	330485	Thos. Hughes	Burslem
9	10	324848	Derby Crown		27	13	330677	T. & R. Boote	Burslem
			Porcelain Co. Ltd.	Derby	28	4	330687	J. Gaskell, Son & Co.	Burslem
9	12	324870–2	Craven, Dunnill &		**1879**				
			Co. Ltd.	Jackfield	Jan 7	7	330920	W. T. Copeland & Sons	Stoke
14	4	325029–34	S. H. Sharp	Leeds	8	11	330965–6	Minton, Hollins & Co.	Stoke
16	9	325094	The Campbell Brick		9	8	330997–8	Wm. Brownfield & Sons	Cobridge
			& Tile Co.	Stoke	14	5	331152	The New Wharf	
23	1	325278	Moore Bros.	Longton				Pottery Co.	Burslem
23	7	325319	J. Dimmock & Co.	Hanley	14	6	331153	The Campbell Brick	
Sept 3	12	325612	G. & L. Wohlauer	Dresden				& Tile Co.	Stoke
5	3	325716	Moore Bros.	Longton	16	3	331228	B. & S. Hancock	Stoke
9	5	325992–4	Wm. Brownfield & Sons	Cobridge	16	13	331342	F. & R. Pratt & Co.	Fenton
10	2	326006	Josiah Wedgwood & Sons	Etruria	20	15	331418–9	Derby Crown	
12	6	326146	J. Bevington	Hanley				Porcelain Co. Ltd.	Derby
13	5	326155	G. L. Ashworth & Bros.	Hanley	22	4	331458	Dunn, Bennett & Co.	Hanley
13	16	326198	The Worcester Royal		28	11	331597	W. T. Copeland & Sons	Stoke
			Porcelain Co. Ltd.	Worcester	29	2	331600	T. Furnival & Sons	Cobridge
20	19	326482	R. Wotherspoon & Co.	Glasgow	29	3	331601	T. Bevington	Hanley
24	3	326785	T. Bevington	Hanley	29	15	331677	E. J. D. Bodley	Burslem
28	5	326970–1	Minton, Hollins & Co.	Stoke					

Date	Parcel No.	Patent No.	Factory, Retailer Wholesaler, etc	Place	Date	Parcel No.	Patent No.	Factory, Retailer Wholesaler, etc	Place
Feb 1	13	331775	Clementson Bros.	Hanley	June 10	4	336030	T. Furnival & Sons	Cobridge
3	1	331777	Josiah Wedgwood & Sons	Etruria	11	8	336075	Thos. Till & Sons	Burslem
5	7	331892–3	Mintons	Stoke	13	13	336132	T. C. Brown–Westhead, Moore & Co.	Hanley
8	1	332030	Mintons	Stoke	18	4	336185	F. W. Grove & J. Stark	Longton
14	4	332251	T. Furnival & Sons	Cobridge	24	11	336415	Josiah Wedgwood & Sons	Etruria
15	2	332266	The Campbell Brick & Tile Co.	Stoke	25	1	336417	Clementson Bros.	Hanley
17	6	332296	McBirney & Armstrong	Belleek	26	13	336471–4	Haviland & Co.	Limoges and London
24	2	332606	W. P. Jervis	Stoke					
24	3	332607–9	W. & T. Adams	Tunstall	27	11	336496	Shorter & Boulton	Stoke
25	4	332642	Mintons	Stoke	30	12	336586–7	Birks Bros. & Seddon	Cobridge
28	1	332823	E. Chetwynd	Stoke	July 2	2	336676	Josiah Wedgwood & Sons	Etruria
28	7	332831	Clementson Bros.	Hanley	7	2	336917	J. F. Wileman	Fenton
Mar 1	1	332837	T. Furnival & Sons	Cobridge	8	1	336930	Mintons	Stoke
4	4	332938	F. W. Grove & J. Stark	Longton	8	16	336967–8	T. C. Brown–Westhead, Moore & Co.	Hanley
6	10	333047	Powell, Bishop & Stonier	Hanley	9	12	337058	idem	Hanley
12	4	333210	Edge, Malkin & Co.	Burslem	10	2	337060	T. Bevington	Hanley
12	12	333235–6	W. T. Copeland & Sons	Stoke	10	3	337061	Moore Bros.	Longton
13	1	333241–4	Wm. Davenport & Co.	Longport	16	4	337157–8	A. Bevington & Co.	Hanley
13	14	333301	Clementson Bros.	Hanley	16	14	337177	T. C. Brown–Westhead, Moore & Co.	Hanley
14	9	333319	E. Clarke	Longport					
17	2	333368	Powell, Bishop & Stonier	Hanley	25	4	337497	Mintons	Stoke
18	1	333431	Josiah Wedgwood & Sons	Etruria	26	6	337536	Minton, Hollins & Co.	Stoke
19	2	333485	J. Hawthorn	Cobridge	31	2	337660	Mintons	Stoke
26	17	333751–2	The Worcester Royal Porcelain Co. Ltd.	Worcester	Aug 2	2	337814	H. M. Williamson & Sons	Longton
28	6	333801	Clementson Bros.	Hanley	5	12	337945–7	J. Mortlock & Co.	London
29	4	333813	Beck, Blair & Co.	Longton	6	6	337958	Wardle & Co.	Hanley
Apr 3	9	334030	T. C. Brown–Westhead, Moore & Co.	Hanley	13	2	338135	F. W. Grove & J. Stark	Longton
4	12	334052–3	Pinder, Bourne & Co.	Burslem	22	4	338559	McBirney & Armstrong	Belleek
9	5	334137	H. Alcock & Co.	Cobridge	27	13	338872	Bates, Gildea & Walker	Burslem
10	12	334200	T. C. Brown–Westhead, Moore & Co.	Hanley	Sept 4	6	339193	T. C. Brown–Westhead, Moore & Co.	Hanley
12	1	334206	The Worcester Royal Porcelain Co. Ltd.	Worcester	10	13	339373	idem	Hanley
					17	4	339685–6	Wm. Brownfield & Sons	Cobridge
15	6	334241–2	T. C. Brown–Westhead, Moore & Co.	Hanley	18	10	339979	T. C. Brown–Westhead, Moore & Co.	Hanley
23	8	334508	T. C. Brown–Westhead, Moore & Co.	Hanley	26	4	340431	J. T. Hudden	Longton
24	3	334531	Josiah Wedgwood & Sons	Etruria	29	3	340569	Edge, Malkin & Co.	Burslem
May 2	5	334803	A. Bevington	Hanley	Oct 9	6	341137	Bates, Gildea & Walker	Burslem
5	1	334860–1	T. Furnival & Sons	Cobridge	10	2	341151	T. C. Brown–Westhead, Moore & Co.	Hanley
5	6	334897	Bates, Gildea & Walker	Burslem	11	5	341229–30	E. J. D. Bodley	Burslem
6	7	334923–5	Sampson Bridgwood & Son	Longton	15	1	341347	Mintons	Stoke
7	11	334978	The Worcester Royal Porcelain Co. Ltd.	Worcester	16	5	341466	J. Roth	London
9	15	335057	idem	Worcester	16	16	341500	Minton, Hollins & Co.	Stoke
13	4	335148–51	Pinder & Bourne & Co.	Burslem	17	2	341502	G. L. Ashworth & Bros.	Hanley
13	8	335167–8	Clementson Bros.	Hanley	18	3	341629	Josiah Wedgwood & Sons	Etruria
14	9	335182	T. C. Brown–Westhead, Moore & Co.	Hanley	23	12	341864	C. Pillivuyt & Co.	London
14	13	335187–8	E. J. D. Bodley	Burslem	24	4	341882–3	The Campbell Brick & Tile Co.	Stoke
19	1	335308–9	Wm. Brownfield & Sons	Cobridge	27	9	341997	E. F. Bodley & Co.	Burslem
21	5	335496	Harvey Adams & Co.	Longton	29	5	342098	Mintons	Stoke
23	2	335551–2	Sampson Bridgwood & Son	Longton	29	7	342100	Clementson Bros.	Hanley
23	14	335608	Harvey Adams & Co.	Longton	29	15	342152	F. D. Bradley	Longton
29	2	335715	John Tams	Longton	30	4	342158	Mintons	Stoke
29	12	335739–40	Pinder, Bourne & Co.	Burslem	Nov 3	12	342396	Minton, Hollins & Co.	Stoke
30	3	335744	McBirney & Armstrong	Belleek	3	14	342398	Tundley, Rhodes & Procter	Burslem
30	10	335791	J. Dimmock & Co.	Hanley					
30	12	335793	F. W. Grove & J. Stark	Longton	6	2	342461	Josiah Wedgwood & Sons	Etruria
31	4	335805	Minton, Hollins & Co.	Stoke	6	3	342462–3	Moore Bros.	Longton
					6	4	342464–72	Burmantofts (Wilcock & Co.)	Leeds

Date	Parcel No.	Patent No.	Factory, Retailer Wholesaler, etc	Place	Date	Parcel No.	Patent No.	Factory, Retailer Wholesaler, etc	Place
12	11	342769	The Worcester Royal Porcelain Co. Ltd.	Worcester	11	10	346344	T. Bevington	Hanley
15	12	342921	C. Ford	Hanley	12	4	346360	W. A. Adderley	Longton
15	16	342925–7	W. T. Copeland & Sons	Stoke	12	7	346363	Wm. Brownfield & Sons	Cobridge
17	2	342929	Powell, Bishop & Stonier	Hanley	14	14	346467	Bates, Gildea & Walker	Burslem
19	5	343017	idem	Hanley	18	12	346594	The Derby Crown Porcelain Co. Ltd.	Derby
20	4	343070–1	Elsmore & Son	Tunstall	24	2	346832	Mintons	Stoke
21	6	343148	Mintons	Stoke	24	11	346870	Wm. Harrop & Co.	Hanley
21	14	343166	Soane & Smith	London	25	18	346920	Clementson Bros.	Hanley
22	7	343219	The Worcester Royal Porcelain Co. Ltd.	Worcester	25	23	346945	Sherwin & Cotton	Hanley
28	5	343530	Wm. Brownfield & Sons	Cobridge	26	6	346952–3	Minton, Hollins & Co.	Stoke
28	6	343531	A. Bevington & Co.	Hanley	26	7	346954	Moore Bros.	Longton
29	3	343585	Mintons	Stoke	Mar 3	6	347138	J. Holdcroft	Longton
29	4	343586	T. C. Brown–Westhead, Moore & Co.	Hanley	4	8	347203	Soane & Smith	London
Dec 1	2	343618	J. Holdcroft	Longton	4	4	347344	T. Furnival & Sons	Cobridge
2	4	343652–3	T. C. Brown–Westhead, Moore & Co.	Hanley	8	10	347360	W. Harrop & Co.	Hanley
2	5	343654	Elsmore & Son	Tunstall	12	4	347476	W. A. Adderley	Longton
2	17	343716	J. Aynsley & Sons	Longton	16	3	347599	J. F. Wileman & Co.	Fenton
6	2	343815–6	T. & R. Boote	Burslem	16	11	347645	Sherwin & Cotton	Hanley
10	14	344077	Clementson Bros.	Hanley	16	12	347646–7	J. Macintyre & Co.	Burslem
11	4	344082–4	Moore Bros.	Longton	17	6	347660	Josiah Wedgwood & Sons	Etruria
17	11	344387	Ridgways	Stoke	18	3	347690–6	Moore Bros.	Longton
19	1	344452	Clementson Bros.	Hanley	22	4	347838	Powell, Bishop & Stonier	Hanley
19	3	344454	Burmantofts (Wilcock & Co.)	Leeds	23	4	347872	Taylor, Tunnicliffe & Co.	Hanley
20	5	344478	Josiah Wedgwood & Sons	Etruria	25	6	348018	Mintons	Stoke
22	2	344503	Mintons	Stoke	30	4	348110	Sherwin & Cotton	Hanley
24	2	344568	Sherwin & Cotton	Hanley	31	3	348114	Thos. Peake	Tunstall
					Apr 12	6	348606–8	Bates, Gildea & Walker	Burslem
1880					15	11	348761	Ridgways	Stoke
Jan 3	1	344838	Sherwin & Cotton	Hanley	19	11	348911–3	The Worcester Royal Porcelain Co. Ltd.	Worcester
7	3	344961–2	T. Bevington	Hanley	22	11	349025–6	Sherwin & Cotton	Hanley
7	4	344963	T. & R. Boote	Burslem	22	5	349027	W. H. Grindley & Co.	Tunstall
7	5	344964–9	Soane & Smith	London	26	1	349221	T. Furnival & Sons	Cobridge
7	8	344972	Minton, Hollins & Co.	Stoke	27	11	349239–41	Moore Bros.	Longton
8	9	344997	The Old Hall Earthenware Co. Ltd.	Hanley	27	13	349318–23	The Worcester Royal Porcelain Co. Ltd.	Worcester
9	3	345003	Sherwin & Cotton	Hanley	29	4	349340–1	Mintons	Stoke
9	12	345045	T. G. Allen	London	30	6	349380	T. Furnival & Sons	Cobridge
13	1	345131	T. C. Brown–Westhead, Moore & Co.	Hanley	May 3	3	349438–43	Wm. Brownfield & Sons	Cobridge
14	11	345184–5	The Worcester Royal Porcelain Co. Ltd.	Worcester	5	13	349528	S. Fielding & Co.	Stoke
16	8	345288	S. Fielding & Co.	Stoke	10	6	349693	Powell, Bishop & Stonier	Hanley
16	14	345299	Brockwell & Son	London	11	15	349791	Soane & Smith	London
21	7	345469–71	Pinder, Bourne & Co.	Burslem	13	8	349852–3	Mintons	Stoke
22	2	345481	Mintons	Stoke	13	15	349869	Minton, Hollins & Co.	Stoke
22	8	345493–4	Minton, Hollins & Co.	Stoke	14	26	349939	Bates, Gildea & Walker	Burslem
23	5	345511	Mintons	Stoke	25	4	350098	Wm. Brownfield & Sons	Cobridge
26	11	345719	Wm. Brownfield & Sons	Cobridge	26	6	350142	Mintons	Stoke
27	13	345798	Wardle & Co.	Hanley	June 1	4	350251	Mintons	Stoke
28	3	345801	T. C. Brown–Westhead, Moore & Co.	Hanley	2	3	350353	Sherwin & Cotton	Hanley
28	4	345802	J. Aynsley & Sons	Longton	7	6	350476	J. Dimmock & Co.	Hanley
28	12	345833	Powell, Bishop & Stonier	Hanley	8	1	350477	Geo. Jones & Sons	Stoke
29	9	345860–1	E. J. D. Bodley	Burslem	10	3	350554	Sherwin & Cotton	Hanley
30	2	345864	Taylor, Tunnicliffe & Co.	Hanley	10	4	350555	E. J. D. Bodley	Burslem
Feb 3	11	345952	Powell, Bishop & Stonier	Hanley	10	12	350613	J. Dimmock & Co.	Hanley
9	18	346202	Whittingham, Ford & Riley	Burslem	11	3	350616	Josiah Wedgwood & Sons	Etruria
10	4	346208–10	Mintons	Stoke	14	12	350842	J. Roth	London
					15	4	350848	Buckley, Wood & Co.	Burslem
					16	3	350972	Wedgwood & Co.	Tunstall
					17	4	351025	Samuel Lear	Hanley
					17	15	351058	Ridgways	Stoke
					17	16	351059	J. Macintyre & Co.	Burslem
					17	20	351063	The Crystal Porcelain Co.	Hanley

Date	Parcel No.	Patent No.	Factory, Retailer Wholesaler, etc	Place	Date	Parcel No.	Patent No.	Factory, Retailer Wholesaler, etc	Place
17	21	351064	J. Dimmock & Co.	Hanley	4	4	357656–7	W. & T. Adams	Tunstall
19	11	351186	Josiah Wedgwood & Sons	Etruria	4	15	357724–5	Minton, Hollins & Co.	Stoke
19	15	351190	J. Roth	London	9	4	357954	Josiah Wedgwood & Sons	Etruria
22	1	351259	W. H. Grindley & Co.	Tunstall	10	2	358062–3	Wilcock & Co. (Burmantofts)	Leeds
26	13	351496–7	The Worcester Royal Porcelain Co. Ltd.	Worcester	10	13	358141	Bednall & Heath	Hanley
July 5	11	351866	Westwood & Moore	Brierley Hill	18	3	358466	S. Radford	Longton
7	4	351909	Sherwin & Cotton	Hanley	18	14	358500	Mintons	Stoke
7	5	351910	Mintons	Stoke	19	15	358552	The Crown Derby Porcelain Co. Ltd.	Derby
7	15	351928	F. J. Emery	Burslem	24	4	358747	F. W. Grove & J. Stark	Longton
12	4	352094	Mintons	Stoke	24	5	358748	Bates, Gildea & Walker	Burslem
13	12	352138	Thos. Barlow	Longton	Dec 6	2	359292	Powell, Bishop & Stonier	Hanley
15	3	352192	Dunn, Bennett & Co.	Hanley	7	10	359321–6	Pinder, Bourne & Co.	Burslem
15	4	352193	F. W. Grove & J. Stark	Longton	8	5	359342–3	Wittmann & Roth	London
16	9	352224	Sherwin & Cotton	Hanley	15	15	359668–71	Wm. Brownfield & Sons	Cobridge
16	10	352225	Moore Bros.	Longton	18	2	359784	Bates, Gildea & Walker	Burslem
16	19	352278	S. Fielding & Co.	Stoke	24	8	359997	T. C. Brown–Westhead, Moore & Co.	Hanley
28	2	352872	The Brownhills Pottery Co.	Tunstall	29	7	360042–4	Doulton & Co.	Lambeth
31	8	353079	The Old Hall Earthenware Co. Ltd.	Hanley	31	1	360100	The Old Hall Earthenware Co. Ltd.	Hanley
Aug 4	3	353108	Pinder, Bourne & Co.	Burslem	31	4	360103–5	Sherwin & Cotton	Hanley
11	14	353543	Clementson Bros.	Hanley	**1881**				
14	12	353713–4	Wm. Davenport & Co.	Longport	Jan 5	7	360326	J. Roth	London
17	6	353746	Sherwin & Cotton	Hanley	6	2	360331	B. & S. Hancock	Stoke
18	3	353818	Josiah Wedgwood & Sons	Etruria	6	8	360355	F. D. Bradley	Longton
21	2	354026	Sherwin & Cotton	Hanley	7	13	360484	Sherwin & Cotton	Hanley
21	10	354081	W. A. Adderley	Longton	12	5	360633	idem	Hanley
23	5	354092	Jackson & Gosling	Longton	14	10	360747	The Worcester Royal Porcelain Co. Ltd.	Worcester
23	6	354093–4	T. C. Brown–Westhead, Moore & Co.	Hanley	14	18	360799	E. J. D. Bodley	Burslem
24	10	354154	E. J. D. Bodley	Burslem	15	4	360806–7	Holmes, Stonier & Hollinshead	Hanley
Sept 3	3	354639	T. C. Brown–Westhead, Moore & Co.	Hanley	20	3	360900	Mintons	Stoke
4	7	354766–7	J. Beech & Son	Longton	21	11	360954	W. & T. Adams	Tunstall
11	3	355091–100	Wm. Brownfield & Sons	Cobridge	26	4	361116–7	Minton, Hollins & Co.	Stoke
14	6	355169	Mintons	Stoke	27	15	361151	The Worcester Royal Porcelain Co. Ltd.	Worcester
15	6	355231	G. L. Ashworth & Bros.	Hanley	28	3	361170	G. Woolliscroft & Son	Hanley
15	12	355255–7	Minton, Hollins & Co.	Stoke	Feb 8	5	361537	F. W. Grove & J. Stark	Longton
23	3	355575	Ambrose Wood	Hanley	8	6	361538–41	Wm. Brownfield & Sons	Cobridge
25	6	355651–4	Minton, Hollins & Co.	Stoke	11	10	361668	F. J. Emery	Burslem
27	5	355745–6	John Marshall & Co.	Bo'ness, Scotland	15	6	361748	W. A. Adderley	Longton
29	3	355947–8	The Brownhills Pottery Co.	Tunstall	16	3	361784	F. D. Bradley	Longton
30	4	355987	The Worcester Royal Porcelain Co. Ltd.	Worcester	17	2	361813	Murray & Co.	Glasgow
Oct 1	3	356014	Wade & Colclough	Burslem	18	3	361868	S. Radford	Longton
6	4	356163	Josiah Wedgwood & Sons	Etruria	19	15	361927	S. S. Bold	Hanley
12	4	356514	Mintons	Stoke	21	4	361937	Taylor, Waine & Bates	Longton
13	5	356532	Josiah Wedgwood & Sons	Etruria	24	8	362086	Wm. Harrop & Co.	Hanley
20	10	356970	Burgess & Leigh	Burslem	25	14	362166	J. Macintyre & Co.	Burslem
21	13	357033–5	The Worcester Royal Porcelain Co. Ltd.	Worcester	28	9	362242	E. J. D. Bodley	Burslem
22	4	357039	E. F. Bodley & Son	Burslem	Mar 3	5	362423	J. Dimmock & Co.	Hanley
22	12	357088	J. Aynsley & Sons	Longton	7	11	362545	J. Aynsley & Sons	Longton
26	13	357298–9	Minton, Hollins & Co.	Stoke	8	3	362548	F. W. Grove & J. Stark	Longton
27	5	357305	Taylor, Tunnicliffe & Co.	Hanley	14	1	362815	E. J. D. Bodley	Burslem
27	20	357429	J. Tams	Longton	17	9	362992	Shorter & Boulton	Stoke
27	21	357430	G. Woolliscroft & Son	Etruria	19	4	363026–7	Mintons	Stoke
28	2	357466	Sherwin & Cotton	Hanley	23	4	363157	Mintons	Stoke
30	6	357560	Jones & Hopkinson	Hanley	24	2	363206–7	T. S. Pinder	Burslem
Nov 2	2	357609	W. H. Grindley & Co.	Tunstall	24	3	363208	W. A. Adderley	Longton
					29	6	363421	T. A. Simpson	Hanley

Date	Parcel No.	Patent No.	Factory, Retailer Wholesaler, etc	Place	Date	Parcel No.	Patent No.	Factory, Retailer Wholesaler, etc	Place
31	2	363461	J. T. Hudden	Longton	2	5	366643	T. Furnival & Sons	Cobridge
Apr 7	2	363720	Sherwin & Cotton	Hanley	6	7	366809	Josiah Wedgwood & Sons	Etruria
7	9	363732	The Old Hall		9	10	366922–3	Wardle & Co.	Hanley
			Earthenware Co. Ltd.	Hanley	14	6	367133–4	T. C. Brown–Westhead,	
8	2	363738	W. Harrop & Co.	Hanley				Moore & Co.	Hanley
8	3	363739	Wedgwood & Co.	Tunstall	15	5	367150	Wm. Corbitt & Co.	Rthrham
8	14	363785	The Worcester Royal		16	3	367213	Trubshaw, Hand & Co.	Longton
			Porcelain Co. Ltd.	Worcester	18	4	367249	G. Hall	Worcester
9	5	363793	R. H. Plant & Co.	Longton	19	2	367259	The Dalehall Brick	
11	1	363800	A. Bevington & Co.	Hanley				& Tile Co.	Burslem
12	4	363849–50	Mintons	Stoke	25	2	367418	J. H. Davis	Hanley
14	10	363975	Mintons	Stoke	28	3	367516	McBirney & Armstrong	Belleek
16	17	364110	J. Marshall & Co.	Bo'ness,	28	4	367517	A. Wood	Hanley
				Scotland	28	14	367538	Ridgways	Stoke
19	3	364116	Sherwin & Cotton	Hanley	29	2	367542–3	Sherwin & Cotton	Hanley
19	5	364118	T. & R. Boote	Burslem	29	3	367544	Whittmann & Roth	London
21	4	364172	Sherwin & Cotton	Hanley	30	3	367549	Sampson Bridgwood & Son	Longton
21	5	364173–4	E. J. D. Bodley	Burslem	30	4	367550	Sherwin & Cotton	Hanley
23	7	364238	J. F. Wileman	Fenton	30	5	367551	Mintons	Stoke
28	12	364488	W. T. Copeland & Sons	Stoke	30	15	367590	W. T. Copeland & Sons	Stoke
30	3	364528	Trubshaw, Hand & Co.	Longton	Aug 2	1	367608	E. J. D. Bodley	Burslem
30	4	364529	Josiah Wedgwood & Sons	Etruria	5	12	367892–3	Pinder, Bourne & Co.	Burslem
May 3	4	364604	Wm. Wood & Co.	Burslem	10	13	368044	The Old Hall	
3	5	364605	Sherwin & Cotton	Hanley				Earthenware Co. Ltd.	Hanley
4	2	364624	idem	Hanley	20	11	368686	The Worcester Royal	
4	3	364625–7	Wm. Brownfield & Sons	Cobridge				Porcelain Co. Ltd.	Worcester
5	2	364648	W. & T. Adams	Tunstall	23	3	368802	F. W. Grove & J. Stark	Longton
6	4	364736	R. H. Plant & Co.	Longton	24	11	368942	T. & R. Boote	Burslem
11	3	364941	J. Tams	Longton	27	3	369202	S. Lear	Hanley
13	2	365005	Mintons	Stoke	27	9	369215–8	Gildea & Walker	Burslem
16	2	365066	Josiah Wedgwood & Sons	Etruria	29	7	369248	W. & T. Adams	Tunstall
17	9	365134–5	J. Mortlock & Co.	London	Sept 2	4	369389	Dale, Page & Goodwin	Longton
20	11	365206	W. A. Adderley	Longton	3	11	369526	T. A. Simpson	Hanley
21	3	365211	Powell, Bishop & Stonier	Hanley	6	1	369538	The Derby Crown	
24	5	365391	G. L. Ashworth & Bros.	Hanley				Porcelain Co. Ltd.	Derby
24	6	365392–3	Mintons	Stoke	7	10	369654	Adams & Sleigh	Burslem
24	7	365394	F. J. Emery	Burslem	9	11	369731	The Worcester Royal	
25	3	365424	Powell, Bishop & Stonier	Hanley				Porcelain Co. Ltd.	Worcester
25	9	365442–4	The Worcester Royal		10	12	369778–81	J. Roth	London
			Porcelain Co. Ltd.	Worcester	16	10	370093	Geo. Jones & Sons	Stoke
25	10	365445–6	Josiah Wedgwood & Sons	Etruria	22	9	370400	Bold & Michelson	Hanley
26	7	365461	G. Woolliscroft & Son	Hanley	23	21	370470–2	Minton, Hollins & Co.	Stoke
30	1	365539	T. Furnival & Sons	Cobridge	27	9	370611	Pinder, Bourne & Co.	Burslem
30	2	365540	The Decorative Art		28	4	370620	E. J. D. Bodley	Burslem
			Tile Co.	Hanley	28	13	370633	Gildea & Walker	Burslem
June 1	3	365730	Mintons	Stoke	29	3	370636	Geo. Jones & Sons	Stoke
1	13	365793	J. Mortlock & Co.	London	30	3	370702–3	Davenports Ltd.	Longport
3	4	365827	S. P. Ledward	Cobridge	30	15	370725–8	Mintons	Stoke
4	3	365852	T. Furnival & Sons	Cobridge	Oct 4	6	370885	Wm. Brownfield & Sons	Cobridge
4	4	365853	The Decorative Art		6	5	370998	J. & R. Boote	Burslem
			Tile Co.	Hanley	6	7	371000	The Campbell Brick	
7	3	365875	E. F. Bodley & Son	Burslem				& Tile Co.	Stoke
7	4	365876–7	The Decorative Art		7	27	371098	Mintons	Stoke
			Tile Co.	Hanley	8	3	371102	Adams & Sleigh	Burslem
7	17	365914–6	The Worcester Royal		11	16	371247	The Worcester Royal	
			Porcelain Co. Ltd.	Worcester				Porcelain Co. Ltd.	Worcester
8	6	365955	The Crystal Porcelain Co.	Hanley	12	14	371330–1	Mintons	Stoke
13	1	366015	S. Lear	Hanley	13	3	371337	Adderley & Lawson	Longton
16	8	366078–9	S. Fielding & Co.	Stoke	13	5	371339	T. & R. Boote	Burslem
18	1	366093	Jackson & Gosling	Longton	20	1	371866	Thos. Begley	Burslem
21	13	366220–2	Birks Bros. & Seddon	Cobridge	20	2	371867	Robinson & Chapman	Longton
21	20	366246	Gildea & Walker	Burslem	22	1	371959	Mintons	Stoke
July 2	1	366634	McBirney & Armstrong	Belleek	26	8	372138	Mintons	Stoke

Date	Parcel No.	Patent No.	Factory, Retailer Wholesaler, etc	Place	Date	Parcel No.	Patent No.	Factory, Retailer Wholesaler, etc	Place
26	16	372171	T. C. Brown–Westhead, Moore & Co.	Hanley	6	4	376764–6	The Campbell Tile Co.	Stoke
27	1	372185	Robinson & Chapman	Longton	7	2	376798	Wm. Mills	Hanley
29	3	372347	T. & R. Boote	Burslem	8	7	376839	Wardle & Co.	Hanley
29	4	372348	Wm. Brownfield & Sons	Cobridge	15	4	377048	F. W. Grove & J. Stark	Longton
29	11	372376	Wardle & Co.	Hanley	16	6	377135–7	Mintons	Stoke
29	14	372379	Minton, Hollins & Co.	Stoke	18	5	377273	J. F. Wileman & Co.	Fenton
31	11	372464	T. A. Simpson	Hanley	23	17	377488–9	Minton, Hollins & Co.	Stoke
Nov 2	1	372489–90	T. C. Brown–Westhead, Moore & Co.	Hanley	24	3	377492	Taylor, Tunnicliffe & Co.	Hanley
					Mar 1	11	377779	The Worcester Royal Porcelain Co. Ltd.	Worcester
3	12	372613	The Worcester Royal Porcelain Co. Ltd.	Worcester	1	12	377780	Minton, Hollins & Co.	Stoke
4	24	372727	idem	Worcester	7	7	378051	idem	Stoke
8	1	372918	T. & R. Boote	Burslem	13	3	378252	J. T. Hudden	Longton
9	6	372979	F. W. Grove & J. Stark	Longton	15	3	378337	Powell, Bishop & Stonier	Hanley
9	7	372980–2	E. J. D. Bodley	Burslem	15	4	378338	Murray & Co.	Glasgow
10	2	372995	Brough & Blackhurst	Longton	20	5	378643	W. A. Adderley	Longton
19	3	373541	Sampson Bridgwood & Son	Longton	23	2	378739	W. & T. Adams	Tunstall
19	12	373573	The Worcester Royal Porcelain Co. Ltd.	Worcester	23	15	378823	T. A. Simpson	Hanley
					27	3	378937	D. Chapman	Longton
21	1	373575	J. Bevington	Hanley	27	10	378959	Shorter & Boulton	Stoke
22	9	373615	J. Tams	Longton	28	12	378988	Ambrose Wood	Hanley
22	17	373647	Ambrose Wood	Hanley	28	16	378993–4	A. Bevington & Co.	Hanley
23	13	373707	Shorter & Boulton	Stoke	30	13	379076	John Rose & Co.	Coalport
25	1	373821	Adams & Sleigh	Burslem	30	17	379080	S. Fielding & Co.	Stoke
25	15	373860	J. Roth	London	31	3	379088	A. Bevington & Co.	Hanley
29	10	374058	The Worcester Royal Porcelain Co. Ltd.	Worcester	Apr 4	2	379212–3	Wm. Brownfield & Sons	Cobridge
					11	6	379434	Geo. Jones & Sons	Stoke
Dec 2	16	374229	J. Roth	London	11	7	379435–6	Minton, Hollins & Co.	Stoke
5	11	374376	John Rose & Co.	Coalport	21	7	379767	Sampson Bridgwood & Son	Longton
8	9	374498	Adderley & Lawson	Longton	27	14	380072	The New Wharf Pottery Co.	Burslem
9	2	374516	E. J. D. Bodley	Burslem	May 2	5	380194	G. L. Ashworth & Bros.	Hanley
10	7	374579	T. C. Brown–Westhead, Moore & Co.	Hanley	3	1	380199	S. Radford	Longton
12	12	374628	John Fell	Longton	5	2	380401	Wood, Hines & Winkle	Hanley
16	3	374782	Mintons	Stoke	6	6	380418	Powell, Bishop & Stonier	Hanley
20	9	374948	Bednall & Heath	Hanley	6	6	380419–20	Whittaker, Edge & Co.	Hanley
21	3	374955	F. Grosvenor	Glasgow	8	18	380549–50	Davenports Ltd.	Longport
21	9	374987	The Worcester Royal Porcelain Co. Ltd.	Worcester	9	3	380553–4	H. Alcock & Co.	Cobridge
24	5	375054	J. Broadhurst	Fenton	9	4	380555	Whittaker, Edge & Co.	Hanley
					9	7	380558	Wm. Brownfield & Sons	Cobridge
					9	11	380564	Minton, Hollins & Co.	Stoke
					10	4	380571–2	John Edwards	Fenton
1882					10	14	380676	S. Fielding & Co.	Stoke
Jan 3	6	375415	Holmes, Plant & Maydew	Burslem	13	6	380789	Geo. Jones & Sons	Stoke
4	2	375426–7	W. T. Copeland & Sons	Stoke	17	2	380869–70	E. J. Bodley	Burslem
4	7	375439	J. Roth	London	24	4	381376	Minton, Hollins & Co.	Stoke
4	9	375444	F. & R. Pratt & Co.	Fenton	24	21	381434	Doulton & Co.	Burslem
7	2	375494	W. H. Grindley & Co.	Tunstall	25	11	381480	W. A. Adderley	Longton
7	11	375580	Ridgways	Hanley	27	3	381568	Samuel Lear	Hanley
10	5	375599	S. Lear	Hanley	30	5	381611	W. H. Grindley & Co.	Tunstall
11	1	375709–12	Minton, Hollins & Co.	Stoke	June 5	6	381805	Mintons	Stoke
13	4	375815–6	The Decorative Art Tile Co.	Hanley	5	7	381806	Wood, Hines & Winkle	Hanley
					9	3	381964	Hall & Read	Burslem
18	10	376032	Robinson & Son	Longton	9	4	381965–6	W. A. Adderley	Longton
26	5	376425	J. T. Hudden	Longton	13	11	382126	A. Shaw & Son	Burslem
26	16	376443	S. Fielding & Co.	Stoke	13	14	382130–1	Wardle & Co.	Hanley
27	8	376461	Craven, Dunnill & Co. Ltd.	Jackfield	21	4	382406	Wm. Lowe	Longton
30	2	376528	Hollinshead & Kirkham	Tunstall	21	5	382407–8	Sampson Bridgwood & Son	Longton
30	3	376529	F. W. Grove & J. Stark	Longton	21	11	382472	The Old Hall Earthenware & Co. Ltd	Hanley
Feb 1	1	376580	Edge, Malkin & Co.	Burslem	23	1	382593–4	Josiah Wedgwood & Sons	Etruria
3	4	376672–3	T. C. Brown–Westhead, Moore & Co.	Hanley	23	5	382598	Burgess & Leigh	Burslem
4	10	376754	Minton, Hollins & Co.	Stoke	28	2	382721	The Derby Crown Porcelain Co.	Derby

Date	Parcel No.	Patent No.	Factory, Retailer Wholesaler, etc	Place	Date	Parcel No.	Patent No.	Factory, Retailer Wholesaler, etc	Place
July 1	8	382829	Taylor, Tunnicliffe & Co.	Hanley	15	7	390004–5	S. Fielding & Co.	Stoke
3	2	382842	Mintons	Stoke	16	3	390023	Taylor, Tunnicliffe & Co.	Hanley
3	3	382843	E. J. D. Bodley	Burslem	21	4	390255	J. Holdcroft	Longton
4	3	382859	Wright & Rigby	Hanley	21	8	390264	Gildea & Walker	Burslem
6	4	383020–1	Wm. Brownfield & Sons	Cobridge	22	11	390285	S. Fielding & Co.	Stoke
14	3	383436–7	Geo. Jones & Sons	Stoke	24	19	390588	Minton, Hollins & Co.	Stoke
14	10	383468	Wardle & Co.	Hanley	27	3	390617	H. Alcock & Co.	Cobridge
14	14	383482	Beech & Tellwright	Cobridge	27	4	390618	The Derby Crown	
17	8	383549	Wood & Son	Burslem				Porcelain Co. Ltd.	Derby
19	7	383641	Wardle & Co.	Hanley	27	5	390619	J. F. Wileman & Co.	Fenton
20	1	383694–6	John Edwards	Fenton	Dec 2	8	390976	Minton, Hollins & Co.	Stoke
22	8	383802	Geo. Jones & Sons	Stoke	4	7	390985	A. Bevington & Co.	Hanley
25	3	383855	F. Grosvenor	Glasgow	6	2	391068–9	T. C. Brown–Westhead,	
25	9	383869–71	The Brownhills Pottery Co.					Moore & Co.	Hanley
			Ltd.	Tunstall	13	4	391361–2	Mintons	Stoke
26	4	383893	Adderley & Lawson	Longton	13	5	391363–4	Josiah Wedgwood	Etruria
28	3	384078	Hawley & Co.	Longton	14	6	391409	S. Lear	Hanley
31	2	384160–1	Sampson Bridgwood & Son	Longton	15	3	391460	The Old Hall	
31	9	384171–2	Mintons	Stoke				Earthenware Co. Ltd.	Hanley
Aug 5	4	384353–4	Wm. Brownfield & Sons	Cobridge	18	9	391596	J. Lockett & Co.	Longton
10	5	384464	Wright & Rigby	Hanley	19	3	391620	H. Kennedy	Glasgow
21	2	385106	John Tams	Longton	21	4	391768	E. J. D. Bodley	Burslem
21	8	385129	Adams & Bromley	Hanley	21	5	391769	Wood, Hines & Winkle	Hanley
25	2	385411	Mintons	Stoke	22	2	391818	F. W. Grove & J. Stark	Longton
26	4	385490	Wm. Wood & Co.	Burslem	22	14	391846	Lorenz Hutschenreuther	Bavaria
28	2	385527	Belfield & Co.	Preston-	23	4	391855	J. F. Wileman	Fenton
				pans	23	12	391917	The New Wharf	
28	9	385544	Mintons	Stoke				Pottery Co.	Burslem
29	12	385623	Wm. Brownfield & Sons	Cobridge	23	14	391922–7	The Worcester Royal	
30	14	385693	The Worcester Royal					Porcelain Co. Ltd.	Worcester
			Porcelain Co. Ltd.	Worcester	27	1	391929	The New Wharf	
31	3	385701	A. Bevington & Co.	Hanley				Pottery Co.	Burslem
Sept 6	2	385954	Hawley & Co.	Longton					
8	5	386085–6	Mintons	Stoke	**1883**				
9	3	386126	Taylor, Tunnicliffe & Co.	Hanley	Jan 2	2	392166	The Derby Crown	
11	4	386178	Adams & Bromley	Hanley				Porcelain Co. Ltd.	Derby
16	2	386388–9	Hulme & Massey	Longton	3	1	392176	Wm. Hines	Longton
19	2	386542	W. H. Grindley & Co.	Tunstall	3	14	392362	T. Furnival & Sons	Cobridge
28	4	387147–8	T. C. Brown–Westhead,		3	18	392388–9	John Rose & Co.	Coalport
			Moore & Co.	Hanley	4	5	392403	T. C. Brown–Westhead,	
28	22	387229	Bridgett & Bates	Longton				Moore & Co.	Hanley
29	2	387231–2	The Brownhills Pottery Co.	Tunstall	8	5	392590	W. T. Copeland & Sons	Stoke
Oct 6	2	387598–	Mintons	Stoke	8	12	392621	The Worcester Royal	
		603						Porcelain Co. Ltd.	Worcester
9	3	387771	W. T. Copeland & Sons	Stoke	9	3	392626	Powell, Bishop & Stonier	Hanley
9	4	387772	Dean, Capper & Dean	Hanley	9	4	392627	E. F. Bodley & Son	Longport
11	3	387958–60	Sampson Bridgwood & Son	Longton	9	5	392628–30	Hall & Read	Hanley
11	4	387961	Wood & Son	Burslem	9	11	392652	Davenports Ltd.	Longport
12	17	388200	T. Furnival & Sons	Cobridge	10	17	392693	Gildea & Walker	Burslem
16	4	388296	Wood & Son	Burslem	12	3	392725	Holmes, Plant & Maydew	Burslem
19	4	388395	Lowe, Ratcliffe & Co.	Longton	13	6	392760	Moore & Co.	Longton
31	2	389136	Wm. Lowe	Longton	13	17	392809	T. & R. Boote	Burslem
Nov 1	14	389201	Stonier, Hollinshead &		16	1	392855	Blair & Co.	Longton
			Oliver	Hanley	17	3	392888	W. H. Grindley & Co.	Tunstall
4	19	389390	The Worcester Royal		23	8	393099	E. F. Bodley & Son	Longport
			Porcelain Co. Ltd.	Worcester	23	10	393102–3	W. T. Copeland & Sons	Stoke
8	2	389554	Mintons	Stoke	24	1	393107	Sampson Bridgwood & Son	Longton
10	10	389793	Ridgways	Stoke	24	2	393108–9	Wm. Brownfield & Sons	Cobridge
10	12	389795–7	Pratt & Simpson	Fenton	25	3	393177	The Brownhills Pottery Co.	Tunstall
11	2	389801	Powell, Bishop & Stonier	Hanley	26	8	393258	Wm. Lowe	Longton
13	1	389893	Edge, Malkin & Co.	Burslem	27	8	393298	G. W. Turner & Sons	Tunstall
13	2	389894	Sampson Bridgwood & Son	Longton	29	6	393310	Wm. Brownfield & Sons	Cobridge
14	3	389911–2	Ed. Steel	Hanley	29	7	393311–2	W. H. Grindley & Co.	Tunstall

Date	Parcel No.	Patent No.	Factory, Retailer Wholesaler, etc	Place
30	1	393323	E. F. Bodley & Son	Longport
30	12	393362	Wedgwood & Co.	Tunstall
31	14	393413	Minton, Hollins & Co.	Stoke
Feb 1	3	393418	Sampson Bridgwood & Son	Longton
1	17	393474	E. J. D. Bodley	Burslem
2	4	393495	S. Hancock	Stoke
2	17	393539	Wedgwood & Co.	Tunstall
3	3	393548	Mintons	Stoke
5	2	393647	J. Holdcroft	Longton
6	1	393668	Wood, Hines & Winkle	Hanley
7	4	393714	Hawley & Co.	Longton
7	5	393715	Mountford & Thomas	Hanley
9	9	393979	E. J. D. Bodley	Burslem
12	3	394086	Dunn, Bennett & Co.	Hanley
14	3	394185	W. H. Grindley & Co.	Tunstall
15	5	394215	J. H. Davis	Hanley
17	13	394371	G. W. Turner & Sons	Tunstall
19	1	394374	W. A. Adderley	Longton
20	13	394443	Davenports Ltd.	Longport
20	17	394448	Gildea & Walker	Burslem
21	3	394452	Geo. Jones & Sons	Stoke
22	6	394556–61	Hall & Read	Hanley
22	20	394599	The Worcester Royal Porcelain Co. Ltd.	Worcester
22	21	394600	The Old Hall Earthenware Co.	Hanley
24	12	394676	Josiah Wedgwood & Sons	Etruria
24	13	394677	The Worcester Royal Porcelain Co. Ltd.	Worcester
26	6	394687	Williamson & Sons	Longton
28	3	394765	Thos. Till & Sons	Burslem
Mar 8	5	395284	M. Massey	Hanley
8	20	395316–7	E. F. Bodley & Son	Longport
14	3	395560	The Derby Porcelain Co. Ltd.	Derby
15	3	395622	T. Furnival & Sons	Cobridge
16	6	395688	J. Broadhurst	Fenton
17	8	395703	Mintons	Stoke
20	3	395818	E. A. Wood	Hanley
20	4	395819	Josiah Wedgwood & Sons	Etruria
24	3	396056	Sampson Bridgwood & Son	Longton
30	1	396200–1	Mintons	Stoke
30	9	396245	Minton, Hollins & Co.	Stoke
Apr 2	3	396313	T. & E. L. Poulson	Castleford
3	3	396316	E. Warburton	Longton
6	14	396576	G. & J. Hobson	Burslem
10	1	396648	Banks & Thorley	Hanley
19	3	397090	R. H. Plant & Co.	Longton
21	1	397227	J. F. Wileman & Co.	Fenton
24	7	397311	G. L. Ashworth & Bros.	Hanley
25	14	397376	Pratt & Simpson	Fenton
27	17	397512	C. Littler & Co.	Hanley
27	18	397513	J. H. Davis	Hanley
27	19	397514	Powell, Bishop & Stonier	Hanley
May 2	4	397609–11	T. C. Brown–Westhead, Moore & Co.	Hanley
5	4	397751	Whittaker, Edge & Co.	Hanley
7	8	397819	S. Fielding & Co.	Stoke
8	6	397829–30	T. G. & F. Booth	Tunstall
11	5	398059	R. H. Plant & Co.	Longton
16	12	398280	T. A. Simpson	Stoke
22	11	398425	Powell, Bishop & Stonier	Hanley
22	12	398426	Burns, Oates	London

Date	Parcel No.	Patent No.	Factory, Retailer Wholesaler, etc	Place
23	7	398436	T. G. & F. Booth	Tunstall
23	8	398437–8	E. A. Wood	Hanley
24	3	398479	The Brownhills Pottery Co.	Tunstall
25	4	398519	W. A. Adderley	Longton
28	2	398577–80	O. G. Blunden	Poling
31	17	398784	Wardle & Co.	Hanley
June 2	9	398849–55	Minton, Hollins & Co.	Stoke
4	8	398877–8	Clementson Bros.	Hanley
8	2	399068	H. Alcock & Co.	Cobridge
9	2	399135–6	Sampson Bridgwood & Son	Longton
9	6	399143	Mintons	Stoke
11	2	399147	F. W. Grove & J. Stark	Longton
11	8	399161	J. Matthews	Weston-s'-Mare
11	9	399162	idem	Weston-s'-Mare
13	3	399319	Belfield & Co.	Preston-pans
13	7	399336	Pratt & Simpson	Stoke
14	2	399367–70	F. W. Grove & J. Stark	Longton
18	11	399554	John Tams	Longton
18	12	399555–9	Wm. Brownfield & Sons	Cobridge
20	3	399640	T. & R. Boote	Burslem
20	4	399641	Mintons	Stoke
20	16	399675	W. & E. Corn	Burslem
21	22	399822	Wardle & Co.	Hanley
23	4	399875	Josiah Wedgwood & Sons	Etruria
25	5	399891	Ford & Riley	Burslem
25	10	399897–8	Wm. Brownfield & Sons	Cobridge
July 2	4	400146	Edge, Malkin & Co.	Burslem
3	3	400176	J. Aynsley & Sons	Longton
3	4	400177	Moore Bros.	Longton
4	7	400348	Wm. Brownfield & Sons	Cobridge
5	6	400367	F. W. Grove & J. Stark	Longton
5	19	400462	T. Furnival & Sons	Cobridge
5	21	400464	Owen, Raby & Co.	Longport
6	2	400467	Blackhurst & Bourne	Burslem
10	9	400582	Ambrose Wood	Hanley
10	11	400583–4	J. Macintyre & Co.	Burslem
11	1	400596	Josiah Wedgwood & Sons	Etruria
19	4	400941	Davenports Ltd.	Longport
19	21	400994	Geo. Jones & Sons	Stoke
20	11	401035	Hollinshead & Kirkham	Tunstall
21	3	401040	Bridgett & Bates	Longton
23	3	401087	Josiah Wedgwood & Sons	Etruria
26	1	401296	W. A. Adderley	Longton
27	4	401410	T. C. Brown–Westhead, Moore & Co.	Hanley
27	13	401426–7	Wm. Bennett	Hanley
30	10	401553	Wm. Brownfield & Sons	Cobridge
31	3	401593	T. & R. Boote	Burslem
Aug 1	3	401623	Wagstaff & Brunt	Longton
1	4	401624	Geo. Jones & Sons	Stoke
1	9	401653	T. C. Brown–Westhead, Moore & Co.	Hanley
2	3	401663–4	Davenports Ltd.	Longport
3	17	401769	E. J. Bodley	Burslem
8	9	401842	J. & E. Ridgway	Stoke
9	15	401897–9	Haviland & Co.	France and London
17	5	402346	E. J. D. Bodley	Burslem
20	8	402514	The Worcester Royal Porcelain Co. Ltd.	Worcester

Date	Parcel No.	Patent No.	Factory, Retailer Wholesaler, etc	Place
22	1	402560–1	The Brownhills Pottery Co.	Tunstall
23	2	402625–6	Grove & Cope	Hanley
24	12	402736	Mountford & Thomas	Hanley
25	11	402839	Wm. Brownfield & Sons	Cobridge
29	3	402950	J. Aynsley & Sons	Longton
31	6	403110	W. & E. Corn	Burslem
31	7	403111	J. F. Wileman & Co.	Fenton
Sept 1	10	403204	S. Fielding & Co.	Stoke
5	3	403298–9	Wm. Brownfield & Sons	Cobridge
7	4	403486	The Derby Crown Porcelain Co. Ltd.	Derby
7	19	403513–4	Powell, Bishop & Stonier	Hanley
11	4	403665	Josiah Wedgwood & Sons	Etruria
13	17	403802–3	H. Aynsley & Co.	Longton
14	1	403805–6	W. & T. Adams	Tunstall
14	2	403807–9	Mintons	Stoke
17	14	403978	The Derby Crown Porcelain Co. Ltd.	Derby
20	12	404171–5	Hall & Read	Hanley
20	13	404176	The Derby Crown Porcelain Co. Ltd.	Derby
21	4	404196	T. C. Brown–Westhead, Moore & Co.	Hanley
24	9	404317	Jones & Hopkinson	Hanley
25	4	404328	F. W. Grove & J. Stark	Longton
25	5	404329–30	Sampson Bridgwood & Son	Longton
27	21	404466	Meigh & Forester	Longton
28	4	404473	Blair & Co.	Longton
28	5	404474	E. J. D. Bodley	Burslem
29	4	404571	Sampson Bridgwood & Son	Longton
Oct 2	15	404643	Mellor, Taylor & Co.	Burslem
2	22	404652–3	Meigh & Forester	Longton
4	4	404745	Sampson Bridgwood & Son	Longton
4	5	404746	Whittaker, Edge & Co.	Hanley
4	24	404809	The Worcester Royal Porcelain Co. Ltd.	Worcester
6	2	404870	W. H. Grindley & Co.	Tunstall
8	1	404900	Hollinson & Goodall	Longton
8	2	404901–2	T. G. & F. Booth	Tunstall
8	3	404903–5	Hall & Read	Hanley
9	9	405016–8	A. Bevington & Co.	Hanley
11	2	405215	Wittmann & Roth	London
12	13	405336	Bridgetts & Bates	Longton
13	3	405341	Wood & Son	Burslem
13	11	405363–4	Wm. Brownfield & Sons	Cobridge
17	5	405466	The New Wharf Pottery Co.	Burslem
17	6	405467–8	Hall & Read	Hanley
20	3	405724	W. A. Adderley	Longton
20	4	405725–9	Wm. Brownfield & Sons	Cobridge
23	6	405855	J. Dimmock & Co.	Hanley
24	11	405946–8	Minton, Hollins & Co.	Stoke
25	17	406032–3	Taylor, Tunnicliffe & Co.	Hanley
26	7	406043	Jones & Hopkinson	Hanley
27	1	406046	The Brownhills Pottery Co.	Tunstall
30	2	406140	J. Marshall & Co.	Bo'ness, Scotland
30	3	406141	The New Wharf Pottery Co.	Burslem
30	17	406187	J. Robinson	Burslem
Nov 1	1	406223	A. Bevington & Co.	Hanley
1	25	406370	Wood, Hines & Winkle	Hanley
1	26	406371	S. Fielding & Co.	Stoke
1	27	406372	Davenports Ltd.	Longport
2	19	406464–9	The Worcester Royal Porcelain Co. Ltd.	Worcester
5	13	406511	H. Alcock & Co.	Cobridge
6	3	406516	E. & C. Challinor	Fenton
7	2	406561	W. & E. Corn	Burslem
10	9	406781	Taylor, Tunnicliffe & Co.	Hanley
10	10	406782	Wm. Brownfield & Sons	Cobridge
13	10	406875	T. G. & F. Booth	Tunstall
14	3	406893	Stonier, Hollinshead & Oliver	Hanley
15	17	407063	T. Furnival & Sons	Cobridge
17	2	407155	The Derby Crown Porcelain Co. Ltd.	Derby
21	3	407333	F. J. Emery	Burslem
22	3	407385	S. Fielding & Co.	Stoke
23	7	407587–8	Minton, Hollins & Co.	Stoke
24	3	407601	Powell, Bishop & Stonier	Hanley
26	2	407623	W. A. Adderley	Longton
26	3	407624	Sampson Bridgwood & Son	Longton
28	12	407805–10	The Worcester Royal Porcelain Co. Ltd.	Worcester
Dec 1	3	407913	idem	Worcester
3	10	407943	James Wilson	Longton
5	2	408035	Malkin, Edge & Co.	Burslem
5	3	408036	The Derby Crown Porcelain Co. Ltd.	Derby
8	8	408136	J. F. Wileman & Co.	Fenton
14	4	408288	The Brownhills Pottery Co.	Tunstall
15	13	408356	T. G. & F. Booth	Tunstall
15	14	408357	Hollinson & Goodall	Longton
29	4	408849	Powell, Bishop & Stonier	Hanley

Holland

Lead-glazed ware decorated with slip-painting or inlay in white clay was made at undetermined centres in Holland from late-medieval times onwards, and is often difficult to distinguish from the contemporary German pottery which was undoubtedly also imported into Holland.

By the second decade of the sixteenth century, and probably earlier, Italian potters and their pupils were at work in the Netherlands making the tin-glazed pottery, painted in colours, to which the name 'maiolica' should be applied in preference to the commonly used but anachronistic term 'Delftware'. The town of Delft did not rise to importance until the seventeenth century.

The sixteenth- and early seventeenth-century wares cannot as a rule be ascribed to particular centres, and the whole class is conveniently known as 'Netherlands maiolica'. Potters of these wares are known to have worked in Haarlem, Rotterdam, Amsterdam, Middleburg (where Joris Andriessen started the earliest recorded North Netherlands maiolica manufacture in 1564), Dordrecht, Leeuwarden and elsewhere in Friesland and at Delft itself. In the course of the century a number of styles were created, differing from the Italian among other features in a certain freshness of colour and in the use of a class of ornament known as *ferronerie*.

During the second quarter of the seventeenth century the town of Delft rose to a leading position, becoming famous more particularly for its imitations in fine tin-glazed earthenware of the Chinese porcelain then being brought to Europe in great quantity by the Dutch East India Company (founded in 1609). The finest Delft ware was made within a hundred years or so of the establishment of the industry; that is to say about 1640 to 1740. This new industry enjoyed such prosperity that by 1667 only fifteen out of a total of a hundred and eighty-two former breweries were at work, and the buildings thus set free had in very many cases been taken over by the potters, who retained the old brewery names such as 'The Three Bells', 'The Rose', 'The Peacock', etc. By about 1725 Delft had begun to decline in face of the renewed competition of porcelain, not only from China but from Germany, where the Meissen factory had begun its great period. A second crisis followed soon after 1760 when the use of Delft faïence rapidly fell away before the technically superior English salt-glazed stoneware and lead-glazed white or cream-coloured earthenware.

In 1764, the Delft potters, united in self-defence, passed an order regularizing the use of marks which thenceforward (and not before) may be accepted as a trustworthy indication of factory. By 1825 only two faïence potters remained in Delft. Apart from Delft the factories at Makkum and Harlingen in Friesland should be noted especially in view of their survival into the nineteenth century.

Parallel with imitations of Chinese white porcelain in tin-glazed faïence was the copying of the red stoneware teapots of Yi-hsing (the so-called *boccaro* ware). These were brought to Europe by the Dutch East Indiamen, accompanying the tea for the brewing of which they were reputed to be particularly suitable. In 1680 seven Delft potters registered their marks for use on red ware, but only the mark of Arij de Milde is at all frequently met with.

The Delft productions of cream-coloured earthenware in the English style date from the nineteenth century and are of little importance. The chief manufacturer was H. A. Piccardt (1800 onward) who not only made earthenware but apparently also decorated in Dutch style imported English wares.

Dutch porcelain is of relatively late date and of little artistic interest. The only eighteenth-century manufactures were that at Weesp (1764–1771), with its successors at Oude Loosdrecht (1771–1784) and Amstel (1784–1810) and that at The Hague (1776–1790). The productions at all factories were of a hard-paste; the Weesp styles showed a marked likeness to the German contemporaries whilst the tendency of the Oude Loosdrecht products was to copy the French. The wares of Amstel were very neo-Classical, as were those at The Hague, which probably began as a decorating establishment of foreign porcelain.

AMSTEL (nr. Amsterdam)
1784–1820
hard-paste porcelain

transferred from
Oude Loosdrecht

Amstel
M. O. L
in blue

Amstel
in black

ARNHEM
faïence
1755–1773

DELFT (nr Rotterdam)
red stoneware
c. 1675–18th century

Arij de Milde
1680–1708

Lambertus van Eenhoorn
c. 1680–1721

Jacobus Caluwe
d. 1730

unidentified

cream-coloured earthenware
19th century

H. A. Piccardt ('The
Porcelain Bottle') (also
decorator of English wares)

PICCARDT

'JAN DERKS (or 'Dirks')
DELFT' (probably importer only)

'JAN DERKS DELFT'

faïence
17th century–

De 3 vergulde Astonne ('The Three
Golden Ashbarrels'), 1655–

Zacharias Dextra
manager, 1712–

Z · DEX

Hendrik van Hoorn
manager, 1759–

HVH
2

mark registered in 1764

3
astonne

De vergulde Blompot
('The Golden Flowerpot')
1654–

blompot

BP
5

mark registered in 1680 by Adriaen
& Jacobus Pijnacker with Albrecht
Keiser, potters at:
De vergulde Blompot
De porcelyn Schotel
De twee Scheepes
De twee Wildemannen

mark registered in 1764

De Blompot

De vergulde Boot ('The Golden
Boat'), 1634–

mark registered in 1680 by Jan Culick, potter at:
De Roos &
De vergulde Boot

Dirck van der Kessel, manager,
1698–1701

D. VK *boot*
1700

mark registered in 1764
by Johannes den Appel

Het Bijltje ('The Hatchet')
1657–1802
mark registered in
1764 by Justus Brouwer

mark of Hugo Brouwer
1775–1788(?)

mark registered in 1680 by Quirinus
Cleynoven, potter at:
De Dissel
De porcelyn Fles
De Grieksche A

De porceleyne Fles
('The Porcelain Bottle')
1655–present

mark registered in 1764
Johann and
Dirk Harlees
c. 1795–1800

H. A. Piccardt
early 19th century

PICCARDT
DELFT
impressed in relief

modern mark

De 3 *porceleyne Flessies* ('The Three Porcelain
Scent-bottles'), 1661–

mark registered in 1764 by Hugo
Brouwer (also of 'The Hatchet')

't Fortuyn ('The Fortune'), 1661–

Joris Mes, *or* Mesch (also of 'The
Heart')

registered in 1764 by widow of Pieter
van den Briel in 1764

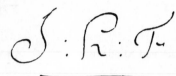

Johannes Hermanus
Frerkingh, 1769–

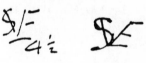

mark registered in 1680 by Martin
Gouda, red-ware potter

De Grieksche A
('The Greek A'), 1658–

Samuel van Eenhoorn
1678–1687

Adriaenus Koeks
1687–1701

Adriaenus Koeks,
son Pieter and his
widow

Jan Theunis Dextra
1759–1765

Jacobus Halder, 1765–

't Hart ('The Heart')
1661–

Joris Mes
(also of 'The Fortune')

De porceleyne Klaeuw ('The Porcelain Claw') 1662–

Cornelia van Schoonhoven *or* Cornelius van Schagen, 1668–1671 or 1695–

various forms of mark registered in 1764:

Hendrick van Middeldijk
1760–

van Putten (also of 'The Three Bells')
1830–1850

De 3 Klokken ('The Three Bells'),
1671–

mark registered by van der Does' widow, 1764

De Lampetkan ('The Ewer')
1637–

variants of marks registered in 1764

mark registered in 1680 by Johannes Mes (or Mesch)

't Jonge Moriaenshooft ('The Young Moor's Head'), 1654–

Rochus Hoppesteyn
1680–1692

Lieve van Dalen
1692–1727

Jan van der Hagen
1732–1764

mark registered in 1764 by widow Van der Strale

't Oude Moriaenshooft ('The Old Moor's Head'), before 1690–

mark registered in 1764 by Geertruy Verstelle

De Paauw ('The Peacock'), 1652–

various late 17th and early 18th-century marks

registered in 1764 by Jacobus de Milde

De metale Pot
('The Metal Pot'), 1638–

Lambertus Cleffius, 1666–1691
(also of 'The White Star')

Lambertus van Eenhorn
1691–1721

registered in 1764
by Pieter Paree

De Romein ('The Rummer')
1613–

Petrus van Marum, 1759–1764

Johannes van der Kloot, 1764

De Roos ('The Rose'), 1662–

various early 18th-century marks

registered by
D. van der Does, 1764

De twee Scheepjes ('The
Two Little Ships'), 1642–

Cornelis Keiser, 1668

Jan Gaal, 1707–1725

A. Pennis, 1759–1770

registered mark of
Anthony Pennis, 1764

De dobbelde Schenckan
('The Double Tankard')
1659–

mark registered in 1764

De porceleyn Schotel
('The Porcelain Dish')
1612–

Ghisbrecht Cruyck
1663–1671

registered by
J. van Duyn, 1764

De witte Starre
('The White Star'), 1660–

registered mark of
Albertus Kiehl, 1761–1772

marks of the last-named

probably Johannes van den
Bergh, 1772–1789

De twee Wildemannen ('The Two
Wild Men'), 1661–

mark of Willem van Beek
1760–1780

HAARLEM
c. 1572–
maiolica

probably Cornelis Lubbertsz

probably Hans Barnaert
Vierleger, c. 1595

MAKKUM (Friesland)
1675–
faïence

Freerk Jans Tichelaar
modern mark of factory

OUDE LOOSDRECHT
1771–1784
hard-paste porcelain
(transferred from Weesp)

 incised

Johannes de Mol

underglaze blue   purple or other
or enamel colour   enamel colour

black or other
enamel colour

HAGUE, THE
c. 1766–1790
hard-paste porcelain
factory started as a decorating-
establishment only of German
porcelain:

underglaze blue
mark of Ansbach
overpainted in blue enamel

in blue   in underglaze
enamel   blue

ROTTERDAM
17th century–
tiles and faïence

Cornelis Boumeester
b. 1652, d. 1733

C:BM

probably Johannes Aelmis

I Aeelmis
1731
C B
*

Rozenburg, modern mark
Factory founded in 1885
by W. W. von Gudenberg,
directed by
Theodorus Colenbrander

probably an independent
porcelain decorator

F . L . S .
A Rotterdam
W.M₆:1812

MAASTRICHT
1883–
hard-paste porcelain

WEESP
1759–1771
hard-paste porcelain
(transferred to
Oude Loosdrecht)

underglaze blue

Hungary

The important type of peasant-maiolica, known as 'Habaner ware', was produced on the borders of Hungary from the late sixteenth and seventeenth centuries onwards.

The only Hungarian faïence factory enjoying aristocratic patronage was Holitsch, the productions were from the beginning inspired by French faïence. Motives drawn from the local peasant-maiolica are later conspicuous in the decoration, and maiolica painted in pallid high-temperature colours in the later Castelli style was also made. In 1786 the factory commenced the manufacture of lead-glazed white and cream-coloured earthenware in English style.

During the nineteenth century many factories commenced the manufacture of wares in hard-paste porcelain; the factory at Herend being a source of imitations of all kinds of Oriental and eighteenth-century European wares.

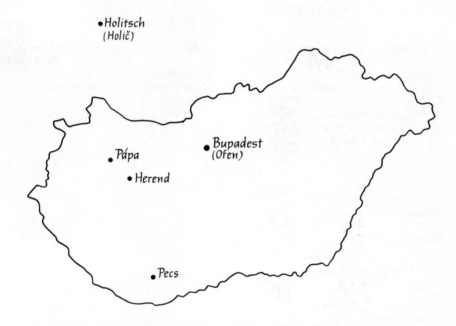

BUDAPEST

Fischer, Emil
1866–
hard-paste porcelain

Hüttl, Theodor
1901–
hard-paste porcelain

Hüttl Tivador
Budapest

'Granit'
1922–
general pottery

GRANIT

HEREND

Fischer, Moritz (*d.* 1880)
1839–
hard-paste porcelain

MF

HEREND

in enamel
usually blue
over the glaze

HOLITSCH
1743–1826
faïence & earthenware

'Holitscher Fabrik'

'Holitscher Herrschaft'

'Holicske Panstvi'

in blue

on cream-coloured earthenware
1786–1813

HOLICS

HOLITSCH   HOLITSH
all impressed

KÖRMÖCZBANYA
1868–
Kossuch, János
general earthenware

KREMNITZ
early 19th century–
cream-coloured earthenware

KREMNITZ   KR
impressed

OFEN
c. 1795–
cream-coloured earthenware

OF

OFEN
impressed

PÁPA
early 19th century
cream-coloured earthenware
Windschügel, K. A.

PAPA

MW
in a crowned shield
impressed

PECS (formerly Fünfkirchen)
1855–
lustre wares

W. Zsolnay
(Now a Hungarian state concern)

ZSOLNAY
PÉCS   *J.J.M.*

Italy

Lead-glazed earthenware with *sgraffiato* decoration appears to have been made in Italy from the late fifteenth and early sixteenth century onwards at many centres, but with the exception of Pavia and Bologna the places have not been identified with certainty. Black- and brown-glazed vases and dishes were made from the later part of the sixteenth century onwards and are variously ascribed to Venice, Montelupo, Siena and Casteldurante.

The only decorated pottery of artistic importance made in Italy at the close of the fourteenth century was painted in green and dark manganese-purple on a more or less imperfect white ground obtained by the use of oxide of tin. The name 'maiolica' was, however, not in contemporary use until the middle of the fifteenth century, when it was first applied to the lustred Spanish pottery and later extended in meaning to include all varieties of tin-glazed earthenware.

The principal centres were at Orvieto (perhaps the earliest), in Tuscany (particularly Siena and Florence) and at Faenza. Rome, Padua, Cortona and Todi were also places of manufacture.

About 1460, fairly close copies of the imported Spanish wares were made in Tuscany, whilst at Faenza a bold and original polychrome style, comparatively free from Spanish influence, was cultivated from about 1470 onwards. The productions of the third great centre of fifteenth-century maiolica, at Deruta, are difficult to identify, one class of great beauty being ascribed to the period from about 1485–1500.

The first decade of the sixteenth century saw the vogue of maiolica already well established, and the custom of adorning the pharmacies with sumptuous services of drug-vases and jars and the fashion for displaying large decorative dishes on sideboards and tables, reached their height in this period.

The art of maiolica reached its highest level of perfection in the work of a number of great individual artists patronized by noblemen in the period between 1505–25.

At Deruta at the latest from 1501 onwards a 'golden' or mother-of-pearl and a ruby lustre were in common use; the latter disappearing from Deruta about 1515, seems to have been passed on to Gubbio.

Apart from Deruta the successive fashionable motives of decoration were to a large extent common to all the factories and the identification of their work can at best be conjectured on the grounds of colour and such incidentals as the rare 'marks' and the patterns on the backs. But each had its favourite, but not exclusive, types of decoration; the designs in concentric circles and the blue-stained enamel (*berettino* or *smaltino*) of Faenza, and the symmetrical (*a candeliere*) formal designs in grey and blue of Casteldurante are instances of this. The predominance of Faenza is indicated by the wide occurrence of its commoner wares in Italy and abroad (bringing the name 'faïence') and by the use elsewhere of the devices or marks associated with its chief factory, the 'Casa Pirota'.

The *istoriato* style or pictorial painting was brought to perfection at Casteldurante by Nicola Pellipario during the first quarter of the sixteenth century. He removed to Urbino in 1528 bringing that centre to the foremost position. The Urbino *istoriato* style was quickly copied in a harder and coarser form at most other Italian factories (and even in France), remaining more or less in vogue until the end of the sixteenth century or even later. Forli and Pesaro appear to have risen to importance only in this later period. Minor factories were also at Rimini and Verona.

Meanwhile, at Venice, about the middle of the century, the Faenza style of painting in blue-and-white on a blue-stained (pale *berettino* or *smaltino*) ground was adapted in many noble and highly original works.

Soon after the middle of the sixteenth century Urbino invented a new type of decoration composed chiefly of small 'grotesques' imitated from Raphael's *Loggie* frescoes, whilst at Faenza a free and unlaboured painting of slight figure-subjects in blue and orange (or pale yellow) on a white ground was adopted.

Still later in the seventeenth and early eighteenth centuries the maiolica tradition was to some extent maintained in original work attributed to Venice and Castelli. Coarser wares were made at Sicily and at Montelupo, and a minor seventeenth-century factory imitating Turkish faïence was at Padua.

The wave of Chinese influence that came in the seventeenth century with the Dutch importations and the rise of Delft brought more or less imitative blue-and-white styles at Savona and elsewhere, while the competition of the French faïence factories and the vogue of Chinese porcelain were largely responsible for the styles adopted at Turin, Lodi, Nove, Bassano, Milan, Pesaro and the later Faenza.

The earliest European attempts towards the imitation of Chinese porcelain are rather obscure but the famous sixteenth-century 'Medici porcelain' of Florence is well attested and of great importance as the first European ware of its kind and the only porcellanous ceramic material to be made in Europe in the Renaissance. It is an artificial soft-paste, as are some rare pieces of slightly later date attributed to Padua.

The short-lived Vezzi factory at Venice (1719 to about 1727 at latest) was started with the help of a Meissen workman, while that of Doccia (1735 onwards) drew its first styles from Vienna. The Capodimonte factory near Naples (1743–59) making a soft-paste of French type, was established by King Charles III and discontinued on his accession to the throne of Spain; the manufacture of porcelain was resumed eventually at Naples itself in 1771.

New factories of Venice (and another at Nove) share with the above the often fantastic Rococo style which is the chief contribution of Italy to the art of European porcelain. A markedly grey colour is characteristic of much Italian porcelain of the eighteenth century; this is shown alike by Venice, Nove, Treviso and Doccia.

Turin
Milan
Pavia
Lodi
Verona
Nove
Bassano
Treviso
Padua
Venice
Este
Vinovo
Mantua
Parma
Modena
Ferrara
Mondovi
Savona
Genoa
Bologna
Ravenna
Imola
Forli
Faenza
Rimini
Florence
Urbino
Pesaro
Cafaggiolo
Montelupo
Casteldurante
Gubbio
TUSCANY
Siena
Fabriano
Deruta
Orvieto
Viterbo
Castelli
Rome
Naples
Palermo
SICILY
Caltagirone

ANGARONO (nr. Bassano)
late 18th century
groups and figures in
creamware

Angaron 1779

'Jacopo', artist

BASSANO (Venezia)
16th–mid-18th century
maiolica

Roman artists at
Bassano about 1725

Antonio Terchi

Bartolomeo Terchi

Bassano
1719

Antonio Terchi
in
Bassano
B° Terchj
Bassano

dated 1514

about 1513

c. 1545–1550, probably
Alessandro Fattorini

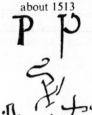

& '*In gafagiolo*'

BOLOGNA
15th century–18th century
lead-glazed earthenware
'*sgraffiato*'

c. 1794–
creamwares

Carlo Aldovrandi

SMV.P.
1674

1675
S.P.P

CARLO ALDOVRANDI
impressed

c. 1530–1540, with
'Medici' arms

dated 1507

c. 1480

dated 1506

probably by 'Jacopo'

orange-red

1849–
reproductions of Italian
Renaissance maiolica

Angelo Minghetti & Son

CAFAGGIOLO (nr. Florence)
early 16th century–
mid-18th century

'SPR' ('Semper'), motto
of Medici family
or
'SF' (Fattorini), potter

AᴧA

'CANDIANA' (nr. Padua)
early 17th century
maiolica & porcellanous
ware

marks on artificial
porcelain

maiolica

IHH
1638

†
G.G.P.F

& '*In Chaffaguolo*'

IᴍH
†
I·G·P·F·1627

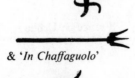

& '*In Chaffagguolo*' & 'SP' monogram

Chandiana·1633 M.G.

CANNETO (Mantova)
Ceramjca Furga
hard-paste porcelain
1872–

 FURGA

Dr. Francesco Antonio
Grue, 1686–1746

fras Ants Grue P

D. Francisci Antonti
Xaveri Grue 1735

Dr. Franc Anton
Grue 1718

CAPODIMONTE
1743–1759
soft-paste porcelain
established by
King Charles III of Spain

impressed

Liborio Grue
b. 1701, *d.* 1776

LGP

about 1745

in gold

Bernardino Gentili
b. 1727, *d.* 1813

Bernardino Gent.p.

Saverio Grue
b. 1731, *d. c.* 1806

SG

on useful wares and
occasionally figures
Also used at Buen Retiro
(Spain)

Carmine Gentile,
b. 1678, *d.* 1763

C G P

Cne Gli P

Gentili

P G

CASTELDURANTE
(renamed Urbania
in 1635)
16th century
maiolica

DERUTA or DIRUTA (Umbria)
c. 1490
maiolica

Nicola Pellipario,
painter, dated 1521

Nicola Pellipario
painter, dated 1528

Nicoſa da
·V·

·LV·

Serial No. (?), by
Nicola Pellipario

c. 1510

on Este-Gonzaga
service

c. 1500–1510

probably Francesco
Durantino

CASTELLI (Abruzzi)
17th and 18th centuries
maiolica

mark of Carthusian
Order, 1697–1727

'Francesco Urbini'
c. 1537–1554

dated 1630

'PETRUS PAULUS
MANCINUS DE DIRUTA'

porcelain style on
maiolica

DOCCIA (nr. Florence)
1735–present
hard-paste porcelain

late 18th and first
half of 19th century

1792–1800

18th-century porcelain
with tin-glaze

in red

on wares of the finest
paste, 1792–1815

about 1810

19th century

1884–1891

1848–
general pottery

1847–1873

1873–1903

1874–1888

imitations of
Capodimonte
and Naples

Richard-Ginori
partnership, late
19th century

'1771 Fabrica di Maiolica
fina di Gregorio
Caselli in Deruta'

all in blue, red or
gold

impressed

     6.

in blue, crimson or purple

10

in green

F
E E
both incised

GI   GIN

'Ginori'
impressed

mark on modern
maiolica

ESTE
1781–late 18th century
porcelain
Fiorina Fabris &
Antonio Costa

1785–
Gerolamo Franchini
creamware

FABRIANO (Duchy of Urbino)
16th century
maiolica

mark on Pellipario
plate

Cesare Miliani
1858–

FAENZA (Emilia)
14th century
maiolica

1480–1490

c. 1490

tiles, dated 1510

probably factory mark
1510–1515

probably Casa Pirota
1490–1500

form of Casa Pirota
mark

Este
G

GF

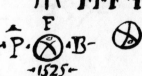

variants of Casa Pirota marks: sometimes used by Faenza painters migrating to other factories

c. 1510

c. 1515, probably Piero Rocca, artist

mark on panel painted by the 'Master of the Resurrection Panel'

initials of Baldassare Manara
c. 1530–1535

attributed to Flaminio Fontano

dated 1546, signed by Giovanni Brame

probably mark of Maestro Virgiliotto Calamelli
d. about 1570

presumed mark of Virgiliotto

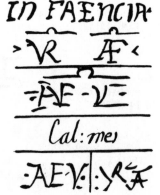

attributed to Don Pino Bettisii, *d.* about 1589

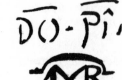

attributed to Antonio Maria Regoli
b. 1707, *d.* 1775

18th-century marks of Ferniani and descendants

A. Farini, 1850–1878
Urbino/Patanazzi style maiolica

1878–

FLORENCE
c. 1575–*c.* 1587
soft-paste porcelain

mark depicting cathedral of Florence and 'F' for 'Firenze' or 'Francesco'

probably signifying 'trial-piece'

FMMDEII ('Franciscus Maria (*or* Medicis) Magnus–Dux Etruriae II')

216

Ulysse Cantagalli (*d.* 1901)
1878–
maiolica reproductions of
early Urbino, Faenza,
Gubbio, Deruta & della
Robbia wares

Fantoni, modern
studio-potter

mark of Maestro
Giorgio with that of
'Maestro N', 1535–1540

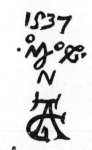

'Maestro N'

probably painted by
Orazio Fontana at
Urbino and lustred
at Gubbio

in lustre

probably only lustred
at Gubbio, dated 1515

FORLI
　mid-16th century
　maiolica

　dated 1542　　　　　*'fata in forli'*

　dated 1545　　　　　**'FU FATA IN FORLI'**
　　　　　　　　　　　(in monogram)

Giovanni Spinaci
c. 1857–1881
reproductions of
'Maestro Giorgio' lustre

Carocci, Fabbri & Co.
19th century

GENOA (*see* Savona)

GUBBIO (Duchy of Urbino)
　c. 1495
　maiolica, especially
　ruby-lustre

　various forms of
　Maestro Giorgio's
　factory mark, 1519–1541

LAVENO
　1856–present
　earthenwares

LODI (Lombardy)
　18th century
　faïence

　Simpliciano Ferreti
　c. 1725

　Morsenchio-Capelletti
　mid-18th century

MILAN
　18th century
　faïence

　Felice Clerici

Pasquale Rubati, 1756

'Fabbrica di Pasquale
Rubati Milano'

Cesare Confalonieri
1770–1775

'*Fabbrica di Santa
Cristina*'

marks attributed to Milan

1833–1873
earthenware
Julius Richard & Co.
at San Cristoforo

1873–
Richard-Ginori
(link with Doccia)

Cacciapuoti
artist-potter in hard-
paste porcelain
modern

MONDOVI (Piedmont)
1808–
cream-coloured earthenware
B. Musso of Savona
1811–
(in family until *c.* 1897)

M.M.
impressed

MONTELUPO (Tuscany)
16th century
maiolica

dated 1627

Raffaello Girolåmo
artist, dated 1639

NAPLES
c. 1684
maiolica

Royal Factory
1771–1806
(1806–1834 continued
under various private
owners and made
biscuit & glazed
figures in Empire
& neo-Classical style)

made at Portici, before
move to Naples in 1775

in blue

F.R.F. monogram (for
'Fabbrica Reale Ferdinandea')
1773–1787

purple, red
or blue

late 18th century

all impressed

underglaze blue or incised

late-18th-century figures
probably Giordano
modeller

incised

Giovine, decorator of
imported wares, 1826–1830

in red

1760–
cream-coloured earthenware
and porcelain

Nicola Giustiniani

GIUSTINIANI

Giustiniani
FN

Biagio Giustiniani (son)
late 18th century

BG   B.G.
N

probably 'Fabbrica
Michele Giustiniani
Napoli'

F M G
N

Antonio and Salvatore
Giustiniani
('*Fratelli Giustiniani*
Napoli')

F G
N

Cherinto del Vecchio
1785–1855
'*Fabbrica del Vecchio*
Napoli'

FDV   *F D V*
N   *N*

del Vecchio
N

'*Gennaro del Vecchio Napoli*'
late mark

G D V N

'modern Giustiniani'

NOVE (Venezia)
1728–
faïence & creamware
soft-paste porcelain
from 1762–1825

mark on faïence
c. 1728–1730

Giovanni Battista
Antonibon & son
Pasquale (from 1738)

rare mark on old faïence
but common on 19th-
century wares

19th century & later
faïence

Giovanni Maria Baccin
c. 1780, creamware

monograms & names of
Giovanni Battista Antonibon
on early porcelain

mark on porcelain after
1781

normal factory mark
from 1781

in red, blue or gold

wares made by
Pasquale Antonibon
1763–1773

in relief

on figures and groups
after 1781

incised

about 1800
with painter's signature

in gold

c. 1800, with an
owner's mark?

in red

Giovanni Baroni period
1801–1825

in gold

late 18th & early 19th
century

incised

19th-century creamware

Bernardi

Cecchetto, G. M.

Viero, G. B.

219

PADUA
late 15th–18th century
maiolica & lead-glazed
sgraffiato earthenware

+

·1555·

×
1563

a *pridoa*

"*Fatto*
in Palermo 1606"

PALERMO, Sicily
late 16th–17th century
maiolica

PAVIA (nr. Milan, Lombardy)
c. 1676–
glazed earthenware
(*sgraffiato*)

Cuzio family, *c.* 1676–
1694

'*Antonio Maria Cuzio*'

'*Giovanni Brizio*'

'*Antonio Maria Antonelli*'

first half of 18th century
faïence

Clara Formenti
(of Santa Chiara)

PESARO (nr. Urbino)
c. 1486–
maiolica

probably 'P(esaro)'
'G(abbice)'
early 16th century

Maestro Girolamo
dated 1542

P   G

'*in la botega di*
mastro Girolame
de le Gabice'

Casali & Galigari, 1763
(with signature of
Lei, painter)

C·C·
Pesaro
1765
P:P:L:
F.A.C.
P

'Filippo Antonio
Callegari, Pesaro'

Callegari
Pesaro

CC

Magrini & Co., 1870–
modern mark on
imitation Urbino

fabbrica Magrin
Pesaro

modern studio-potter

MOLARONI
M.G.
PESARO
ITALY

PISA (Tuscany)
c. 1587–
maiolica
Niccolò Sisti

'PISA'

G. Palme & Co.
creamware
second half of 19th
century

PORDENONE
19th century
creamware
Giuseppe Carlo Galvani

1823–1845

1845–1850

WEDGWOOD
A

1850–1860

1860–1874

1883

1883

RIMINI
15th–16th century
maiolica

'*in Rimino*'

RIVIGNANO
19th century
creamware
Pertoldeo

ROME
14th–17th century
maiolica

'FATTO . IN . BOTEGA .
DE . M . DIOMEDE .
DURANTE . IN . ROMA .'

'ALMA ROMA 1623'

'FATTO . IN . ROMA .
DA . GIO . PAULO .
SAVONI . MDC .'

1761–1784
porcelain
Filippo Cuccumos

'ROMA MAG 1769'
incised

on piece inscribed
'*Roma l⁰ Maggio* 1769'

1785–1831
porcelain (up to 1818)
and earthenware

Giovanni Volpato

G. VOLPATO
ROMA
impressed

Bartolomeo Terchi
painter, *c.* 1736

Bar: Terchi Roma
no

SAN CRISTOFORO (*see* Milan)

SAN QUIRICO D'ORCIA (nr. Siena)
1693–18th century
maiolica
arms of Cardinal Chigi
founder

Bartolommeo Terchi
painter

'*Bar. Terchi Romano
in S. Quirico*'

SAVONA (nr. Genoa, Liguria)
16th–18th century
maiolica

shield of arms of Savona

'Girolamo Salomini'
17th-century potter

the ducal 'berretto'

ducal 'berretto', 'BC'
for 'Conrade' or
'Corrado', potters

cross from the arms
of Savoy

'pentagram' or 'Solomon's
seal', probably mark of
Girolamo Salomini or
Siccardi

'fortress' mark, ascribed
to Guidobono, painter

Levantino family of
Albissola
(beacon-light from
Genoa harbour)

mark of Chiodo
potter

Luigi Levantino
late 17th–early 18th
century

Agostino Levantino

Giordano

Sebastiano Folco
18th–19th century

Pescetto, late 17th century

Salomini *or* Salamone
17th–18th century

unexplained initials
on undoubted pieces
of Savona faïence

on pieces signed by
Agostino Ratti, painter
c. 1720

Giacomo Boselli
painter & potter, last
quarter of 18th century
creamware

19th-century makers
of creamware:

Antonio Musso
c. 1830
(branch of Mondovi
factory)

Antonio Folco
1856–
creamware

Sebastiano Ricci
pre-1860
creamware   impressed

Marcenaro
19th-century creamware

Francesco Ferro
1852–
primarily pipes   impressed

SESTO FIORENTINO
1907–
reproductions of
maiolica
Ceramics Artistica
Ciulli
Bruno Fantani

SIENA (Tuscany)
15th and 16th century
maiolica

16th century probably
owners' or series
marks

Maestro Benedetto
c. 1515–1520

*'fata T Siena
da m° benedetto'*

TREVISO (Venezia)
late 18th century–1840
soft-paste porcelain

*'Guiseppe Andrea
Fratelli, Fontebasso'*

'Fratelli Fontebasso'
dated 1779

G.A.F.F
Treviso

F.F.

19th-century earthenware

Fontebasso

1851–

1830–1850

1853–

1856–

WEGWOOD

R.FABB..FON..TREV.

1860–
'Royal Fabrique,
Fontebasso'

1873–

FERRARA
R.F. F.T.

TRIESTE
maiolica, 1776
creamware, *c.* 1780–1797
Pietro Lorenzi

PL)

P★L

1783–early 19th century
creamware
Guiseppe Sinibaldi
Lodovico Santini

S S

SS

1788–
creamware
Mattia Filippuzzi

M F

TURIN (Piedmont)
16th century–
maiolica

*'Fatta in Torino
adi 12 d
Setebre 1577*

probably Parco factory
1646–

shield of Savoy

'Torino-Rossetti'
(Giorgio Rossetti
di Macello), 1725

Giorgio Rossetti
(also porcelain
1737–*c.* 1745)
G. A. Ardizzone
c. 1765

slipware
19th century
D. Gionetti

in black

TUSCANY
late 14th-early 15th century
maiolica

Siena-Orvieto type

marks found on
'oak-leaf' jars

on 'pomegranate-
pattern' wares

on 'Spanish' foliage wares

armorial vase

on 'Hispano-Moresque'
and 'Gothic' foliage
wares

marks on pieces with
'Gothic' foliage, pomegranate,
and peacock's-feather
decoration

URBANIA
late-19th-century
reproductions of early
maiolica
Castelbarco Albani

impressed

URBINO
c. 1520–18th century
maiolica

signatures of Francesco
Xanto Avelli of Rovigo
dated 1530–1542

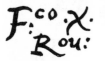

marks of Orazio Fontana
mid-16th century

attributed to Flaminio
Fontana, dated 1583

·A·F·A·

handwriting of Nicola
Pellipario

handwriting of Francesco
Xanto

Patanazzi family
c. 1584

probably Giovanni
Antonio Maria Roletti
c. 1770

'*Fabrica Roletti
Taurinorum*'

·F·F·

·O·A·
P·P
1548

'*Mo Antoni Patanzi,
Vrbini 1580*'

'ALF . P . F
VRBINO . 1606'

'*in botega di Jos.
Batista Boccione
1607*'

'*Fabrica di
maiolica fina di
Monsiur Rolet in
Urbino*'

16th century
maiolica

late 17th–early 18th
century

18th century
hard-paste porcelain

Vezzi factory
c. 1719–1727

also imitated on later
Doccia in gold or black

VEN:

underglaze blue

V=ᵃ

red or gold

Ven·

red

1758–1763
hard-paste porcelain
Nathaniel Friedrich
Hewelcke

'*In Venetia in
Cotrada di Sᵗᵒ Polo
in Botego di Mᵒ
Lodovico*'

incised

VeneziA.

in blue

Ven:ᵃ

in underglaze blue
red, blue enamel or gold,

in red, green or blue

Ven:⁻

red

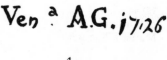

V   V

incised & painted red

1764–1765 to 1812
hybrid soft-paste

Geminiano Cozzi

*'1765 Venezia
Faba Geminiano
Cozzi'*

in red

VERONA
16th century
maiolica

*'Gio Giovani
Batista da Faenza
In Verona M . . .'*

'1547 in Verona'

VICENZA
1788–early 19th century
creamware
Vicentini del Giglio
(porcelain from 1791)

Todescan, *c.* 1820
Otto, Count
(Societa Ceramica di
Vicenza, 1871)

Sebellin Baldissera
before 1816–early 20th century
creamware

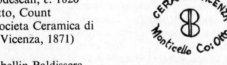

peasant pottery
of Vicenza & Nove

19th century

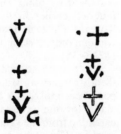

VINOVO (nr. Turin)
1776–1820
hybrid soft-paste

cross from arms of Savoy

initials of Dr. Gioanetti
1780–1815

all usually in under-
glaze blue or incised,
rare in other colours
or gold

Lomello, 1815–1820

VISCHE (nr. Turin)
1765–1766
faïence & porcelain

cross 'V' mark attributed
to factory

VITERBO (Roma)
16th century
maiolica

*'In Viterbo
Diomeo 1544'*

Japan

The Japanese first became aware of the aesthetic appeal of pottery through the ancient tea-ceremony which was originally inspired by a Buddhist sect in the twelfth century, and called for ceremonial vessels of both beauty and simplicity.

According to the legend, a potter named Kato Shirozaemon (also called Toshiro) returned from China in the thirteenth century and made pottery of brown-glazed *temmoku* type at Seto in the province of Owari, which became the pottery centre of Japan, using the T'ang wares and celadons and later Korean types as models.

The earliest Seto productions are uncertainly identified but it may be said that the period extended over the thirteenth, fourteenth and first half of the fifteenth century ending in 1472 when the rules of the tea-ceremony were formulated and a period of sophistication began. But fine pottery of the same sort was undoubtedly still made in the sixteenth and seventeenth centuries and even later in country places untouched by the prevailing fashions.

In addition to the early group of brown and yellowish-glazed stoneware many versions of the later Korean inlaid ('mishima') ware are ascribed to Seto.

To the phase following the formal establishment of the tea-ceremony in 1472, belong most of the older productions of the Satsuma factories, which besides some admirable wares inspired by the Korean and close copies of T'ang three-colour ('bekko') and of Sawankhalok ware ('Sunkoroku'), include some of the worst kinds of pseudo-primitive horror, such as the revolting 'dragon-skin' glaze, Soma wares (made for the prince of that name at Nakamura, Iwaki province) and the wares of Shidoro (province of Totomi) which include the tea-bowls showing the characteristic affectation of primitive roughness.

About 1580 in the neighbourhood of Kyoto, the capital, in the province of Yamashiro, Chojiro, the son of a Korean potter, began the production of a soft, uneven-surfaced, low-fired, lead-glazed ware known as *'raku'*, sometimes thrown but more often hand-modelled. There were two distinct kinds of this ware: 'black *raku*', a coarse and hardish dark red-brown or black-glazed ware; and 'red *raku*', a very soft salmon-red ware touched with white, green, and other coloured slips showing through a waxen-looking glaze. Chojiro was rewarded by the war-lord Hideyoshi with a seal for use on his wares, inscribed *'raku'* meaning enjoyment.

Also in the neighbourhood of Kyoto, at Awata and elsewhere, was developed in the early seventeenth century, a cream-glazed grey or brownish earthenware which has continued to be produced to the present day.

With the peace of the seventeenth century, we find famed Kyoto artists such as Koyetsu and Kenzan making *'raku'* ware, the latter also making Awata ware, whilst later in the century worked the celebrated Ninsei and his followers including several members of the Donachi family who practised enamelling. A greyish crackled ware similar to that of Awata is associated with Kiyomizu, a neighbouring Kyoto district.

The once greatly admired 'brocaded' export wares of the province of Satsuma with their crowded designs and extravagant gilding and enamelling on a cream-coloured crackled ground are often confused with the Kyoto export wares. Both were developments, well calculated to appeal to the nineteenth-century taste, of the slightly decorated enamelled Satsuma first made at the Tadeno factory in Kagoshima about 1795.

Porcelain makes its first appearance in Japan during the early seventeenth century with the early Arita wares painted in greyish underglaze blue and the primitive red and green enamels; other seventeenth-century products include the export ware brought to Europe by the Dutch, these being of greyish porcelain painted in purple-toned underglaze blue with panelled decoration in late Ming style and large quantities of Imari wares with crowded decoration of flowers, scrolls and panelling painted in underglaze blue and thick dark red and gilding, the latter continuing into the early eighteenth century.

The so-called Kakiemon wares include both the finest and most familiar Japanese porcelain and date from the late seventeenth century.

The very different porcelain of Kutani in the province of Kaga dates from about 1664. In that year Goto Saijiro and a fellow potter are said to have learnt to make porcelain at Arita and returned to start a factory at Kutani near which china-stone had been found some years before. But the Kutani wares are of a totally different character from those of Arita. The earliest and most important phase of activity saw the production of the 'green Kutani' ware. The ware itself is a heavy porcelain, often coarse in texture, but the nineteenth-century egg-shell and other porcelain from the district often bears the name of the pottery and of the potter.

The porcelain known as Nabeshima ware was made at Okawachi in Hizen for a prince of that name. The factory was started about 1660 with the help of other potters from other Hizen factories which had been founded earlier in the seventeenth century by the Koreans. The technique suggests that its best work was contemporary with the reign of Yung-chêng (1723–35).

The pottery started by the Koreans in the seventeenth century at Mikawachi in Hizen did not make porcelain until 1712 when the wares executed were made for the princes of Hirado whose patronage extended from the years 1751 to 1843, but were never marked. The later nineteenth-century Mikawachi porcelain was marked with the name, but was of inferior quality. Celadon porcelain was made at Mikawachi as well as at Arita and at Sanda in the province of Settsu.

The porcelain of Kyoto was the work of a host of clever potters, mostly copyists. Much of the work shows the characteristic nineteenth-century cleverness and prettiness for which modern Japanese commercial pottery is notorious.

The modern Japanese artist-potters have produced close reproductions in the Chinese and Korean styles, their achievements covering a wide range of fine wares. It has been argued that it is a sentimental revival and as such is doomed to failure for want of economic conditions which gave reality and meaning to the works of the early potters, and that it would have been better to accept the conditions of the modern industrial world and seek to create within them new forms of ceramic art as authentic as the old.

JAPANESE POTTERS' NAMES AND PLACE-NAMES SOMETIMES USED AS MARKS

Japanese marks are very numerous and misleading. Besides those formed on the same lines as the Chinese and often copied from them, a host of artists' signatures and other names or words are found, in the form of impressed seals on the base or side of a piece, or painted in freely written characters, often in the field of the decoration.

Such signatures are no more to be taken at their face-value than Chinese reign-names; but even in genuine examples they are hard to interpret, since a potter may have used, besides his family name, one or more 'art-names', comparable with the hall-names on Chinese porcelain, granted to him by a patron or adopted by him on setting up a new workshop or the like occasion. An artist-potter commonly bequeathed the right to use his marks to his 'sons' or pupils; thus the same mark may appear on the pottery made by several generations all working in the same style. Place-names and the names of princely patrons were also used and add to the confusion. It would obviously be pointless and unsuitable to give here more than a few typical examples of the Japanese marks.

Japanese porcelain of the eighteenth century and earlier seldom bears a mark of origin, though Chinese marks, especially Ming reign-names, were sometimes added. Cyclical dates, like the Chinese, were used occasionally, as well as the Japanese period-names (*nengo*), but most of the fine Kutani, Kakiemon, Nabeshima and Hirado porcelains bear no mark at all. Various forms of the word *fuku* (happiness) were characteristically added to early Kutani, but the full six-, eight-, or even ten-character Kutani mark, including the name of a hall or potter, appears only on bad nineteenth-century porcelain. In fact all the marks beginning Dai Nippon ('Great Japan'), as in the *Eiraku* mark below, indicates a nineteenth- or twentieth-century date. Such marks, and some earlier ones, end with the same characters as the Chinese *chih* and *tsao*, which in Japanese are read *sei* and *tsukuru* (or *zo*).

 fuku (happiness)

 fuku (happiness)

 Kutani

 dai Nippon Eiraku tsukuru ('Great Japan Eiraku made') 19th century

Kanzan sei (19th century)

seal: *raku*

impressed signature of Ninsei

signature of Kenzan

signature of Dohachi

seal of Banko

Luxembourg

The only factory worthy of note in Luxembourg is that at Septfontaines: founded in about 1766, this factory had become very prosperous by 1795 and still exists as 'Villeroy & Boch'.

White and cream-coloured earthenware (*faïence fine*) are commonest among the productions of the late eighteenth and early nineteenth century; biscuit figures in the style of Sèvres were also made.

(See map on page 25)

SEPTFONTAINES

c. 1766–
white and cream-
coloured wares

in blue

**BL
2 1**

impressed

impressed

Boch, Jean-François, 1795   **JFB & Cie**

early 19th century

general pottery

Villeroy & Boch

Boch and Villeroy families united in 1836

Norway

The outstanding Norwegian contribution to European pottery during the eighteenth century was the faïence produced at Herrebøe, near Friedrichshald. The factory was founded in 1757. The Herrebøe decoration is among the most remarkable manifestations of the Rococo style; the only colours used were blue and manganese-purple, save for rare instances of *bianco sopra bianco*.

The objects made include wall-cisterns and basins, large tureens and 'bishop-bowls', besides the usual tablewares.

(See map on page 20)

HERREBØE (nr. Friedrichshald)
   1757–*c.* 1772
   faïence

'HB' (for Herre Bøe') and probably initial of Hosenfeller (artist)

mark most commonly found

probably initials of H. C. F. Hosenfeller

probably signature of Joseph and Gunder Large

PORSGRUNN
   1887–
   hard-paste porcelain
   Porsgrunds Porzelaenfabrik

Poland

The Belvedere faïence factory in Warsaw was erected by King Stanislas Poniatowski in 1774. The wares were marked 'Varsovie', and the usual style of decoration adopted seems to have derived from the Chinese through the medium of German porcelain. A faïence factory specializing in stoves was conducted at Telechany from the end of the eighteenth century. (The important group of faïence wares made during the eighteenth century at Proskau is shown under the German section.)

Hard-paste porcelain was made towards the end of the eighteenth century at several factories in Poland which lasted well through the nineteenth century. The wares of Baranovka, Korodnitza, Korzec and Tomaszów which were the principal factories, were much in keeping with those of the Russian Imperial factory, especially during the Empire period.

See map on page 57)

BARANOVKA (Volhynia)
1801–1895
porcelain

Baranùwka

in black, brown, etc.

in blue

Michael Mezer (*d.* 1825)

WARSAW
1774–
faïence

The Belvedere factory

·B   ℬ

Varsovie

'Varsovie'

Wolff, 1783–

W

KORZEC (*or* Koretzki)
1790–1797
hard-paste porcelain
(continued in
Gorodnitza until 1870)

Korzçc

TELECHANY
late 18th century
faïence

Count Michael Oginski

C O
3

TOMASZÓW
c. 1805–1810
hard-paste porcelain

Michael Mezer

Tomaszów

in black or other
colour

incised

230

Portugal

The Portuguese maiolica of the Renaissance period cannot easily be distinguished from that of Italy, Spain and the Netherlands. Tilework in particular, of all periods, is abundant and of amazing quality, but has until lately been little studied.

In the seventeenth century the Portuguese trade with China quickly brought the influence of blue-and-white porcelain; and designs from late Ming wares were adapted on what is perhaps the most distinctive class of Portuguese maiolica, believed to have been made at Lisbon or Braga.

In the eighteenth century faïence tablewares and figures were made at the royal factory of Rato and at other centres, such as Viana Darque, Aveiro, Santo Antonio, Coimbra, Miragaya, etc., as well as at Lisbon itself, where many excellent faïence tiles were also made.

A manufacture of porcelain was started in 1773 at the Military Arsenal at Lisbon. Medallion portraits, tablets with inscriptions, and reliefs, were made in sometimes slightly glossy white biscuit on a lilac or white ground. A further porcelain factory was founded in 1824 at Vista Alegre, near Oporto and is still in production.

(See map on page 235)

AVEIRO (Portugal)
c. 1785
faïence

'Fabrica Aveiro'

CALDAS DA RAINHA
1853–
imitation Palissy ware

Mafra & Son

impressed

COIMBRA
18th and 19th centuries
faïence

LISBON
1773–
hard-paste porcelain

signature of sculptor
Figueireido

IOÃO DE FIG^{DO}

MIRAGAYA (nr. Oporto)
late 18th century
faïence

late 18th century

RATO (nr. Lisbon)
1767–19th century
faïence

T. Brunetto, 1767–1771

S. de Almeida, 1771–1814 (?)

SANTO ANTONIO DO VALE DE PIEDADE
c. 1785–
faïence

Francisco Rossi

'Ri'

VIANNA DO CASTELLO (Darque)
1774–
faïence

in blue

VISTA ALEGRE (nr. Oporto)
1824–present
hard-paste porcelain

Russia

No faïence of artistic importance seems to have been made during the eighteenth century within the boundaries of Russia as at present defined, though minor factories apparently existed at St. Petersburg and elsewhere. At Kiev and Morje important faïence was made in the first half of the nineteenth century.

The most considerable porcelain factory was the Imperial factory at St. Petersburg, which did not commence regular production until 1758 and under Catherine II (1762–96) good porcelain was made in the French, German and Viennese styles, often with violet or blue grounds and elaborate gilding together with an important series of figure models featuring Russian folk-types. Other large manufactures worthy of note were at Verbilki and Gorbunovo, both near Moscow.

Minor establishments of the reign of Alexander I (1801–25) were at St. Petersburg (Batenin's factory) and at Moscow (Raschkin's, Formin's, Vsevolojsky's and Polivanoff's and Nassonoff's). In this period the industry was protected by duties on imported wares and after 1812 the notable and characteristic Russian variant of the Empire style reached its full development.

ARKHANGELSKOIE
1814–31
porcelain

ARKHANGELSKOIE

DOMKINO (Tver)
1809–
faïence

АУЕРБАХЬ

KIEV
1798–
faïence and porcelain

КIЕВЬ

∴

МЕЖИГОРЬЕ

ФГ

ГУАИНА

M. Gulina (porcelain)

MORJE (St. Petersburg)
early 19th century-
faïence

С.ПОСКОЧИН

MOSCOW
hard-paste porcelain
c. 1765–

Francis Gardner
c. 1765–1891

G　G　Г

all in blue

early 19th century

ГАРАНЕРZ

impressed

mid-19th century

printed in red

ГАРАНЕРZ

impressed

Popoff factory, c. 1800–1872

ЯП

Raschkin brothers
early 19th century

БРАТЬЕВЬ
РАУКИНЫХЬ

Fomin, c. 1800–

ПЕТРА
ФОМИНА

Vsevolojsky and
Polivanoff, 1813–55

БП

in colour or
incised

Fabrique de Wsevolojsky

F W

marks of Sipiagin
1820–

S

В.СИПАГИНА

Novik brothers
1820–

Н

БРАТЬЕВЬ
НОВЫХЬ

Nassonoff, 1811–c. 1813

АН

Kiriakoff, 1813–c. 1816

АК

Safronoff
c. 1820–

САФРОНОВА

С　　С

Dunashoff, 1830–

МФВ
ДУНАШОВА

Kozloff's factory
c. 1820–1856

ГК

incised

козловыхъ

ST. PETERSBURG (later Petrograd,
now Leningrad)
1744–
hard-paste porcelain

impressed

Russian Imperial
Porcelain-Factory
period of Elizabeth, 1741–1762

wares made from the Gjelsk clay·

wares made from
the Orenburg clay

both impressed
or incised

mark of Catherine II
1762–1796

in blue

Court inventory marks **П:К.**

Придвор:

marks of Paul I
1796–1801

marks of Alexander I
1801–1825

mark of Nicholas I
1825–1855

mark of Alexander II
1855–1881

mark of Alexander III
1881–1894

mark of Nicholas II
1894–1917

mark of Soviet regime
1917–

Batenin's factory
c. 1812–1820

С.З.К.Б **Б**

ВРАТЬЕВЪ

Korniloff's factory
1835–

КорниловыхЪ

Spain

The only medieval pottery of artistic importance made in Spain belongs to the period and places of the Arab occupation—to the Andalusian cities of Cordova and the neighbouring Medina az-Zahra and Medina el-Vira in the ninth to eleventh centuries, and to Malaga and Granada in the thirteenth and fourteenth centuries. This pottery strictly belongs to Islamic rather than European art. Much pottery of Moorish type (such as the great oil-jars and well-heads with impressed relief decoration, often heraldic) was made at Seville, and at neighbouring places in Andalusia, as well as at Toledo.

From the fifteenth century the lead in pottery-making was taken by Valencia, more particularly its suburbs, Paterna and Manisses. Lustreware was made there in the light of Andalusian technique and tradition, but the Moorish design was quickly succeeded by floral and heraldic elements, especially among the blue-painted wares.

Beginning in the early sixteenth century polychrome tilework and pottery in Renaissance style was first made at Seville and later at Talavera, the latter flourishing in the seventeenth century when the Savona Chinese blue-and-white styles were also much imitated. Minor centres were at the neighbouring Toledo and Puente del Arzobispo.

Belonging to the eighteenth century and of French influence, is the pottery of the Count of Aranda at Alcora, where some highly individual styles of great importance were created. Cream-coloured ware and *terre de pipe* in English style were made from the latter part of the eighteenth century onwards at Alcora.

The chief porcelain of Spain was that of Buen Retiro, a factory in Madrid originally established in 1760 as a private manufacture by the Bourbon King Charles III (previously of Naples), in continuation of that of Capodimonte. By far the most important period of the factory falls within the lifetime of Charles III, who died in 1788. The Rococo and chinoiserie styles lasted only a few years and the best and most characteristic Buen Retiro porcelain of about 1765–80 is in a variant of the *Louis Seize* style. After the closing down of Buen Retiro in 1808 the old stock and moulds were used in an unimportant factory started by Ferdinand VII at La Moncloa (1817–50). Hard-paste porcelain of indifferent quality was made also at Alcora from about 1775.

ALCORA (Valencia)
c. 1726–
faïence, c. 1727–c. 1785
hard-paste porcelain, c. 1775–
cream-coloured wares, c. 1775–

marks used
1784 or later

A

in brown or black

A incised   **A** in gold

early 19th century

printed in
red

probably mark of
Vicente Cros, faïence
painter, 1735–1750

probably Vicente Ferrer
faïence painter, 1727–1743

Fer.

BUEN RETIRO (Madrid)
1760–1808
porcelain
soft-paste, 1760–1804
hard-paste, 1804–1808
Charles III Bourbon,
King of Naples

1760–1804, various forms of the
usual factory mark, the Bourbon
fleur-de-lys, also used at
Capodimonte   all in blue

rare mark

incised

probably a repairer's mark

incised

1804–1808, 'Sureda period'

          'MADRID'

in red

LA MONCLOA
(*or* Florida, nr. Madrid)
1817–1850
porcelain

Ferdinand VII

impressed

this Buen Retiro mark
also used

MADRID (*see* Buen Retiro and La
Moncloa)

MANISES
1941–
hard-paste porcelain
Ceramicas Hispania

SARGADELOS
1804–1875
cream-coloured and
white earthenware

1804–1829

1835–1842

1845–1862

SEVILLE (Andalusia)
19th century
faïence

M. Francesco
de Aponte and
Pickman & Co

Sweden

One of the principal and most flourishing Scandinavian potteries was that of Rörstrand near Stockholm; it commenced the manufacture of faïence in 1725, its most prosperous period being from 1753–73. The early wares painted only in blue resembled those of Copenhagen; whilst 1760 onwards brought imitations of Marieberg; the best results being obtained with the use of high-temperature colours.

From 1773 tin-glazed faïence slowly gave way to the lead-glazed earthenware of English type, known in Sweden as '*flintporslin*'. Nothing of great artistic importance was made from that time onwards until the modern revivals.

Marieberg was best known for its admirable faïence, its early wares being decorated with a unique marbled glaze and enamel colours of great beauty, high temperature colours being rarely used. Figures of birds and Italian Comedy figures also featured among its productions. From about 1766 transfer-prints in black, red or dark-brown were used in the decoration of useful wares and Classical vases.

From 1769 cream-coloured earthenware of very light weight was made, decorated either by moulded design or transfer-prints.

The early soft-paste products of Marieberg from 1766–69 were similar in style to those of Mennecy, reeded custard-cups being one of their most popular models; this paste was followed by a hybrid brittle porcelain and was finally succeeded in 1778 by a true hard-paste.

The wares of Gustavsberg (1786–97) were very much in the style of Marieberg, of which the factory was virtually a continuation. Glazed earthenware of English type was made from 1820, the mark used being the name impressed. Black basaltes, buff-and-red stoneware and other pottery in Wedgwood style (in 1819 it was in fact called '*Wedgwood-Fabriker*') was made at Ulfsunda from the late eighteenth century onwards.

Faïence was also made at Sölvesborg and Pålsjö during the second half of the eighteenth century.

(See map on page 20)

GÄVLE
1850–1910 earthenware
1910–   hard-paste
porcelain 'GEFLE-PORSLIN'

GUSTAVSBERG (*or* Vänge-Gustafs-
berg, nr. Bredsjö)
1786–1860
faïence and semi-porcelain,
glazed earthenware from 1820

1786–1797

these initials when
accompanying the mark are said to be:

Carl Erik   'CE'

Carl Forsling   'CF'

Carl Petter   'CP'

Carl Petter Löfström   'CPL'

                                   impressed

1820–1860

1822–
hard-paste porcelain
1910–40

1930–

HACKEFORS
1929–
hard-paste porcelain
Nilson, J. O.

LIDKHÖPING
1910–1939 (absorbed by
Rörstrand)
hard-paste porcelain

MARIEBERG (nr. Stockholm)
1758–
faïence

Johann Eberhard
Ludwig Ehrenreich
1760–1766

Pierre Berthevin
1766–1769

mark with signature
in enamel colour of
the painter J. O. Frantzen

Henrik Sten, 1769–1788

Sten
M B
impressed

porcelain
1766–

Pierre Berthevin   impressed
1766–1769 (soft-paste)

Henrik Sten
1769–1788 (hybrid porcelain)

and
Jacob Dortu
1777–1778 (hard-paste)

in red; the
dots in blue.

·.·

in blue

≡≡
MB

in red

PÅLSJÖ (nr. Helsingborg)
faïence
1765–1774

'Palsjö Fabrik'
dated 1774

$P\,F$

$17\frac{25}{3}74$

painted in blue
or manganese

RÖRSTRAND (nr. Stockholm)
1725–
faïence

various forms
of factory marks
including dates:

1797– hard-paste porcelain

1850–

1837–

1850–

1852–

1859–

1878–

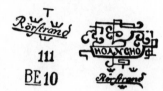

1884–

cream-coloured wares
Jacob Ohrn, 1763–1782

RÖRSTRAND
impressed

SÖLVESBORG
1773–1793
faïence

'Sölves-Borg'

S. B

ULFSUNDA
late 18th-19th century
faïence and
'Wedgwood' style wares

C A L

Christian Arvid Linning
d. 1843

Ulfsunda
impressed

Switzerland

The Italian maiolica technique was quickly adopted by the numerous *Hafner* or makers of stoves who were the chief potters in Switzerland at the beginning of the sixteenth century, and dated pieces probably made at Lucerne are recorded from 1542.

The chief centre of manufacture, both of stoves and pottery vessels, from about 1600 onwards to the middle of the eighteenth century was at Winterthur. Other eighteenth-century factories were at Lenzburg, Steckborn, Zurich, Berne and Bero-Münster. *Sgraffiato* and other peasant pottery was made at Langnau, Heimberg, Simmenthal and Bäriswyl.

Soft-paste porcelain of creamy-white tone was made at Zurich for a short time only and is consequently rare. Hard-paste was made from about 1765, and for ten years or so after this date Zurich produced some of the most beautiful European porcelain of the eighteenth century.

Hard-paste porcelain was also made at Nyon from about 1780, the wares were of a cold-white technically perfect hard-paste and decorated in the prevailing Paris styles, with diapers, butterflies, sprigs, garlands, trophies and Classical borders, all painted with skill and taste but without much originality.

BERNE
18th century
faïence

Emanuel J. 'Früting
of Berne'

E.i.F
1772

Emanuel J. Frisching
mid-18th century

'B'
in brown

BERO-MÜNSTER
c. 1769–1780
faïence

Andreas Dolder
(transferred to Lucerne
about 1780)

ℳ　.M.i
for Münster

CAROUGE (nr. Geneva)
19th century
cream-coloured earthenware

Jacob Dortu
1813–c. 1820

'DORTU VERET B'

Abraham Baylon, 1812–

'BAYLON'

'BAYLON & CIE'

all impressed

GENEVA
19th century
porcelain

mark of Jean-Pierre
Mulhauser, outside-
decorator of white Nyon
porcelain, 1805–1818

P M
Genève

LANGENTHAL
1906–present
porcelain

mark on hand-
decorated wares

SUISSE
S
LANGENTHAL

L

LENZBURG
18th century
faïence

L2　L2

Marcus
Hunerwadel,
A. H. & H. C. Klug
c. 1767

H.
B.

presumed mark of
H. C. Klug

Hans Jacob Frey
1774–1796

L B　　L B

presumed mark of Frey

Hf

NYON (nr. Geneva)
c. 1780–1860
hard-paste porcelain and later,
general pottery

typical forms of
Nyon mark

in underglaze
blue

early 19th-century

'*Dortu & Cie*'
impressed

earthenware
mid-19th century

'*Poterie fine
Bonnard et Gonin*'

Pfluger Bros. & Co.
19th century

THOUNE
present
'peasant-pottery'

incised

ZÜRICH
1763–1897
porcelain and faïence
also cream-coloured
earthenware from 1778

Z　　Z

Z　　3

in blue　　incised